THE PRICE
OF COMPASSION

THE PRICE OF COMPASSION

Assisted Suicide and Euthanasia

EDITED BY MICHAEL STINGL

broadview press

Library and Archives Canada Cataloguing in Publication

The price of compassion : assisted suicide and euthanasia / edited by Michael Stingl.

Includes bibliographical references.
ISBN 978-1-55111-883-3

1. Assisted suicide—Canada—Textbooks. 2. Assisted suicide—United States—Textbooks.
3. Euthanasia—Canada—Textbooks. 4. Euthanasia—United States—Textbooks.
I. Stingl, Michael, 1955-

R726.P75 2010   179.7   C2010-901016-7

Broadview Press is an independent, international publishing house, incorporated in 1985. Broadview believes in shared ownership, both with its employees and with the general public; since the year 2000 Broadview shares have traded publicly on the Toronto Venture Exchange under the symbol BDP.

We welcome comments and suggestions regarding any aspect of our publications—please feel free to contact us at the addresses below or at broadview@broadviewpress.com.

North America
PO Box 1243, Peterborough, Ontario, Canada K9J 7H5
2215 Kenmore Ave., Buffalo, New York, USA 14207
Tel: (705) 743-8990; Fax: (705) 743-8353
email: customerservice@broadviewpress.com

UK, Europe, Central Asia, Middle East, Africa, India, and Southeast Asia
Eurospan Group, 3 Henrietta St., London, WC2E 8LU, United Kingdom
Tel: 44 (0) 1767 604972; Fax: 44 (0) 1767 601640
email: eurospan@turpin-distribution.com

Australia and New Zealand
NewSouth Books
c/o TL Distribution
15-23 Helles Avenue, Moorebank, NSW, Australia 2170
Tel: (02) 8778 9999; Fax: (02) 8778 9944
email: orders@tldistribution.com.au

www.broadviewpress.com

Broadview Press acknowledges the financial support of the Government of Canada through the Book Publishing Industry Development Program (BPIDP) for our publishing activities.

Copy-edited by Martin Boyne

Designed by Chris Rowat Design, Daiva Villa

This book is printed on paper containing 100% post-consumer fibre.

PRINTED IN CANADA

CONTENTS

INTRODUCTION

Why another book on euthanasia, and, in particular, a book that emphasizes both voluntary and nonvoluntary forms of medically assisted death? And why address such questions in the comparative context of the Canadian and US health and legal systems?

The purpose of this book is to focus on one important strand of the debate on medically assisted death—the so-called slippery-slope argument—and, in particular, on one important aspect of the downward slope of this argument: hastening the death of those individuals who appear to be suffering greatly from their medical condition but who are unable to ask us to do anything about that suffering because of their diminished mental capacities. Slippery-slope concerns have been raised in many countries, including Britain, the Netherlands, the United States, and Canada. To maintain its focus, this book concentrates most of its attention on the latter two countries. The similarities and differences between these two countries regarding medically assisted death and health services more generally provide an interesting and important basis for understanding what compassion may (or may not) require of us in responding to the unbearable medical suffering of others, whether they are our family members or our fellow citizens.

The past several decades have seen a good many books, and a good deal of legal activity, directed toward the idea of physician-assisted suicide. In the US, there have been two important Supreme Court decisions regarding physician-assisted suicide and several important state-level initiatives to decriminalize and regulate its practice.[1] Physician-assisted suicide has appeared to be a safer response to unbearable suffering in a medical context than has voluntary euthanasia, both as a medical practice harder to abuse and easier to regulate than voluntary

---

[1] Both US Supreme Court decisions are excerpted in Part I of this book. Oregon has legally permitted physician-assisted suicide since 1998, Washington State since March 2009. The situation in Oregon is discussed in Part IV of this book.

1

euthanasia, and as a medical practice less morally problematic than voluntary euthanasia. In physician-assisted suicide, the physician does not kill the patient, as in voluntary euthanasia, but makes available to the patient the means of taking his or her own life. For some, this is a crucial moral difference, particularly because suicide itself has been decriminalized in both the US and Canada. Under the right circumstances, helping someone commit suicide might thus be seen to be morally and legally legitimate, even if killing someone at his or her explicit request, in similar medical circumstances, is not.

The main argument in favour of physician-assisted suicide is that just as people should be allowed to make individual decisions about the manner in which they will lead their lives, so too should they have individual sovereignty over the manner of their deaths. In the past, it was much harder to control the timing and manner of one's death; now, with modern medical technology, many people will live past the time when they might otherwise have died. Sometimes, and indeed often, this extra time is experienced as a benefit; in some cases, however, it is experienced as unbearable. When this is the case, competent patients, as individual decision-makers taking charge of their own lives, should be allowed to ask their physicians for assistance in ending their lives. The medical treatments that have kept them alive are no longer of any benefit to them, and so now it is up to medicine to provide the last benefit that it can, namely a swift and easy death.

This is the best-case scenario for allowing physician-assisted suicide: the patients requesting it are fully competent to make decisions about their lives, their medical treatments, and their deaths. They find themselves in medical circumstances which, according to the beliefs and values that have guided their lives, they judge to be unbearable. Other treatment alternatives have been exhausted, either because they are not medically indicated or because the patient's individual beliefs and values rule them out as a better alternative to physician-assisted suicide. For such patients, given their current circumstances, and the beliefs and values that have structured and defined their lives, death is better than continued life. Their deaths, like their lives, are theirs and theirs alone to decide.

The most frequent argument against physician-assisted suicide, somewhat surprisingly, grants the preceding point. It agrees that on grounds of individual sovereignty, or individual autonomy, patients like those described above should be allowed to choose physician-assisted suicide. In this regard, physician-assisted suicide is undeniably a morally good thing. But moral goods have to be balanced against moral harms, and in the case of physician-assisted suicide there is an important social harm that may ensue, were its practice to be legally allowed. The harm is that if we allow physician-assisted suicide, we may soon find ourselves allowing voluntary euthanasia and, from there, nonvoluntary euthanasia, and perhaps even involuntary euthanasia (the distinction between the latter two forms of euthanasia is explained below). Since this potential for social harm outweighs the individual goods that physician-assisted suicide might otherwise bring about, the argument concludes that physician-assisted suicide should not be allowed, all things considered. This is the slippery-slope argument against allowing physician-assisted suicide or voluntary euthanasia. Allowing something that might be considered morally legitimate on its own puts us on a slippery slope which has, at its bottom, things that are not morally legitimate; and, given the slipperiness of the slope and the nastiness of what awaits us downhill, the best thing we can do is not to venture out onto the top of the slope.

In thinking about this argument, we need to be careful to distinguish between nonvoluntary euthanasia and involuntary euthanasia. In nonvoluntary euthanasia, a decision is made to end an individual's life when that individual is not competent to make the decision for him or herself. The parallel here is to decisions that are made not to proceed with life-saving treatments for non-competent patients, or even to withdraw a life-saving treatment from such a patient once it has been started. There are two ways in which such non-treatment decisions are currently made. First, for a patient who was once competent, an appropriate proxy decision-maker may be able to ascertain what the patient would have wanted in the condition he or she is now in. Second, for a patient who was never competent, an appropriate proxy decision-maker may be able to ascertain that in this patient's condition, no reasonable person would wish to be treated, or if treatment has started, for the treatment to continue. In the first sort of case, decisions are made on the basis of what is called the "substituted judgment" standard of decision making for patients who are not competent to make their own medical decision about the treatment in question. In the second sort of case, the standard involved is one of "best interests," where such interests are measured against what a reasonable person would want in the medical circumstances in which the non-competent patient finds him or herself. In Part II of this book we will find ourselves confronted with a case of this second kind.

The strongest case for nonvoluntary euthanasia sees it as being a similarly appropriate response to the suffering of non-competent patients: hopeless suffering is hopeless suffering, whether the patient is competent or not. This argument has nothing to do with involuntary euthanasia, where patients are euthanized against their will. Involuntary euthanasia may happen in more or less subtle sorts of ways. In Nazi Germany, involuntary euthanasia was not so subtle: people who expressly did not want to be euthanized were euthanized for the supposed greater good of German society and the Aryan race. But more subtle forms of involuntary euthanasia are also possible, when, for example, a competent patient might be pressured to ask for euthanasia in circumstances where he or she, given more freedom to make a better personal judgment regarding his or her medical condition, would not otherwise ask for it. And of course such pressures may themselves be more or less socially subtle: some may be the direct result of a relative or family member who is tired of caring for the patient, while others may stem from the patient's more generally impoverished social circumstances. Particularly worrisome here are circumstances involving disability, where patients may have a prior history of sustained social discrimination based on their disabilities.

According to some opponents of euthanasia, all cases of nonvoluntary euthanasia are in fact cases of involuntary euthanasia, since if we cannot ask a patient if death is preferable to continued life, we must always assume the opposite. But given the fact that we currently stop or refrain from starting life-saving treatments on the basis of the best-interests standard, so strong a claim about nonvoluntary euthanasia does not seem credible. In a similar vein, some people make the quick argument that the example of Nazi Germany proves that if you start with physician-assisted suicide, you will wind up with something like Auschwitz. This is a serious example, but it is a weak analogy to current questions of assisted death in liberal societies like those of the US and Canada. Nazi Germany began with a fascist political ideology, one which held that it was right and good to sacrifice individual lives to the greater glory of the state and the race. In accord with this ideology, the country did not *end up* with a justification for involuntary euthanasia—they *started* with one. Patients' lives were ended not for their own carefully considered good, but for the ill-considered good of the state and the race. The cornerstone of liberal societies is their belief in the fundamental importance of individual liberty. Unless one is deeply pessimistic about the future of liberalism as a political institution in the developed world, the analogy of Nazi Germany seems completely misplaced.

Although the preceding points may be fairly easy to dismiss, more general worries behind the slippery-slope argument are not so readily dismissible. If we allow physician-assisted suicide, which might in itself be a morally non-problematic practice, will we, by incremental steps, find ourselves gradually sliding down a slippery slope that has, at its bottom, practices that might be just as clearly morally problematic, if not downright or even horribly wrong? What about people with disabilities, who face sustained social messages that their lives are not fully worth living? Will they sometimes find an assisted death their best option, not because it is, but because of the limited resources otherwise made available to them? What about people with few social or economic resources? Will the social and economic limits of their situations make assisted death appear to be a better health-care option than it otherwise might be? And what about palliative care? If good-quality palliative care were readily available to everyone who might benefit from it, would that many people really be interested in any form of assisted death? Finally, what about those individuals who are so deeply disabled that others will be placed in positions to decide whether they live or die? Can anyone make this sort of decision for another?

As we will see in Part I of this book, both sides of the slippery slope argument have had their day in court. The argument has loomed large in legal reasoning over whether physician-assisted suicide, or voluntary euthanasia, should be allowed in either the US or Canada as a constitutionally guaranteed right, a right regarding individuals' fundamental liberty to live out their lives as they please. In its Glucksberg decision, included in Part I of this book, the US Supreme Court considered slippery-slope concerns to be of sufficient weight that a ban on assisted suicide in Washington State could not be declared unconstitutional simply because it limited an individual's liberty to end his or her life in the face of what the individual judged to be unbearable suffering. Delivering the opinion of the court, Chief Justice Rehnquist noted that given current arguments about potential harms to others, allowing physician-assisted suicide could reasonably be expected to threaten various vulnerable groups with euthanasia, such as the disabled, the depressed, the suicidal, those not competent to make their own medical decisions, and those for whom adequate palliative or other forms of health care were not being provided. The reality of these threats was a matter for continued public debate, not for the Court to decide as a matter of constitutional law. In the meantime, it had not been proven that the right to die was protected by the US Constitution as a fundamental liberty right.

Neither, of course, had it been proven that there was not such a right, as Justice Stevens's concurring opinion makes clear in a point to which we will return below.

A similar if slightly less open-ended argument was given by the Supreme Court of Canada in the Sue Rodriguez case. The details of the case are discussed more fully below, and the decision itself is also included in Part I of this book. While the majority of the court found that Sue Rodriguez did have a fundamental liberty interest in dying as she wished, it also found that this liberty interest could be limited by concerns over potential harms to other individuals more vulnerable than she was herself. In other words, not all liberty interests are liberty rights. Section 7 of the Canadian Charter of Rights and Freedoms says that everyone has the right to life, liberty, and security of his or her person, but it also says that this right may be limited by principles of fundamental justice. Such principles are a matter of general consensus over what values are fundamental to Canadian society. The Court found that while there was no general consensus that assisted suicide should be allowed, the criminalization of assisted suicide had been a provision of Canada's Criminal Code since its inception, and, moreover, this prohibition was consistent with a general Canadian regard for the sanctity of human life, a regard also to be found in the prohibition against capital punishment. So while the Court implicitly left it open as to whether the social consensus against assisted suicide might one day change, it found that Rodriguez's liberty interest in assisted suicide was not a right guaranteed by the Charter.

The practical result of these cases in both the US and Canada has been to return the questions of physician-assisted suicide and voluntary euthanasia to other levels of democratic authority in each country. In the US, the Supreme Court has returned the question of physician-assisted suicide to state legislatures, which can, as they see fit, assess the power of the slippery-slope argument and develop whatever regulations of the practice of physician-assisted suicide they deem necessary, including, of course, continuing to criminalize it. Alternatively, such measures can be the subject of state referenda. In Canada, the Supreme Court has returned the question of voluntary euthanasia to the federal parliament, where, as in US state legislatures, the power of the slippery-slope argument can be more fully assessed, and voluntary euthanasia either regulated or criminalized (as it now is).

The unquestioned assumption on both of the main lines of the current public arguments—for and against physician-assisted suicide in the US, and for and against voluntary euthanasia in Canada—is that nonvoluntary euthanasia is wrong, or at least so morally problematic that it cannot even be considered in drafting regulations for physician-assisted suicide or voluntary euthanasia. Nonvoluntary euthanasia stands near or at the bottom of the slippery slope, and, as such, it is something to be strenuously avoided.

In Canada, an important legal and moral challenge has arisen against this assumption. In 1993, in a small town in the Canadian Prairies, Robert Latimer killed his daughter, Tracy Latimer, because of her medical condition. In light of the much louder public debate about physician-assisted suicide and voluntary euthanasia in both the US and Canada, this case is especially interesting for a number of reasons. It suggests not only that nonvoluntary euthanasia and voluntary euthanasia cannot be morally separated from each other as easily as many defenders of physician-assisted suicide and voluntary euthanasia assert, but also that nonvoluntary euthanasia may be just as important a response to hopeless suffering as physician-assisted suicide or voluntary euthanasia. Why should the suffering of those who are unable to consent to euthanasia ultimately count for anything less than the suffering of those who are?

When she died, Tracy Latimer was 12 years old. She had cerebral palsy and functioned mentally at the level of a four-month-old. Because of ongoing problems with uneven muscle and bone growth, along with seizures, she had had a series of operations in which muscles and ligaments had been cut and metal rods inserted into her back. Her current problem was a dislocated hip, and the only solution, the Latimers were told, was to remove her thigh bone, leaving her lower leg hanging as a flail limb. Tracy had been in pain, was in pain, and was likely to continue to be in pain. The only painkiller that the Latimers could give her was Tylenol, because of worries that stronger painkillers might interfere with her other medications. It is an interesting and open question whether Tracy was receiving the best palliative care possible; as far as the Latimers knew, she was—by means of the series of operations and the Tylenol. This issue of access to adequate levels of palliative care will resonate through a number of the chapters of this book, in a variety of interestingly different ways.

But even if better palliative measures were a possibility in theory, they were not a possibility for the Latimers as they had been led to understand their daughter's condition. This much was clear about the case, as were several other things. First, Tracy was in continuing pain,

THE PRICE OF COMPASSION

the point of which she clearly could not understand. Second, Robert Latimer loved his daughter. Third, on a Sunday morning in late October, Robert placed Tracy in the cab of his pickup truck and ran a hose from the exhaust pipe of the truck into the cab. He testified that he was prepared to remove Tracy from the truck were she to show any signs of discomfort, but she did not, and so he did not. After Tracy was dead, Robert placed her in her bed, called the police, and told them that she had died in her sleep.

Although this proved to be untrue, there has been little doubt about Robert Latimer's motive in killing his daughter. For those who have argued against clemency for Latimer, three lines of argument have been important. First, it is claimed that no one can judge for another whether he or she is in unbearable pain, or whether, on such grounds, his or her life is worth living. Second, the life of a disabled person is equal to the life of a non-disabled person, so the sentence for murder should be the sentence for murder, regardless of who has been killed. It is thirdly claimed, in true slippery-slope fashion, that were the law against murder not to be so enforced, the resulting situation would be one of an "open season" on the lives of the disabled.

For all their support, these arguments have also faced a good deal of public resistance. In particular, a majority of Canadians seem to feel that Latimer's sentence was much too harsh. In the immediate aftermath of the discovery and investigation of his daughter's death, Latimer was charged with first-degree murder but was convicted only of second-degree murder. This conviction was ultimately quashed by the Supreme Court of Canada on grounds of interference in the selection of jurors by the prosecution. A new trial was ordered, and Latimer was once again convicted of second-degree murder. The jury was visibly upset, however, when they were told that their recommendation for sentencing must start with the mandatory minimum sentence in Canada for second-degree murder: life in prison, with no chance of parole for ten years. The jury nonetheless recommended one year in prison, followed by another year during which Latimer would be confined to his farm, which his family was in danger of losing. And indeed the trial judge, despite being bound by federal law to disregard the jury and to impose at least the minimum sentence on Latimer, sentenced him instead to one year in prison followed by one year of parole to his farm. Portions of this ruling, written by Judge Noble, conclude the legal background provided in Part I of this book. The prosecution appealed Judge Noble's ruling, and this appeal was ultimately upheld by the

Supreme Court of Canada, which found that the minimum sentencing requirements did not, in this case, violate the Canadian Charter of Rights and Freedoms, the Canadian equivalent of the US Constitution. If Latimer wanted clemency, the Court noted, he would have to seek it from the federal government in the form of a pardon. In January 2001, Robert Latimer drove himself to jail to begin serving his sentence. Asked by a scrum of reporters as he got into his car at his farm about the possibility of a pardon, Latimer replied, with his usual rural circumspection, "politicians won't touch this with a ten-foot pole."

In Canada, the Latimer case has been closely tied to the earlier case of Sue Rodriguez. The importance of these cases goes beyond Canada, for what the Rodriguez case shows is how quickly the question of allowing physician-assisted suicide can extend to the question of allowing voluntary euthanasia, and what the Latimer case shows is how quickly this second question can extend to the question of allowing nonvoluntary euthanasia. Both the Rodriguez and Latimer cases focus our attention squarely on disability and equality before the law, and thus both cases confront the slippery-slope argument against physician-assisted suicide or voluntary euthanasia head on.

Sue Rodriguez was a fully competent patient with amyotrophic lateral sclerosis, or ALS, commonly known as Lou Gehrig's disease. ALS leads to a gradual loss of muscle control and in its final stages may result in difficulty breathing and eventual suffocation. While Rodriguez found the idea of this sort of death unbearable, she valued her life in her current circumstances. Her fear was that by the time she wanted to take her own life she would be unable to do so. Her argument before the Supreme Court of Canada was that, as a disabled person, she would not be given equal benefit of the law that had decriminalized suicide in Canada. Were she able bodied, she would be able to commit suicide if the final stages of her medical condition became unbearable. But it was highly likely that at such a stage she would not in fact be able bodied, and hence, without assistance in committing suicide, she would not be able to end her life in accord with her own values and her own decision-making capacity.

The Supreme Court of Canada did not find this equality right in the Charter of Rights and Freedoms. Just as Sue Rodriguez's interest in liberty could be overridden by potential harms to others, so could her interest in equality. However, four of the nine judges dissented from the majority decision precisely on the point of Rodriguez's disability. As two of these judges (L'Heureux-Dubé and McLachlin) put the point,

Parliament had allowed suicide, but in so doing it had denied this option to those who were not physically able to commit suicide without the assistance of others. This was an arbitrary limitation of the disabled individual's interest in the security of his or her own person.

Even if this minority view did not prevail, there are still several important reasons to consider the meaning of this judgment in the context of North American legal and health systems. First, as in the Rodriguez case, the more recent US Supreme Court decisions, in particular the *Glucksberg* decision, have also relied on the slippery-slope argument as a significant counterweight to each individual's liberty to lead, or not to lead, his or her life as he or she sees fit. Indeed, in the Notes to Justice Rehnquist's Opinion of the Court in *Glucksberg*, the Rodriguez decision is prominently mentioned. But Sue Rodriguez herself is an interesting challenge to some of the main slippery-slope concerns raised in Rehnquist's Opinion, which states that the interest in individual liberty represented by those who request physician-assisted suicide must be balanced against risks to those in society who are vulnerable, such as the disabled. The disabled, the Opinion tells us, must be protected from "societal indifference" (quotes in the original), and their suicidal impulses should thus be interpreted and treated the same way as everybody else's. But this was exactly Sue Rodriguez's own argument before the Supreme Court of Canada, an argument over which the judges divided five to four.

This point is especially important if we consider the main conceptual line that divides physician-assisted suicide and euthanasia from cases where life-saving treatment is withheld or withdrawn, the distinction between killing and allowing to die. This distinction is well ensconced in US law, as the US Supreme Court makes clear in the second of the two decisions included in Part I of this book, *Vacco v. Quill*. But as many would argue, including Bryson Brown in Chapter 9, this distinction fails to mark a genuine moral difference.[1] Were we to allow physician-assisted suicide, we would in effect be giving in to arguments like Brown's: killing is not so far outside the legitimate aims of medicine. Killing, in other words, is not such a bad thing: under the right circumstances, patients can do it to themselves, and indeed, physicians can help them. But it is precisely here that Sue Rodriguez's predicament

---

1   For another argument to this effect, one that takes into account the reasoning in the *Vacco* decision, see Lance K. Stell, "Physician-Assisted Suicide: To Decriminalize or Legalize, That Is the Question," *Physician Assisted Suicide: Expanding the Debate*, ed. Margaret P. Battin, Rosamond Rhodes, and Anita Silvers (New York: Routledge, 1998).

becomes extremely important: some patients will be so disabled that, although mentally competent, they will be physically unable to kill themselves. If killing is permissible in such situations, and if equality matters to us, why should we not be required to do for such patients what they cannot do for themselves? It is here that the moral point of the distinction between killing and allowing to die will be seriously eroded, something that will surely affect our thinking about those non-competent patients from whom we think it appropriate to withhold or withdraw lifesaving treatments. If it is sometimes permissible to allow such patients to die, and sometimes permissible for us to kill patients who cannot kill themselves, why shouldn't it sometimes be permissible to kill noncompetent patients in the sorts of circumstances where we would already allow them to die? In at least some of these circumstances, killing may bring about a quicker end to a patient's suffering than standing by and allowing the patient to die.

Arguments against the moral coherence of the distinction between killing and allowing to die may become especially important as the US continues to struggle to reform its health-care system. The basis of the legal distinction between killing and letting die given in *Vacco* is in essence a difference between negative and positive political rights. In the US, negative political rights, i.e., rights to non-interference, are of paramount importance. The general idea is that no one can do anything to anyone without the other person's consent. In medicine more specifically, the general principle is that a physician cannot do anything to a patient without the patient's consent, even if what the physician might do would save the patient's life. There is, on the other hand, no general political right for persons to be benefited by the practice of medicine in the US. Nearly one fifth of the US population has no health insurance, and many more Americans have health insurance that would be considered inadequate by Canadian standards. Thus the US Supreme Court can say, on the one hand, that allowing someone to die by refusing treatment is a right well protected by prior Court decisions involving the inviolability of persons, while saying, on the other hand, that allowing someone to die in this way has absolutely nothing to do with providing any health benefit to that person, such as an alleged "right to die" in the face of an unbearable medical condition. Americans have negative political rights not to be interfered with, but not nearly as many positive political rights to receive the sorts of benefits that might be essential for living their lives according to their own liberty interests and values.

If, however, the US moves in the direction of insuring some form of health-care benefits for all its citizens, cases like that of Sue Rodriguez will become more interesting from the point of view of political rights. If one guaranteed benefit of universal health insurance is having a life-saving treatment stopped when death is preferable to continued life, it is hard to see how this politically guaranteed benefit could not turn into a politically guaranteed right to die, assuming there to be no deeper moral distinction between killing and allowing to die. Without any deeper moral significance to this distinction, if positive political rights to health-care benefits become generally mandated by a law such as the Canada Health Act, release from an unbearable medical condition through a refusal of life-saving treatment would seem to be not only a matter of non-interference with the person of another, but also a gen-uine benefit that patients might ask for as part of managing their end-of-life care.

On the other hand, if the US does not reform its health system in the direction of the Canadian system, where health benefits are guaranteed to all by the Canada Health Act, the other main argument against physi-cian-assisted suicide becomes much harder to sustain. In addition to the slippery-slope argument, the other main argument against physi-cian-assisted suicide is that instead of making physician-assisted sui-cide widely available, adequate palliative care should be made widely available to all patients who need it. Health reforms to one side, there are other problems with this general line of argument, such as the fact that for some patients, palliative care is only part of a more general medical situation that for them is still one of unbearable suffering, and that for some of these patients, as well as others, the only palliative option may be terminal sedation.[1] But the argument becomes weaker still if, as a matter of social policy, the full range of palliative options is not guaranteed to all patients through some form of universal health care. To the extent that significant reform of the US health system does not seem likely in the foreseeable future, the argument that physician-assisted suicide is unnecessary because better palliative options are always preferable seems to be at best disingenuous.

These last points may be especially important in light of Judge Stevens's concurring judgment in *Glucksberg*, included in Part I of this book. At the end of his judgment, Stevens says, "[t]he purpose of termi-

---

[1]   For a good initial discussion of terminal sedation and related issues, see the Forum on Slow Euthanasia, *Journal of Palliative Care* 12.4 (1996): 21-46.

nal sedation is to ease the suffering of the patient and comply with her wishes, and the actual cause of death is the administration of heavy doses of lethal sedatives."[1] He goes on to say that even though the challenges to the distinction between killing and letting die presented by *Vacco* are not strong enough in themselves to ground a constitutional right to die based on the right of equal protection under the law, new challenges might succeed where these have failed. So while state legislatures are currently free, in the US, to regulate physician-assisted suicide as they see fit, the recent judgments of the US Supreme Court have not closed the door on future judgments regarding not just a negative right to refuse life-saving treatment, but a positive right to die.

In February of 1994, six months after losing her case before the Supreme Court of Canada, Sue Rodriguez died as she wanted, with the help of a physician, at a point in her illness when she could no longer take her own life. She died in the arms of a member of the federal parliament, Svend Robinson, who in the course of Rodriguez's protracted legal battle had become both a staunch champion of her cause and a good friend. Immediately following her death, Robinson held a press conference to tell Canadians in general terms what had happened. No prosecution followed because of a lack of any corroborating evidence that a physician had been in attendance at Rodriguez's death. According to the prosecutor's office, no one had actually seen a physician entering or leaving Rodriguez's residence around the time of her death. And why believe either politicians or press conferences without corroborating evidence?

A similar result occurred in the US in the case of Dr. Timothy Quill and a patient named Diane. In 1991 in *The New England Journal of Medicine*, Quill published a moving account of his having assisted the suicide of Diane, a patient of eight years who was diagnosed with an acute form of leukemia.[2] For a variety of well-considered personal reasons, Diane opted for non-treatment of her cancer, which meant that she would have at most a few months of life remaining to her. After careful consideration of palliative care options (Quill was a former director of a hospice program), Diane requested sufficient barbiturates to take her own life if her suffering became too great in her final days.

---

[1]   For a second forum on the some of the more detailed aspects of sedation at the end of life, see Susan Fohr, "The Double Effect of Pain Medication: Separating Myth From Reality," *Journal of Palliative Medicine* 1.4 (1998): 315-28, together with editorial responses from Howard Brody (329-31) and Timothy Quill (333-36).

[2]   T.E. Quill, "Death and Dignity: A Case of Individualized Decision Making," *The New England Journal of Medicine* 324 (1991): 691-94.

Quill prescribed the barbiturates and Diane ultimately used them to take her life. Called to examine her by family members, Quill reported to the medical examiner that Diane had died of acute leukemia. When a prosecutor asked a US grand jury to indict Quill on the charge of assisting a suicide, it refused to do so.

A similar legal outcome might have occurred in the Latimer case. That it did not is perhaps little more than a turn of the wheel of fortune: good fortune if one has fears about an "open season" on the lives of the disabled, bad fortune if one considers Latimer's genuine love for his daughter and the loss to the other members of the Latimer family of a husband, father, and farm. The prosecutor in the Latimer case might have charged Latimer with administering a noxious substance, which might have led to his being sentenced in the way that both the jury and the judge in his second trial thought he ought to be, based on the evidence before them. Alternatively, given the fact that Latimer was charged at his second trial with second-degree murder, had the jury known, or been informed, that the minimum sentence was life in prison, they might have failed to convict him of that offence on the basis of the evidence before them. In the Latimer case none of these things happened, even though they might have happened. For this reason, neither side of the debate on physician-assisted suicide, voluntary euthanasia, and nonvoluntary euthanasia can rest easy with the Latimer decision. After serving ten years in prison, Robert Latimer is now on parole, a decision that was vociferously protested by disability-rights activists, but just as vociferously defended by a large number of voices on the other side. An important point at issue was Latimer's steadfast and matter-of-fact denial that he had done anything wrong. In ending his daughter's life, he did the only thing he could do for her in the face of her ongoing suffering.

Despite his own equanimity, Latimer has paid a high price for his compassion. Others, in cases like Rodriguez and Diane, have acted compassionately but have not had to pay the high price of a lengthy prison term, or the loss of a family farm. And still others have failed to do what compassion seemed to demand of them, incurring costs of a very different kind. But against all such compassionate concerns are the concerns of the slippery-slope argument: were we to start by ending some lives where compassion seems to demand it, would we finish by ending many other vulnerable lives in situations where we most definitely should not? Is the ultimate cost of killing for compassionate reasons too high a price to pay?

THE STRUCTURE OF THE BOOK

Part I contains selections from four important court cases in the US and Canada. We begin with two related decisions from the US Supreme Court, *Glucksberg* and *Vacco*. The two cases deal with the distinction between killing and allowing to die and with the government's interest in preserving life and protecting the vulnerable. Both cases involve physicians, rather than particular patients, and both cases involve general challenges to state bans on physician-assisted suicide. The next case, in Chapter 3, centrally involves the situation of a particular Canadian patient, Sue Rodriguez. While the Canadian judges on both sides of this decision reflect compassion for Rodriguez's situation, the majority of the judges (five to four) find against her. Concluding Part I is the reasoning of the trial judge in Robert Latimer's second trial, where Latimer was successfully convicted of second-degree murder and eventually sentenced to life in prison with no chance of parole for ten years. According to the trial judge, based on the evidence presented at the second trial, this punishment was entirely inappropriate. In finding that the democratically enacted penalty for second-degree murder was not in violation of the Canadian Charter of Rights and Freedoms, however, the Supreme Court of Canada overruled the trial judge and found against Latimer.

Part II of the book begins with two selections from outside Canada and the US which nevertheless offer a good background account of the worries about nonvoluntary euthanasia that are an important part of the slippery-slope argument against allowing physician-assisted suicide or voluntary euthanasia. While withdrawing or withholding life-saving treatment from competent adults who refuse such treatment is now standard medical practice in many countries, physicians and societies are still grappling with issues involved in withholding or withdrawing life-saving treatments from patients who cannot competently refuse them but for whom there is strong reason to believe that were they able to, they would. One such class of individuals comprises severely impaired newborns. In addition to offering guidance for when life-saving treatments can be withheld or withdrawn from severely impaired newborns, the recent report from the Nuffield Council on Bioethics, presented in Chapter 5, serves as a useful introduction to the fundamental moral concepts that are at issue in making such life-and-death decisions. More to the point of the slippery-slope argument, the report worries about the consequences of actively taking the lives of severely impaired newborns, a practice it rejects. Were we to allow the active euthanasia of adults in intolerable medical situations, it is unclear why we should not then also allow the active euthanasia of severely impaired newborns in intolerable medical situations. In fact, this is just what the Groningen Protocol argues in the next selection, in Chapter 6. Since Dutch law allows euthanasia for competent patients whose suffering cannot be adequately controlled, why should it not also allow for the euthanasia of severely impaired newborns whose medical situation is similar? But then why, as the Nuffield report wonders, should we stop with infants? Why not allow the euthanasia of any noncompetent person whose best interests would seem to be served by such an act?

Thus might we be led, step by step, from the permissibility of voluntary euthanasia to the apparent permissibility of more and more forms of nonvoluntary euthanasia. In examining the underlying logical structure of this general sort of argument in Chapter 7, John Woods finds it to be deeply ambiguous. Slippery-slope arguments depend on an accumulation of logical steps, where no one step makes all the difference to the issue at hand, such as the moral permissibility or impermissibility of euthanasia. The basic problem with such arguments, according to Woods, is that they work equally as well in both directions. Suppose that the presumed moral permissibility of voluntary euthanasia does lead, via a slippery-slope argument, to the moral permissibility of a number of forms of nonvoluntary euthanasia. If we think no form of nonvoluntary euthanasia is ever permissible, this might lead us to conclude that we should simply not allow ourselves to suppose that voluntary euthanasia is ever permissible. But why not suppose that what the argument really shows, as a new and surprising conclusion, is that many forms of nonvoluntary euthanasia are in fact morally permissible, and that we have until now been wrong in thinking otherwise? The underlying logic of the slippery-slope argument itself works just as well in either direction.

For reasons that have little directly to do with logic, Woods thinks that once we accept the moral permissibility of some forms of voluntary euthanasia, we will find ourselves, as a society, faced with the new and undeniable truth that some forms of nonvoluntary euthanasia are also permissible. What we really face in the euthanasia debate is not, according to Woods, a slippery-slope argument from voluntary to nonvoluntary euthanasia, but an eroding taboo against the taking of innocent human lives. What is at stake in allowing any form of euthanasia is what Justice Sopinka calls in his Rodriguez opinion the sanctity of human life.

In my own piece in Chapter 8, I argue that there is a way to prevent the logical slide from voluntary to nonvoluntary euthanasia. The argument is based on the claim that for voluntary euthanasia to be morally permissible, the patient must be suffering unbearably, where what counts as "unbearable suffering" is something that must be measured by the patient's own values. Since patients who were never competent never had any values, it follows that they can never suffer unbearably. If there are reasons for nonvoluntary euthanasia, they must be entirely separate from our primary reason for accepting voluntary euthanasia.

In Part III, Bryson Brown takes this line of argument to task in Chapter 9, arguing that while noncompetent patients may be unable to make judgments about the value of their continued existence, they may well find themselves experiencing unrelenting physical pain. In the face of such pain, what are our obligations, as health professionals and as family members? Brown argues that as a society we have an obligation to allow but to monitor closely nonvoluntary euthanasia in certain extraordinary circumstances. Against my own line of argument, Brown argues that while informed consent is an important part of the debate over voluntary euthanasia, a better understanding of when and why informed consent is important should lead us to adopt a permissive, albeit conservative, view of nonvoluntary euthanasia.

With Brown's argument, we begin to move into the individual and social contexts in which physician-assisted suicide, voluntary euthanasia, or nonvoluntary euthanasia would take place and have to be regulated, were they allowed in contemporary North American society. Against this background, in Chapter 10 John Baker constructs an extended argument that given current standards of medical practice, physicians should never kill their patients, regardless of a patient's level of suffering or pain, and regardless of their own views about the moral legitimacy of euthanasia. But by the same argument, Baker feels pushed to conclude that the moral prohibition against physicians killing their patients cannot be extended to patients' family members. In extreme circumstances, it may be morally permissible, or perhaps even a duty, for a family member to do what a doctor cannot. Baker thus turns what some have perceived to be the common wisdom regarding assisted death on its head. Some believe that if the pain and suffering get bad enough, physicians can help to end their patients' lives, but only if they do not draw attention to what they are doing. That this is now happening in both the Canadian and US health systems is indisputable. Baker argues that it should not happen, but by the same argument, that

THE PRICE OF COMPASSION

family members should, in extreme circumstances, be morally allowed to do what physicians cannot.

Against views like those of Brown and Baker, Kira Tomsons and Susan Sherwin argue in Chapter 11 that closer attention to the overall social context in which any form of euthanasia might be implemented makes otherwise straightforward appeals to individual autonomy or substituted consent by family members deeply problematic. Tomsons and Sherwin describe and explore two different feminist approaches to questions of euthanasia, one based on a critical analysis of oppressive social relationships and one based on an ethics of care. In both approaches, individual autonomy and substituted consent prove to be problematic ethical concepts. On the one hand, individual autonomy is typically limited for members of oppressed groups, and so, in general, the more individual autonomy members of oppressed groups are allowed, the better. But on the other hand, how one individual is allowed to use his or her autonomy may have wider and more significant negative effects on the autonomy of other members of the individual's group. Thus, what is good for Sue Rodriguez, or Tracy Latimer, might not be good for other women or girls in related circumstances.

Part IV takes us from the arguments of earlier parts of the book to some of the most significant of the current medical and social realities that bear on these arguments.

A key group in the slippery-slope argument is people living with disabilities. The selection in Chapter 12 addresses what members of this group might themselves think about assisted suicide or euthanasia. Given the vocal opposition of disability-rights activists to both assisted suicide and euthanasia, the results reported on in this chapter are surprising: as a group, disabled people seem to be as deeply divided by these issues as everyone else. While the disability-rights movement has spoken with one voice in the sorts of documents that were submitted to the courts in the cases included in Part I, the research reported on by Fadem and her colleagues suggests that opinions may be much more divided among disabled people themselves. While many of the disabled people who were questioned wanted physician-assisted death available to them, should they want or need it, they were wary of making such a choice widely available to others. Their main area of concern was the huge amount of discrimination that they and other disabled individuals faced on a regular basis, discrimination that suggested to them that from the outside, they lives weren't considered worth living. While this sort of consideration has most directly to do with worries regarding social pressures that might lead to more or less subtle forms of involuntary euthanasia, they are hardly irrelevant to worries about nonvoluntary euthanasia in cases like Tracey Latimer's.

Interestingly, factors like race, religious affiliation, and gender seem not to make a difference in the research results reported on by Fadem and her colleagues. Along with disabilities, race and economic position are two of the other important factors entering into the slippery-slope argument and its worries about vulnerable populations. If assisted suicide or euthanasia were to be allowed, would members of these groups figure disproportionately in the number of people asking for and receiving such treatments?

Addressing such concerns, Chapter 13 turns to Oregon, which has allowed physician-assisted suicide since 1997. In the past decade, most of those who have availed themselves of this option have been white, male, financially secure, and better educated than the population as a whole. Although 15 per cent of those who are dying in Oregon consider hastening their death, only 1 per cent request assistance, and only about 1 in 700 of those who are dying actually use the medication supplied by their physician to end their lives. The legislation requires, among other things, that patients and their physicians consider alternatives to assisted suicide, and there is evidence to suggest that the quality of palliative care in Oregon has improved since assisted suicide has been allowed. Talking about assisted suicide means talking about alternatives, and most people don't want to die before they have to.

To examine this point more closely in the context of end-of-life care, we may turn to the final chapter of this book. Focusing on a patient who requests but does not receive terminal sedation, in Chapter 14 Philip Higgins and Terry Altilio examine what palliative care might (or might not) be able to do for such patients. As an alternative to assisted suicide or euthanasia, palliative care is clearly an important option to consider. Moreover, a frequent adjunct to the slippery-slope argument against euthanasia is the argument that what is really needed for those suffering unbearably from medical conditions is better palliative care. If we had better palliative care, no one, or almost no one, would ever really want assisted suicide or euthanasia.

In light of the palliative care option, and the argument against assisted suicide and euthanasia that goes along with it, the final chapter in this book raises several extremely important points to consider in assessing the moral and legal permissibility of assisted suicide or euthanasia.

First and perhaps most importantly, the chapter gives us a detailed picture of what good-quality palliative care can look like. Written from a social-work perspective, the chapter focuses on the point that good-quality palliative care needs to respond to the suffering of the whole person. When many of us think about hopeless or unbearable suffering in a medical context, we typically think about physical pain. The final chapter makes clear that while hopeless suffering may well include intractable physical pain, it includes more comprehensively the patient's response to his or her entire medical situation, whatever the level of physical pain the patient might be suffering from.[1]

Second, while the chapter shows us what good palliative care might look like, it also reminds us of the limitations of such care. Sometimes, despite our best efforts to alleviate it, suffering is experienced by a patient as hopeless, or in the case of a noncompetent patient, judged by the patient's family members to be hopeless. Depending on the situation, it is current practice, in both the US and Canada, to offer the end-of-life option that we have been referring to as terminal sedation. Terminal sedation may hasten death, and when it is combined with the withdrawal of nutrition and hydration, this treatment option seems even more likely to hasten death.[2]

Finally, although Chapter 14 argues that terminal sedation should not be confused with assisted suicide or euthanasia, its arguments in this regard return us to central concerns of earlier chapters that such arguments are themselves confused. Reasons for terminal sedation look like the same sorts of reasons that might be given in favour of assisted suicide or euthanasia. Moreover, terminal sedation ends the patient's conscious life, and it may also be accompanied by removal of nutrition

---

[1] For a brief overview and discussion of future prospects of palliative care in the US, see Kathleen M. Foley, "The Past and Future of Palliative Care," *Improving End of Life Care: Why Has It Been So Difficult? Hastings Center Report Special Report* 35, no. 6 (2005): S42-S46. For similar discussions relating to Canada, see Deborah Dudgeon, Vida Vaitonis, Hsien Seow, Susan King, Helen Angus and Carol Sawka, "Ontario, Canada: Using Networks to Integrate Palliative Care Province-Wide," *Journal of Pain and Symptom Management* 33.5 (2007): 640-44, and Robin L. Fainsinger, Carleen Brenneis and Conrad Fassbinder, "Edmonton, Canada: A Regional Model of Palliative Care Development," *Journal of Pain and Symptom Management* 33.5 (2007): 634-39.

[2] See again the sources mentioned in n.1, p. 13 above. For an interesting recent effort to reach a consensus on guidelines regarding terminal sedation in intensive care units (ICUs), see Laura A. Hawryluck, William R.C. Harvey, Louise Lemieux-Charles and Peter A. Singer, "Consensus Guidelines on Analgesia and Sedation in Dying Intensive Care Unit Patients," *BMC Medical Ethics* 3.3 (2002): 1-6, <http:www.biomedcentral.com/1472-6939/3/3>. According to these guidelines, there should be no upper limit to the sedatives that may be appropriately administered when patients face intractable suffering at the end of life.

and hydration, which may ultimately be a factor in the biological death of the patient. For all intents and purposes, the patient's life, insofar as it might matter to the patient, is over, and biological death occurs when and as it does because of medical decision making. So we are back to the questions of earlier chapters: does the doctrine of the double effect, or the distinction between acts and omissions, bear the moral weight required of it in allowing terminal sedation, but not assisted suicide or euthanasia? If we are prepared to allow terminal sedation, even for those who cannot make this decision for themselves, should we not also be prepared to allow for the moral permissibility of assisted suicide, voluntary euthanasia, and even nonvoluntary euthanasia?

By the end of this book, readers should be better able to understand and participate in the ongoing debates in Canada and the US over these questions. The top courts of both countries have made these issues a matter for democratic decision making, a process that, at its best, requires vigourous and well-informed public debate. As concerned and compassionate members of the public, we need to join that debate.

PART I

PHYSICIAN-ASSISTED SUICIDE, EUTHANASIA AND THE LAW

Chapter 1

WASHINGTON ET AL. v.
GLUCKSBERG ET AL.

*Decided June 1997**

[...]

Chief Justice Rehnquist delivered the opinion of the Court.

The question presented in this case is whether Washington's prohibition against "caus[ing]" or "aid[ing]" a suicide offends the Fourteenth Amendment to the United States Constitution. We hold that it does not....

Petitioners in this case are the State of Washington and its Attorney General. Respondents Harold Glucksberg, MD, Abigail Halperin, MD, Thomas A. Preston, MD, and Peter Shalit, MD, are physicians who practice in Washington. These doctors occasionally treat terminally ill, suffering patients, and declare that they would assist these patients in ending their lives if not for Washington's assisted-suicide ban. In January 1994, respondents, along with three gravely ill, pseudonymous plaintiffs who have since died and Compassion in Dying, a nonprofit organization that counsels people considering physician-assisted suicide, sued in the United States District Court, seeking a declaration that Wash. Rev. Code § 9A.36.060(1) (1994) is, on its face, unconstitutional....

I

We begin, as we do in all due process cases, by examining our Nation's history, legal traditions, and practices.... In almost every State—indeed, in almost every western democracy—it is a crime to assist a

---

* For ease of reading, portions of this judgment have been omitted. All omissions are indicated by "...". The full judgment, with its complete references, can be found online at <http://www.supremecourtus.gov/opinions/boundvolumes/521bv.pdf>, pages 702-92.

suicide. The States' assisted-suicide bans are not innovations. Rather, they are longstanding expressions of the States' commitment to the protection and preservation of all human life.... Indeed, opposition to and condemnation of suicide—and, therefore, of assisting suicide—are consistent and enduring themes of our philosophical, legal, and cultural heritages....

More specifically, for over 700 years, the Anglo-American common-law tradition has punished or otherwise disapproved of both suicide and assisting suicide.... In the 13th century, Henry de Bracton, one of the first legal-treatise writers, observed that "[j]ust as a man may commit felony by slaying another so may he do so by slaying himself." 2 Bracton on Laws and Customs of England 423 (f. 150) (G. Woodbine ed., S. Thorne transl., 1968). The real and personal property of one who killed himself to avoid conviction and punishment for a crime were forfeit to the King; however, thought Bracton, "if a man slays himself in weariness of life or because he is unwilling to endure further bodily pain...[only] his movable goods [were] confiscated." Id., at 423-424 (f. 150). Thus, "[t]he principle that suicide of a sane person, for whatever reason, was a punishable felony was...introduced into English common law." Centuries later, Sir William Blackstone, whose Commentaries on the Laws of England not only provided a definitive summary of the common law but was also a primary legal authority for 18th- and 19th-century American lawyers, referred to suicide as "self-murder" and "the pretended heroism, but real cowardice, of the Stoic philosophers, who destroyed themselves to avoid those ills which they had not the fortitude to endure...." 4 W. Blackstone, Commentaries *189. Blackstone emphasized that "the law has...ranked [suicide] among the highest crimes," ibid., although, anticipating later developments, he conceded that the harsh and shameful punishments imposed for suicide "borde[r] a little upon severity." Id., at *190.

For the most part, the early American Colonies adopted the common-law approach. For example, the legislators of the Providence Plantations, which would later become Rhode Island, declared, in 1647, that "[s]elf-murder is by all agreed to be the most unnatural, and it is by this present Assembly declared, to be that, wherein he that doth it, kills himself out of a premeditated hatred against his own life or other humor: ...his goods and chattels are the king's custom, but not his debts nor lands; but in case he be an infant, a lunatic, mad or distracted man, he forfeits nothing." The Earliest Acts and Laws of the Colony of Rhode

Island and Providence Plantations 1647-1719, p. 19 (J. Cushing ed. 1977). Virginia also required ignominious burial for suicides, and their estates were forfeit to the Crown. A. Scott, Criminal Law in Colonial Virginia 108, and n. 93, 198, and n. 15 (1930).

Over time, however, the American Colonies abolished these harsh common-law penalties. William Penn abandoned the criminal-forfei-ture sanction in Pennsylvania in 1701, and the other Colonies (and later, the other States) eventually followed this example.... Zephaniah Swift, who would later become Chief Justice of Connecticut, wrote in 1796:

> "There can be no act more contemptible, than to attempt to pun-ish an offender for a crime, by exercising a mean act of revenge upon lifeless clay, that is insensible of the punishment. There can be no greater cruelty, than the inflicting [of] a punishment, as the forfeiture of goods, which must fall solely on the innocent off-spring of the offender.... [Suicide] is so abhorrent to the feelings of mankind, and that strong love of life which is implanted in the human heart, that it cannot be so frequently committed, as to become dangerous to society. There can of course be no necessity of any punishment." 2 Z. Swift, A System of the Laws of the State of Connecticut 304 (1796).

This statement makes it clear, however, that the movement away from the common law's harsh sanctions did not represent an acceptance of suicide; rather, as Chief Justice Swift observed, this change reflected the growing consensus that it was unfair to punish the suicide's family for his wrongdoing.... Nonetheless, although States moved away from Blackstone's treatment of suicide, courts continued to condemn it as a grave public wrong....

That suicide remained a grievous, though nonfelonious, wrong is confirmed by the fact that colonial and early state legislatures and courts did not retreat from prohibiting assisting suicide. Swift, in his early 19th-century treatise on the laws of Connecticut, stated that "[i]f one counsels another to commit suicide, and the other by reason of the advice kills himself, the advisor is guilty of murder as principal." 2 Z. Swift, A Digest of the Laws of the State of Connecticut 270 (1823). This was the well-established common-law view, see In re Joseph G., 34 Cal. 3d 429, 434-435, 667 P. 2d 1176, 1179 (1983); Commonwealth v. Mink, 123 Mass. 422, 428 (1877) ("'Now if the murder of one's self is felony, the

accessory is equally guilty as if he had aided and abetted in the murder'")
(quoting Chief Justice Parker's charge to the jury in *Commonwealth v.
Bowen*, 13 Mass. 356 (1816)), as was the similar principle that the consent of a homicide victim is "wholly immaterial to the guilt of the person who cause[d] [his death]," 3 J. Stephen, A History of the Criminal
Law of England 16 (1883); see 1 F. Wharton, Criminal Law §§ 451-452
(9th ed. 1885); *Martin v. Commonwealth*, 184 Va. 1009, 1018-1019, 37 S.
E. 2d 43, 47 (1946) ("'The right to life and to personal security is not
only sacred in the estimation of the common law, but it is inalien-
able'"). And the prohibitions against assisting suicide never contained
exceptions for those who were near death. Rather, "[t]he life of those to
whom life ha[d] become a burden—of those who [were] hopelessly
diseased or fatally wounded—nay, even the lives of criminals condemned to death, [were] under the protection of the law, equally as the
lives of those who [were] in the full tide of life's enjoyment, and anxious
to continue to live." *Blackburn v. State*, 23 Ohio St. 146, 163 (1872); see
Bowen, supra, at 360 (prisoner who persuaded another to commit suicide could be tried for murder, even though victim was scheduled
shortly to be executed).

The earliest American statute explicitly to outlaw assisting suicide
was enacted in New York in 1828...and many of the new States and
Territories followed New York's example.... Between 1857 and 1865, a
New York commission led by Dudley Field drafted a criminal code that
prohibited "aiding" a suicide and, specifically, "furnish[ing] another
person with any deadly weapon or poisonous drug, knowing that such
person intends to use such weapon or drug in taking his own life."...By
the time the Fourteenth Amendment was ratified, it was a crime in
most States to assist a suicide.... The Field Penal Code was adopted in
the Dakota Territory in 1877 and in New York in 1881, and its language
served as a model for several other western States' statutes in the late
19th and early 20th centuries.... California, for example, codified its
assisted-suicide prohibition in 1874, using language similar to the Field
Code's. In this century, the Model Penal Code also prohibited "aiding"
suicide, prompting many States to enact or revise their assisted-suicide
bans. The code's drafters observed that "the interests in the sanctity of
life that are represented by the criminal homicide laws are threatened by
one who expresses a willingness to participate in taking the life of
another, even though the act may be accomplished with the consent, or
at the request, of the suicide victim." American Law Institute, Model

Penal Code § 210.5, Comment 5, p. 100 (Official Draft and Revised Comments 1980).

Though deeply rooted, the States' assisted-suicide bans have in recent years been reexamined and, generally, reaffirmed. Because of advances in medicine and technology, Americans today are increasingly likely to die in institutions, from chronic illnesses. President's Comm'n for the Study of Ethical Problems in Medicine and Biomedical and Behavioral Research, Deciding to Forego Life-Sustaining Treatment 16-18 (1983). Public concern and democratic action are therefore sharply focused on how best to protect dignity and independence at the end of life, with the result that there have been many significant changes in state laws and in the attitudes these laws reflect. Many States, for example, now permit "living wills," surrogate health-care decisionmaking, and the withdrawal or refusal of life-sustaining medical treatment.... At the same time, however, voters and legislators continue for the most part to reaffirm their States' prohibitions on assisting suicide.

The Washington statute at issue in this case, Wash. Rev. Code § 9A.36.060 (1994), was enacted in 1975 as part of a revision of that State's criminal code. Four years later, Washington passed its Natural Death Act, which specifically stated that the "withholding or withdrawal of life-sustaining treatment... shall not, for any purpose, constitute a suicide" and that "[n]othing in this chapter shall be construed to condone, authorize, or approve mercy killing...." Natural Death Act, 1979 Wash. Laws, ch. 112, § 8(1), p. 11 (codified at Wash. Rev. Code §§ 70.122.070(1), 70.122.100 (1994)). In 1991, Washington voters rejected a ballot initiative which, had it passed, would have permitted a form of physician assisted suicide. Washington then added a provision to the Natural Death Act expressly excluding physician-assisted suicide. 1992 Wash. Laws, ch. 98, § 10; Wash. Rev. Code § 70.122.100 (1994).

California voters rejected an assisted-suicide initiative similar to Washington's in 1993. On the other hand, in 1994, voters in Oregon enacted, also through ballot initiative, that State's "Death With Dignity Act," which legalized physician-assisted suicide for competent, terminally ill adults. Since the Oregon vote, many proposals to legalize assisted-suicide have been and continue to be introduced in the States' legislatures, but none has been enacted. And just last year, Iowa and Rhode Island joined the overwhelming majority of States explicitly prohibiting assisted suicide.... Also, on April 30, 1997, President Clinton signed the Federal Assisted Suicide Funding Restriction Act of 1997, which prohibits the use of federal funds in support of physician-assisted suicide....[†]

Thus, the States are currently engaged in serious, thoughtful examinations of physician-assisted suicide and other similar issues. For example, New York State's Task Force on Life and the Law—an ongoing, blue-ribbon commission composed of doctors, ethicists, lawyers, religious leaders, and interested laymen—was convened in 1984 and commissioned with "a broad mandate to recommend public policy on issues raised by medical advances." ... Over the past decade, the Task Force has recommended laws relating to end-of-life decisions, surrogate pregnancy, and organ donation.... After studying physician-assisted suicide, however, the Task Force unanimously concluded that "[l]egalizing assisted suicide and euthanasia would pose profound risks to many individuals who are ill and vulnerable.... [T]he potential dangers of this dramatic change in public policy would outweigh any benefit that might be achieved."

Attitudes toward suicide itself have changed since Bracton, but our laws have consistently condemned, and continue to prohibit, assisting suicide. Despite changes in medical technology and notwithstanding an increased emphasis on the importance of end-of-life decisionmaking, we have not retreated from this prohibition. Against this backdrop of history, tradition, and practice, we now turn to respondents' constitutional claim.

II

The Due Process Clause guarantees more than fair process, and the "liberty" it protects includes more than the absence of physical restraint. *Collins* v. *Harker Heights*, 503 U.S. 115, 125 (1992) (Due Process Clause "protects individual liberty against 'certain government actions regardless of the fairness of the procedures used to implement them'") (quoting *Daniels v. Williams*, 474 U.S. 327, 331 (1986)). The Clause also provides heightened protection against government interference with

---

† Other countries are embroiled in similar debates: The Supreme Court of Canada recently rejected a claim that the Canadian Charter of Rights and Freedoms establishes a fundamental right to assisted suicide, *Rodriguez v. British Columbia* ...; the British House of Lords Select Committee on Medical Ethics refused to recommend any change to Great Britain's assisted suicide provision.... New Zealand's Parliament rejected a proposed "Death with Dignity Bill" that would have legalized physician assisted suicide...and the Northern Territory of Australia legalized assisted suicide and voluntary euthanasia in 1995.... On March 14, 1997, however, the Australian Senate voted to overturn the Northern Territory's law....

certain fundamental rights and liberty interests.... In a long line of cases, we have held that, in addition to the specific freedoms protected by the Bill of Rights, the "liberty" specially protected by the Due Process Clause includes the rights to marry, *Loving v. Virginia*, 388 U.S. 1 (1967); to have children, *Skinner v. Oklahoma ex rel. Williamson*, 316 U.S. 535 (1942); to direct the education and upbringing of one's children, *Meyer v. Nebraska*, 262 U.S. 390 (1923); *Pierce v. Society of Sisters*, 268 U.S. 510 (1925); to marital privacy, *Griswold v. Connecticut*, 381 U.S. 479 (1965); to use contraception, *ibid.*; *Eisenstadt v. Baird*, 405 U.S. 438 (1972); to bodily integrity, *Rochin v. California*, 342 U.S. 165 (1952), and to abortion, *Casey, supra*. We have also assumed, and strongly suggested, that the Due Process Clause protects the traditional right to refuse unwanted lifesaving medical treatment. *Cruzan*, 497 U.S., at 278-279.

But we "ha[ve] always been reluctant to expand the concept of substantive due process because guideposts for responsible decisionmaking in this unchartered area are scarce and open-ended." ... By extending constitutional protection to an asserted right or liberty interest, we, to a great extent, place the matter outside the arena of public debate and legislative action. We must therefore "exercise the utmost care whenever we are asked to break new ground in this field," ... lest the liberty protected by the Due Process Clause be subtly transformed into the policy preferences of the Members of this Court....

Our established method of substantive-due-process analysis has two primary features: First, we have regularly observed that the Due Process Clause specially protects those fundamental rights and liberties which are, objectively, "deeply rooted in this Nation's history and tradition," ...; *Snyder v. Massachusetts*, 291 U.S. 97, 105 (1934) ("so rooted in the traditions and conscience of our people as to be ranked as fundamental"), and "implicit in the concept of ordered liberty," such that "neither liberty nor justice would exist if they were sacrificed," *Palko v. Connecticut*, 302 U.S. 319, 325, 326 (1937). Second, we have required in substantive-due-process cases a "careful description" of the asserted fundamental liberty interest.... Our Nation's history, legal traditions, and practices thus provide the crucial "guideposts for responsible decisionmaking," *Collins, supra*, at 125, that direct and restrain our exposition of the Due Process Clause. As we stated recently in *Flores*, the Fourteenth Amendment "forbids the government to infringe... 'fundamental' liberty interests *at all*, no matter what process is provided, unless the infringement is narrowly tailored to serve a compelling state interest." 507 U.S., at 302.

Justice Souter, relying on Justice Harlan's dissenting opinion in *Poe v. Ullman*, 367 U.S. 497 (1961), would largely abandon this restrained methodology, and instead ask "whether [Washington's] statute sets up one of those 'arbitrary impositions' or 'purposeless restraints' at odds with the Due Process Clause of the Fourteenth Amendment," *post*, at 752 (quoting *Poe*, *supra*, at 543 [Harlan, J., dissenting]). In our view, however, the development of this Court's substantive-due-process jurisprudence, described briefly *supra*, at 719-720, has been a process whereby the outlines of the "liberty" specially protected by the Fourteenth Amendment — never fully clarified, to be sure, and perhaps not capable of being fully clarified — have at least been carefully refined by concrete examples involving fundamental rights found to be deeply rooted in our legal tradition. This approach tends to rein in the subjective elements that are necessarily present in due process judicial review. In addition, by establishing a threshold requirement — that a challenged state action implicate a fundamental right — before requiring more than a reasonable relation to a legitimate state interest to justify the action, it avoids the need for complex balancing of competing interests in every case.

Turning to the claim at issue here, the Court of Appeals stated that "[p]roperly analyzed, the first issue to be resolved is whether there is a liberty interest in determining the time and manner of one's death," 79 F. 3d, at 801, or, in other words, "[i]s there a right to die?," *id.*, at 799. Similarly, respondents assert a "liberty to choose how to die" and a right to "control of one's final days," Brief for Respondents 7, and describe the asserted liberty as "the right to choose a humane, dignified death," *id.*, at 15, and "the liberty to shape death," *id.*, at 18. As noted above, we have a tradition of carefully formulating the interest at stake in substantive due-process cases. For example, although *Cruzan* is often described as a "right to die" case, see 79 F. 3d, at 799; *post*, at 745 (Stevens, J., concurring in judgments) (*Cruzan* recognized "the more specific interest in making decisions about how to confront an imminent death"), we were, in fact, more precise: We assumed that the Constitution granted competent persons a "constitutionally protected right to refuse lifesaving hydration and nutrition." *Cruzan*, 497 U.S., at 279; *id.*, at 287 (O.Connor, J., concurring) ("[A] liberty interest in refusing unwanted medical treatment may be inferred from our prior decisions"). The Washington statute at issue in this case prohibits "aid[ing] another person to attempt suicide," Wash. Rev. Code § 9A.36.060(1) (1994), and, thus, the question before us is whether the "liberty" specially protected by the Due Process Clause includes a right to commit suicide which itself includes a right to assistance in doing so.18

We now inquire whether this asserted right has any place in our Nation's traditions. Here...we are confronted with a consistent and almost universal tradition that has long rejected the asserted right, and continues explicitly to reject it today, even for terminally ill, mentally competent adults. To hold for respondents, we would have to reverse centuries of legal doctrine and practice, and strike down the considered policy choice of almost every State. See *Jackman v. Rosenbaum Co.*, 260 U.S. 22, 31 (1922) ("If a thing has been practised for two hundred years by common consent, it will need a strong case for the Fourteenth Amendment to affect it"); *Flores*, 507 U.S., at 303 ("The mere novelty of such a claim is reason enough to doubt that 'substantive due process' sustains it").

Respondents contend, however, that the liberty interest they assert *is* consistent with this Court's substantive-due-process line of cases, if not with this Nation's history and practice. Pointing to *Casey* and *Cruzan*, respondents read our jurisprudence in this area as reflecting a general tradition of "self-sovereignty," Brief for Respondents 12, and as teaching that the "liberty" protected by the Due Process Clause includes "basic and intimate exercises of personal autonomy," *id.*, at 10; see *Casey*, 505 U.S., at 847 ("It is a promise of the Constitution that there is a realm of personal liberty which the government may not enter"). According to respondents, our liberty jurisprudence, and the broad, individualistic principles it reflects, protects the "liberty of competent, terminally ill adults to make end-of-life decisions free of undue government interference." Brief for Respondents 10. The question presented in this case, however, is whether the protections of the Due Process Clause include a right to commit suicide with another's assistance. With this "careful description" of respondents' claim in mind, we turn to *Casey* and *Cruzan*.

In *Cruzan*, we considered whether Nancy Beth Cruzan, who had been severely injured in an automobile accident and was in a persistive vegetative state, "ha[d] a right under the United States Constitution which would require the hospital to withdraw life-sustaining treatment" at her parents' request. 497 U.S., at 269. We began with the observation that "[a]t common law, even the touching of one person by another without consent and without legal justification was a battery." *Ibid.* We then discussed the related rule that "informed consent is generally required for medical treatment." *Ibid.* After reviewing a long line of relevant state cases, we concluded that "the common-law doctrine of informed consent is viewed as generally encompassing the right of a competent individual to refuse medical treatment." *Id.*, at 277. Next, we reviewed our own cases on the subject, and stated that "[t]he principle that a competent person has a constitutionally protected liberty interest in refusing unwanted medical treatment may be inferred from our prior decisions." *Id.*, at 278. Therefore, "for purposes of [that] case, we assume[d] that the United States Constitution would grant a competent person a constitutionally protected right to refuse lifesaving hydration and nutrition." *Id.*, at 279; see *id.*, at 287 (O.Connor, J., concurring). We concluded that, notwithstanding this right, the Constitution permitted Missouri to require clear and convincing evidence of an incompetent patient's wishes concerning the withdrawal of life-sustaining treatment. *Id.*, at 280-281.

Respondents contend that in *Cruzan* we "acknowledged that competent, dying persons have the right to direct the removal of life-sustaining medical treatment and thus hasten death," Brief for Respondents 23, and that "the constitutional principle behind recognizing the patient's liberty to direct the withdrawal of artificial life support applies at least as strongly to the choice to hasten impending death by consuming lethal medication," *id.*, at 26. Similarly, the Court of Appeals concluded that "*Cruzan*, by recognizing a liberty interest that includes the refusal of artificial provision of life-sustaining food and water, necessarily recognize[d] a liberty interest in hastening one's own death." 79 F. 3d, at 816.

The right assumed in *Cruzan*, however, was not simply deduced from abstract concepts of personal autonomy. Given the common-law rule that forced medication was a battery, and the long legal tradition protecting the decision to refuse unwanted medical treatment, our assumption was entirely consistent with this Nation's history and constitutional traditions. The decision to commit suicide with the assistance of another may be just as personal and profound as the decision to refuse unwanted medical treatment, but it has never enjoyed similar legal protection. Indeed, the two acts are widely and reasonably regarded as quite distinct. See *Quill v. Vacco....* In *Cruzan* itself, we recognized that most States outlawed assisted suicide—and even more do today—and we certainly gave no intimation that the right to refuse unwanted medical treatment could be some how transmuted into a right to assistance in committing suicide. 497 U.S., at 280.

Respondents also rely on *Casey*. There, the Court's opinion concluded that "the essential holding of *Roe v. Wade* [410 U.S. 113 (1973),] should be retained and once again reaffirmed." 505 U.S., at 846. We held, first, that a woman has a right, before her fetus is viable, to an abortion "without undue interference from the State"; second, that States may restrict postviability abortions, so long as exceptions are made to protect a woman's life and health; and third, that the State has legitimate interests throughout a pregnancy in protecting the health of the woman and the life of the unborn child. *Ibid.* In reaching this con-clusion, the opinion discussed in some detail this Court's substantive-due-process tradition of interpreting the Due Process Clause to protect certain fundamental rights and "personal decisions relating to mar-riage, procreation, contraception, family relationships, child rearing, and education," and noted that many of those rights and liberties "involv[e] the most intimate and personal choices a person may make in a lifetime." *Id.*, at 851.

The Court of Appeals, like the District Court, found *Casey* "'highly instructive'" and "'almost prescriptive'" for determining "'what liberty interest may inhere in a terminally ill person's choice to commit suicide'":

> "Like the decision of whether or not to have an abortion, the deci-sion how and when to die is one of 'the most intimate and per-sonal choices a person may make in a lifetime,' a choice 'central to personal dignity and autonomy.'" 79 F. 3d, at 813-814.

Similarly, respondents emphasize the statement in *Casey* that:

> "At the heart of liberty is the right to define one's own concept of existence, of meaning, of the universe, and of the mystery of human life. Beliefs about these matters could not define the attributes of personhood were they formed under compulsion of the State." 505 U.S., at 851.

Brief for Respondents 12. By choosing this language, the Court's opin-ion in *Casey* described, in a general way and in light of our prior cases, those personal activities and decisions that this Court has identified as so deeply rooted in our history and traditions, or so fundamental to our concept of constitutionally ordered liberty, that they are protected by the Fourteenth Amendment. The opinion moved from the recogni-tion that liberty necessarily includes freedom of conscience and belief about ultimate considerations to the observation that "though the abortion decision may originate within the zone of conscience and belief, it is *more than a philosophic exercise.*" *Casey*, 505 U.S., at 852 (emphasis added). That many of the rights and liberties protected by the Due Process Clause sound in personal autonomy does not warrant the sweeping conclusion that any and all important, intimate, and personal decisions are so protected, *San Antonio Independent School Dist. v. Rodriguez*, 411 U.S. 1, 33-35 (1973), and *Casey* did not suggest otherwise.

The history of the law's treatment of assisted suicide in this country has been and continues to be one of the rejection of nearly all efforts to permit it. That being the case, our decisions lead us to conclude that the asserted "right" to assistance in committing suicide is not a fundamental liberty interest protected by the Due Process Clause. The Constitution also requires, however, that Washington's assisted suicide ban be rationally related to legitimate government interests.... This requirement is unquestionably met here. As the court below recognized ... Washington's assisted-suicide ban implicates a number of state interests....

First, Washington has an "unqualified interest in the preservation of human life." *Cruzan*, 497 U.S., at 282. The State's prohibition on assisted suicide, like all homicide laws, both reflects and advances its commitment to this interest. See *id.*, at 280; Model Penal Code § 210.5, Comment 5, at 100 ("[T]he interests in the sanctity of life that are represented by the criminal homicide laws are threatened by one who expresses a willingness to participate in taking the life of another"). This interest is symbolic and aspirational as well as practical:

> "While suicide is no longer prohibited or penalized, the ban against assisted suicide and euthanasia shores up the notion of limits in human relationships. It reflects the gravity with which we view the decision to take one's own life or the life of another, and our reluctance to encourage or promote these decisions." New York Task Force 131-132.

Respondents admit that "[t]he State has a real interest in preserving the lives of those who can still contribute to society and have the potential to enjoy life." Brief for Respondents 35, n. 23. The Court of Appeals also recognized Washington's interest in protecting life, but held that the "weight" of this interest depends on the "medical condition and the wishes of the person whose life is at stake." 79 F. 3d, at 817. Washington, however, has rejected this sliding-scale approach and, through its assisted-suicide ban, insists that all persons' lives, from beginning to end, regardless of physical or mental condition, are under the full protection of the law. See *United States v. Rutherford*, 442 U.S. 544, 558 (1979) ("... Congress could reasonably have determined to protect the terminally ill, no less than other patients, from the vast range of self-styled panaceas that inventive minds can devise"). As we have previously affirmed, the States "may properly decline to make judgments about the 'quality' of life that a particular individual may enjoy," *Cruzan, supra*, at 282. This remains true, as *Cruzan* makes clear, even for those who are near death.

Relatedly, all admit that suicide is a serious public-health problem, especially among persons in otherwise vulnerable groups. See Washington State Dept. of Health, Annual Summary of Vital Statistics 1991, pp. 29-30 (Oct. 1992) (suicide is a leading cause of death in Washington of those between the ages of 14 and 54); New York Task Force 10, 23-33 (suicide rate in the general population is about one percent, and suicide is especially prevalent among the young and the elderly). The State has an interest in preventing suicide, and in studying, identifying, and treating its causes. See 79 F. 3d, at 820; *id.*, at 854 (Beezer, J., dissenting) ("The state recognizes suicide as a manifestation of medical and psychological anguish")....

Those who attempt suicide—terminally ill or not—often suffer from depression or other mental disorders. See New York Task Force 13-22, 126-128 (more than 95% of those who commit suicide had a major psychiatric illness at the time of death; among the terminally ill, uncontrolled pain is a "risk factor" because it contributes to depression); Physician-Assisted Suicide and Euthanasia in the Netherlands: A Report of Chairman Charles T. Canady to the Subcommittee on the Constitution of the House Committee on the Judiciary, 104th Cong., 2d Sess., 10-11 (Comm. Print 1996); cf. Back, Wallace, Starks, & Pearlman, Physician-Assisted Suicide and Euthanasia in Washington State, 275 JAMA 919, 924 (1996) ("[I]ntolerable physical symptoms are not the reason most patients request physician-assisted suicide or euthanasia"). Research indicates, however, that many people who request physician-assisted suicide withdraw that request if their depression and pain are treated. H. Hendin, Seduced by Death: Doctors, Patients and the Dutch Cure 24-25 (1997) (suicidal, terminally ill patients "usually respond well to treatment for depressive illness and pain medication and are then grateful to be alive"); New York Task Force 177-178. The New York Task Force, however, expressed its concern that, because depression is difficult to diagnose, physicians and medical professionals often fail to respond adequately to seriously ill patients' needs. *Id.*, at 175. Thus, legal physician-assisted suicide could make it more difficult for the State to protect depressed or mentally ill persons, or those who are suffering from untreated pain, from suicidal impulses.

The State also has an interest in protecting the integrity and ethics of the medical profession. In contrast to the Court of Appeals' conclusion that "the integrity of the medical profession would [not] be threatened in any way by [physician-assisted suicide]," 79 F. 3d, at 827, the American Medical Association, like many other medical and physicians' groups, has concluded that "[p]hysician-assisted suicide is fundamentally incompatible with the physician's role as healer." American Medical Association, Code of Ethics § 2.211 (1994); see Council on Ethical and Judicial Affairs, Decisions Near the End of Life, 267 JAMA 2229, 2233 (1992) ("[T]he societal risks of involving physicians in medical interventions to cause patients' deaths is too great"); New York Task Force 103-109 (discussing physicians' views). And physician-assisted suicide could, it is argued, undermine the trust that is essential to the doctor-patient relationship by blurring the time-honored line between healing and harming. Assisted Suicide in the United States, Hearing before the Subcommittee on the Constitution of the House Committee on the Judiciary, 104th Cong., 2d Sess., 355-356 (1996) (testimony of Dr. Leon R. Kass) ("The patient's trust in the doctor's whole-hearted devotion to his best interests will be hard to sustain").

Next, the State has an interest in protecting vulnerable groups—including the poor, the elderly, and disabled persons—from abuse, neglect, and mistakes. The Court of Appeals dismissed the State's concern that disadvantaged persons might be pressured into physician-assisted suicide as "ludicrous on its face." 79 F. 3d, at 825. We have recognized, however, the real risk of subtle coercion and undue influence in end-of-life situations. *Cruzan*, 497 U.S., at 281. Similarly, the New York Task Force warned that "[l]egalizing physician-assisted suicide would pose profound risks to many individuals who are ill and vulnerable.... The risk of harm is greatest for the many individuals in our society whose autonomy and well-being are already compromised by poverty, lack of access to good medical care, advanced age, or membership in a stigmatized social group." New York Task Force 120; see *Compassion in Dying*, 49 F. 3d, at 593 ("An insidious bias against the handicapped—again coupled with a cost-saving mentality—makes them especially in need of Washington's statutory protection"). If physician assisted suicide were permitted, many might resort to it to spare their families the sub-stantial financial burden of end of life health-care costs.

The State's interest here goes beyond protecting the vulnerable from coercion; it extends to protecting disabled and terminally ill people from prejudice, negative and inaccurate stereotypes, and "societal indif-ference." 49 F. 3d, at 592. The State's assisted-suicide ban reflects and reinforces its policy that the lives of terminally ill, disabled, and elderly people must be no less valued than the lives of the young and healthy, and that a seriously disabled person's suicidal impulses should be inter-preted and treated the same way as anyone else's. See New York Task Force 101-102; Physician-Assisted Suicide and Euthanasia in the Netherlands: A Report of Chairman Charles T. Canady, *supra*, at 9, 20 (discussing prejudice toward the disabled and the negative messages euthanasia and assisted suicide send to handicapped patients).

Finally, the State may fear that permitting assisted suicide will start it down the path to voluntary and perhaps even involuntary euthanasia. The Court of Appeals struck down Washington's assisted-suicide ban only "as applied to competent, terminally ill adults who wish to hasten their deaths by obtaining medication prescribed by their doctors." 79 F. 3d, at 838. Washington insists, however, that the impact of the court's decision will not and cannot be so limited. Brief for Petitioners 44-47. If suicide is protected as a matter of constitutional right, it is argued, "every man and woman in the United States must enjoy it." *Compassion in Dying*, 49 F. 3d, at 591; see *Kevorkian*, 447 Mich., at 470, n. 41, 527 N. W. 2d, at 727-728, n. 41. The Court of Appeals' decision, and its expan-sive reasoning, provide ample support for the State's concerns. The court noted, for example, that the "decision of a duly appointed surro-gate decision maker is for all legal purposes the decision of the patient himself," 79 F. 3d, at 832, n. 120; that "in some instances, the patient may be unable to self-administer the drugs and...administration by the physician...may be the only way the patient may be able to receive them," *id.*, at 831; and that not only physicians, but also family members and loved ones, will inevitably participate in assisting suicide, *id.*, at 838, n. 140. Thus, it turns out that what is couched as a limited right to "physician-assisted suicide" is likely, in effect, a much broader license, which could prove extremely difficult to police and contain. Washing-ton's ban on assisting suicide prevents such erosion.

This concern is further supported by evidence about the practice of euthanasia in the Netherlands. The Dutch government's own study revealed that in 1990, there were 2,300 cases of voluntary euthanasia (defined as "the deliberate termination of another's life at his request"), 400 cases of assisted suicide, and more than 1,000 cases of euthanasia without an explicit request. In addition to these latter 1,000 cases, the study found an additional 4,941 cases where physicians administered lethal morphine overdoses without the patients' explicit consent. Physician-Assisted Suicide and Euthanasia in the Netherlands: A Report of Chairman Charles T. Canady, *supra*, 12-13 (citing Dutch study). This study suggests that, despite the existence of various reporting procedures, euthanasia in the Netherlands has not been limited to competent, terminally ill adults who are enduring physical suffering, and that regulation of the practice may not have prevented abuses in cases involving vulnerable persons, including severely disabled neonates and elderly persons suffering from dementia. *Id.*, at 16-21; see generally C. Gomez, Regulating Death: Euthanasia and the Case of the Netherlands (1991); H. Hendin, Seduced By Death: Doctors, Patients, and the Dutch Cure (1997). The New York Task Force, citing the Dutch experience, observed that "assisted suicide and euthanasia are closely linked," New York Task Force 145, and concluded that the "risk of... abuse is neither speculative nor distant," *id.*, at 134. Washington, like most other States, reasonably ensures against this risk by banning, rather than regulating, assisted suicide. See *United States v. 12 200-ft. Reels of Super 8MM. Film*, 413 U.S. 123, 127 (1973) ("Each step, when taken, appear[s] a reasonable step in relation to that which preceded it, although the aggregate or end result is one that would never have been seriously considered in the first instance").

We need not weigh exactingly the relative strengths of these various interests. They are unquestionably important and legitimate, and Washington's ban on assisted suicide is at least reasonably related to their promotion and protection. We therefore hold that Wash. Rev. Code § 9A.36.060(1) (1994) does not violate the Fourteenth Amendment, either on its face or "as applied to competent, terminally ill adults who wish to hasten their deaths by obtaining medication prescribed by their doctors." 79 F. 3d, at 838.

* * *

Throughout the Nation, Americans are engaged in an earnest and profound debate about the morality, legality, and practicality of physician-assisted suicide. Our holding permits this debate to continue, as it should in a democratic society. The decision of the en banc Court of Appeals is reversed, and the case is remanded for further proceedings consistent with this opinion. *It is so ordered.*

Justice Stevens, concurring in the judgments.

... The morality, legality, and practicality of capital punishment have been the subject of debate for many years. In 1976, this Court upheld the constitutionality of the practice in cases coming to us from Georgia, Florida, and Texas. In those cases we concluded that a State does have the power to place a lesser value on some lives than on others; there is no absolute requirement that a State treat all human life as having an equal right to preservation. Because the state legislatures had sufficiently narrowed the category of lives that the State could terminate, and had enacted special procedures to ensure that the defendant belonged in that limited category, we concluded that the statutes were not unconstitutional on their face. In later cases coming to us from each of those States, however, we found that some applications of the statutes were unconstitutional.

... just as our conclusion that capital punishment is not always unconstitutional did not preclude later decisions holding that it is sometimes impermissibly cruel, so is it equally clear that a decision upholding a general statutory prohibition of assisted suicide does not mean that every possible application of the statute would be valid. A State, like Washington, that has authorized the death penalty, and thereby has concluded that the sanctity of human life does not require that it always be preserved, must acknowledge that there are situations in which an interest in hastening death is legitimate. Indeed, not only is that interest sometimes legitimate, I am also convinced that there are times when it is entitled to constitutional protection.

... In *Cruzan v. Director, Mo. Dept. of Health,* 497 U.S. 261 (1990), the Court assumed that the interest in liberty protected by the Fourteenth Amendment encompassed the right of a terminally ill patient to direct the withdrawal of lifesustaining treatment. As the Court correctly observes today, that assumption "was not simply deduced from abstract concepts of personal autonomy." *Ante,* at 725. Instead, it was supported by the common-law tradition protecting the individual's general right to refuse unwanted medical treatment. *Ibid.* We have recognized, however, that this common-law right to refuse treatment is neither absolute nor always sufficiently weighty to overcome valid countervailing state interests. As Justice Brennan pointed out in his *Cruzan* dissent, we have upheld legislation imposing punishment on persons refusing to be vaccinated, 497 U.S., at 312, n. 12, citing *Jacobson* v. *Massachusetts*, 197 U.S. 11, 26-27 (1905), and as Justice Scalia pointed out in his concurrence, the State ordinarily has the right to interfere with an attempt to commit suicide by, for example, forcibly placing a bandage on a self-inflicted wound to stop the flow of blood. 497 U.S., at 298. In most cases, the individual's constitutionally protected interest in his or her own physical autonomy, including the right to refuse unwanted medical treatment, will give way to the State's interest in preserving human life.

Cruzan, however, was not the normal case. Given the irreversible nature of her illness and the progressive character of her suffering, Nancy Cruzan's interest in refusing medical care was incidental to her more basic interest in controlling the manner and timing of her death. In finding that her best interests would be served by cutting off the nourishment that kept her alive, the trial court did more than simply vindicate Cruzan's interest in refusing medical treatment; the court, in essence, authorized affirmative conduct that would hasten her death. When this Court reviewed the case and upheld Missouri's requirement that there be clear and convincing evidence establishing Nancy Cruzan's intent to have life-sustaining nourishment withdrawn, it made two important assumptions: (1) that there was a "liberty interest" in refusing unwanted treatment protected by the Due Process Clause; and (2) that this liberty interest did not "end the inquiry" because it might be outweighed by relevant state interests. *Id.*, at 279. I agree with both of those assumptions, but I insist that the source of Nancy Cruzan's right to refuse treatment was not just a common-law rule. Rather, this right is an aspect of a far broader and more basic concept of freedom that is even older than the common law. This freedom embraces not merely a person's right to refuse a particular kind of unwanted treatment, but also her interest in dignity, and in determining the character of the memories that will survive long after her death. In recognizing that the State's interests did not outweigh Nancy Cruzan's liberty interest in refusing medical treatment, *Cruzan* rested not simply on the common-law right to refuse medical treatment, but—at least implicitly—on the even more fundamental right to make this "deeply personal decision," *id.*, at 289 (O'Connor, J., concurring).

Thus, the common-law right to protection from battery, which included the right to refuse medical treatment in most circumstances, did not mark "the outer limits of the substantive sphere of liberty" that supported the Cruzan family's decision to hasten Nancy's death.

Planned Parenthood of Southeastern Pa. v. Casey, 505 U.S. 833, 848 (1992). Those limits have never been precisely defined. They are generally identified by the importance and character of the decision confronted by the individual, *Whalen v. Roe*, 429 U.S. 589, 599-600, n. 26 (1977). Whatever the outer limits of the concept may be, it definitely includes protection for matters "central to personal dignity and autonomy." *Casey*, 505 U.S., at 851. It includes

> "the individual's right to make certain unusually important decisions that will affect his own, or his family's, destiny. The Court has referred to such decisions as implicating 'basic values,' as being 'fundamental,' and as being dignified by history and tradition. The character of the Court's language in these cases brings to mind the origins of the American heritage of freedom—the abiding interest in individual liberty that makes certain state intrusions on the citizen's right to decide how he will live his own life intolerable." *Fitzgerald v. Porter Memorial Hospital*, 523 F. 2d 716, 719-720 (CA7 1975) (footnotes omitted), cert. denied, 425 U.S. 916 (1976).

The *Cruzan* case demonstrated that some state intrusions on the right to decide how death will be encountered are also intolerable. The now-deceased plaintiffs in this action may in fact have had a liberty interest even stronger than Nancy Cruzan's because, not only were they terminally ill, they were suffering constant and severe pain. Avoiding intolerable pain and the indignity of living one's final days incapacitated and in agony is certainly "[a]t the heart of [the] liberty...to define one's own concept of existence, of meaning, of the universe, and of the mystery of human life." *Casey*, 505 U.S., at 851.

While I agree with the Court that *Cruzan* does not decide the issue presented by these cases, *Cruzan* did give recognition, not just to vague, unbridled notions of autonomy, but to the more specific interest in making decisions about how to confront an imminent death. Although there is no absolute right to physician-assisted suicide, *Cruzan* makes it clear that some individuals who no longer have the option of deciding whether to live or to die because they are already on the threshold of death have a constitutionally protected interest that may outweigh the State's interest in preserving life at all costs. The liberty interest at stake in a case like this differs from, and is stronger than, both the common-law right to refuse medical treatment and the unbridled interest in deciding whether to live or die. It is an interest in deciding how, rather than whether, a critical threshold shall be crossed.

... In New York, a doctor must respect a competent person's decision to refuse or to discontinue medical treatment even though death will thereby ensue, but the same doctor would be guilty of a felony if she provided her patient assistance in committing suicide. Today we hold that the Equal Protection Clause is not violated by the resulting disparate treatment of two classes of terminally ill people who may have the same interest in hastening death. I agree that the distinction between permitting death to ensue from an underlying fatal disease and causing it to occur by the administration of medication or other means provides a constitutionally sufficient basis for the State's classification. Unlike the Court, however, see *Vacco, post*, at 801-802, I am not persuaded that in all cases there will in fact be a significant difference between the intent of the physicians, the patients, or the families in the two situations.

There may be little distinction between the intent of a terminally ill patient who decides to remove her life support and one who seeks the assistance of a doctor in ending her life; in both situations, the patient is seeking to hasten a certain, impending death. The doctor's intent might also be the same in prescribing lethal medication as it is in terminating life support. A doctor who fails to administer medical treatment to one who is dying from a disease could be doing so with an intent to harm or kill that patient. Conversely, a doctor who prescribes lethal medication does not necessarily intend the patient's death — rather that doctor may seek simply to ease the patient's suffering and to comply with her wishes. The illusory character of any differences in intent or causation is confirmed by the fact that the American Medical Association unequivocally endorses the practice of terminal sedation — the administration of sufficient dosages of pain-killing medication to terminally ill patients to protect them from excruciating pain even when it is clear that the time of death will be advanced. The purpose of terminal sedation is to ease the suffering of the patient and comply with her wishes, and the actual cause of death is the administration of heavy doses of lethal sedatives. This same intent and causation may exist when a doctor complies with a patient's request for lethal medication to hasten her death.

Thus, although the differences the majority notes in causation and intent between terminating life support and assisting in suicide support the Court's rejection of the respondents' facial challenge, these distinctions may be inapplicable to particular terminally ill patients and their doctors. Our holding today in *Vacco v. Quill, post*, p. 793, that the Equal Protection Clause is not violated by New York's classification, just like our holding in *Washington v. Glucksberg* that the Washington statute is not invalid on its face, does not foreclose the possibility that some applications of the New York statute may impose an intolerable intrusion on the patient's freedom.

There remains room for vigorous debate about the outcome of particular cases that are not necessarily resolved by the opinions announced today. How such cases may be decided will depend on their specific facts. In my judgment, however, it is clear that the so-called "unqualified interest in the preservation of human life," *Cruzan*, 497 U.S., at 282; *ante*, at 728, is not itself sufficient to outweigh the interest in liberty that may justify the only possible means of preserving a dying patient's dignity and alleviating her intolerable suffering.

Justice Souter, concurring in the judgment.

... The State claims interests in protecting patients from mistakenly and involuntarily deciding to end their lives, and in guarding against both voluntary and involuntary euthanasia. Leaving aside any difficulties in coming to a clear concept of imminent death, mistaken decisions may result from inadequate palliative care or a terminal prognosis that turns out to be error; coercion and abuse may stem from the large medical bills that family members cannot bear or unreimbursed hospitals decline to shoulder. Voluntary and involuntary euthanasia may result once doctors are authorized to prescribe lethal medication in the first instance, for they might find it pointless to distinguish between patients who administer their own fatal drugs and those who wish not to, and their compassion for those who suffer may obscure the distinction between those who ask for death and those who may be unable to request it. The argument is that a progression would occur, obscuring the line between the ill and the dying, and between the responsible and the unduly influenced, until ultimately doctors and perhaps others would abuse a limited freedom to aid suicides by yielding to the impulse to end another's suffering under conditions going beyond the narrow limits the respondents propose. The State thus argues, essentially, that respondents' claim is not as narrow as it sounds, simply because no recognition of the interest they assert could be limited to vindicating those interests and affecting no others. The State says that the claim, in practical effect, would entail consequences that the State could, without doubt, legitimately act to prevent.

The mere assertion that the terminally sick might be pressured into suicide decisions by close friends and family members would not alone be very telling. Of course that is possible, not only because the costs of care might be more than family members could bear but simply because they might naturally wish to see an end of suffering for someone they love. But one of the points of restricting any right of assistance to physicians would be to condition the right on an exercise of judgment by someone qualified to assess the patient's responsible capacity and detect the influence of those outside the medical relationship.

The State, however, goes further, to argue that dependence on the vigilance of physicians will not be enough. First, the lines proposed here (particularly the requirement of a knowing and voluntary decision by the patient) would be more difficult to draw than the lines that have limited other recently recognized due process rights. Limiting a State from prosecuting use of artificial contraceptives by married couples posed no practical threat to the State's capacity to regulate contraceptives in other ways that were assumed at the time of *Roe* to be legitimate; the trimester measurements of *Roe* and the viability determination of *Casey* were easy to make with a real degree of certainty. But the knowing and responsible mind is harder to assess. Second, this difficulty could become the greater by combining with another fact within the realm of plausibility, that physicians simply would not be assiduous to preserve the line. They have compassion, and those who would be willing to assist in suicide at all might be the most susceptible to the wishes of a patient, whether the patient was technically quite responsible or not. Physicians, and their hospitals, have their own financial incentives, too, in this new age of managed care. Whether acting from compassion or under some other influence, a physician who would provide a drug for a patient to administer might well go the further step of administering the drug himself; so, the barrier between assisted suicide and euthanasia could become porous, and the line between voluntary and involuntary euthanasia as well. The case for the slippery slope is fairly made out here, not because recognizing one due process right would leave a court with no principled basis to avoid recognizing another, but because there is a plausible case that the right claimed would not be readily containable by reference to facts about the mind that are matters of difficult judgment, or by gatekeepers who are subject to temptation, noble or not.

Respondents propose an answer to all this, the answer of state regulation with teeth. Legislation proposed in several States, for example, would authorize physician-assisted suicide but require two qualified physicians to confirm the patient's diagnosis, prognosis, and competence; and would mandate that the patient make repeated requests witnessed by at least two others over a specified timespan; and would impose reporting requirements and criminal penalties for various acts of coercion. See App. to Brief for State Legislators as *Amici Curiae* 1a-2a.

But at least at this moment there are reasons for caution in predicting the effectiveness of the teeth proposed. Respondents' proposals, as it turns out, sound much like the guidelines now in place in the Netherlands, the only place where experience with physician-assisted suicide and euthanasia has yielded empirical evidence about how such regulations might affect actual practice. Dutch physicians must engage in consultation before proceeding, and must decide whether the patient's decision is voluntary, well considered, and stable, whether the request to die is enduring and made more than once, and whether the patient's future will involve unacceptable suffering. See C. Gomez, Regulating Death 40-43 (1991). There is, however, a substantial dispute today about what the Dutch experience shows. Some commentators marshall evidence that the Dutch guidelines have in practice failed to protect patients from involuntary euthanasia and have been violated with impunity. See, e.g., H. Hendin, Seduced By Death 75-84 (1997) (noting many cases in which decisions intended to end the life of a fully competent patient were made without a request from the patient and without consulting the patient); Keown, Euthanasia in the Netherlands: Sliding Down the Slippery Slope?, in Euthanasia Examined 261, 289 (J. Keown ed. 1995) (guidelines have "proved signally ineffectual; non-voluntary euthanasia is now widely practised and increasingly condoned in the Netherlands"); Gomez, *supra*, at 104-113. This evidence is contested. See, e.g., R. Epstein, Mortal Peril 322 (1997) ("Dutch physicians are not euthanasia enthusiasts and they are slow to practice it in individual cases"); R. Posner, Aging and Old Age 242, and n. 23 (1995) (noting fear of "doctors' rushing patients to their death" in the Netherlands "has not been substantiated and does not appear realistic"); Van der Wal, Van Eijk, Leenen, and Spreeuwenberg, Euthanasia and Assisted Suicide, 2, Do Dutch Family Doctors Act Prudently?, 9 Family Practice 135 (1992) (finding no serious abuse in Dutch practice). The day may come when we can say with some assurance which side is right, but for now it is the substantiality of the factual disagreement, and the alternatives for resolving it, that matter. They are, for me, dispositive of the due process claim at this time.

I take it that the basic concept of judicial review with its possible displacement of legislative judgment bars any finding that a legislature has acted arbitrarily when the following conditions are met: there is a serious factual controversy over the feasibility of recognizing the claimed right without at the same time making it impossible for the State to engage in an undoubtedly legitimate exercise of power; facts necessary to resolve the controversy are not readily ascertainable through the judicial process; but they are more readily subject to discovery through legislative factfinding and experimentation. It is assumed in this case, and must be, that a State's interest in protecting those unable to make responsible decisions and those who make no decisions at all entitles the State to bar aid to any but a knowing and responsible person intending suicide, and to prohibit euthanasia. How, and how far, a State should act in that interest are judgments for the State, but the legitimacy of its action to deny a physician the option to aid any but the knowing and responsible is beyond question.

The capacity of the State to protect the others if respondents were to prevail is, however, subject to some genuine question, underscored by the responsible disagreement over the basic facts of the Dutch experience. This factual controversy is not open to a judicial resolution with any substantial degree of assurance at this time. It is not, of course, that any controversy about the factual predicate of a due process claim disqualifies a court from resolving it. Courts can recognize captiousness, and most factual issues can be settled in a trial court. At this point, however, the factual issue at the heart of this case does not appear to be one of those. The principal enquiry at the moment is into the Dutch experience, and I question whether an independent front-line investigation into the facts of a foreign country's legal administration can be soundly undertaken through American courtroom litigation. While an extensive literature on any subject can raise the hopes for judicial understanding, the literature on this subject is only nascent. Since there is little experience directly bearing on the issue, the most that can be said is that whichever way the Court might rule today, events could overtake its assumptions, as experimentation in some jurisdictions confirmed or discredited the concerns about progression from assisted suicide to euthanasia.

Legislatures, on the other hand, have superior opportunities to obtain the facts necessary for a judgment about the present controversy.

Not only do they have more flexible mechanisms for factfinding than the Judiciary, but their mechanisms include the power to experiment, moving forward and pulling back as facts emerge within their own jurisdictions. There is, indeed, good reason to suppose that in the absence of a judgment for respondents here, just such experimentation will be attempted in some of the States....

I do not decide here what the significance might be of legislative foot dragging in ascertaining the facts going to the State's argument that the right in question could not be confined as claimed. Sometimes a court may be bound to act regardless of the institutional preferability of the political branches as forums for addressing constitutional claims.... Now, it is enough to say that our examination of legislative reasonableness should consider the fact that the Legislature of the State of Washington is no more obviously at fault than this Court is in being uncertain about what would happen if respondents prevailed today. We therefore have a clear question about which institution, a legislature or a court, is relatively more competent to deal with an emerging issue as to which facts currently unknown could be dispositive. The answer has to be, for the reasons already stated, that the legislative process is to be preferred. There is a closely related further reason as well.

One must bear in mind that the nature of the right claimed, if recognized as one constitutionally required, would differ in no essential way from other constitutional rights guaranteed by enumeration or derived from some more definite textual source than "due process." An unenumerated right should not therefore be recognized, with the effect of displacing the legislative ordering of things, without the assurance that its recognition would prove as durable as the recognition of those other rights differently derived. To recognize a right of lesser promise would simply create a constitutional regime too uncertain to bring with it the expectation of finality that is one of this Court's central obligations in making constitutional decisions. See *Casey*, 505 U.S., at 864-869.

Legislatures, however, are not so constrained. The experimentation that should be out of the question in constitutional adjudication displacing legislative judgments is entirely proper, as well as highly desirable, when the legislative power addresses an emerging issue like assisted suicide. The Court should accordingly stay its hand to allow reasonable legislative consideration. While I do not decide for all time that respondents' claim should not be recognized, I acknowledge the legislative institutional competence as the better one to deal with that claim at this time.

Chapter 2

VACCO, ATTORNEY GENERAL OF NEW YORK, ET AL. v. QUILL ET AL.*

Argued January 8, 1997 — Decided June 26, 1997

[...]

Chief Justice Rehnquist delivered the opinion of the Court.

In New York, as in most States, it is a crime to aid another to commit or attempt suicide, but patients may refuse even lifesaving medical treatment. The question presented by this case is whether New York's prohibition on assisting suicide therefore violates the Equal Protection Clause of the Fourteenth Amendment. We hold that it does not.

Petitioners are various New York public officials. Respondents Timothy E. Quill, Samuel C. Klagsbrun, and Howard A. Grossman are physicians who practice in New York. They assert that although it would be "consistent with the standards of [their] medical practice[s]" to prescribe lethal medication for "mentally competent, terminally ill patients" who are suffering great pain and desire a doctor's help in taking their own lives, they are deterred from doing so by New York's ban on assisting suicide.... Respondents, and three gravely ill patients who have since died, sued the State's Attorney General in the United States District Court. They urged that because New York permits a competent person to refuse life-sustaining medical treatment, and because the refusal of such treatment is "essentially the same thing" as physician-assisted suicide, New York's assisted-suicide ban violates the Equal Protection Clause....

---

* For ease of reading, portions of this judgment have been omitted. All omissions are indicated by "...". The full judgment, with its complete references, can be found online at <http://www.supremecourtus.gov/opinions/boundvolumes/521bv.pdf>, pages 793-810.

The District Court disagreed: "[I]t is hardly unreasonable or irrational for the State to recognize a difference between allowing nature to take its course, even in the most severe situations, and intentionally using an artificial death producing device." ... The court noted New York's "obvious legitimate interests in preserving life, and in protecting vulnerable persons," and concluded that "[u]nder the United States Constitution and the federal system it establishes, the resolution of this issue is left to the normal democratic processes within the State."

The Court of Appeals for the Second Circuit reversed.... The court determined that, despite the assisted-suicide ban's apparent general applicability, "New York law does not treat equally all competent persons who are in the final stages of fatal illness and wish to hasten their deaths," because "those in the final stages of terminal illness who are on life-support systems are allowed to hasten their deaths by directing the removal of such systems; but those who are similarly situated, except for the previous attachment of life-sustaining equipment, are not allowed to hasten death by self-administering prescribed drugs." ... In the court's view, "[t]he ending of life by [the withdrawal of life-support systems] is *nothing more nor less than assisted suicide.*" ... The Court of Appeals then examined whether this supposed unequal treatment was rationally related to any legitimate state interests, and concluded that "to the extent that [New York's statutes] prohibit a physician from prescribing medications to be self-administered by a mentally competent, terminally-ill person in the final stages of his terminal illness, they are not rationally related to any legitimate state interest."

The Equal Protection Clause commands that no State shall "deny to any person within its jurisdiction the equal protection of the laws." This provision creates no substantive rights.... Instead, it embodies a general rule that States must treat like cases alike but may treat unlike cases accordingly.... If a legislative classification or distinction "neither burdens a fundamental right nor targets a suspect class, we will uphold [it] so long as it bears a rational relation to some legitimate end."

New York's statutes outlawing assisting suicide affect and address matters of profound significance to all New Yorkers alike. They neither infringe fundamental rights nor involve suspect classifications.... These laws are therefore entitled to a "strong presumption of validity."

On their faces, neither New York's ban on assisting suicide nor its statutes permitting patients to refuse medical treatment treat anyone differently from anyone else or draw any distinctions between persons. *Everyone*, regardless of physical condition, is entitled, if competent, to refuse unwanted lifesaving medical treatment; *no one* is permitted to assist a suicide. Generally speaking, laws that apply evenhandedly to all "unquestionably comply" with the Equal Protection Clause....

The Court of Appeals, however, concluded that some terminally ill people—those who are on life-support systems—are treated differently from those who are not, in that the former may "hasten death" by ending treatment, but the latter may not "hasten death" through physician-assisted suicide.... This conclusion depends on the submission that ending or refusing lifesaving medical treatment "is nothing more nor less than assisted suicide."... Unlike the Court of Appeals, we think the distinction between assisting suicide and withdrawing life-sustaining treatment, a distinction widely recognized and endorsed in the medical profession and in our legal traditions, is both important and logical; it is certainly rational. See *Feeney, supra*, at 272 ("When the basic classification is rationally based, uneven effects upon particular groups within a class are ordinarily of no constitutional concern").

The distinction comports with fundamental legal principles of causation and intent. First, when a patient refuses life-sustaining medical treatment, he dies from an underlying fatal disease or pathology; but if a patient ingests lethal medication prescribed by a physician, he is killed by that medication....

Furthermore, a physician who withdraws, or honors a patient's refusal to begin, life-sustaining medical treatment purposefully intends, or may so intend, only to respect his patient's wishes and "to cease doing useless and futile or degrading things to the patient when [the patient] no longer stands to benefit from them."... The same is true when a doctor provides aggressive palliative care; in some cases, painkilling drugs may hasten a patient's death, but the physician's purpose and intent is, or may be, only to ease his patient's pain. A doctor who assists a suicide, however, "must, necessarily and indubitably, intend primarily that the patient be made dead."... Similarly, a patient who commits suicide with a doctor's aid necessarily has the specific intent to end his or her own life, while a patient who refuses or discontinues treatment might not. See, e. g., *Matter of Conroy, supra*, at 351, 486 A. 2d, at 1224 (patients who refuse life-sustaining treatment "may not harbor a specific intent to die" and may instead "fervently wish to live, but to do so free of unwanted medical technology, surgery, or drugs"); *Superintendent of Belchertown State School v. Saikewicz*, 373 Mass. 728, 743, n. 11, 370 N. E. 2d 417, 426, n. 11 (1977) ("[I]n refusing treatment the patient may not have the specific intent to die").

The law has long used actors' intent or purpose to distinguish between two acts that may have the same result. See, e. g., *United States v. Bailey*, 444 U.S. 394, 403-406 (1980) ("[T]he ... common law of homicide often distinguishes ... between a person who knows that another person will be killed as the result of his conduct and a person who acts with the specific purpose of taking another's life").... Put differently, the law distinguishes actions taken "because of" a given end from actions taken "in spite of" their unintended but foreseen consequences. *Feeney*, 442 U.S., at 279; *Compassion in Dying v. Washington*, 79 F. 3d 790, 858 (CA9 1996) (Kleinfeld, J., dissenting) ("When General Eisenhower ordered American soldiers onto the beaches of Normandy, he knew that he was sending many American soldiers to certain death.... His purpose, though, was to ... liberate Europe from the Nazis").

Given these general principles, it is not surprising that many courts, including New York courts, have carefully distinguished refusing life-sustaining treatment from suicide....

This Court has also recognized, at least implicitly, the distinction between letting a patient die and making that patient die. In *Cruzan v. Director, Mo. Dept. of Health* ... we concluded that "[t]he principle that a competent person has a constitutionally protected liberty interest in refusing unwanted medical treatment may be inferred from our prior decisions," and we assumed the existence of such a right for purposes of that case.... But our assumption of a right to refuse treatment was grounded not, as the Court of Appeals supposed, on the proposition that patients have a general and abstract "right to hasten death," ... but on well-established, traditional rights to bodily integrity and freedom from unwanted touching.... In fact, we observed that "the majority of States in this country have laws imposing criminal penalties on one who assists another to commit suicide." ... *Cruzan* therefore provides no support for the notion that refusing life-sustaining medical treatment is "nothing more nor less than suicide."

For all these reasons, we disagree with respondents' claim that the distinction between refusing lifesaving medical treatment and assisted suicide is "arbitrary" and "irrational." ... Granted, in some cases, the line between the two may not be clear, but certainty is not required, even were it possible. Logic and contemporary practice support New York's judgment that the two acts are different, and New York may therefore, consistent with the Constitution, treat them differently. By permitting everyone to refuse unwanted medical treatment while prohibiting anyone from assisting a suicide, New York law follows a longstanding and rational distinction.

New York's reasons for recognizing and acting on this distinction — including prohibiting intentional killing and preserving life; preventing suicide; maintaining physicians' role as their patients' healers; protecting vulnerable people from indifference, prejudice, and psychological and financial pressure to end their lives; and avoiding a possible slide towards euthanasia — are discussed in greater detail in our opinion in *Glucksberg, ante*. These valid and important public interests easily satisfy the constitutional requirement that a legislative classification bear a rational relation to some legitimate end.

The judgment of the Court of Appeals is reversed. *It is so ordered.*

Chapter 3

SUE RODRIGUEZ v. BRITISH COLUMBIA

September 1993[1]

[This case divided the Supreme Court of Canada five to four against Sue Rodriguez's appeal that she be allowed to choose the time and manner of her death, something she was prevented from doing by the Canadian law against assisted suicide. Presented here are some of the reasons of Chief Justice Lamer, dissenting from the Court's decision, and Justice Sopinka, reasoning in favour of the Court's decision against Rodriguez.]

LAMER C.J. (dissenting) —

I. FACTS

The facts of this case are straightforward and well known. Sue Rodriguez is a 42-year-old woman living in British Columbia. She is married and the mother of an 8½-year-old son. Ms. Rodriguez suffers from amyotrophic lateral sclerosis (ALS), which is widely known as Lou Gehrig's disease; her life expectancy is between 2 and 14 months but her condition is rapidly deteriorating. Very soon she will lose the ability to swallow, speak, walk and move her body without assistance. Thereafter she will lose the capacity to breathe without a respirator, to eat without a gastrotomy and will eventually become confined to a bed.

Ms. Rodriguez knows of her condition, the trajectory of her illness and the inevitability of how her life will end; her wish is to control the circumstances, timing and manner of her death. She does not wish to

---

[1]   For ease of reading, portions of this judgment have been omitted. All omissions are indicated by "…". The full judgment may be found at <http://scc.lexum.umontreal.ca/en/1993/1993rcs3-519/1993rcs3-519.html>.

die so long as she still has the capacity to enjoy life. However, by the time she no longer is able to enjoy life, she will be physically unable to terminate her life without assistance. Ms. Rodriguez seeks an order which will allow a qualified medical practitioner to set up technological means by which she might, by her own hand, at the time of her choosing, end her life....

II. RELEVANT STATUTORY PROVISIONS

The relevant provision of the *Criminal Code* is as follows:

241. Every one who

(a) counsels a person to commit suicide, or

(b) aids or abets a person to commit suicide,

whether suicide ensues or not, is guilty of an indictable offence and liable to imprisonment for a term not exceeding fourteen years.

The relevant sections of the *Charter* are as follows:

1. The Canadian Charter of Rights and Freedoms guarantees the rights and freedoms set out in it subject only to such reasonable limits prescribed by law as can be demonstrably justified in a free and democratic society.

7. Everyone has the right to life, liberty and security of the person and the right not to be deprived thereof except in accordance with the principles of fundamental justice.

12. Everyone has the right not to be subjected to any cruel and unusual treatment or punishment.

15. (1) Every individual is equal before and under the law and has the right to the equal protection and equal benefit of the law without discrimination and, in particular, without discrimination based on race, national or ethnic origin, colour, religion, sex, age or mental or physical disability.

[...]

IV. CONSTITUTIONAL QUESTIONS

The following constitutional questions were stated by order of this Court on March 25, 1993:

> 1. Does s. 241(*b*) of the *Criminal Code* of Canada infringe or deny, in whole or in part, the rights and freedoms guaranteed by ss. 7, 12 and 15(1) of the *Canadian Charter of Rights and Freedoms*?

> 2. If so, is it justified by s. 1 of the *Canadian Charter of Rights and Freedoms* and therefore not inconsistent with the *Constitution Act, 1982*?

V. ANALYSIS

I find that s. 241(*b*) of the *Criminal Code* infringes s. 15(1) of the *Charter*. In my view, persons with disabilities who are or will become unable to end their lives without assistance are discriminated against by that provision since, unlike persons capable of causing their own deaths, they are deprived of the option of choosing suicide. I further find that s. 1 of the *Charter* does not save s. 241(*b*) of the *Criminal Code*. The means chosen to carry out the legislative purpose of preventing possible abuses do not in my opinion impair as little as reasonably possible the right to equality enshrined in s. 15(1) of the *Charter*....

... Can the right to choose at issue here, that is the right to choose suicide, be described as an advantage of which the appellant is being deprived? In my opinion, the Court should answer this question without reference to the philosophical and theological considerations fuelling the debate on the morality of suicide or euthanasia. It should consider the question before it from a legal perspective—*Tremblay v. Daigle*, [1989] 2 S.C.R. 530—while keeping in mind that the *Charter* has established the essentially secular nature of Canadian society and the central place of freedom of conscience in the operation of our institutions. As Dickson J. said in *Big M Drug Mart, supra*, at p. 336:

> A truly free society is one which can accommodate a wide variety of beliefs, diversity of tastes and pursuits, customs and codes of conduct. A free society is one which aims at equality with respect

to the enjoyment of fundamental freedoms and I say this without any reliance upon s. 15 of the *Charter*.

He went on to add (at p. 346):

> It should also be noted...that an emphasis on individual con-science and individual judgment also lies at the heart of our dem-ocratic political tradition. The ability of each citizen to make free and informed decisions is the absolute prerequisite for the legiti-macy, acceptability, and efficacy of our system of self-government.

In medical matters, the common law recognizes to a very large degree the right of each individual to make decisions regarding his or her own person, despite the sometimes serious consequences of such choices. In *Ciarlariello v. Schacter*, [1993] 2 S.C.R. 119, Cory J., for this Court recently restated the right of a patient to decide on the treatment he is prepared to undergo (at p. 135):

> It should not be forgotten that every patient has a right to bodily integrity. This encompasses the right to determine what medical procedures will be accepted and the extent to which they will be accepted. Everyone has the right to decide what is to be done to one's own body. This includes the right to be free from medical treatment to which the individual does not consent. This concept of individual autonomy is fundamental to the common law....

Like the *Charter* itself in several of its provisions, therefore, the com-mon law recognized the fundamental importance of individual auton-omy and self-determination in our legal system. That does not mean that these values are absolute. However, in my opinion s. 15(1) requires that limitations on these fundamental values should be distributed with a measure of equality.

In this connection, and without expressing any opinion on the moral value of suicide, I am forced to conclude that the fact that persons unable to end their own lives cannot choose suicide because they do not legally have access to assistance is—in legal terms—a disadvantage giv-ing rise to the application of s. 15(1) of the *Charter*. Is this disadvantage based on a personal characteristic covered by s. 15(1)?

...In *Andrews, supra*, McIntyre J. stated that the first characteristic of discrimination is that it is "a distinction...based on grounds relating to personal characteristics of the individual or group" (p. 174). Can it be said that the distinction here is "based" on grounds relating to a personal characteristic covered by s. 15(1)? In my view, if s. 15(1) is to be applied to adverse effect discrimination, as McIntyre J. implies, the definition given in *Andrews* should not be taken too literally. I adopt in this regard the observations of Linden J.A., who said in dissent in *Egan and Nesbit v. Canada* (1993), 153 N.R. 161 (F.C.A.), at p. 196:

> While a distinction must be based on grounds relating to personal characteristics of the individual or group in order to be discriminatory, the words "based on" do not mean that the distinction must be designed with reference to those grounds. Rather, the relevant consideration is whether the distinction affects the individual or group in a manner related to their personal characteristics....

In other words, the difference in treatment must be closely related to the personal characteristic of the person or group of persons. In the case at bar, there can be no doubt as to the existence of such a connection. It is only on account of their physical disability that persons unable to commit suicide unassisted are unequally affected by s. 241(*b*) of the *Criminal Code*. The distinction is therefore unquestionably "based" on this personal characteristic. Is it a characteristic covered by s. 15(1)?

A physical disability is among the personal characteristics listed in s. 15(1) of the *Charter*. There is therefore no need to consider at length the connection between the ground of distinction at issue here and the general purpose of s. 15, namely elimination of discrimination against groups who are victims of stereotypes, disadvantages or prejudices. No one would seriously question the fact that persons with disabilities are the subject of unfavourable treatment in Canadian society, a fact confirmed by the presence of this personal characteristic on the list of unlawful grounds of this discrimination given in s. 15(1) of the *Charter*. In *Andrews*, *supra*, McIntyre J. said (at p. 175):

> The enumerated grounds do...reflect the most common and probably the most socially destructive and historically practised bases of discrimination and must, in the words of s. 15(1), receive particular attention.

There is also no need to undertake any lengthy demonstration in order to show that persons so physically disabled that they are or will become unable to end their own lives without assistance, even assuming that all the usual means of committing suicide are available to them, fall within the classes of persons with disabilities covered by s. 15(1) of the *Charter*, which contains no definition of the phrase "physical disability." Persons whose movement is so limited are even to some degree the classic case of what is meant by a person with a disability in ordinary speech. I prefer to postpone to a later occasion the task of defining the meaning of the phrase "physical disability" for the purposes of s. 15(1).

It is moreover clear that the class of persons with physical disabilities is broader than that of persons unable to end their lives unassisted. In other words, some persons with physical disabilities are treated unequally by the effect of s. 241(*b*) of the *Criminal Code*, but not all persons, nor undoubtedly the majority of persons with disabilities, are so treated. The fact that this is not a bar to a remedy under s. 15(1) seems to me to have been clearly decided by *Brooks v. Canada Safeway Ltd.*, [1989] 1 S.C.R. 1219, and *Janzen v. Platy Enterprises Ltd.*, [1989] 1 S.C.R. 1252.

In *Brooks*, the question was whether unfavourable treatment on account of pregnancy could be regarded as sex discrimination. Responding to the argument that this was not so because all women were not affected by this discriminatory provision, Dickson C.J. said (at p. 1247):

> I am not persuaded by the argument that discrimination on the basis of pregnancy cannot amount to sex discrimination because not all women are pregnant at any one time. While pregnancy-based discrimination only affects part of an identifiable group, it does not affect anyone who is not a member of the group. Many, if not most, claims of partial discrimination fit this pattern. As numerous decisions and authors have made clear, this fact does not make the impugned distinction any less discriminating.

In *Janzen* this Court had to determine whether sexual harassment was a form of sex discrimination. The Court of Appeal had accepted the argument that since all women were not affected by this type of behaviour, no discrimination had resulted. Dickson C.J. rejected this argument as follows (at pp. 1288-89):

If a finding of discrimination required that every individual in the affected group be treated identically, legislative protection against discrimination would be of little or no value. It is rare that a discriminatory action is so bluntly expressed as to treat all members of the relevant group identically.

... I conclude that s. 241(*b*) of the *Criminal Code* infringes the right to equality guaranteed in s. 15(1) of the *Charter*. This provision has a discriminatory effect on persons who are or will become incapable of committing suicide themselves, even assuming that all the usual means are available to them, because due to an irrelevant personal characteristic such persons are subject to limitations on their ability to take fundamental decisions regarding their lives and persons that are not imposed on other members of Canadian society. I now turn to considering s. 241(*b*) in light of s. 1.

... The onus under s. 1 is on the state to demonstrate that an infringement on a *Charter* right is demonstrably justified in a free and democratic country. The standard that the state must satisfy under s. 1 is now well established and consists of the two branches first outlined in *R. v. Oakes*, [1986] 1 S.C.R. 103. The first branch of the test considers the validity of the legislative objective, while the second branch considers the validity of the means chosen to achieve that objective.

... The appellant does not appear to dispute that the legislation in question is aimed at the protection of persons who may be vulnerable to the influence of others in deciding whether, when and how to terminate their lives. The trial judge referred to this constituency in the following terms:

> ... those who may at a moment of weakness, or when they are unable to respond or unable to make competent value judgments, may find themselves at risk at the hand of others who may, with the best or with the worst of motives, aid and abet in the termination of life. Section 241 protects the young, the innocent, the mentally incompetent, the depressed, and all those other individuals in our society who at a particular moment in time decide the termination of their life is a course that they should follow for whatever reason.

I accept this characterization. However, while s. 241(*b*) has always been intended for the protection of such vulnerable people, the context in which this provision operated was altered when, in 1972, Parliament removed the offence of attempted suicide from the *Criminal Code*. The evidence suggests that the offence of attempted suicide was repealed in order to reflect the prevailing societal view that suicide was an issue related more to health and social policy than to the ambit of the criminal justice system. Parliament by so doing was acknowledging that the threat of jail offered minimal deterrence to a person intent on terminating his or her life.

I also take the repeal of the offence of attempted suicide to indicate Parliament's unwillingness to enforce the protection of a group containing many vulnerable people (i.e., those contemplating suicide) over and against the freely determined will of an individual set on terminating his or her life. Self-determination was now considered the paramount factor in the state regulation of suicide. If no external interference or intervention could be demonstrated, the act of attempting suicide could no longer give rise to criminal liability. Where such interference and intervention was present, and therefore the evidence of self-determination less reliable, the offence of assisted suicide could then be triggered.

As I noted above, however, s. 241(*b*), while remaining facially neutral in its application, now gave rise to a deleterious effect on the options open to persons with physical disabilities, whose very ability to exercise self-determination is premised on the assistance of others. In other words, can it be said that the intent of Parliament in retaining s. 241(*b*) after repealing the offence of attempted suicide was to acknowledge the primacy of self-determination for physically able people alone? Are the physically incapacitated, whether by reason of illness, age or disability, by definition more likely to be vulnerable than the physically able? These are the vexing questions posed by the continued existence of the offence of assisted suicide in the wake of the repeal of the attempted suicide provision.

The objective of s. 241(*b*) also must be considered in the larger context of the legal framework which regulates the control individuals may exercise over the timing and circumstances of their death. For example, it is now established that patients may compel their physicians not to provide them with life-sustaining treatment (*Malette v. Shulman* (1990), 72 O.R. (2d) 417 (C.A.)); and patients undergoing life-support treatment may compel their physicians to discontinue such treatment (*Nancy B. v. Hôtel-Dieu de Québec* (1992), 86 D.L.R. (4th) 385 (Que. S.C.)), even where such decisions may lead directly to death. The rationale underlying these decisions is the promotion of individual autonomy; see *Ciarlariello, supra,* at p. 135. An individual's right to control his or her own body does not cease to obtain merely because that individual has become dependent on others for the physical maintenance of that body; indeed, in such circumstances, this type of autonomy is often most critical to an individual's feeling of self-worth and dignity. As R. Dworkin concisely stated in his recent study, *Life's Dominion: An Argument About Abortion, Euthanasia, and Individual Freedom* (1993), at p. 217: "Making someone die in a way that others approve, but he believes a horrifying contradiction of his life, is a devastating, odious form of tyranny."

... It was argued that if assisted suicide were permitted even in limited circumstances, then there would be reason to fear that homicide of the terminally ill and persons with physical disabilities could be readily disguised as assisted suicide and that, as a result, the most vulnerable people would be left most exposed to this grave threat. There may indeed be cause for such concern. Sadly, increasingly less value appears to be placed in our society on the lives of those who, for reason of illness, age or disability, can no longer control the use of their bodies. Such sentiments are often, unfortunately, shared by persons with physical disabilities themselves, who often feel they are merely a burden and expense to their families or on society as a whole. Moreover, as the intervener COPOH (Coalition of Provincial Organizations of the Handicapped) observed in its written submissions, "[t]he negative stereotypes and attitudes which exist about the lack of value and quality inherent in the life of a person with a disability are particularly dangerous in this context because they tend to support the conclusion that a suicide was carried out in response to those factors rather than because of pressure, coercion or duress."

The principal fear is that the decriminalization of assisted suicide will increase the risk of persons with physical disabilities being manipulated by others. This "slippery slope" argument appeared to be the central justification behind the Law Reform Commission of Canada's recommendation not to repeal this provision. The Commission stated the following in its Working Paper 28, *Euthanasia, Aiding Suicide and Cessation of Treatment* (1982), at p. 46:

> The principal consideration in terms of legislative policy, and the deciding one for the Commission, remains that of possible abuses. There is, first of all, a real danger that the procedure developed to allow the death of those who are a burden to themselves may be

gradually diverted from its original purpose and eventually used as well to eliminate those who are a burden to others or to society. There is also the constant danger that the subject's consent to euthanasia may not really be a perfectly free and voluntary act.

While I share a deep concern over the subtle and overt pressures that may be brought to bear on such persons if assisted suicide is decriminalized, even in limited circumstances, I do not think legislation that deprives a disadvantaged group of the right to equality can be justified solely on such speculative grounds, no matter how well intentioned. Similar dangers to the ones outlined above have surrounded the decriminalization of attempted suicide as well. It is impossible to know the degree of pressure or intimidation a physically able person may have been under when deciding to commit suicide. The truth is that we simply do not and cannot know the range of implications that allowing some form of assisted suicide will have for persons with physical disabilities. What we do know and cannot ignore is the anguish of those in the position of Ms. Rodriguez. Respecting the consent of those in her position may necessarily imply running the risk that the consent will have been obtained improperly. The proper role of the legal system in these circumstances is to provide safeguards to ensure that the consent in question is as independent and informed as is reasonably possible.

The fear of a "slippery slope" cannot, in my view, justify the overinclusive reach of the *Criminal Code* to encompass not only people who may be vulnerable to the pressure of others but also persons with no evidence of vulnerability, and, in the case of the appellant, persons where there is positive evidence of freely determined consent. Sue Rodriguez is and will remain mentally competent. She has testified at trial to the fact that she alone, in consultation with her physicians, wishes to control the decision-making regarding the timing and circumstances of her death. I see no reason to disbelieve her, nor has the Crown suggested that she is being wrongfully influenced by anyone. Ms. Rodriguez has also emphasized that she remains and wishes to remain free *not* to avail herself of the opportunity to end her own life should that be her eventual choice. The issue here is whether Parliament is justified in denying her the ability to make this choice lawfully, as could any physically able person.

While s. 241(*b*) restricts the equality rights of all those people who are physically unable to commit suicide without assistance, the choice for a mentally competent but physically disabled person who additionally suffers from a terminal illness is, I think, different from the choice of an individual whose disability is not life-threatening; in other words, for Ms. Rodriguez, tragically, the choice is not whether to live as she is or to die, but rather when and how to experience a death that is inexorably impending. I do not, however, by observing this distinction, mean to suggest that the terminally ill are immune from vulnerability, or that they are less likely to be influenced by the intervention of others whatever their motives. Indeed, there is substantial evidence that people in this position may be susceptible to certain types of vulnerability that others are not. Further, it should not be assumed that a person with a physical disability who chooses suicide is doing so only as a result of the incapacity. It must be acknowledged that mentally competent people who commit suicide do so for a wide variety of motives, irrespective of their physical condition or life expectancy.

… I agree with the importance of distinguishing between the situation where a person who is aided in his or her decision to commit suicide and the situation where the decision itself is a product of someone else's influence. However, I fail to see how preventing against abuse in one context must result in denying self-determination in another. I remain unpersuaded by the government's apparent contention that it is not possible to design legislation that is somewhere in between complete decriminalization and absolute prohibition.

… To summarize, then, I would make a constitutional exemption available to Ms. Rodriguez, and others, on the following conditions:

1. the constitutional exemption may only be sought by way of application to a superior court;
2. the applicant must be certified by a treating physician and independent psychiatrist, in the manner and at the time suggested by McEachern C.J., to be competent to make the decision to end her own life, and the physicians must certify that the applicant's decision has been made freely and voluntarily, and at least one of the physicians must be present with the applicant at the time the applicant commits assisted suicide;
3. the physicians must also certify:
   (i) that the applicant is or will become physically incapable of committing suicide unassisted, and (ii) that they have informed him or her, and that he or she understands, that he or she has a continuing right to change his or her mind about terminating his or her life;

4. notice and access must be given to the Regional Coroner at the time and in the manner described by McEachern C.J.;
5. the applicant must be examined daily by one of the certifying physicians at the time and in the manner outlined by McEachern C.J.;
6. the constitutional exemption will expire according to the time limits set by McEachern C.J.; and
7. the act causing the death of the applicant must be that of the applicant him- or herself, and not of anyone else.

I wish to emphasize that these conditions have been tailored to the particular circumstances of Ms. Rodriguez. While they may be used as guidelines for future petitioners in a similar position, each application must be considered in its own individual context....

[...]

SOPINKA J. —

I have read the reasons of the Chief Justice and those of McLachlin J. herein. The result of the reasons of my colleagues is that all persons who by reason of disability are unable to commit suicide have a right under the *Canadian Charter of Rights and Freedoms* to be free from government interference in procuring the assistance of others to take their life. They are entitled to a constitutional exemption from the operation of s. 241 of the *Criminal Code*, R.S.C., 1985, c. C-46, which prohibits the giving of assistance to commit suicide (hereinafter referred to as "assisted suicide")....

... The appellant argues that, by prohibiting anyone from assisting her to end her life when her illness has rendered her incapable of terminating her life without such assistance, by threat of criminal sanction, s. 241(*b*) deprives her of both her liberty and her security of the person. The appellant asserts that her application is based upon (a) the right to live her remaining life with the inherent dignity of a human person, (b) the right to control what happens to her body while she is living, and (c) the right to be free from governmental interference in making fundamental personal decisions concerning the terminal stages of her life....

... I find more merit in the argument that security of the person, by its nature, cannot encompass a right to take action that will end one's life as security of the person is intrinsically concerned with the well-being of the living person. This argument focuses on the generally held and deeply rooted belief in our society that human life is sacred or inviolable (which terms I use in the non-religious sense described by Dworkin (*Life's Dominion: An Argument About Abortion, Euthanasia, and Individual Freedom* (1993)) to mean that human life is seen to have a deep intrinsic value of its own). As members of a society based upon respect for the intrinsic value of human life and on the inherent dignity of every human being, can we incorporate within the Constitution which embodies our most fundamental values a right to terminate one's own life in any circumstances? This question in turn evokes other queries of fundamental importance such as the degree to which our conception of the sanctity of life includes notions of quality of life as well.

Sanctity of life ... has been understood historically as excluding freedom of choice in the self-infliction of death and certainly in the involvement of others in carrying out that choice. At the very least, no new consensus has emerged in society opposing the right of the state to regulate the involvement of others in exercising power over individuals ending their lives.

The appellant suggests that for the terminally ill, the choice is one of time and manner of death rather than death itself since the latter is inevitable. I disagree. Rather it is one of choosing death instead of allowing natural forces to run their course. The time and precise manner of death remain unknown until death actually occurs. There can be no certainty in forecasting the precise circumstances of a death. Death is, for all mortals, inevitable. Even when death appears imminent, seeking to control the manner and timing of one's death constitutes a conscious choice of death over life. It follows that life as a value is engaged even in the case of the terminally ill who seek to choose death over life.

Indeed, it has been abundantly pointed out that such persons are particularly vulnerable as to their life and will to live and great concern has been expressed as to their adequate protection, as will be further set forth.

I do not draw from this that in such circumstances life as a value must prevail over security of person or liberty as these have been understood under the *Charter*, but that it is one of the values engaged in the present case....

The effect of the prohibition in s. 241(*b*) is to prevent the appellant from having assistance to commit suicide when she is no longer able to do so on her own. She fears that she will be required to live until the deterioration from her disease is such that she will die as a result of choking, suffocation or pneumonia caused by aspiration of food or secretions. She will be totally dependent upon machines to perform her bodily functions and completely dependent upon others. Throughout this time, she will remain mentally competent and able to appreciate all that is happening to her. Although palliative care may be available to ease the pain and other physical discomfort which she will experience, the appellant fears the sedating effects of such drugs and argues, in any event, that they will not prevent the psychological and emotional distress which will result from being in a situation of utter dependence and loss of dignity. That there is a right to choose how one's body will be dealt with, even in the context of beneficial medical treatment, has long been recognized by the common law. To impose medical treatment on one who refuses it constitutes battery, and our common law has recognized the right to demand that medical treatment which would extend life be withheld or withdrawn. In my view, these considerations lead to the conclusion that the prohibition in s. 241(*b*) deprives the appellant of autonomy over her person and causes her physical pain and psychological stress in a manner which impinges on the security of her person. The appellant's security interest (considered in the context of the life and liberty interest) is therefore engaged, and it is necessary to determine whether there has been any deprivation thereof that is not in accordance with the principles of fundamental justice.

... In this case, it is not disputed that in general s. 241(*b*) is valid and desirable legislation which fulfils the government's objectives of preserving life and protecting the vulnerable. The complaint is that the legislation is over-inclusive because it does not exclude from the reach of the prohibition those in the situation of the appellant who are terminally ill, mentally competent, but cannot commit suicide on their own. It is also argued that the extension of the prohibition to the appellant is arbitrary and unfair as suicide itself is not unlawful, and the common law allows a physician to withhold or withdraw life-saving or life-maintaining treatment on the patient's instructions and to administer palliative care which has the effect of hastening death. The issue is whether, given this legal context, the existence of a criminal prohibition on assisting suicide for one in the appellant's situation is contrary to principles of fundamental justice.

... The issue here, then, can be characterized as being whether the blanket prohibition on assisted suicide is arbitrary or unfair in that it is unrelated to the state's interest in protecting the vulnerable, and that it lacks a foundation in the legal tradition and societal beliefs which are said to be represented by the prohibition.

Section 241(*b*) has as its purpose the protection of the vulnerable who might be induced in moments of weakness to commit suicide. This purpose is grounded in the state interest in protecting life and reflects the policy of the state that human life should not be depreciated by allowing life to be taken. This policy finds expression not only in the provisions of our *Criminal Code* which prohibit murder and other violent acts against others notwithstanding the consent of the victim, but also in the policy against capital punishment and, until its repeal, attempted suicide. This is not only a policy of the state, however, but is part of our fundamental conception of the sanctity of human life. The Law Reform Commission expressed this philosophy appropriately in its Working Paper 28, *Euthanasia, Aiding Suicide and Cessation of Treatment* (1982), at p. 36:

> Preservation of human life is acknowledged to be a fundamental value of our society. Historically, our criminal law has changed very little on this point. Generally speaking, it sanctions the principle of the sanctity of human life. Over the years, however, law has come to temper the apparent absolutism of the principle, to delineate its intrinsic limitations and to define its true dimensions.

As is noted in the above passage, the principle of sanctity of life is no longer seen to require that all human life be preserved at all costs. Rather, it has come to be understood, at least by some, as encompassing quality of life considerations, and to be subject to certain limitations and qualifications reflective of personal autonomy and dignity....

... Canadian courts have recognized a common law right of patients to refuse consent to medical treatment, or to demand that treatment, once commenced, be withdrawn or discontinued (*Ciarlariello v. Schacter*, [1993] 2 S.C.R. 119). This right has been specifically recognized to exist even if the withdrawal from or refusal of treatment may result in death (*Nancy B. v. Hôtel-Dieu de Québec* (1992), 86 D.L.R. (4th) 385 (Que. S.C.); and *Malette v. Shulman* (1990), 72 O.R. (2d) 417 (C.A.)). The United States Supreme Court has also recently recognized that the right to refuse life-sustaining medical treatment is an aspect of the liberty interest protected by the Fourteenth Amendment in *Cruzan v. Director, Missouri Health Department* (1990), 111 L. Ed. 2d 224. However, that Court also enunciated the view that when a patient was unconscious and thus unable to express her own views, the state was justified in requiring compelling evidence that withdrawal of treatment was in fact what the patient would have requested had she been competent.

... The distinction between withdrawing treatment upon a patient's request, such as occurred in the *Nancy B.* case, on the one hand, and assisted suicide on the other has been criticized as resting on a legal fiction — that is, the distinction between active and passive forms of treatment. The criticism is based on the fact that the withdrawal of life supportive measures is done with the knowledge that death will ensue, just as is assisting suicide, and that death does in fact ensue as a result of the action taken. See, for example, the *Harvard Law Review* note "Physician-Assisted Suicide and the Right to Die with Assistance" (1992), 105 *Harv. L. Rev.* 2021, at pp. 2030-31.

Other commentators, however, uphold the distinction on the basis that in the case of withdrawal of treatment, the death is "natural" — the artificial forces of medical technology which have kept the patient alive are removed and nature takes its course. In the case of assisted suicide or euthanasia, however, the course of nature is interrupted, and death results *directly* from the human action taken (E.W. Keyserlingk, *Sanctity of Life or Quality of Life in the Context of Ethics, Medicine and Law* (1979), a study paper for the Law Reform Commission of Canada's Protection of Life Series). The Law Reform Commission calls this distinction "fundamental" (at p. 19 of the Working Paper 28).

Whether or not one agrees that the active vs. passive distinction is maintainable, however, the fact remains that under our common law, the physician has no choice but to accept the patient's instructions to discontinue treatment. To continue to treat the patient when the patient has withdrawn consent to that treatment constitutes battery (*Ciarlariello* and *Nancy B., supra*). The doctor is therefore not required to make a choice which will result in the patient's death as he would be if he chose to assist a suicide or to perform active euthanasia.

The fact that doctors may deliver palliative care to terminally ill patients without fear of sanction, it is argued, attenuates to an even greater degree any legitimate distinction which can be drawn between assisted suicide and what are currently acceptable forms of medical treatment. The administration of drugs designed for pain control in dosages which the physician knows will hasten death constitutes active contribution to death by any standard. However, the distinction drawn here is one based upon intention — in the case of palliative care the intention is to ease pain, which has the effect of hastening death, while in the case of assisted suicide, the intention is undeniably to cause death. The Law Reform Commission, although it recommended the continued criminal prohibition of both euthanasia and assisted suicide, stated, at p. 70 of the Working Paper, that a doctor should never refuse palliative care to a terminally ill person only because it may hasten death. In my view, distinctions based upon intent are important, and in fact form the basis of our criminal law. While factually the distinction may, at times, be difficult to draw, legally it is clear. The fact that in some cases, the third party will, under the guise of palliative care, commit euthanasia or assist in suicide and go unsanctioned due to the difficulty of proof cannot be said to render the existence of the prohibition fundamentally unjust.

The principles of fundamental justice cannot be created for the occasion to reflect the court's dislike or distaste of a particular statute. While the principles of fundamental justice are concerned with more than process, reference must be made to principles which are "fundamental" in the sense that they would have general acceptance among reasonable people. From the review that I have conducted above, I am unable to discern anything approaching unanimity with respect to the issue before us. Regardless of one's personal views as to whether the distinctions drawn between withdrawal of treatment and palliative care, on the one hand, and assisted suicide on the other are practically compelling, the fact remains that these distinctions are maintained and can be persuasively defended. To the extent that there is a consensus, it is that human life must be respected and we must be careful not to undermine the institutions that protect it.

This consensus finds legal expression in our legal system which prohibits capital punishment. This prohibition is supported, in part, on the basis that allowing the state to kill will cheapen the value of human life and thus the state will serve in a sense as a role model for individuals in society. The prohibition against assisted suicide serves a similar purpose. In upholding the respect for life, it may discourage those who consider that life is unbearable at a particular moment, or who perceive themselves to be a burden upon others, from committing suicide. To permit a physician to lawfully participate in taking life would send a signal that there are circumstances in which the state approves of suicide.

… Section 241(*b*) protects all individuals against the control of others over their lives. To introduce an exception to this blanket protection for certain groups would create an inequality. As I have sought to demonstrate in my discussion of s. 7, this protection is grounded on a substantial consensus among western countries, medical organizations and our own Law Reform Commission that in order to effectively protect life and those who are vulnerable in society, a prohibition without exception on the giving of assistance to commit suicide is the best approach. Attempts to fine tune this approach by creating exceptions have been unsatisfactory and have tended to support the theory of the "slippery slope." The formulation of safeguards to prevent excesses has been unsatisfactory and has failed to allay fears that a relaxation of the clear standard set by the law will undermine the protection of life and will lead to abuses of the exception. The recent Working Paper of the Law Reform Commission, quoted above, bears repeating here:

> The probable reason why legislation has not made an exception for the terminally ill lies in the fear of the excesses or abuses to which liberalization of the existing law could lead. As in the case of "compassionate murder," decriminalization of aiding suicide would be based on the humanitarian nature of the motive leading the person to provide such aid, counsel or encouragement. As in the case of compassionate murder, moreover, the law may legitimately fear the difficulties involved in determining the true motivation of the person committing the act.

The foregoing is also the answer to the submission that the impugned legislation is overbroad. There is no halfway measure that could be relied upon with assurance to fully achieve the legislation's purpose; first, because the purpose extends to the protection of the life of the terminally ill. Part of this purpose, as I have explained above, is to discourage the terminally ill from choosing death over life. Secondly, even if the latter consideration can be stripped from the legislative purpose, we have no assurance that the exception can be made to limit the taking of life to those who are terminally ill and genuinely desire death.

... I agree with the sentiments expressed by the justices of the British Columbia Court of Appeal—this case is an upsetting one from a personal perspective. I have the deepest sympathy for the appellant and her family, as I am sure do all of my colleagues, and I am aware that the denial of her application by this Court may prevent her from managing the manner of her death. I have, however, concluded that the prohibition occasioned by s. 241(*b*) is not contrary to the provisions of the *Charter*.

Chapter 4

JUDGE NOBLE'S RULING

December 1, 1997*

Upon the jury returning a verdict of "guilty" to the charge of second degree murder counsel for the accused brought a motion seeking a declaration of this Court that in the circumstances of this case it would be cruel and unusual punishment to apply the mandatory minimum sentence prescribed by ss. 235 and 745 of the Criminal Code in sentencing Mr. Latimer.

... If I might be permitted to summarize the basis of Mr. Latimer's motion at this point it is this:

(a) he acknowledges the jury has found him guilty of second degree murder in the death of his daughter Tracy.

(b) he seeks relief from the mandatory minimum sentence of life imprisonment without parole for ten years on the ground that having regard to the circumstances surrounding Tracy's death and his admitted role in it such a sentence is harsh and more than excessive.

(c) the legal instrument he is asking the Court to invoke to overcome the minimum sentence he faces is the concept of a constitutional exemption from the ten-year requirement before parole is available to him.

(d) for the Court to grant his request it must conclude first, that the minimum sentence breaches his Charter right not to be subjected to cruel and unusual punishment; secondly, that the extent of the breach

---

*   For ease of reading, portions of this judgment have been omitted. All omissions are indicated by "...". The full judgment can be found online at <http://robertlatimer.net/court_transcripts/judge_nobles_ruling.pdf>.

of this right entitles him to a constitutional exemption from the ten-year minimum thereby allowing the Court to substitute a penalty pursuant to s. 24 of the Charter that it considers "appropriate and just."

...I next turn to the criteria which the Supreme Court has decided must be established to find that a sentence is so grossly disproportionate that it violates s. 12 of the Charter. The leading case in this regard is R. v. Smith....

...In the Smith case we are told that in assessing what is a grossly disproportionate sentence the Court must look at four aspects of the crime:

- the personal characteristics of Mr. Latimer—the gravity of the offence—the particular circumstances of this case, and—the effect of or consequences of the sentence actually imposed

The object of the examination being to determine what sentence would be appropriate to punish, rehabilitate or deter him or to protect the public from him.

...Before I discuss the four factors relating to the issue of disproportionality, I want to first consider the principal argument of Crown counsel in defence of this motion. It is that the majority decision of our Court of Appeal following the first trial of Mr. Latimer was that he was not entitled in the circumstances of the case before them to the benefit of a constitutional exemption from the prescribed sentences for second degree murder. Counsel contends that applying the doctrine of stare decisis I am bound by that ruling.

I am unable to accept this position for a number of reasons. Strictly speaking it is only an appeal court's pronouncements on rules of law which are binding on a lower court. The conclusion of the majority of our Court of Appeal was arrived at after it drew certain inferences of fact from the evidence in the first trial. I am not bound by their factual findings and indeed I do not necessarily agree with some of the inferences they drew when I weigh them against the evidence presented to the jury in this trial. One example is the inference the Court drew that Mr. Latimer would never have considered taking Tracy's life had she not been handicapped and in extreme pain. This suggests that his decision was at least in part prompted by Tracy's tragic physical debilitation by virtue of her cerebral palsy. That may have been a fair inference for the Court of Appeal to draw from the evidence they were considering but I am bound to say that on the basis of the evidence presented at this trial there is no suggestion, by any witness who testified or for that matter by Crown counsel that he was motivated in any way by her disability. All of the evidence points to his concern for the pain which he saw flowing from her illness. So on the evidence I heard I could not conclude Mr. Latimer ever considered killing his daughter because she was disabled. In addition the history of his 12-year relationship with her completely negates such a conclusion.

There were other significant differences between the first trial and this one. Take for example the Crown's determination in the first trial to depict the accused as a cold-blooded killer. Counsel in his jury address described Mr. Latimer as "foul, callous, cold, calculating and not motivated by anything other than making his own life easier." I am not aware of the strategy employed by counsel for the Crown on the appeal of the first trial but I can say that Mr. Neufeld, as counsel on this trial took the position throughout that Tracy's pain is what motivated Mr. Latimer but he argued, quite rightly, in my view — that in relation to the issue of his guilt or innocence of the murder charge what compelled him to do it was irrelevant.

Another difference between the two trials relates to the evidence presented to the jury. I am not aware of all the evidence admitted at the first trial although I do know that the accused's statement to the police formed a significant part of the case against him just as it did in this trial. The evidence of Dr. Dzus was the same evidence in this trial as she gave at the first trial. We know that at this trial additional evidence was brought forward. For example, Tracy's doctor, two of her caregivers and two sisters of the accused. There was also the opinion evidence of Dr. Robin Menzies, a forensic psychiatrist, who examined Mr. Latimer, his background and his motives in taking Tracy's life and confirmed that in his opinion he was compelled to do what he did out of concern for her present and future pain. We cannot judge what affect this new evidence had on the jury's verdict but it is arguable that it raised in the minds of the jurors some sympathy for Mr. Latimer even though they had concluded that in accordance with the law I gave them he was guilty.

This brings me to the fourth incident that differentiates this trial from the first one. That is the significance of the questions the jury sent to the Court after it began its deliberations. Just briefly, the jury had been out for some time when it returned with some questions. The first question read, "Is there any possible way we can have input into a recommendation for sentencing?" My response was the usual one which simply stated is that they were not to concern themselves with penalty. Later after returning a verdict of guilty and I announced that in accordance with s. 745 of the Criminal Code that I must sentence the accused to life imprisonment but that I needed them to consider whether or not his eligibility for parole should exceed the ten years minimum it was apparent that some of the jurors were emotionally upset. A fair inference to be drawn from that fact is that they were unaware of the mandatory minimum sentence for murder or if any of them were aware it had not been raised during their deliberations. The jury retired again and after a few minutes sent the following question to the Court: "Can we recommend less than ten years before parole? We want to be clear on this as there is some confusion." I again explained to them that s. 745 only calls for a recommendation with respect to eligibility for parole over the ten years specified but that they could make any recommendation they chose to. When they returned for the last time they recommended that the accused be eligible for parole after one year. Counsel for the accused contends that the jury was telling the Court they thought the sentence of life imprisonment without parole for ten years was in the circumstances of the evidence they heard harsh and excessive, and did not fit the crime he had committed. Counsel for the Crown argued that the jury's recommendation was not in conformity with s. 745 and should be ignored. Perhaps, but given the manner in which the jury stated their position would it be fair to ignore the implications of it? It is a fair inference to be drawn from the first question that they were considering finding the accused guilty at the time they asked it. The second question indicated their concern for the length of the sentence the law required for second degree murder. To just ignore the message they appeared to be sending the Court would in the eyes of many citizens bring the administration of justice into disrepute. I am not prepared to pretend it did not happen.

I return to consider the four factors which govern the consideration of whether or not the mandatory minimum sentence facing the accused is grossly disproportionate. I shall consider the personal characteristics of

Mr. Latimer first; then the gravity of the offence together with the circumstances surrounding it; and finally the effects that imposing the
minimum sentence on the accused would have. In discussing each of
these factors I do not propose to review the evidence before me at
length. That evidence is on the record and need not be repeated here
beyond summarizing what I believe the evidence to be.

As a person Mr. Latimer is depicted as a responsible and hard-working
farmer from the Wilkie area where he has lived his entire life. With his
wife Laura they had four children, the oldest of which was Tracy, born
with a very severe form of cerebral palsy which left her permanently
incapacitated and in order to sustain her life she required constant
ongoing total care. The evidence reveals the enormity of their task in
caring for Tracy on a day-to-day basis but establishes that Mr. Latimer
shared in providing for her needs. Not only his wife but his sisters
described his love and devotion to this child. When asked about the
standard of care the Latimers provided Tracy her doctor said "excellent." So the evidence does not suggest that Mr. Latimer did not do his
share in caring for Tracy so far as his other responsibilities to his farm
and family would allow him. He came across as a devoted family man
with a loving and caring nature. Beyond that it is apparent he was well
regarded in his community. He has virtually no criminal record (an
alcohol-related driving offence some 20 years ago) long before he married Laura. It is also clear from the ongoing history of this whole case
that he is not a threat to society nor does he require any rehabilitation.
In summary the evidence establishes he is a caring and responsible person and that his relationship with Tracy was that of a loving and protec-
tive parent. On the evidence it is difficult to believe that there is anything
about Mr. Latimer that could be called sinister or malevolent or even
unkind towards other people.

I move on to consider the gravity of the offence and the circumstances
which led the accused to taking his daughter's life. The gravity of murder need not be stated. It is recognized in our society as the most serious crime of all and that is reflected in the penalty that has always been
attached to its commission. Having said that an act of murder like any
other crime is committed in countless ways by people with countless
reasons for doing it. There is in the commission of murder as there is in
the commission of any crime varying degrees of culpability revealed by
the evidence and circumstances surrounding the act. Since murder

involves the taking of a human life, Parliament has said that the penalty shall be life imprisonment in all cases but that if it is first degree murder the offender is denied parole for 25 years (subject to the so-called faint hope clause) and ten years if the conviction is second degree. The distinction between first and second degree by itself indicates first degree murder is classified in law as more serious than second degree murder. In that regard s. 745 of the Criminal Code mandates that a trial judge (as I did in this case) ask a jury who convicts an offender of second degree murder if they are of the opinion that the ten-year period should be extended upward. This again suggests that Parliament recognized that some second degree murders might be more sinister or malevolent than others. So we know the law recognizes that the moral culpability or the moral blameworthiness of murder can vary from one convicted offender to another. The degree of variance in acts of murder can range on a scale of one to ten to something akin to manslaughter at the lowest end of the scale in terms of culpability; to the high end which is usually akin to a vengeful, hateful and violent act designed specifically to accomplish the death of the victim. So in all crimes it can be said the gravity of a crime — even murder — is determined by the moral culpability of the person committing it.

Mr. Latimer's moral culpability in killing his daughter can only be placed on that scale of one to ten by briefly reviewing what happened including how and why he did it. From the moment he was arrested he told the police he did it because he wanted to put her out of her pain. The extent of the pain Tracy was suffering in the months leading up to October 12, 1993 is well documented by the evidence of her mother, the outside caregivers who attended on her and Dr. Dzus — the surgeon who had announced to Laura Latimer on October 12, 1993 that to alleviate Tracy's pain radical surgery to her right hip had to be done very soon. The extent of her concern is enhanced by her decision to move the surgery up to November 4. We know Tracy had surgery before this to alleviate her condition. At four years they cut the muscles and tendons in her hips and she was left with a flail limb she could no longer control. While every effort was made to keep her muscles as flexible as possible it must be remembered that Tracy save for her head and one arm was incapable of movement on her own, a fact which illustrates again the constant attention she required. At age nine she required further cutting of her muscles and tendons to ease the pressure on her joints. This time she was placed in a cast from chest to toes for a period of six months.

In 1992 her body had become so twisted out of shape that the surgeon placed steel rods in her back to straighten her body. After this surgery Tracy suffered severe pain because her right hip was dislocating regularly. This was 13 months before she died. By the time Dr. Dzus saw her on October 12, 1993 her pain was pretty well unremitting. All in all the evidence indicates that her health was slowly but steadily deteriorating. In the summer of 1993 she was in a respite home in Battleford and while there lost several pounds by the time she came home.

When Laura Latimer told her husband on October 12 that Tracy needed more surgery to alleviate the right hip problem and that there was no guarantee it would stop the pain and that Tracy faced further surgery as she got older just to alleviate her suffering Robert Latimer took the decision to take the matter of Tracy's pain into his own hands. He considered a number of ways of putting her out of her misery but finally settled on putting her to sleep with carbon monoxide gas as the most gentle way of accomplishing his goal. We know that on Sunday, October 24 he carried out his plan.

Why did he do it? He consistently said his only concern was Tracy's ongoing pain and that he could not see any possible way she could ever be freed of the pain by the surgery which was scheduled to be done November 4 or that any future surgery designed to reduce her ongoing pain was anything more than pain management—certainly not a cure or anything close to it. In support of his explanation the defence called Dr. Robin Menzies who testified that he examined Mr. Latimer against a background of information he gathered from several sources including the evidence of some of the witnesses the jury heard from. He found him to be a candid, responsible perhaps a somewhat stubborn and single-minded person who had no symptoms of mental disorder. He said Mr. Latimer expressed to him a growing dissatisfaction of the medical care Tracy had received as she went from one surgery to another with no end in sight. He told Dr. Menzies he believed her pending surgery on November 4 would be torture and that is why he took the decision he did. In his opinion Latimer was motivated entirely by Tracy's pain because he saw no other way to alleviate her from it.

As I indicated earlier it is my opinion that the evidence establishes Mr. Latimer was motivated solely by his love and compassion for Tracy and the need—at least in his mind—that she should not suffer any more pain. The decision he made was in clear conflict with the law and he knew it but he did not seem to care so long as he accomplished his goal. There are different ways of characterizing his decision to take Tracy's life. The Court of Appeal saw him as "assuming the role of a surrogate decision maker" who then decided to terminate her life. I would characterize it by saying that he (and his wife) became the surrogates of Tracy at her birth and that twelve years later he decided when faced with the despairing news that her pain would continue unremitting that he must do his duty as her father to relieve her of that prospect. It is significant in my opinion that the jurors indicated through the questions submitted to the Court that they too felt he should not have killed Tracy but they sympathized to a significant degree with why he had done it. I repeat again that in my opinion the evidence does not in any way suggest he killed his daughter because she was so severely disabled. It is admittedly a difficult task to prove what motivates a person to carry out such a grave act as murder that was not somehow related to self interest, malevolence, hate or violence. But in my view of the evidence presented in this case which is for the most part clear and uncontradicted we have that rare act of homicide that was committed for caring and altruistic reasons. That is why for want of a better term this is called compassionate homicide.

It is therefore my conclusion that Mr. Latimer's place on the scale of culpability I spoke of is very near the low end. By way of comparison I would refer briefly to the four cases that Chief Justice Bayda describes in his dissenting judgment on the accused's appeal from his earlier conviction. These are examples of compassionate homicides committed elsewhere in Canada (See: Dissenting judgment in R. v. Latimer (supra) at pp. 662 to 669). The first — R. v. Mataya concerned a nurse who administered a lethal dose of potassium chloride to a comatose patient to shorten his agony. While he was originally charged with first degree murder he eventually was allowed to plead guilty to administering a noxious substance with intent to endanger life. This offence calls for a maximum sentence of 14 years. Mataya was placed on probation and forced to give up the practice of nursing.

In R. v. de la Roche the accused, a doctor injected potassium chloride into a dying patient to end her life and faced a charge of second degree murder and a separate charge of administering a noxious substance with intent to end her life. He pleaded guilty to the second charge and was discharged with a three-year term of probation.

In R. v. Myers—a Nova Scotia case where the two accused, who were married, smothered the wife's father who was dying of cancer with a pillow. They were charged with second degree murder but in the circumstances were permitted to plead to the lesser offence of manslaughter. They were placed on three years probation and ordered to perform 150 hours community service.

In R. v. Brush (reported on Quicklaw (1995) OJ No. 656), Mrs. Brush, an 81-year-old woman had been happily married to Mr. Brush for 58 years. Her husband's health was failing (Alzheimer's disease) and it increased the difficulties she had in trying to care for him. They first attempted joint suicide but did not succeed. So later Mrs. Brush stabbed her husband causing his death but her attempts to take her own life failed. She was charged with murder which was later reduced to manslaughter. The trial judge saw no purpose in incarcerating her and suspended sentence.

I note also that just recently a doctor in Halifax, Nova Scotia was charged with first degree murder of a patient in the hospital where she works. Ironically, while this trial was in progress the Crown agents in that province reduced the charges against the doctor to manslaughter. Her trial is yet to come.

These are all examples of euthanasia-type mercy killings and while there are differences one can discern in comparing them to the facts of this case there are also many similarities, the most important of which is the compassionate motivation of each accused. All of these accused were seen by the Crown authorities to have a degree of culpability at the minimal end of the scale used to determine the gravity of their offences. It can be argued, as Chief Justice Bayda so forcefully does that Robert Latimer's compassionate homicide of his daughter falls into much the same degree of culpability.

The fourth and final aspect of this assessment to be measured is the effect of imposing the mandatory minimum sentence on Mr. Latimer. Since the sentence was imposed upon him after his first trial we can look at the public reaction which occurred at that time and to some degree since his conviction in this Court. There is no doubt that the sentence provoked an unprecedented public reaction against the severity of the punishment which the law prescribed. In the material filed by the accused's counsel there are hundreds of letters from all over Canada and beyond protesting the harshness of the mandatory sentence. Those letters were to the Latimers, to members of Parliament, to the Ministers of Justice, the Prime Minister and even the Governor General. Many of the letters of support came from people who were themselves handicapped. Some came from church groups. Many of these people enclosed money to help Mr. Latimer's fight what the writers seemed to consider the injustice of his conviction but more particularly the harshness of the sentence required by law. If as the Supreme Court said in defining the phrase "cruel and unusual" in the context of punishment it depends on "whether the punishment prescribed is so excessive as to outrage standards of decency"—then it seems to me there is considerable evidence that this case and the life sentence without parole for ten years imposed (or to be imposed) on Mr. Latimer is seen by the public who responded in this manner as an outrage. In my opinion the jury saw the prescribed punishment in the same light. This is important because that jury also represented the public and it heard all of the evidence.

Another effect of the ten-year minimum sentence is the one pointed out by Bayda C.J. with respect to the wide discrepancy between the punishment Mr. Latimer faces for committing compassionate homicide and the manner in which the Crown and the courts in other provinces handled the four compassionate homicides he describes as noted above. As he points out the inequality of the penalty imposed in the handling of those cases and that which Mr. Latimer is facing is stark to say the least.

Does this analysis of the factors to be weighed and considered in determining whether or not the ten-year mandatory minimum sentence without parole for ten years which the accused is facing is so grossly disproportionate to what is appropriate in all of the circumstances of this case as to constitute cruel and unusual punishment? After much reflection I have concluded that the answer to that question is "yes." It is my judgment that even though the offence of murder is the gravest of all crimes in our law that the circumstances established by the evidence as to why and how he committed this compassionate act of homicide when taken together with his personal characteristics, the caring role he played as Tracy's father and as an otherwise law-abiding citizen who is respected within his home community despite what he did, his conviction does not warrant the imposition of the ten-year minimum sentence because it would be unjust, unfair and far too excessive....

PART II

THE SLIPPERY SLOPE ARGUMENT AND NONVOLUNTARY EUTHANASIA

EXCERPTS FROM THE NUFFIELD COUNCIL ON BIOETHICS REPORT: CRITICAL CARE DECISIONS IN FETAL AND NEONATAL MEDICINE: ETHICAL ISSUES

Nuffield Council on Bioethics 2006[1]

THE VALUE OF THE LIFE OF A FETUS OR NEWBORN BABY

2.8 One important question that all those involved in critical care decision making need to address concerns the value of the life of a fetus or a newborn baby. Is it equal to that of an adult person with fully developed mental capacity? And if not, to what extent would this matter for critical care decisions? Two important distinctions are made in the discussion that follows. First we examine the view that all human life has absolute value and that everything possible must always be done to prolong life. We then examine arguments that support the view that humans have different value (or moral status) at different developmental stages.

---

[1] The full report is available online at <http://www.nuffieldbioethics.org/go/ourwork/neonatal/publication_406.html>.

"SANCTITY OF LIFE" OR "QUALITY OF LIFE"?

2.9 According to the doctrine of the "sanctity of life,"[1] taking human life is categorically wrong, as all humans are of equal intrinsic value and should be treated with the same respect. There are different interpretations that can be distinguished within the doctrine. Some people think that "sanctity of life" means that although life is of exceptional value, there may be cases in which it can be permissible not to strive to keep a person alive. Others believe the doctrine to be sufficient to underpin an absolute right to life, in both moral and legal terms. We term this the absolutist position. Human life may be said to be sacrosanct for different reasons. Whatever interpretation is put on "sanctity of life," the position is often defended in religious terms, although it can be held without referring to religion. One influential line of argument refers to the view that man is made in the image of God,[2] and only God may take life.[3] The sanctity of life view can be contrasted with a "quality of life" view that does not recognise an absolute right to life nor a duty to preserve it, but rather judges whether a life is worth preserving (or having in the first place) in terms of its quality.[4]

2.10 Both views face inherent difficulties. For those who would place great importance upon quality of life, and that includes many consequentialists, it is difficult to make decisions on this basis as the quality of life is "hard to define and even harder to measure."[5] Judgements of what constitutes a life of sufficient quality are notoriously variable. Some people would view life with severe mental or physical impairments as not worth living. However, many severely disabled individuals report that they are content with their lives, which they do not regard as having less value than the lives of others.... Thus judgements on the quality of life may reveal prejudices or conclusions based on anxieties

---

[1] See J. Finnis (1980) *Natural Law and Natural Rights* (Oxford: Oxford UP); H. Kuhse (2001) "A Modern Myth: That Letting Die is Not the Intentional Causation of Death," in *Bioethics: An Anthology*, H. Kuhse and P. Singer (editors) (Oxford: Blackwell).

[2] Genesis 1: 26-27, 1 Corinthians 11: 7.

[3] 1 Corinthians 3: 16-17; Job 1: 21. See also J. Wyatt (1998) "When Is a Person? Christian Perspective on the Beginning of Life," in *Matters of Life and Death* (Leicester: Intervarsity P).

[4] See J. Glover (1977) *Causing Death and Saving Lives* (Penguin); H. Kuhse and P. Singer (1985) "Is All Human Life of Equal Worth?," in *Should the Baby Live? The Problem of Handicapped Infants* (Oxford: Oxford UP), pp. 18-47.

[5] P. Boddington and T. Podpadec (1999) "Measuring Quality of Life in Theory and in Practice," in *Bioethics: An Anthology*, H. Kuhse and P. Singer (editors) (Oxford: Blackwell), pp. 273-82.

or preconceptions. It should also be noted that disability is at least in part a socially created and conditioned state....[1]

2.11 As we acknowledge above...we should not expect complete unanimity on issues of fundamental moral concern and members of the Working Party hold differing personal and philosophical positions in relation to "sanctity" or "quality" of life. The Working Party, however, agreed that in relation to the newborn baby there are some circumstances in which imposing or continuing treatments to sustain a baby's life results in a level of irremediable suffering such that there is no ethical obligation to act in order to preserve that life. The Working Party struggled, as have others, to identify the criteria that should determine when the degree of suffering outweighs the baby's interest in continuing to live, and to find the appropriate language to describe the threshold at which any obligation to prolong life cedes to a duty to provide palliative care. Following deliberation, **the Working Party adopted the concept of "intolerability." It would not be in the baby's best interests to insist on the imposition or continuance of treatment to prolong the life of the baby when doing so imposes an intolerable burden upon him or her.**

2.12 In seeking to understand what may be meant by an intolerable burden the Working Party reviewed the guidance in the Framework of the Royal College of Paediatrics and Child Health (RCPCH) on withholding and withdrawing life-sustaining treatment (see Box 2.1). In considering what constitutes "intolerability," we noted that the RCPCH distinguishes between three situations: "no chance," " no purpose," and "unbearable." Where treatment offers "no chance" of survival other than for a short period of time, the best interests of the baby focus on the relief of any suffering and a peaceful death. We consider that to mandate distressing and futile interventions that can do no more than delay death would be a clear case of an intolerable burden.

2.13 Much more difficult are cases where evidence suggests that treatments to prolong life may have either "no purpose" (as defined by the RCPCH) or result in "unbearable" suffering. In those cases, establishing what constitutes a level of "intolerability" is more complex and controversial. The concept of "no purpose" is suggested by the RCPCH for

---

[1] There is a substantial literature on the ethics of disability. For an introduction to this topic, which is not addressed in this Report, see (2005) "Symposium of Disability," *Ethics* 116 (1).

cases in which treatment may secure the survival of a baby or child but only for him or her to endure such an "impossibly poor" life that it would be unreasonable to expect him or her to bear it. For example, the clinical evidence may indicate that any future existence for the baby will be a life bereft of any of those features that give meaning and purpose to human life (for example, being aware of his or her surroundings or other people). Implementing burdensome treatments when faced with such a prospect may be seen as imposing an "intolerable" existence, even in the absence of evidence of great pain or distress.

2.14 An "unbearable situation" emphasises that there may be cases where treatment secures the survival of the baby but only for him or her to endure a life of great suffering and the family believes that further treatment is more than can be borne, irrespective of medical opinion that it may be of some benefit. While the RCPCH recommends that consensus should be sought (as does the Working Party, see paragraph 2.16), the "unbearable" situation would appear to give more weight to the judgement of the parents in decision making. Unlike the "no purpose" situation described above, babies in an "unbearable" situation may have greater inherent awareness and potential capacities to relate to others, but suffer extreme and irremediable pain. An example of such a distressing condition might be the most severe form of the incurable inherited skin condition, junctional epidermolysis bullosa (discussed in Chapter 6, Case 8). The intractable pain and consequent disability imposed on a child with this extreme form of the condition could be said to make continuing life "intolerable." The Working Party concluded that in both "no purpose" and "unbearable" situations, continuing life-sustaining interventions could result in maintaining a life that imposed an "intolerable" burden on the baby.

2.15 There are also a number of situations that are both "no purpose" and "unbearable." For example, a baby may show indicators of severe and unrelievable pain that is likely to persist, and at the same time he or she may be incapable of sustaining any meaningful relations with other people and lack any potential for an independent existence. The baby's suffering is significant and there is no prospect of benefits to him or her in continuing life to offset that suffering. Cases in which the life of a baby in such a condition could continue only by means of intrusive and invasive treatments may be also described as "intolerable."

2.16 Our use of "intolerability" embraces all three situations recognised by the RCPCH, as well as those that have features of more than one of these categories. We take "intolerability" to encompass an extreme level of suffering or impairment which is either present in the baby or may develop in the future, and may be given more weight in the judgement of parents or doctors. In proposing "intolerability" as a threshold to justify decisions not to insist on life-prolonging treatments, the Working Party acknowledges the fallibility of language and the uncertainty of interpretation of evidence. Reasonable people may disagree both about what constitutes "intolerability" and/or when a particular baby's condition meets that condition. In applying this concept, we acknowledge, however, that in each case an assessment must be made of the individual baby. The Working Party regards it as crucial that assessments both of what purpose a baby may find in his or her life and of the degree of suffering endured by a baby are made jointly by parents and healthcare professionals.... **We conclude at this stage that, although a presumption in favour of life is rightly at the root of all medical care** (paragraph 2.36), **it cannot be absolute in situations where there are clear indications that the life to be experienced will be an intolerable burden on the child** (for an illustration of such a situation, see Chapter 6, Case 8).

[...]

BEST INTERESTS

2.21 The principle of the best interests of the child is central to medical practice, child protection and disputes about child custody. **The Working Party concludes that the best interests of a baby must be a central consideration in determining whether and how to treat him or her.** In legal terms the concept is enshrined in the important legislative and political instruments in the UK that are concerned with children.[1]

---

[1] For example, these instruments include in the UK the Children Act 1989, the Children (Northern Ireland) Order 1995 and the Children (Scotland) Act 1995. Internationally there is the United Nations Convention on the Rights of the Child (UNCRC) (see paragraphs 3.44 and 8.2), which gives all children a right to have their best interests be the primary consideration in matters affecting them (Article 3). It is noteworthy that the Children Act does not refer to *best interests* but only to the child's *welfare*, which might be understood to be less demanding on those who make decisions for children. The instruments also differ in the weight they accord to a child's interest: the UNCRC stipulates that the child's interests are "a primary consideration"; the Children Act states that the child's welfare should be "paramount."

However, the interpretation and application of the principle are far from straightforward.

What Does It Mean to Have Interests?

2.22 For the purpose of this discussion, interests can be understood in terms of the factors that affect a person's quality of life.[1] They are the constitutive elements of wellbeing: a person's wellbeing prospers or declines as their interests grow or wane.[2] A person benefits from having their interests promoted and suffers from having their interests neglected.

2.23 In determining how to treat an individual so that their interests are promoted, we may be able to discuss possible courses of action with them and then ask them about their preferences. These preferences also form a crucial element in seeking consent in medical decision making, provided the person has a good understanding of what the treatment involves. However, there are situations where a person may be unable to express preferences, for example where they have temporarily or permanently lost the capacity to understand or to reason or, as in the case of fetuses and newborn babies, where they have not yet developed these faculties. It is in these cases that the concept of best interests has most relevance, and where it is the most challenging to apply.

Interpretation of Best Interests

2.24 How do we know what is in the best interests of a person who may not experience self-consciousness? Parents often talk about their baby "fighting for her life" or, say that a baby has "had enough." Certainly more attention is now paid to a baby's signals and to recognizing that his or her actions may indicate preferences. However, such behaviour is often held to be instinctive and not consciously formulated. It follows that adults must choose for the baby and in doing so they must attempt

---

[1]   We leave aside here more subtle discussions about whether promoting someone's best interests requires promoting *all* of their interests to *the highest degree*, or promoting, for example, only a *subset* such that a basic level of wellbeing is achieved. In general when we speak of "best interests" in this Report, we are not referring to a distinct subset of a person's interests. Rather we are saying that what is in a person's interests is promoted to the greatest extent possible and that this may be understood in several different ways.

[2]   J. Feinberg (1984) "Harm to Others," in *The Moral Limits of the Criminal Law*, Volume 1 (Oxford: Oxford UP), p. 34.

to determine the baby's best interests on the basis of the available information. The main types of problem that influence the interpretation of what might be in the best interests of a fetus, a newborn baby or a child are explored below. We begin by considering philosophical issues and what is meant by pain and suffering. We then examine which parties are involved and consider the interests of other parties.

2.25 There are fundamental philosophical and scientific issues concerning knowledge about pain and suffering in other people. Assessments of these states are of great importance in many of the situations considered in this Report. We take for granted that a life free from pain and suffering is in a person's best interests. In the case of adults, medical information, empathy, and the possibility of asking a person to describe their state can support inferences about how they feel. At the same time, pain and suffering are highly subjective, and difficult to quantify in objective terms. These problems are further complicated in the case of fetuses and the newborn, where reliance is placed on information such as body temperature or blood pressure, and where empathy has limited scope. This uncertainty is particularly important in those cases where parties might argue that it is against a newborn baby's best interests to be resuscitated. Here, the implicit assumption is usually that, from the perspective of the newborn baby, it would be preferable not to continue to live. Such a view would appear to require a high degree of certainty that the state of pain and suffering is indeed intolerable. Moreover, these decisions concern what will happen in the future, and often we cannot know with certainty, or indeed with any real degree of assurance, the outcome of each choice we might make.

2.26 There are different parties involved in the assessment of best interests, and even if they agree about the current condition of a child, they may disagree, profoundly and irreconcilably, in their judgements about whether the life the baby might have in the future would be better or worse.[1] Healthcare professionals, parents and lawyers have different relationships with a fetus or newborn baby whose interests are being considered. Cases may become more complicated where, for example, the mother has a different view from the father. All parties draw on

---

[1] S. Parker (1994) "The Best Interests of the Child," in *The Best Interests of the Child: Reconciling Culture and Human Rights*, P. Alston (editor) (Oxford: Clarendon), pp. 26-41.

different facts and emotions in forming their decisions, and may give these attributes different weights.

2.27 Even if there is agreement on what is in the best interests of a fetus, a newborn baby or child, there can be conflicts with the interests of other parties, as we consider below in more detail (see paragraphs 2.29-2.30). For now, we conclude that although there are problems in interpreting and assessing best interests, it is clear that a fetus and a newborn baby have interests and that they must be taken into account.... It also makes sense in certain circumstances to ask whether it is in the best interests of a newborn baby to continue all possible treatment, for example when death is thought to be inevitable, or when the quality of life is intolerable (see paragraph 2.16).

The Weight of Best Interests, and Interests of Different Parties

2.28 Acknowledging that a baby has interests is one matter; deciding what weight should be given to these interests is another. Should they be "paramount" as might be implied by the Children Act 1989? If so, best interests might be said to "trump" other principles or considerations. Alternatively, should they be regarded simply as "a primary consideration" as suggested in provisions of the United Nations Convention on the Rights of the Child (UNCRC)? And how should the best interests of the fetus or newborn baby be considered in relation to the interests of others involved in the decision-making process?

2.29 Any decision in respect of a baby will have implications for his or her parents and other members of the family who also all have interests. The Working Party does not consider that the baby's interests should invariably take precedence over the interests of these other parties. Hence our view is that those who make decisions in respect of a child must carefully consider the interests of all those who may be affected, most usually other family members, old or young, who will live with the child, care for him or her, or are dependent upon the immediate family in other ways. Consider for instance the interests of the parents of a baby who is born with a severe disability. There is no doubt that the interests of a baby are bound up with those of his or her parents, in that the degree of care that parents can devote to their child can make a very substantial difference to the quality of life that he or she can expect to enjoy. While often the adjustments that families have to make when a child has disabilities can readily be overcome, having a seriously disabled child can make a very substantial difference to the kind of life the parents can expect to enjoy.... Caring for a seriously disabled child may significantly and deleteriously affect the lives of his or her parents: it can mean giving up employment, economic hardship, marital discord and divorce, great unhappiness, stress and ill health for which help from the state is limited (paragraphs 3.35 and Box 7.2). **The Working Party is clear that parents have interests and that it is reasonable for these interests to be given some weight in any relevant deliberations about critical care decisions for a child who is, or who will become, severely ill.**

2.30 Impartiality requires that equivalent interests of morally relevant parties of equal status have the same moral importance, and have equal weight. However, the nature of competing interests requires further scrutiny because not all of an individual's interests are equally important. In the circumstances concerning the decisions addressed by this Report, the interests of a baby which are at stake are often those of his or her very existence, whether he or she lives or dies, and of the quality of any life he or she might enjoy. These are usually a baby's very central or basic interests.[1] **Thus, in according particular weight to the best interests of a baby, we are not viewing the baby as more important than other persons; rather we view his or her interests in living or dying, or in avoiding an "intolerable" life (see paragraph 2.16), as more important than the interests that others may have in any significant decisions made about him or her.**

2.31 Decisions about whether to continue or to cease providing life-sustaining treatments are decisions between two mutually exclusive options. However, many clinical decisions are more complex and involve many possible options such as what kinds of treatment are most appropriate, and for how long should a treatment be tried. In these cases the best interests of a baby may be harder to determine and to agree upon. This does not mean that the principle of best interests ceases to be relevant, only that it is more difficult to apply.

---

[1]   See footnote 1, p. 93.

2.32 If, after careful consideration, all involved in the decision-making process have come to the conclusion that it might be in the best interests of a baby to cease life-sustaining treatment, a question arises as to what may permissibly be done. Are withholding and withdrawing treatment equally acceptable options in moral terms? Do they differ from deliberately ending the life of a newborn child?

WITHHOLDING AND WITHDRAWING TREATMENT

2.33 The Working Party examined whether there was any case to say that withholding or withdrawing treatment are morally equivalent.[1] In our view, when healthcare professionals withhold or withdraw treatment in the context of critical care decisions, when guided by the best interests of a baby, they substitute one form of care for another. They may refuse to start or continue a particular treatment when they know that doing so can bring about no benefit to patients or may actively harm them. In these cases, other forms of care or palliative care would routinely be substituted. For example, when mechanical ventilation to support breathing is withdrawn in a patient whose quality of life is described as intolerable (see paragraph 2.16), the medical staff implement palliative care to minimise any discomfort associated with any ensuing difficulty in breathing. **Although many people, including clinicians, perceive a moral difference between withholding and withdrawing treatment, the Working Party concludes that there are no good reasons to draw a moral distinction between them, provided these actions are motivated in each case by an assessment of the best interests of the baby. Either withholding or withdrawing treatment would be an acceptable course of action depending on the circumstances of each case. We note that the RCPCH has reached the same conclusion (see Box 2.1).[2]**

---

[1] Some commentators might think discussions of "acts and omissions" could be relevant to the discussions on end-of-life decision making in this Report. However, the Working Party takes the view that when medical staff withhold or withdraw treatment, they do not fail to act, they substitute one form of care for another. The classic critique of the acts and omissions doctrine in the context of taking life is J. Rachels (1975) "Active and Passive Euthanasia," *N Engl J Med* 292: 78-80.

[2] The RCPCH notes that "Ethically the withholding and the withdrawal of life sustaining treatment are equivalent but emotionally they are sometimes poles apart." Royal College of Paediatrics and Child Health (2004) *Withholding or Withdrawing Life Sustaining Treatment in Children: A Framework for Practice*, 2nd edition (London: RCPCH). See Appendix 9.

Box 2.1: Royal College of Paediatrics and Child Health Framework on Withholding or Withdrawing Life-Sustaining Treatment

The Royal College of Paediatrics and Child Health first published guidance on withholding or withdrawing treatment in 1997, recognising that there was a need for guidance in dealing with these difficult decisions. A revised edition was published in 2004.* The guidance suggests five situations in which it may be ethical and legal to consider withholding or withdrawing a child's treatment:

- the brain-dead child;†
- the permanent vegetative state;
- the "no chance" situation: "the child has such severe disease that life-sustaining treatment simply delays death without significant alleviation of suffering. Treatment to sustain life is inappropriate";
- the "no purpose" situation: "although the patient may be able to survive with treatment, the degree of physical or mental impairment will be so great that it is unreasonable to expect them to bear it"; and
- the "unbearable" situation: "the child and/or family feel that in the face of progressive and irreversible illness further treatment is more than can be borne. They wish to have a particular treatment withdrawn or to refuse further treatment irrespective of the medical opinion that it may be of some benefit."

In a situation where the conditions for one of these categories are not met, where there is disagreement, or where there is uncertainty

---

* Royal College of Paediatrics and Child Health (2004) *Withholding or Withdrawing Life Sustaining Treatment in Children: A Framework for Practice*, 2nd edition (London: RCPCH), available at: <http://www.rcpch.ac.uk/publications/recent_publications/ Witholding.pdf>, accessed on 12 September 2006.[1]
† The guidance notes that definitions of brain death are typically not applied to young babies because of uncertainty about the maturity of the brain at this age.

---

[1] Note that the URL listed in the report no longer links to the site. See <http://www.rcpch.ac.uk/Publications/Publications-list-by-title#W>.

over the degree of future impairment, the RCPCH advises that the child's life should always be safeguarded until these issues are resolved. The guidance notes that withdrawal or withholding of life-sustaining treatment "does not imply that the child will receive no care," and highlights the need for provision of palliative care in order to ensure that the remainder of the child's life is as comfortable as possible.[‡]

---

‡   The guidance describes palliative care as including treatment for alleviation of symptoms and care to maintain dignity and comfort.

2.34 It is important to clarify that the observations above have no bearing on when to make the decision that it would be appropriate to withhold or withdraw treatment. In practice, in many cases it will be preferable to continue to treat until healthcare professionals can decide with a reasonable degree of certainty that withholding or withdrawing treatment would be preferable.

DELIBERATELY ENDING LIFE

2.35 Viewing withholding and withdrawing treatment as morally equivalent and acceptable in certain circumstances invites the question of whether the deliberate ending of life should also be seen as equally morally acceptable, given that the outcomes of all three options may be the same. **On balance, the Working Party rejects the argument that they are equally morally acceptable, as we explain below.**[1] Consider the case of a seriously ill premature newborn child with no realistic prospect of survival and whose life can reasonably be thought of as one of intolerable suffering (see paragraph 2.16). Why might it be thought permissible to allow a baby to die by withdrawing or withholding life-saving treatment, but impermissible to take the life of a baby deliberately, for example by means of a lethal injection?

---

1   In what follows the Working Party must be understood to be speaking about what can reasonably be foreseen as the consequences of continuing treatment, withholding treatment, withdrawing treatment, or of actively seeking to hasten death. We are clear that the possibility of a dramatic life-saving scientific discovery does not fall within the scope of what can reasonably be foreseen. Equally if doctors act with a well-grounded conviction that a baby will die as a consequence of their actions, they cannot be condemned if the actual outcome is otherwise.

2.36 In principle, doctors have a professional obligation to preserve life where and when they can,[1] using the appropriate course of action to achieve that end.... By contrast, taking intentional measures to end the life of a newborn baby, even one whose condition is reasonably judged as one of intolerable suffering (see paragraph 2.16) with no prospect of survival or improvement, is commonly regarded as a violation of the duty to protect the life of the patient.[2] The professional guidelines of the RCPCH sanction the withdrawal of life-prolonging treatment in appropriate situations but remain opposed to "causing death by intended lethal action."[3] While reference to legal and professional instruments cannot by itself be sufficient to settle the moral question of the responsibility of doctors, these guidelines appear to reflect the current UK consensus on these matters and give expression to the ethos of healthcare professionals, factors that the Working Party holds as important.[4] Furthermore, although we recognise that evidence on such matters is difficult to obtain, we take the view that permitting doctors to end life deliberately would be likely to have a negative impact not only upon those doctors psychologically but on how the medical profession is perceived more widely. This is especially relevant where parents may lose trust in the impartiality of advice provided by doctors during the decision-making process.

2.37 There is also a problem of ensuring consistency.... A newborn baby cannot express his or her wishes. It is therefore appropriate to appeal to what is believed to be in his or her best interests. If it were permissible to take the life of a newborn baby on the grounds that it was in his or her best interests to do so, we have to ask why would it not be permissible to kill an incompetent adult on the same grounds. Those who

---

[1] "A physician shall always bear in mind the obligation of preserving human life." World Medical Association (1949, as amended) *International Code of Medical Ethics.* Doctors are not obliged to provide what they consider to be futile treatment.

[2] For a brief introductory discussion of the intentional ending of life by a doctor see H. Kuhse (1991) "Euthanasia," in *A Companion to Ethics,* P. Singer (editor) (Oxford and Massachusetts: Blackwell), pp. 294-302 and M. Tooley (2003) "Euthanasia and Assisted Suicide," in *A Companion to Applied Ethics,* R.G. Frey and C.H. Wellman (editors) (Oxford: Blackwell), pp. 326-41.

[3] Royal College of Paediatrics and Child Health (2004) *Withholding or Withdrawing Life Sustaining Treatment in Children: A Framework for Practice,* 2nd edition (London: RCPCH). The RCPCH also notes that "withdrawal of life sustaining treatment in appropriate circumstances is not viewed by the courts as active killing, nor as a breach of the right of life under article 2 of the European Convention on Human Rights."

[4] British Medical Association (2006) *Assisted Dying—A Summary of the BMA's Position,* available at: <http://www.bma.org.uk/ap.nsf/Content/assisteddying?OpenDocument&High light=2, euthanasia, accessed on: 12 Oct 2006>.

reject adult euthanasia but who are sympathetic to the proposition that it is permissible actively to end the life of a newborn child whose life is intolerable, would need to show that, further to the fact that the adult has had many life experiences and has entered into social relationships, there is a morally relevant difference. **In summary, the Working Party unreservedly rejects the active ending of neonatal life even when that life is "intolerable."**

RELIEVING PAIN AND CAUSING DEATH: THE DOCTRINE OF THE DOUBLE EFFECT

2.38 Measures to end life could include the administration of a chemical that has no other purpose than to end life, such as a lethal injection of potassium chloride. Medicines such as sedatives and analgesics can also have the effect of hastening death, particularly if given at higher doses. Death may therefore occur in cases where doctors provide such treatments with the intention of reducing pain and suffering. The acceptability of administering pain-relieving drugs that may also bring about death is debated under the doctrine of double effect (see Box 2.2). **The Working Party takes the view that, provided treatment is guided by the best interests of a baby, and has been agreed in the joint decision-making process (paragraphs 2.42-2.57), potentially life-shortening but pain-relieving treatments are morally acceptable.**

Box 2.2: Doctrine of Double Effect

This principle governs the permissibility of actions that have two outcomes, one good and the other bad. The principle states that an action of this kind may be permissible provided the bad outcome is only foreseen, not intended, and is proportionate, that is, the bad that could be caused is not such as to outweigh the good intended.* The principal critics of the doctrine question whether there is a robust moral difference between intending and merely foreseeing an outcome, a difference which would be sufficient to show the permissibility of the act or to excuse the agent.† How

---

* J.K. Mason and G.T. Laurie (2005) "Double Effect," in *Mason and McCall Smith's Law and Medical Ethics*, 7th edition (Oxford: Oxford UP), pp. 634-35.

† H. Kuhse and P. Singer (1985) "The Doctrine of Double Effect," in *Should the Baby Live? The Problem of Handicapped Infants* (Oxford: Oxford UP), pp. 85-86.

---

ever, it is important to acknowledge that the principle does not permit cases in which an action has two outcomes, both intended. Thus administering a high dose of pain relief with no intention to kill but with an awareness of the possibility of it hastening death is permitted under this principle, provided the foreseen possibility of death is viewed as "proportionate." By contrast, administration of the same dosage of analgesic with the clear and deliberate intention of bringing about death would not be permitted. Hence if a doctor administers a high dose of pain relief to a newborn baby aiming to hasten death, then what the doctor does could reasonably be described as a deliberate act of killing. The principle of double effect would not be applicable in such a case. The British Medical Association (BMA) has noted that doctors may fear that their motives in providing pain relief could be misinterpreted, but advises that "if the intention is clearly to relieve pain and distress and the dosage provided is commensurate with that aim, the action will not be unlawful."‡ The BMA also emphasises the importance of good symptom control.

---

‡ British Medical Association Ethics Department (2004) Medical Ethics Today: The BMA's Handbook of Ethics and Law, 2nd edition (London: BMJ Books).

[...]

Case 8: Freddie — Pain Relief and the Consequence that Death is Hastened

Freddie

Freddie was born by normal vaginal delivery after a nine month pregnancy. It rapidly became apparent that he had the incurable rare inherited skin condition, recessive junctional (Herlitz type) epidermolysis bullosa (EB), which is lethal in infancy. The diagnosis was confirmed by skin biopsy and DNA analysis. Here is a description by a mother of a child with this most serious form of the condition:[1]

---

[1] See <http://www.ebinfoworld.com>.

> "A child with painful wounds similar to burns covering most of his or her body. Having to wrap each tiny little infant finger with Vaseline gauze and then cover it with gauze to prevent the hand from webbing and contracting. Never being able to hold your child tight because if you did, their skin would blister or shear off. A child who will never know what it's like to run, skip or jump, or to play games with other children because even the slightest physical contact will injure his or her skin. A child who screams out each time it is bathed because the water touching its open wounds creates incredible pain. A diet of only liquids or soft foods because blistering and scarring occur in the oesophagus. An active baby with his knees soaked in blood from the normal act of crawling."

Freddie's parents read this description, and others, on the Internet.[1] They realised that the severity of the condition varied and that there were different forms. Other sufferers might not be as badly affected. However, it was clear that their son had the most serious form, which occurs in only a small proportion of babies with epidermolysis bullosa. They accepted advice from doctors, who consulted specialists in the disorder, that there was no treatment for their son's condition. It was obvious that Freddie was suffering and he was given morphine[2] for pain relief. The dose was increased to control the pain, until the point came that his breathing started to be affected. The parents were still very concerned that their child might be in severe pain and asked the medical staff to continue to increase the dose of morphine, which was done. They did not want him to be mechanically ventilated if he stopped breathing, and the clinicians agreed to this request. The parents were present when Freddie died peacefully.

---

[1] For example DebRA online, available at <http://www.debra.org.uk/>. Organisations with websites such as this can provide information on particular conditions, enable people and families who are affected to establish contact, raise funds for research and raise awareness of the condition.

[2] Morphine is widely used for pain relief in neonates. Other painkillers used for severe pain, including diamorphine, pethidine and fentanyl, would have similar effects on breathing.

Best Interests

6.36 Arguments presented for Freddie's best interests were based on the concern about existing and future pain he would suffer and the poor prognosis for this incurable condition. For him, was survival worse than death? All those involved in the decision-making process agreed that Freddie's condition was "intolerable" (paragraph 2.16). This condition is very distressing to witness, not just for the parents but also for clinical staff. It is crucially important that the diagnosis is correct and not confused with another type of the skin disorder which has a better prognosis, such as epidermolysis bullosa simplex.

The Doctrine of Double Effect

6.37 Freddie's case illustrates the doctrine of double effect (paragraph 2.38) which becomes relevant where an action is taken with two outcomes, one good and the other bad. For such an action to be acceptable, the bad caused should not outweigh the good intended. The point at which the doctrine of double effect came to apply was when the dose of medication for pain had been increased to the point that Freddie's breathing became affected. The parents and the doctors wanted pain relief to be continued so that he should not suffer, but they also knew that increasing the dose would suppress his respiration. Here, giving morphine was intended to relieve pain but in the knowledge of the possibility of hastening death. While some people view such actions as equivalent to deliberately ending a life, others would disagree. **The Working Party takes the view that, provided the treatment in this case has been guided by the best interests of the baby, and has been agreed through joint decision making, pain-relieving treatments are morally acceptable, even if potentially life-shortening (paragraph 2.38).**

Active Ending of Life

6.38 Some might argue that Freddie should be given a lethal injection under sedation to allow him to die quickly. However, unlike voluntary euthanasia in adults, which is sometimes defended on the grounds that competent adults have a basic right to exercise choice, a baby cannot let his or her wishes be known. Thus any decision to end life would be on the basis of what others judged to be his or her best interests. This case also raises the question (accepting that it is not permissible by law) of whether it is ever morally acceptable actively to end life. Our position is that it is not ..., and that to allow this practice would erode trust in doctors and the neutrality of their advice....

Decision Making

6.39 All those involved in the decision-making process agreed that to continue life-sustaining treatment was not in Freddie's best interests, and arrangements were made to support his parents and for them to be with him while he was dying. Clear communication between the parents and the healthcare team about Freddie's condition and the options for clinical management was crucial to avoid later confusion or psychological distress if the parents subsequently experienced guilt in having "allowed" Freddie to die.

Chapter 6

THE GRONINGEN PROTOCOL: EUTHANASIA IN SEVERELY ILL NEWBORNS

Eduard Verhagen and Pieter J.J. Sauer[1]

Of the 200,000 children born in the Netherlands every year, about 1000 die during the first year of life. For approximately 600 of these infants, death is preceded by a medical decision regarding the end of life. Discussions about the initiation and continuation of treatment in newborns with serious medical conditions are one of the most difficult aspects of pediatric practice. Although technological developments have provided tools for dealing with many consequences of congenital anomalies and premature birth, decisions regarding when to start and when to withhold treatment in individual cases remain very difficult to make. Even more difficult are the decisions regarding newborns who have serious disorders or deformities associated with suffering that cannot be alleviated and for whom there is no hope of improvement.

Suffering is a subjective feeling that cannot be measured objectively, whether in adults or in infants. But we accept that adults can indicate when their suffering is unbearable. Infants cannot express their feelings through speech, but they do so through different types of crying, movements, and reactions to feeding. Pain scales for newborns, based on changes in vital signs (blood pressure, heart rate, and breathing pattern) and observed behavior, may be used to determine the degree of discomfort and pain. Experienced caregivers and parents are able to evaluate the degree of suffering in a newborn, as well as the degree of relief afforded by medication or other measures. In the Netherlands,

---

[1] Originally published in *The New England Journal of Medicine* 352: 10 (2005): 959-62.

euthanasia for competent persons older than 16 years of age has been legally accepted since 1985. The question under consideration now is whether deliberate life-ending procedures are also acceptable for newborns and infants, despite the fact that these patients cannot express their own will. Or must infants with disorders associated with severe and sustained suffering be kept alive when their suffering cannot be adequately reduced?

In the Netherlands, as in all other countries, ending someone's life, except in extreme conditions, is considered murder. A life of suffering that cannot be alleviated by any means might be considered one of these extreme conditions. Legal control over euthanasia in newborns is based on physicians' own reports, followed by assessment by criminal prosecutors. To provide all the information needed for assessment and to prevent interrogations by police officers, we developed a protocol, known as the Groningen protocol, for cases in which a decision is made to actively end the life of a newborn. During the past few months, the international press has been full of blood-chilling accounts and misunderstandings concerning this protocol.

Infants and newborns for whom such end-of-life decisions might be made can be divided into three categories.[1] First, there are infants with no chance of survival. This group consists of infants who will die soon after birth, despite optimal care with the most current methods available locally. These infants have severe underlying disease, such as lung and kidney hypoplasia.

Infants in the second group have a very poor prognosis and are dependent on intensive care. These patients may survive after a period of intensive treatment, but expectations regarding their future condition are very grim. They are infants with severe brain abnormalities or extensive organ damage caused by extreme hypoxemia. When these infants can survive beyond the period of intensive care, they have an extremely poor prognosis and a poor quality of life.

Finally, there are infants with a hopeless prognosis who experience what parents and medical experts deem to be unbearable suffering. Although it is difficult to define in the abstract, this group includes patients who are not dependent on intensive medical treatment but for whom a very poor quality of life, associated with sustained suffering, is

---

[1]   P.J. Sauer, "Ethical Dilemmas in Neonatology: Recommendations of the Ethics Working Group of the CESP (Confederation of European Specialists in Paediatrics)," *Eur J Pediatr* 2001; 160: 364-68.

predicted. For example, a child with the most serious form of spina bifida will have an extremely poor quality of life, even after many operations. This group also includes infants who have survived thanks to intensive care but for whom it becomes clear after intensive treatment has been completed that the quality of life will be very poor and for whom there is no hope of improvement.

Deciding not to initiate or to withdraw life-prolonging treatment in newborns with no chance of survival is considered good practice for physicians in Europe and is acceptable for physicians in the United States. Most such infants die immediately after treatment has been discontinued.

Neonatologists in the Netherlands and the majority of neonatologists in Europe are convinced that intensive care treatment is not a goal in itself. Its aim is not only survival of the infant, but also an acceptable quality of life. Forgoing or not initiating life-sustaining treatment in children in the second group is acceptable to these neonatologists if both the medical team and the parents are convinced that treatment is not in the best interest of the child because the outlook is extremely poor.

Confronted with a patient in the third category, it is vital for the medical team to have as accurate a prognosis as possible and to discuss it with the parents. All possible measures must be taken to alleviate severe pain and discomfort. There are, however, circumstances in which, despite all measures taken, suffering cannot be relieved and no improvement can be expected. When both the parents and the physicians are convinced that there is an extremely poor prognosis, they may concur that death would be more humane than continued life. Under similar conditions, a person in the Netherlands who is older than 16 years of age can ask for euthanasia. Newborns, however, cannot ask for euthanasia, and such a request by parents, acting as the representatives of their child, is invalid under Dutch law. Does this mean that euthanasia in a newborn is always prohibited? We are convinced that life-ending measures can be acceptable in these cases under very strict conditions: the parents must agree fully, on the basis of a thorough explanation of the condition and prognosis; a team of physicians, including at least one who is not directly involved in the care of the patient, must agree; and the condition and prognosis must be very well defined. After the decision has been made and the child has died, an outside legal body should determine whether the decision was justified and all necessary procedures have been followed.

A national survey of neonatologists in the Netherlands has shown that each year there are 15 to 20 cases of euthanasia in newborn infants who would be categorized in the third group.[1] According to Dutch law, it is a doctor's duty to file a death certificate when a patient has died from natural causes. If a death is due to euthanasia, it cannot be certified as "natural." The doctor must inform the coroner, who inspects the body and, in turn, informs the district attorney, whose office reviews each case in light of the applicable laws or jurisprudence. The district attorney presents the case, together with his or her own opinion, to the College of Attorneys General, whose four members manage the national public prosecution department and provisionally decide whether or not to prosecute. The final decision is made by the minister of justice.

Two court cases, decided in the mid-1990s, regarding euthanasia in infants in the Netherlands provide some guidance for both judges and physicians. In the first case, a physician ended the life of a newborn who had an extreme form of spina bifida. In the second case, a physician ended the life of a newborn who had trisomy 13. Both cases involved a very limited life expectancy and extreme suffering that could not be alleviated. In their verdicts, the courts approved the procedures as meeting the requirements for good medical practice. Although these rulings have given some guidance, many organizations have repeatedly pleaded for clearer guidelines, arguing that a committee with multidisciplinary (medical, legal, and ethical) expertise would be more capable than judges of assessing such cases. Physicians would be expected to be much more willing to report procedures to such a committee than they are to report to a district attorney. The Dutch government, however, has neither created a committee nor offered other guidance, despite having promised repeatedly, since 1997, to do so.

Twenty-two cases of euthanasia in newborns have been reported to district attorneys' offices in the Netherlands during the past seven years. Recently, we were allowed to review these cases.[2] They all involved infants with very severe forms of spina bifida. In most cases (17 of the 22), a multidisciplinary spina bifida team was consulted. In the remaining five cases, at least two other independent medical experts were consulted. The physicians based their decisions on the presence of severe

---

[1]   A. van der Heide , P.J. van der Maas, G. van der Wal , et al, "Medical End-of-Life Decisions Made for Neonates and Infants in the Netherlands," *Lancet* 1997; 350: 251-55.

[2]   A.A.E. Verhagen, J.J. Sol, O.F. Brouwer, P.J. Sauer, "Actieve levensbeeindiging bij pasgeborenen in Nederland, Een analyse van alle meldingen van 1997-2004," *Ned Tijdschr Geneeskd* 2005; 149: 183-88.

suffering without hope of improvement (see Table 1). The decisions were always made in collaboration with, and were fully approved by, both parents. The prosecutor used four criteria to assess each case: the presence of hopeless and unbearable suffering and a very poor quality of life, parental consent, consultation with an independent physician and his or her agreement with the treating physicians, and the carrying out of the procedure in accordance with the accepted medical standard. The conclusion in all 22 cases was that the requirements of careful practice were fulfilled. None of the physicians were prosecuted.

Table 1: Considerations Used to Support the Decision to End the Life of a Newborn in 22 Cases*

Consideration	No. of Cases (%)
Extremely poor quality of life (suffering) in terms of functional disability, pain, discomfort, poor prognosis, and hopelessness	22 (100)
Predicted lack of self-sufficiency	22 (100)
Predicted inability to communicate	18 (82)
Expected hospital dependency	17 (77)
Long life expectancy†	13 (59)

*   Data are from Verhagen et al.
†   The burden of other considerations is greater when the life expectancy is long in a patient who is suffering.

Given that the national survey indicated that such procedures are performed in 15 to 20 newborns per year, the fact that an average of three cases were reported annually suggests that most cases are simply not being reported. We believe that all cases must be reported if the country is to prevent uncontrolled and unjustified euthanasia and if we are to discuss the issue publicly and thus further develop norms regarding euthanasia in newborns. With that aim, we developed a protocol in 2002, in close collaboration with a district attorney. The protocol contains general guidelines and specific requirements related to the decision about euthanasia and its implementation. Five medical requirements must be fulfilled; other criteria are supportive, designed to clarify the decision and facilitate assessment (see Table 2). Following the protocol does not guarantee that the physician will not be prosecuted. Since implementing this protocol, our group has reported four cases in which we performed a deliberate life-ending procedure in a newborn. None have resulted in prosecution.

Dilemmas regarding end-of-life decisions for newborns with a very poor quality of life and presumably unbearable suffering and no hope of improvement are shared by physicians throughout the world. In the Netherlands, obligatory reporting with the aid of a protocol and subsequent assessment of euthanasia in newborns help us to clarify the decision-making process. This approach suits our legal and social culture, but it is unclear to what extent it would be transferable to other countries.

Table 2: The Groningen Protocol for Euthanasia in Newborns

Requirements that Must be Fulfilled
The diagnosis and prognosis must be certain
Hopeless and unbearable suffering must be present
The diagnosis, prognosis, and unbearable suffering must be confirmed by at least one independent doctor
Both parents must give informed consent
This procedure must be performed in accordance with the accepted medical standard

Information Needed to Support and Clarify the Decision about Euthanasia
Diagnosis and Prognosis
Describe all relevant medical data and the results of diagnostic investigations used to establish the diagnosis
List all the participants in the decision-making process, all opinions expressed, and the final consensus
Describe how the prognosis regarding long-term health was assessed
Describe how the degree of suffering and life expectancy were assessed
Describe the availability of alternative treatments, alternative means of alleviating suffering, or both
Describe treatments and the results of treatment preceding the decision about euthanasia

Euthanasia Decision

Describe who initiated the discussion about possible euthanasia and at what moment

List the considerations that prompted the decision

List all the participants in the decision-making process, all opinions expressed, and the final consensus

Describe the way in which the parents were informed and their opinions

Consultation

Describe the physician or physicians who gave a second opinion (name and qualifications)

List the results of the examinations and the recommendations made by the consulting physician or physicians

Implementation

Describe the actual euthanasia procedure (time, place, participants, and administration of drugs)

Describe the reasons for the chosen method of euthanasia

Steps Taken after Death

Describe the findings of the coroner

Describe how the euthanasia was reported to the prosecuting authority

Describe how the parents are being supported and counseled

Describe planned follow-up, including case review, postmortem examination, and genetic counseling

Chapter 7

LIFE, DEATH, AND SLIPPERY SLOPES

John Woods[1]

Euthanasia is but one of a class of practices that are susceptible to factors of degree. Also included is abortion and, as we shall see, pedophilia. Thus some people hold that patients whose quality of life is extremely low are candidates for permissible termination, fetuses that are quite young are liable to permissible abortion, and persons who aren't too young and who exhibit high degrees of informed consent may permissibly enter into sexual relations with adults. All these appear to be intrinsically *gradualist* practices.

Since antiquity, it has widely been thought that gradualist phenomena fall naturally within the ambit of forms of reasoning that pivot on the factor of degree. The two most prominent and venerable of such arguments are the *sorites argument* (or the *argument of the heap*) and the *slippery slope* argument. This leaves us oddly positioned. Sorites and slippery slope arguments appear to have been tailor-made for the examination and analysis of gradualist phenomena, and yet the received view is that there is something gravely wrong with these kinds of arguments. The problem would seem to be that our most natural way of analyzing these phenomena is unsound. If this is right, it would follow that beings like us have a natural disposition to misconceive and misanalyze practices and states of affairs to which factors of degree are intrinsic. Given the moral and psychological gravamen that attaches to euthanasia, abortion, and pedophilia, it is genuinely alarming that we are, or appear to be, prone to misconceive them.

What I shall attempt to do in this chapter is to take the measure of

---

[1] Department of Philosophy, University of British Columbia, Department of Computer Science, King's College, and Department of Philosophy, University of Lethbridge.

this alarm, and to determine whether there are ways of avoiding the intellectual and moral corruptions that it purports to sound against.

In working through this task, it is necessary to begin at the beginning, with the nuts and bolts of the arguments here in question. So in section 1, I shall examine the structure of sorites arguments, and in section 3 that of slippery slope arguments. Once those investigations have been made, I shall then move to discuss, in order, the sexual revolution, pedophilia, abortion, euthanasia, and murder.

1. SORITES ARGUMENTS

There are classes of attributes that hang on metrical considerations. A person's height is always some number of units, and a taller person is guaranteed to have more of them. There is widespread agreement today that the question of impermissible abortion is also in part a metrical affair. If we take it that abortion is morally impermissible at time t (just before birth, say), then the common understanding is that the range of impermissibility stretches temporally downwards from t to t_{-1}, t_{-2}, and so on, to some terminal t_n. What distinguishes t_n as a node in the descent is that it is the temporal unit at which *reapplication* of what we might call the minus-1 rule constitutes a *sorites* fallacy.

Early Greek philosophers were well aware of this fallacy: "sorites" is the Greek word for heap. Taking its cue from the classical examples of the Heap and the Bald Man, a sorites argument employs something like the principle of mathematical induction to generate all the nonnegative integers less than some fixed one. Let K be a collection of grains G. Then the allegedly inductive principle is:

I: If K is a heap H and, for all H, H-1G is an H, then all sub-collections of K are Hs.

Removing grains one by one (-1G) from K, eventually we run out of grains. But by **I**, the empty set of grains is a sub-collection of K, and hence still a heap H.[1] But since no grains remaining means no heap remaining, **I** is clearly defective.[2] In its application to impermissible

---

[1] For those who dislike the idea of empty *collections*, as opposed to sets or classes, the unit set of grains will do for present purposes.

[2] To simplify our discussion, I omit consideration of topographical factors, which are as essential to heaphood as the cardinality of its grains, and of the distribution pattern of hairs, which is as essential to baldness as their number.

abortion, the minus-1 operation, now applied to days (-1D), takes us from, say, the day before birth, straight down to the day of conception. Full-width anti-abortionists will find no fallacy here, because it yields a conclusion to which they are already pledged. But a fallacy they will surely have committed if they rest their sweeping prohibition on the legitimacy of a principle like **I**. Anti-abortionists and those not wanting to quantify over zero-grained heaps share a problem, though it comes at them from different directions. People who refuse the existence of zero-grained heaps must not only produce a demonstration that the -1G operation fails to preserve the property of heapiness, but they must determine where in the chain of descent it fails, and on what account. Much of the current literature on sorites is devoted to whether such a task can be performed, and if it can, how.[1] Full-width anti-abortionists meet with a variation of the same problem. Since their version of **I** is likewise invalid, they must produce an independent demonstration that, even so, the -1D operation does indeed preserve the impermissibility property *as if* the relevant principle were sound. Much of the current literature on abortion is devoted to determining whether such a task can be brought off and, if so, how.

In the heap case, the challenge is to find constitutive features of heapiness which the -1G operation does not preserve. In the abortion case, it is to show that all constitutive features of the impermissibility of abortion *are* preserved under the -1D operation. The classic problem in each case is to demonstrate the existence and function of those additional constitutive features.

It should be said, however, that *classical* sorites arguments invite a certain complacency that it would be wise to try to guard against.[2] I illustrate the point with an imaginary dialogue between S, a sorites-lover, and A, who is antagonistic toward such arguments:

A: Well, you see at once that the sorites argument to the effect that no one becomes bald, i.e., that there are hirsute heads with zero hairs on them, is preposterous.

S: No, I don't see that at all. The argument is valid at every step and it originates in an obvious truth. So what we have here is a

---

[1] See, for example, Timothy Williamson's book on *Vagueness*.

[2] A classical sorites argument is one whose conclusion is by common consent false or absurd. Standard examples include Heap and Bald Man.

proof of a surprising truth, and correspondingly we must change our concept of baldness.

A: Whatever are you talking about?

S: I mean that we must *now* understand that baldness can only be an *original* condition of a head. It cannot be the result of losing one hair at a time.

A: Are you mad? Have you forgotten that there is *another* sorites argument—the *reverse* of the one you like so much—which concludes that no originally bald head becomes hirsute, one hair at a time?

S: Oh, yes. I forgot.

A: So is the second argument also sound?

S: Well, yes it is. It too is a proof of a very surprising truth!

A: And so it shows that hirsuteness, like baldness, can only be an original condition of a head, and that you can never get from the one to the other by gaining or losing hairs?

S: Exactly.

A: Who do you think you're kidding, Mac?

Let us illustrate this point with a further example. Suppose that S and A are arguing about freedom of the will. Consider the following argument.

1. Human actions are (non-micro) natural events.
2. All non-micro natural events have a cause.[1]
3. If there are any free actions, they are uncaused.
4. Therefore, there are no free actions.

---

[1] Some physicists and philosophers of science are of the view that the law of causality fails in the microdomain, i.e., in that part of nature described by quantum mechanics. But few doubt that the causal law holds in the *non*-microdomain. I assume this qualification here.

It is easy to see that we can react to this argument in one of two ways. We might hold that the argument is sound and that, notwithstanding its extreme counterintuitiveness, its conclusion is a truth. It is, so to speak, a *surprising* truth. On the other hand, we might see this same argument as a *reductio ad absurdum* of the premises that imply it. On this view, the conclusion, far from being a surprising truth, is an utter and transparent falsehood. Suppose that S sees the argument in the first of these two ways. Then S is a determinist. Suppose that A sees the argument in the second way. Then A is a non-determinist. Although S and A disagree strongly about whether human actions are free, it is necessary to emphasize that there is something on which they agree. They agree that the argument is valid, that its conclusion is a strict logical consequence of its premises.

What this tells us is that one person's *reductio ad absurdum* of a set of premises can be another person's sound demonstration of a surprising (even an apparently impossible) truth. It is a nice question as to how these conflicting interpretations are to be adjudicated without each party begging the question against the other. We can represent the determinist S as holding the following:

a. The above argument <(1), (2), (3), (4)> is valid.
b. Its premises (1), (2), (3) are all true.
c. So its conclusion is also true. (There are no free human actions.)

And we can represent the anti-determinist A as making the different claim:

i) The above argument <(1), (2), (3), (4)> is valid.
ii) But its conclusion is false (or absurd, impossible, etc.).
iii) So either premise (1) is false or premise (2) is false or premise (3) is false.

Now notice that the cases made here by S and A are question-begging against each other. S's case invokes a premise (namely, (b)) that contradicts A's conclusion (namely, (iii)). On the other hand, A's case invokes a premise (namely, (ii)) that contradicts S's conclusion (namely, (c)).

It is easy to see that the same difficulty applies to our dispute between S and A about the sorites argument. Nearly everyone sides with A in thinking that the sorites argument is a *reductio* of at least one of the steps preceding its conclusion. S in effect plumps for the interpretation in which the sorites is a sound demonstration of a surprising truth. Of course, nearly everyone thinks that S is mad—or, at best, naïve. But, as in the example just above, in siding with A we beg the question against S, just as in siding with S, we beg the question against A.

This makes it clear why S's naiveté is so difficult to defeat. A is not able to charge S with an invalid argument since it is equivalent to A's own argument, assuming that he sees S's argument as a successful *reductio*. This leaves A with no option but to query the truth of one or more of S's premises. This is hard to do. S and A both agree that S begins with a true premise, and that S's argument is valid if A's is. But validity preserves truth, doesn't it? Small wonder that our dialogue ends in such a shambles.

The fact remains that hardly anyone believes the conclusions of classical sorites arguments, whether they involve existence of zero-grained heaps, or zero-haired non-bald heads, or whatever else. But the problem takes on a certain gravamen when non-classical sorites arguments produce conclusions concerning whose falsehood there is a significant lack of consensus in populations of apparently competent persons of apparently good will. I develop this point in the sections to follow.

2. ARGUMENTS FROM DISCOUNTABLE DISSIMILARITIES

It is a metaphysical commonplace that things of certain kinds are so organized that certain of their properties are preserved under various kinds of difference.[1] A watch without a working battery, for example, is still a watch. Facts instantiating this metaphysical commonplace underwrite arguments of a kind that I shall call *arguments from discountable dissimilarities* (ADDs, for short). One particular form of the ADD is the sorites argument.

Sorites arguments produce *accumulations*, that is to say, accumulations of differences. This is a metaphysical fact of deep significance for ADDs, since accumulations of differences have a high likelihood of being target-property *preservation-busters*.[2] If I remove the defective battery from my watch, and along with it enough other pieces, at some

---

[1] Of course, as the classical fallacies of composition and division attest, property preservation often fails under the difference between wholes and parts.

[2] This is not invariably true, of course. The property of deductive validity is preserved under arbitrary iterations of the or-introduction rule, to take just one example. Nor is it the case that analogical arguments go wrong only when they involve iteration. But I am not considering such cases here.

point I cease to have a watch. Imagine that after a fair bit of ill-advised tinkering, all that you have left of your watch is the empty watch case and band. You can hardly take what you have left to the repair shop and ask the watchmaker to fix your watch. What you've got left, after the ill-advised accumulation of differences, now lacks the target-property of *being a watch*.

Arguments from discountable dissimilarities are frequently deployed in discussions of what is permissible, prudent or possible to do. But as we have seen, sorites arguments are chains of subarguments. The chain is solid only if its subarguments to date are solid. But as the chain enlarges, the iterations of differences approach the status of preservation-busting accumulations. It is widely but not uncontestedly thought that one of the chief tasks of a sorites logic is the principled identification of the degree of accumulation at which target-property preservation breaks down. If this is taken to mean "At what *single* iteration is preservation lost?," some theorists say that the question is incompetent. Its incompetence inheres, they say, in the indeterminacy that such metaphysical arrangements underwrite. Others will say that the indeterminacy is not a metaphysical fact, but rather the marker of an epistemic limitation: as a matter of metaphysical fact, preservation *does* break down at one particular step in the argument. The problem is, given our epistemic limitations, we can *never know* at exactly what step in the argument this in fact happens.

However this difference gets sorted out, ADDs of the kind we are talking about here go bad when they exhibit the structure of an *argumentum ad falsum*. In a common form, *argumenta ad falsum* are arguments that seem to (or actually do) start out well, only to go disastrously wrong in transit. *Argumenta ad falsum* are difficult to identity in a principled way, as we have seen. The difficulty is that one of the functions of arguments is to defeat the antecedent or received view that a given proposition is false. When arguments of this sort work, they are demonstrations of the truth of a counterintuitive consequence. Again, the difficulty is that there is no obvious *general* way of discerning when an argument is an *argumentum ad falsum* rather than a proof of a surprising truth. Subduing this difficulty is one of the tasks of a comprehensive logic of practical reasoning. It is a difficulty that bears on issues to be dealt with here, as we shall shortly see.[1]

---

[1] For a more detailed discussion, see Woods, "Pluralism About Logical Consequence."

ADDs of the kind we are talking about here, arguments that concern *what should be done*, present a second important difficulty. *If* they are defective, they nonetheless contain subsequences that are not defective. Further, *if* they are defective, then at some point what they argue for is morally indefensible. It is important to avoid what is morally indefensible, so it is important that we develop and harness the means of identifying defective iterated ADDs. It is good to bear in mind that the class of defective ADDs we are discussing are those that appear to contain untrue conclusions and yet at the same time acceptable subarguments. It would appear that *sorites* arguments are arguments that go wrong at a point. But if the indeterminacy issue is correctly understood, whether metaphysically or epistemically, then either there *is* no point at which they go wrong or it cannot be *known* where that point is in the argument chain. Either way, we lack the means of saying in a principled way what it is that makes such an argument an *argumentum ad falsum* as opposed to a sound proof of a surprising result.

Our problem is that we appear to lack the resources to demonstrate whether an ADD is an *ad falsum* argument or the sound proof of a surprising truth. In many real-life situations, this doesn't matter. Nothing particularly urgent depends on whether we can know the point at which Uncle Frank becomes bald.

3. SLIPPERY SLOPES

Arguments have the *slippery slope factor* when and to the extent that they are practical ADDs of the kind that we have been discussing. They are arguments that appear to be defective, appear to have sound subarguments, and about which we lack the resources to demonstrate that they are *ad falsum* arguments, rather than sound demonstrations of surprising truths. When such arguments are about things that matter, it also matters that they display the slippery slope factor. For the presence of that factor means that we lack the resources effectively to discourage people from accepting bad arguments that have slipped attractively into badness from impeccable or anyhow uncontested beginnings.

We now have the resources to characterize a *slippery slope argument*. It is not everyone's conception of it, but as we will see, it has the attraction of bearing some real theoretical weight in the context of disputations about public policy. It is a definition that does some *practical* work for us. So I shall say that

A subject S makes a *slippery slope argument* if and only if, or to the extent that,

1. S holds that P is an acceptable policy or practice.
2. There exists an ADD originating with the purported acceptability of P which apparently licenses policy or practice P* by parity of argument.
3. S holds that P* is not acceptable.
4. S asserts that the ADD in question has the slippery slope factor, hence that he (and the rest of us, too) lacks the resources to pinpoint the defectiveness of the ADD.
5. In consequence, S proposes that it is ill-advised to conform our practice to the *sound subarguments of ADD.*

Applied to the euthanasia debate, we might fill in this argument form as follows:

1. Voluntary euthanasia, with all the appropriate safeguards, is arguably an acceptable social policy.
2. However, no accumulation of individually discountable dissimilarities will enable us to distinguish between this policy and a series of increasingly permissive policies, the last one of which would allow clearly impermissible cases of nonvoluntary euthanasia.
3. Such an outcome is simply not socially acceptable.
4. But the argument in (2) has the slippery slope factor, so it is unavoidable.
5. In consequence, even if there is a permissible voluntary euthanasia policy, one for which some increasingly permissive extensions might be legitimate, we should not adopt this policy.

As conceived of here, slippery slope arguments are risk-averse arguments. They are arguments against acting on sound arguments that license acceptable deviations from acceptable practice on grounds that parity of reasoning considerations may take us to further deviations whose unacceptability we lack the resources to demonstrate. My conception of slippery slope arguments closely resembles that of Douglas Walton, at least in its most basic sense. As Walton says,

A slippery slope argument is a kind of argument that warns you [that] if you take a first step, you will find yourself involved in a sticky sequence of consequences from which you will be unable to extricate yourself, and eventually you will wind up speeding faster and faster towards some disastrous outcome.[1]

What I want to do now is to examine this conception of slippery slope and slippery slope arguments in contexts of social change that I shall characterize as *collapsing taboos*.

4. TABOOS

I begin by taking some lexical liberties with the word "taboo." Its actual (European) anthropological lineage appears to have originated in Captain James Cook's mention of the word in Tongan, Tahitian, and Hawaiian variations, in the journal of his third Pacific voyage in the late 1780s. We owe our fuller understanding of the word to the work of various students of the practices it denotes, most notably perhaps in books by Sahlens and by Valeri.[2] It is not my purpose to recount this interesting history here, except to remark that in the Hawaiian case, taboos originated as something divine or closely connected with divinity, and that after the substantial encroachments of European influence, they were merely what is out of bounds. Some of this spread of meaning is reflected in my stipulation, as we shall now see.

In my usage, a taboo is a deep cultural protection of a value, underwritten by broad and largely tacit societal consensus. So conceived, a taboo is an ordered pair <P,X> in which P is a principle protecting a value—usually a prohibition—and X is an exclusion, an embedded practice which excludes P itself from free enquiry, from the rough-and-tumble of dialectical probing. Sometimes the X-factor also precludes the mere *mention* in polite society of the practice prohibited by P; but its more general implication is to avert discussion of P's merits, whether it is a justified prohibition, and, if so, by virtue of what. If, for example, P is the principle that prohibits incest, then X is the habit of not exposing P to critical reflection or scrutiny. In the absence of the X-factor, P

---

[1] Walton, *Slippery Slope Arguments*, 1. Notwithstanding the similarity of our basic conceptions, Walton and I understand the comprehensive logic of such arguments in rather different ways, which I lack the space to detail here.

[2] Sahlens, *Islands of History*; Valeri, *Kingship and Sacrifice.*

cannot be a taboo. In societies such as ours there is a principle that strenuously discourages urinating in public, but it is no taboo in my sense. Except in the most delicate of circles, there is no corresponding bar against explanation and justification, or against meeting arguments that might be marshalled against the prohibition (e.g., that there is no such prohibition for males in Japan). Taboos, then, are special cases of principles or points of view attended by dialectically weak—or even non-existent—track records. It is true that there are whole classes of dialectically impotent statements, whose lack of justificatory vigour is a reflection of the fact that they are seen as not *needing* defence or justification. They are "self-evident" or "common knowledge," or some such thing. With taboos, however, dialectical impotence is less a matter of judging that a defence is not needed than that it should not even be *attempted*. (I return to this point.)

Many taboos were once religious proscriptions. This helps in understanding both the X-factor and the dialectical impotence that attaches to taboos even after they have lost their religious sanctions. Though shorn of this expressly religious backing, we seem to retain them out of cultural inertia. When they were religious laws, they required no justification by us; indeed, to raise the question of whether something commanded by God might require our justification is to risk the sin of hubris. These features are retained as the X-factor and the pallid dialectical track record this gives rise to.

Other taboos, such as the one against the eating of pork, may be seen as risk-averse generalizations from genuinely factual data. Epistemically, the generalizations are hasty; prudentially, they are safe. Risk-averse behaviour is tailor-made for taboos. A good deal of risk-averse behaviour involves holding generalizations that we don't know how to justify or that we subconsciously see as having no epistemological alethic justification. Again, it doesn't follow that risk-averse *behaviour* is likewise without strategic justification. Hence our disinclination to raise the question of how these generalizations are justified, and the consequent lightness of the dialectical track record.

Taboos come in degrees, though not exactly on a scale of one to ten. At the high end we could expect to find the cannibalism taboo; slightly lower down, perhaps, the incest taboo; and—almost another thing entirely—the prohibition in 1949, say, of homosexuality. These differences are reflected mainly in our response to violations of a P, rather than of an X. No one in my neighbourhood, to my knowledge, is a

THE PRICE OF COMPASSION

cannibal, but I daresay that the discovery of a cannibalistic cult next door would be met with utter outrage and outright condemnation.[1] Incest differs on two counts. Comparatively speaking, there is quite a lot of it around; and when it is discovered it is prosecuted, and it may be the object of substantial, even though less sweeping than in the case of cannibalism, public disapproval. The prohibition against homosexuality was much sinned against even in 1949; but except for errant celebrities, a homosexual's defections were the object of local rather than wholly general public condemnation. For all the differences, these prohibitions retained their status as taboos by virtue of the X-factor, the factor that inhibits any enquiry into the permissibility of P-hood of a sort that might result in downgrading the prohibited practice from its standing as a *public wrong*. In certain cases, therefore, taboos are a kind of social hypocrisy. They lend, in any event, hefty encouragement to discretion. It is an interesting dynamic, in which getting caught is sometimes the greater wrong than what one was caught at.

In some respects, taboos resemble conventions. Conventions I take in David Lewis's way; they are solutions of co-ordination problems.[2] In a classic example, the conventions on driving—on the right in countries such as Canada and on the left in countries such as Japan—coordinate traffic's ebb and flow. In such cases, there is no prior fact of the matter as to which side of the road is the correct side to drive on in Canada, or in Japan. The only facts of the matter are the facts that our respective conventions constitute. If taboos resemble conventions closely enough, there is reason to think that, in some cases at least, they will imbibe this feature of them. If so, the existence of the X-factor can now be seen to be a well-motivated constituent of such taboos. Taboos

---

[1] Against this it might be doubted that there is any taboo against cannibalism. In countries like Canada, there is no economic or sacerdotal motive for people even to consider the cannibalistic option. So they don't; and that they don't is reflected in the uniformity of their behaviour. If a taboo always involves a prohibition, we may wonder whether it is possible to prohibit what no one seems to have the slightest interest in doing. This suggests that Canadian avoidance of cannibalism is not the result of a taboo.

    On the other hand, no one in Canada wears Elizabethan garb. One could say that non-Elizabethan dress is the settled Canadian practice. There is nothing to say for there being a prohibition against Elizabethan costuming, and nothing for there being a taboo against it. Even so, the two cases harbour a significant difference. If people started dressing in this fashion, others might approve or disapprove; but there would be no prohibition. If people started setting up Hell's Angels' Cannibal clubs, there would be outrage and universal condemnation. The taboo which was only counterfactually in play would now be realized.

[2] Lewis, *Convention*.

carry the cachet of high moral dudgeon and of confident certainty; under their sway, people are easily disgusted and quick to dismiss contrary views out of hand. If a taboo is a convention or sufficiently like a convention, there is no prior fact of the matter that the taboo reports or honours. The X-factor inhibits open enquiry. It does so for a reason, as we now see. Open inquiry might well disclose that the taboo records no prior fact, hence no fact which could be seen as sustaining it. This in turn affords an explanation of the dialectical impotence of taboos, for to scrutinize a taboo is to collapse it.

Taboos sometimes have something of the character of the first principles or absolute presuppositions of normal science. As such, they resemble Kuhnian paradigms: if a paradigm cracks, nothing less then a chunk of normal science is in the balance, and a scientific revolution may well be in store. If a taboo cracks, events of like gravamen portend: the collapse of a large chunk of case law, or of public morality, with the prospect, even, of a more sweeping axiological revolution. Indeed, taboos are the natural enemy of other principles we hold dear. One of these is our admiration of free and open inquiry. Taboos embed principles P under the protection of dialectical exclusions X. The Ps of our <P, X>s have not had occasion to win their dialectical spurs. This makes them especially vulnerable to attack, should indeed they chance to be attacked. Needless to say, taboos also sometimes crack; sometimes they just wear out. When this happens, violations of the X-factor are made in ways that are tolerated or even sponsored by decision-makers and shapers of public opinion. So a practice heretofore constrained by a taboo might become the subject of a Government White Paper, a series of editorials in the *Times*, or even the "full hour" with Larry King. More significantly still, it might be given a less than hostile "treatment" in a network sitcom or drama.[1] When the X-factor is violated by dominant élites, there is a good chance that this alone constitutes its retirement, and the P in question has immediately lost its status as a taboo. It is now fair game for dialectical attack, which its *prior* status as a taboo has given it scant fire-power now to resist.

This is a point worth emphasizing. So I ask you, the reader, a blunt question: "What precisely would *you* say to demonstrate that cannibalism

---

[1] A few years ago, when the main character in the ABC sitcom *Ellen* emerged, to much anticipation and hype, as a lesbian, the show would shortly be cancelled. It appears that plummeting ratings were not a reaction to Ellen's lesbianism, but rather to the program's boring didacticism about it.

is an abomination?" If I might answer my own question, apart from the fact that I intensely dislike the very idea of it, *I haven't a clue.*

5. THE SEXUAL REVOLUTION

Some taboos prohibit what people in any event have little interest in or stomach for, as we have seen. Others prohibit what lots and lots of people are keen to do and would do but for the prohibition. Let us think of the former as *pro forma* and the latter as *substantial* taboos. Let me now suggest that the collapse of a substantial taboo constitutes a slippery slope. In our usage here, slippery slopes aren't arguments, at least not in any sense that a logician would want for his technical appropriations. Rather, they are historical stretches of dialectic, patterns of public and private acceptance and rejection, having, to be sure, arguments as constituent elements, as well as the structural features that I shall now try to describe. It will facilitate exposition if I take as an example a slope that has been slipped down pretty nearly as far as can be, a complex social event of the last fifty years.

Let us re-visit or, as the case may be, imagine the year 1949. The more or less settled consensus about sexual relations was that they were forbidden except under the following conditions:

> Marriage and *therefore* heterosexuality, adulthood and monogamy; as well as consent, privacy, and the "penile-vaginal modality" (if the linguistic barbarism can be forgiven).

I do not say that this consensus had the status of a taboo in 1949. In fact, it was by then a mere convention under attack. And the attack, too, was modest. It proposed a small relaxation of these conditions. Marriage would be displaced by *engagement*, or *going steady* or some such thing, hence by a simulacrum of marriage. Yet in the space of a dozen years, only the conditions of heterosexuality, adulthood, consent, and privacy would remain, and the adulthood condition was in the process of re-interpretation as biological maturity.

This was the beginning of the sexual revolution. Once the only-in-marriage condition lapsed, it became increasingly difficult to sustain the conditions implied by it.[1] Even as the sexual revolution was in full

---

[1]   Until the pill, timely marriage was also a fail-safe strategy against illegitimacy. It is difficult to overestimate the influence of contraceptive technologies in the heterosexual sector of the sexual revolution. The story of this influence is well understood and need not be developed here.

flower, two taboos remained, though they endured with differential tenacity: one was the prohibition against homosexuality, the other against pedophilia. All the same, the taboo against homosexuality was fraying. How could it not have done? If the marriage condition had lapsed, and the penile-vaginal condition[1] too, there remained little to say for the heterosexuality condition that those constraints imply. The heterosexuality condition was now on its own. The conditions that were left in force bore all the weight of our disapproval of sexual licence: adulthood, consent, and privacy, supplemented perhaps by the desiderata of tenderness and respect.

The original prohibition (see below) was against all sexual relations save in marriage. When marriage ceased being a sacrament and was well on its way to what a "pre-nup" would provide—"a mere piece of paper" as the saying has it—what was there to say for its *utter dominance* as a constraint? What was to be said for it *at all* as a constraint? With the marriage-condition gone, I say again that the other specifically anti-homosexuality conditions lost their most secure mooring.

6. DIALECTICAL SLIPPAGE

The permissibility that came to attach to heterosexual relations outside of marriage was not transmitted to homosexuality by the relation of logical consequence. When the only-in-marriage condition was in effect, it did indeed make homosexual relations impermissible on the received, and still widely held, view of marriage. But to infer the permissibility of homosexual relations from the collapse of the only-in-marriage condition would be the ancient fallacy of denying the antecedent.

Historical accuracy demands a qualification, however. Even Christian marriage was not always a necessary condition of permissible sexual union. For many years St. Augustine lived with a concubine, who bore him a son. The union was not condemned; it was the functional equivalent of what today would be seen as a monogamous common-law marriage. Sacramental marriage would not have been possible in this particular case, not because of the woman's status as Augustine's mistress, but because of Augustine's superior social rank. The Church forbade such marriages. It is also true that, in his *Confessions*, Augustine was troubled by the wickedness of his youth. He deeply regretted his

---

[1] Itself a casualty of the displacement of the only-in-marriage condition, as it relates to procreative intent.

former Manicheanism; he regretted leaving his mistress and their son; but he regretted most of all the theft of a pear, an act of stealing attended by neither hunger nor temptation (it was *une acte gratuite*). But he did not regret his sexual union with the mother of his son.

Even so, the only-in-marriage factor came to acquire the status of a necessary condition of morally permissible sex for Christians. In the account that I am trying to develop, it is not necessary that the prohibition was also a taboo. It suffices that it was a standard of conduct, deviations from which triggered, in the last half of the twentieth century, the collapse of other sex-related prohibitions that did indeed have the status of taboos.

The linkage that I am describing is not a logical but rather a dialectical one. To see how this is so, the inference we have denounced could be redeemed with a replacement premise, however implausible on its face, to the effect that:

> The marriage-condition is the only valid prohibitor of homosexual practice.[1]

The question now is whether there is any reason to suppose that those who advocated for the sexual revolution were actually disposed to accept this premise, and if so, why? Actual dialectical experience suggests that they were in a classic situation *ad ignorantiam*, as we ourselves are today. Short of the only-in-marriage condition, we found ourselves without convincing or plausible cases to press against homosexuality. It is a situation in which continued resistance takes on a texture of arbitrariness and prejudice. It is a situation in which our failure to find a convincing case against homosexuality eventuates in a disposition to suppose that no such case exists. It is disposition, that is to say, to favour an argument *ad ignorantiam*:[2]

---

[1] Something of the tenacity of the condition, though not of what it has historically implied, can be seen in the recent success of those who advocate for the social and legal (and no doubt, metaphysical) legitimacy of homosexual marriage.

[2] John Locke is the originator of the name "*ad ignorantiam*," which means "to ignorance." In the concluding paragraphs of chapter 17 of his *Essay Concerning Human Understanding* (1690), Locke describes the *argumentum ad ignorantiam* as follows: "Another way that men ordinarily use to drive others and force them to submit their judgements and receive the opinion in a debate is to require the adversary to admit what they allege as a proof, or to assign a better." Thus, if you are ignorant of such a proof, you must yield; and my argument against you is directed *to* that *ignorance*. Locke did not think that *ad ignorantiam* arguments were fallacious, but this has not stopped writers of the present day taking the opposite view.

1. We don't know of a convincing case against homosexuality.
2. Therefore, there is no such case.

Ad ignorantiam arguments are sometimes fallacious, needless to say. But they commit no fallacy where interpretable *either* as an autoepistemic argument such as

a. If there were a convincing case against homosexuality, we would know what it is (by now).
b. But we don't.
c. So there isn't.

or as an abductive argument such as:

i) The best explanation of our not having a convincing case against homosexuality is that there is no such case.
ii) We haven't, in fact, a convincing case against homosexuality.
iii) So it is plausible to conjecture that no such case exists.

The autoepistemic argument is valid by *modus tollens*; and while the abductive argument is invalid if construed deductively, this is not the intended construal, as the tentativeness of its conclusion makes clear. In each case, the main weight of the argument is borne by the first premise. It is one thing to know whether these premises are actually true; it is another and easier thing to suppose that in our failure to find a convincing case against homosexuality, we might come to believe that they are true. The key factor in this dynamic is *dialectical fatigue*. With the lapse of the marriage-only condition we find that we have nothing effective to say against homosexuality. This produces a dialectical lassitude which, in turn, delivers the key premise in the autoepistemic and abductive arguments here sketched.

Euthanasia exhibits an interestingly different logico-dialectical structure. No one seriously proposes that killing human beings is not as such a terrible wrong, albeit defeasibly. If the day ever came when something recognizable as a *case* against the generic prohibition of homicide

---

On a common contemporary conception of it, an *ad ignorantiam* is an argument whose elementary form is:

1. It is not known that not-P.
2. Therefore, P.

came to be pressed, those loyal to the prohibition might be surprised to find that they had little in the way of a coherent defence to mount, a defence in which the inherent wrongfulness of homicide could actually be demonstrated. Even so, for now the default position is that killing human beings is indeed morally wrong as such. Those who favour euthanasia favour it as an exception that leaves this rule intact. In this they are exploiting a critically important feature of generic statements. Although killing people is wrong, sometimes it is not, as with self-defence and—some say—suicide.

There is thus a body of supportive thought about euthanasia that ties its fortunes to the moral permissibility of self-death. If everyone has the right to life, everyone has the collateral right to waive it. The suicide is someone who, having waived his right to life, has ended it. This is a fact that the euthanasist wants to make something of. In the clearest cases, he simply does something for another person that the other person was unable to do for himself, making what is done a kind of agent-suicide, a right to which passes to the perpetrator in the way that any right of a principal passes to any duly constituted agent.[1]

Whatever the constraints that may fall on this presumed right, euthanasia is dialectically interesting beyond their range. If we are not careful, we will resort to it freely just when we sincerely think that this is what the patient would tell us if he could. At the crux of such imaginings is the difference between what the patient would tell us about *remaining* in his present conditions of life and what we ourselves think about *falling into* those same conditions. Either there is a difference or there is not. If there is not, then *our* view prevails, for it is also *his* view. If there is a difference, no one has yet managed to tell us what it is and how its presence or absence might be discerned. In time, we may come to see such differences as unimaginable, finding ourselves faced with a recurrence of the same dialectical tension between a risk-averse approach in which we are never satisfied by our efforts to imagine the patient's condition, and an *ad ignorantiam* approach in which we come to think that the unimaginability of the difference between how the patient sees his plight and how we see it on his behalf is grounds for denying the difference. If we take the first approach, we will never sanction assisted suicide by implied consent; and if we take the second approach we will sanction it whenever someone suitably placed feels badly enough on the patient's behalf.

---

[1]   Concerning suicide, see Woods, *Engineered Death*, chapter 6.

It is utterly important to know whether we have the means to adjudicate the conflict between these two approaches. If not, that failure *itself* will occasion reactivation of the self-same dialectical rivalry. Risk-averse people will make a risk-averse argument for the tricky option, while others, noting our failure to determine which is the better approach, may reason abductively that neither is. But for this to be true, it must also be true that there *is* no best approach, that there is no fact of the matter about how best to judge assisted suicide in such cases. Either way, we have deep slopes and radical slippages—upwards in the one case to the point of total prohibition, and downwards in the second in ways approximating to licence. These are things to keep an eye on.

7. PUTTING DOWN

Let me open this section by quoting in full Lord McColl's letter to the London *Times* of 13 August 1999.

Dutch Warning

Sir—It comes as little surprise that the Dutch parliament will shortly contemplate the extension of its euthanasia policy to children as young as 12 (report, August 11). It gives further proof of what a growing body of medical opinion suspects: that the Dutch have embarked on a very slippery slope.

There is evidence that during this decade euthanasia has been practiced in the Netherlands not only on those who asked, but also on patients who had not or were not able to request it. As one court case revealed, even the depressed have been given euthanasia. If only 18 percent of euthanasia cases are reported, one wonders about the circumstances of those not reported.

It was the 1984 decision of the Royal Dutch Medical Association to produce guidelines on voluntary euthanasia which began this process. I hope the ethics department of the British Medical Association will use this latest news to take a long look at the Netherlands as it prepares for its own conference on the issue next year.

Prof. Lord McColl of Dulwich, London, SW1

If there is one respect in which nonvoluntary euthanasia seems a less divisive matter than abortion, it is that it would appear to be the sort of case in which a human being suffers greatly and unstoppably and without having had the cognitive resources even to conceptualize this plight or therefore to regret it. Where the cognitive deficit has been a permanent trait of the individual, there is no need and no occasion to reckon counterfactual consent. It suffices to invoke the guidance of the analogy of "putting to sleep" an irrecoverably and greatly suffering pet. The analogy is important; at any rate it raises an important question. No one seriously believes that the morality of putting one's dog to sleep, of putting him down, has anything to do with his consent or preference. Neither is it merely a question of moral permissibility. The received view is that of a moral *obligation* to put the poor wretch out of his misery.

Here, then, is a case to consider. As we know, Tracy Latimer was killed by her father through carbon-monoxide asphyxiation at their home in rural Saskatchewan. Twelve years of age at the time of her death, Tracy suffered from severe cerebral palsy. Her condition was so serious as to deny her any cognitive or conceptual awareness of it. The question this raises is the obvious one. Wasn't Tracy's case an *analogue* of the putting-down paradigm? If so, was there not an obligation to end her suffering? If, on the other hand, the analogy fails, why does it fail? If it holds, the analogy requires no determination of the properties essential to personhood. All that is required is an estimate of the degree of suffering, of the likelihood of its stoppage, and of the extent and permanency of the cognitive deficit. No one should underestimate the seriousness of these questions. But they aren't *metaphysical* questions; they are questions fully within our technological competence to answer.

It is not difficult to see why the Crown Prosecutor charged Tracy's father with first-degree murder. Less easy to understand is the jury's conviction of murder in the second degree. If this was murder by the criteria of the Criminal Code of Canada, it could only have been murder in the first degree. Even less understandable was the judge's sentence, a very much lighter sentence than is mandated by the Criminal Code. If this wasn't judicial misconduct, what would be?

Upon reflection after the fact, we may see things with greater clarity. The Criminal Code underwrites a taboo. The full force of that taboo, or of what remains of it, is summed up in the laws of murder in the first degree. The judge in the Tracy Latimer case took that taboo head on, and was aided and abetted by the jury's conviction on the lesser charge. In effect, Mr. Justice Noble challenged us to show the *disanalogy* between putting a loved pet to sleep and putting Tracy to sleep (although there isn't in his reasons for judgement the slightest recognition of this analogy). This is a case that liberates justifiable homicide from the constraints of grievance or consent. It sanctions, or at least leaves room for, homicide when there is not a whiff of a suggestion of the subject's consent, no matter how counterfactual, and not the slightest hint of a response to threat or any other kind of grievance on the part of the killer. Time will tell about how slippery a slope this case has created. But there is a particular issue to keep an eye on. What ultimately is the difference between never having had cognitive resources for conceptualizing one's own plight, and not having them *now*? If Tracy Latimer was in the relevant respects like my dog all her life, and made that way by certain deficits that afflict human beings, why cannot anyone *turn into* the moral equivalent of my dog, here too by virtue of the later acquisition of those same deficits? Given that there is an obligation to put Tracy to sleep, why is there not the same obligation toward anyone who comes to find him or herself in Tracy's position?

8. MURDER

In the past several paragraphs I have been readying myself to take the measure of the secularization of the prohibition of murder. In the long ago it was a matter of divine forbearance—and is so to this day for a great many people. But the dominant view is that it is also a valid secular prohibition, tenable even if God is dead. An also dominant sister-idea is the secularization of death itself; the view that death is one's irreversible metaphysical extinction. And there can be little doubt that much of the secular taboo against murder is still in force. The taboo against murder resembles the taboo against cannibalism: there isn't much general taste for it, and so it looks like, or something like, what we called a *pro forma* taboo. Another feature that the two taboos appear to share is the dialectical impotence of the proof that murder and cannibalism are both an abomination. The whole secular case against murder is either a question-begging retreat to self-evidence or a case built on collateral factors such as consequences and ways and means. The *pure* question about murder is this: Suppose that certain human beings could be dispatched privately, and without any fear, anxiety or suffering to them and, further, without loss, damage, or grief to family or friends (for the reason, say, that sadly they have no family or friends). Bearing in mind the secular view of death as utter metaphysical destruction— once dead no one exists who *is* dead—then murder which constitutes a secular death creates the condition in which there is no survivor of it.

Who, then, is the *victim* of it? Is there any case to be made against such a murder, never mind what our feelings might be? Of course, people will point out that whether there is a case or not, the conditions embedded in our question's assumptions all but guarantee that *you and I* would not be endangered by such homicidal permissibility as may attach to our example, for we don't meet the conditions the alleged permissibility requires and rests upon.

But what is true of us is precisely untrue of the class members of *homo sapiens* we call "fetuses." People who favour selective feticide will nearly always try to find a justification in the metaphysics of personhood or in a theory of rights in which fetuses lose out to mothers. We should wonder about this. How sound, how *safe*, can it be to hold our practical policies on the life and death of one another to the successful resolution of immensely difficult problems in metaphysics? I conjecture that all this philosophical to-and-fro about whom it is all right to kill is a delusion of philosophers, that it plays no causal role in the cultural transformations we have lately observed in relation to killing. I offer a different conjecture. Let us again ask ourselves:

What is the largest class of human beings who fulfill the conditions imposed by our example?
Answer: Human fetuses.
Ask ourselves now whether there exists a concurrence between the secularization of the murder taboo and the liberalization of abortion.
Answer: Of course.
A further question: Did various factors of our social revolution call that taboo into question?
Answer: Yes, obviously.
In that case, given that the murder taboo was in process of X-factor violation, is it reasonable to expect a concurrent manifestation of dialectical impotence? And was this the case, in fact?
Answer: It was.
Is there a class of humans virtually defined by our inability to mount a convincing case against homicide in certain conditions?
Answer: Yes, the class of human fetuses.

My conjecture, then, is that the actual, though largely tacit, social etiology of liberal abortion is neither a metaphysical nor an ethical affair, but is a consequence of the indefensibility of the prohibition of murder, under precisely those conditions that all but specify the fetal class of *homo sapiens*, once the secular taboo against murder was shaken by the advocacy politics of the seventies. The slippage to free abortion has had wholly *dialectical* etiology. It is the same etiology that presently creeps its way into the precincts of nonvoluntary euthanasia. If the empirical record to date is anything to go by, the contest between risk-averse policies and abductively motivated policies will be won decisively by the latter. If so, we may expect to see the not necessarily slow disappearance of the factor of presumed consent as a policy parameter in matters affecting the taking of human life at any stage of the adventure from conception to the grave.

9. CONCLUDING REMARKS

When a substantial taboo crashes, the prohibition it once protected suffers an elimination of a condition. If this happens, it is rather likely that we will not have the dialectical means of preventing a further such elimination, should it be pressed for in an appropriately public way. At each stage downwards, the weakened prohibition either meets with public acquiescence or not. If not, *the process stops*. If so, it is likely to continue, collecting in its wake new waves of public acquiescence. Public acquiescence is important; it is compatible with private certainties to the contrary. As I said, the private constituencies of the sexual liberation dynamic might not be able to abide one another, but even so, public acquiescence establishes that what the acquiescence converges upon is *not a public wrong*. The fragmentation between private morality (what you or I think is right for people) and public morality (what may be justifiably imposed upon people other than you or me) leads inexorably to moral relativism whenever such fragmentation meets the conditions of the Hypertolerance Theorem: "Wrong for me; not wrong for others in a way that there is anything *right* that I can do to prevent it." We can say this succinctly. The death of substantial taboos induces with high probability an unstoppable moral relativism in which the role of private moral conviction is little more than declaring and acting on one's dislike of bananas.[1] Such is the logic of the slope induced by the collapse of taboos.

---

[1] And with it comes the possibility, if not the likelihood, of *slow and indirect* disfunctionality. See again Woods, "Deep Disagreements and Public Demoralization" and "Public Policy and Standoffs of Force Five."

When good and evil were matters of what God commands, it sufficed in the general case to know what God *does* command. For this there were legions of experts, theological specialists, whose *obiter dicta* would supplement established teaching. What was unneeded was sustained, rigorous, highly specialized training in *ethical* thinking. The hard work that was required was theological thinking. When all this collapsed, and when moral content started leaching into the sands of change, what was then needed was indeed sustained, rigorous, highly specialized training in ethical thinking. True, ancient models existed and offered some prospect of adaptation, but none fitted the texture of modernity in convincing ways. Slightly overstating our predicament, we found the utter want of what was now required. The implosion of religiously sanctioned ethics resembled the collapse of a taboo; and I have been saying that one of the effects of making a taboo of something is to place it beyond the reach of our standard habits of case-making and justification. So, again, once a taboo collapses, people find that they lack the dialectical savvy to defend its moral content, never having had to do so before. So morality *changes*. Even so, what was lacking for ethics was vigorously present for politics and law—high levels of theoretically sophisticated thought that cut its teeth in seeking intellectually coherent and socially stable accommodations of *difference*. This left a gap for the stuff of morality to flow into. In the old way, moral disagreement was something for a sound ethical understanding to *eliminate*; but now it was for a sound political theory to *accommodate*, something it could do with relish. That being the case, we have an explanation for the suddenness and sheer scope of the abandonment of fetuses. It is that fetuses leave *no* political footprint, that they are, in this universe of endlessly negotiated self-demand, a constituency wholly without voice and without story.[1]

---

[1] This paper is a considerably revised version of an initial draft read to the Philosophy Colloquium, University of Lethbridge, in January 1998; the Philosophy Club, King's College London, in the following February; and the Department of Philosophy Graduate Club, McMaster University, in March of the same year. Another version was presented to the Fourth International Conference on Argumentation Theory, University of Amsterdam, in June of the same year. After further revision, it was read to the Philosophy Club of Hunter College, CUNY, in February 1999.

In addition to acknowledgments already made in the text, I extend my thanks for helpful comments to Paul Viminitz and Goldie Morgentaler in Lethbridge; to Barry Allen and David Hitchcock in Hamilton; to Michael Gabbay in London; to Lawrence Powers, Hans Hansen, and Ralph Johnson in Windsor; to Maarten van der Tol and Frans van Eemeren in Amsterdam; and to James Freeman and Marco Tomaschett in New York.

REFERENCES

Lewis, David K. *Convention: A Philosophical Study.* Cambridge, MA: Harvard UP, 1969.

Sahlens, Marshall. *Islands of History.* Chicago: U of Chicago P, 1985.

Valeri, Valerio. *Kingship and Sacrifice.* Chicago: U of Chicago P, 1985.

Walton, Douglas. *Slippery Slope Arguments.* Oxford: Clarendon P, 1992.

Williamson, Timothy. *Vagueness.* London: Routledge, 1994.

Woods, John. "Deep Disagreements and Public Demoralization." Reprinted in Woods, *The Death of Argument: Fallacies in Agent-Based Reasoning.* Dordrecht and Boston: Kluwer, 2004 [1996].

——. "Public Policy and Standoffs of Force Five." Reprinted in Woods, *The Death of Argument: Fallacies in Agent-Based Reasoning.* Dordrecht and Boston: Kluwer, 2004 [1992].

——. "Pluralism About Logical Consequence: Conflict Resolution in Logic." *Logical Consequences: Rival Approaches.* Ed. John Woods and Bryson Brown. Oxford: Hermes Scientific, 2001.

——. *Engineered Death: Abortion, Suicide, Euthanasia and Senecide.* Ottawa: U of Ottawa P, 1978.

Research underwriting this chapter started as early as 1990 when I was Fellow-in-Residence at the Netherlands Institute for Advanced Study. My team leader was Frans van Eemeren. Other members were Rob Grootendorst, Sally Jackson, Scott Jacobs, Agnès van Rees, Agnes Verbiest, Douglas Walton, and Charles Willard. My gratitude to all. Further support has been provided by research grants from the Social Sciences and Humanities Research Council of Canada; by then-dean of arts and sciences, Professor Bhagwan Dua, University of Lethbridge; and by the Vakgroep Taalbeheersing, Argumentatietheorie en Rhetorica, University of Amsterdam, for which my enduring thanks. Finally, my thanks to Dawn Collins, Michael Stingl, and Carol Woods for technical support, and Michael Stingl for assiduous editing. I have drawn this last paragraph, with permission, from my "Respondeo," in Kent A. Peacock and Andrew D. Irvine, eds., *Mistakes of Reason* (Toronto: U of Toronto P, 2006), pp. 507-08.

A related version of this paper appeared as "Slippery Slopes and Collapsing Taboos," *Argumentation* 14 (2000): 107-34.

Chapter 8

VOLUNTARY AND NONVOLUNTARY EUTHANASIA: IS THERE REALLY A SLIPPERY SLOPE?

Michael Stingl[1]

1. SOME SLIPPERY LEGAL DECISIONS AND A PURPORTEDLY SLIPPERY SLOPE

I take as my point of departure the slippery slope argument used by the Supreme Court of Canada to deny Sue Rodriguez a constitutional right to voluntary euthanasia. From 1992, when she asked a parliamentary committee studying changes to the Criminal Code the pointed question "Whose body is this?," until her death in 1994, Rodriguez was the most publicly visible proponent of voluntary euthanasia in Canada. In September 1993, a slim majority of the Court found that although Rodriguez's body was her own as far as the Charter of Rights was concerned, she nevertheless did not have a charter right to voluntary euthanasia because her exercise of such a right might be expected to jeopardize the rights of others to their own security of person. In short, the argument was that if Sue Rodriguez were allowed the right to voluntary euthanasia, then other patients, vulnerable in ways that Rodriguez was not, might well become the victims of other, less than fully voluntary acts of euthanasia.

---

[1]   Department of Philosophy, University of Lethbridge.

Despite this decision, Rodriguez was apparently helped to take her own life in February 1994. Several days after her death, Svend Robinson, then-Member of Parliament and a friend of Rodriguez, called a press conference to say that he had held her in his arms as she died, and that she had died according to her own wishes. Yet despite the evidence of this national press conference, the decision was made not to prosecute either Robinson or the unnamed doctor for breaking the Canadian law against assisting suicide. So while the law was clear, the will of prosecutors to enforce the law was not.

Matters became even less clear with the case of Robert and Tracy Latimer. In October 1993, Robert Latimer pumped carbon monoxide from the exhaust pipe of his truck into its cab, where his twelve-year-old daughter Tracy fell asleep and died. Tracy, who had the mental development of a child of less than a year, faced a painful surgical procedure to treat a deformity of her body due both to cerebral palsy and to prior surgical interventions. Robert Latimer was apparently not prepared to watch his daughter go through yet another such procedure, with no clear end to such procedures in sight. In the Latimer case, the prosecutor's office showed no reluctance in laying charges. Having waited until a Sunday morning when the rest of his family was in church, and having initially attempted to conceal his actions from police, Latimer was charged with first-degree murder. While the jury convicted him of only second-degree murder, that conviction was overturned by the Supreme Court on the grounds that the prosecutor had unfairly interfered with the selection of the jury. In a second trial, Latimer was again convicted of second-degree murder.

It is interesting that he was not charged with administering a noxious substance, a charge that would have carried with it a more appropriate sentence, both in terms of widespread public feeling about the case, and in terms of the sentence actually suggested by the jurors and imposed by the judge in the second trial. Rejecting the automatic sentence of life in prison with no possibility of parole for ten years, the mandatory legislated penalty in Canada for second-degree murder, the judge, citing Charter reasons regarding cruel and unusual punishment, sentenced Latimer to one year of imprisonment followed by one year of house arrest on his farm. In finding Latimer guilty of second-degree murder, at least some of the jurors were apparently unaware of the mandatory life sentence for this offense in the Criminal Code of Canada, since several of them were visibly shocked when the jury learned that it could not recommend the sentence that the judge himself eventually imposed. The judge's sentencing decision was, however, overturned by a subsequent decision of the Supreme Court, which found that mandatory sentences for murder did not count as cruel and unusual punishment, and hence were not ruled out by the Canadian Charter of Rights.[1] The Court also found that the sentence, as a public denunciation of Latimer's conduct, was consistent with valid penological goals, especially since his victim had been a vulnerable individual due to her physical and mental disabilities. The decision was strongly supported by a number of disability-rights groups, many of whom had been interveners in the case. But many other Canadians did not see matters in the same way, including, it would seem, some members of the jury that was responsible for finding Latimer guilty of second-degree murder.

These two cases suggest that regardless of the decision of the Supreme Court in the Rodriguez case, the social, moral, and legal situation in Canada is in a slippery state when it comes to euthanasia: lots of slipperiness when it comes to voluntary euthanasia, and some lesser but still significant degree of slipperiness when it comes to nonvoluntary euthanasia. It is reasonable to suppose that the current state of slipperiness is due in no small part to public opinion, which seemed to be squarely behind Sue Rodriguez but sharply divided in the Latimer case. The Supreme Court found such slipperiness to be a sufficient reason for deciding against a constitutional right to voluntary euthanasia, but it left the door open for such a right to be legislated into legal existence. As noted in the introductory chapter, the situation is much the same in the US.

Thus the main question of this paper: Is the slippery slope argument regarding nonvoluntary euthanasia strong enough, by itself, to legitimately block any legislative initiative that would allow voluntary euthanasia? Looking for an answer to this question forces us onto our skis and out onto the slope.

2. JUST HOW SLIPPERY IS THE SLIPPERY SLOPE?

Must voluntary euthanasia inevitably lead us to nonvoluntary euthanasia? Is it really impossible for us to allow someone like Sue Rodriguez to control her own death without thereby slipping into a situation where people like Tracy Latimer face a greater chance of being killed, if not by

---

[1]   This decision, along with other material related to Robert and Tracy Latimer, can be found at <http://robertlatimer.net/documents/criminalr.pdf>.

their fathers in their farmyards, then by trained physicians in more carefully monitored medical surroundings? Somewhat paradoxically, I want to argue yes and no. On the one hand, allowing voluntary euthanasia will not require us, logically, legally, or morally, to allow nonvoluntary euthanasia for patients like Tracy Latimer. But there might be other reasons, independent of our reasons for allowing voluntary euthanasia, that would allow for such a form of nonvoluntary euthanasia. "Might" is the operative word here, since whether nonvoluntary euthanasia for patients who were never competent is allowable is a completely independent question from that of voluntary euthanasia. Or so I will argue below.

The argument will be complicated by the fact that not all forms of nonvoluntary euthanasia are alike. There are three important categories of patients for whom nonvoluntary euthanasia might be considered an option: patients who are no longer competent but who have left a clear advance directive; patients who are no longer competent and for whom there is some evidence of what they would have wanted, were they now able to tell us; and patients who were never competent. Tracy Latimer fell into this last category of patients, and as I will argue below, it is the most morally troubling of the three categories.

But before proceeding any further, we must also consider a further complication involved in the question of whether voluntary euthanasia must inevitably lead to nonvoluntary euthanasia. On the one hand, the slippery slope question can be raised in a purely logical form: can we draw a line that will coherently and consistently justify allowing voluntary euthanasia without thereby allowing other, nonvoluntary forms of euthanasia? But on the other hand, if a logical line of demarcation can in fact be drawn, will that line be understood appropriately by the public and by the various actors in the legal system, to allow for cases like that of Sue Rodriguez but not for cases like that of Tracy Latimer? This second aspect of the slippery slope question depends not on the crisp logic of rational argument, but on the rather more muddled social reasonableness of the public in accepting limits established by rational argument; these two things, alas, cannot always be depended upon to coincide with each other. And indeed, for those Canadians opposed to euthanasia in any of its forms, this is exactly the situation with legal matters as they now stand: confused public opinion is distorting the clear and reasonable lines of the current law against euthanasia. So it is not enough to have clear laws; we must also have a public that is prepared to understand those laws as they are meant to be understood and, indeed, *should* be understood, morally speaking.

3. NO NECESSARY SLIDE IN LOGIC FROM RODRIGUEZ TO LATIMER

In this section I will argue that there is no reason to suppose that once we have allowed voluntary euthanasia we must also, to be logically consistent, allow nonvoluntary euthanasia, properly understood. Such a reason would obtain, of course, if our argument for allowing voluntary euthanasia applied with equal force to nonvoluntary euthanasia, and if there were no countervailing arguments in the second case that had not already been defeated in the first. My reasoning here is more straightforward: the best argument for allowing voluntary euthanasia is at the same time an important (but not necessarily decisive) argument against allowing nonvoluntary euthanasia.

The best argument in favour of voluntary euthanasia can be developed as follows. In the Netherlands, voluntary euthanasia has been allowed for the last several decades. For many years the Dutch legal situation was in some ways a nice parallel to the Rodriguez situation, for while there was a law against euthanasia in the Netherlands, it was not enforced in cases of voluntary euthanasia. But in stark contrast to the handling of the Rodriguez case, a series of court decisions in the Netherlands resulted in a set of conditions under which voluntary euthanasia would not be prosecuted. Among the most important of these conditions were that the patient's request for euthanasia should be enduring and that the patient's condition should be one of unbearable suffering. Few of the patients who actually met these conditions were, however, in a situation of unbearable pain. In a landmark 1990 study on euthanasia in the Netherlands, pain was the most important reason for requesting euthanasia in only about 5 per cent of cases, and since then, pain has increasingly become less important in requests for euthanasia.[1] In 2002, the Dutch parliament acted to legalize euthanasia in accord with the evolving practices of the courts and Dutch medical practice.

The empirical data from the Netherlands suggest that the best reason for voluntary euthanasia is not unbearable pain, but unbearable suffering. Unbearable suffering is not to be found directly in a patient's medical condition, but rather in the all-things-considered judgement of the

---

[1] Marquet et al., "Twenty-Five Years of Requests"; Onwuteaka-Philipsen et al., "Euthanasia and other End-of-Life Decisions in the Netherlands"; van der Maas et al., "Euthanasia, Physician-Assisted Suicide, and Other Medical Practices"; van der Maas et al., "Euthanasia and other Medical Decisions Concerning the End of Life." The last of these, reporting on the 1990 study, is often called the Remmelink Report, for the Dutch official who requested it.

patient in regard to his or her medical condition, complete with all the treatments, palliative or otherwise, that may be a part of that condition. When and where palliative care is effective, it may be that few patients would find their condition unbearable. In Canada it is hard to know the answer to this question, because we do not know how many patients are receiving palliative care that is completely effective. There is some reason to suppose that in large urban centers, palliative care is fully available and completely effective. Once outside of urban centers, however, there is reason to suppose that palliative care is neither fully available nor completely effective.

Nevertheless, we must remember that palliative treatments are medical treatments, and like all medical treatments, their medical benefits may not be worth the psychological burden of the patient's condition to the patient him or herself. Whether a fully treated medical condition is worth enduring depends on the patient's values and, most importantly, on what the patient considers to be a life worth continuing, given his or her fundamental beliefs about the value of life. What the data from the Netherlands suggest, and what Sue Rodriguez's own testimony and actions suggest, is that even with completely effective palliative treatments, some patients will not find their medical condition worth prolonging. Such situations of unbearable suffering are thus a function of a competent patient's considered judgment that his or her situation is unbearable, given his or her beliefs about the value of life.

Let us suppose, then, that this is our best argument for allowing voluntary euthanasia. The competent patient's body is nobody's body but his or her own, and if the competent patient finds prolonged life in that body unbearable, then it is the competent patient's decision and no one else's to put an end to the situation. But if this is our understanding of unbearable suffering and the competent patient's right to decide to put an end to it, then it is just as clear that no such situation exists for patients like Tracy Latimer. The very condition that makes such patients noncompetent precludes unbearable suffering, where the unbearability of such suffering is measured by the patient's values and no one else's. For the patient who has never been competent, there can be no autonomous decision, based on the patient's own beliefs about the value of life, that his or her medical condition is not worth prolonging. This is simply because for noncompetent patients there can be no autonomous judgments regarding the disvalue, for them, of life-saving medical treatments.

So contrary to the requirements of the argument for voluntary euthanasia outlined above, there can be no unbearable suffering for patients who were never competent. It follows that the argument for allowing voluntary euthanasia does not logically extend to at least one important class of potential candidates for nonvoluntary euthanasia, namely the class of patients who, like Tracy Latimer, were never competent. Does this mean that euthanasia for such patients must always remain impermissible? Of course not, since there may be other, completely independent lines of argument for supposing that in some cases euthanasia might be appropriate medical treatment for such patients. Given adequate palliative care, these cases might be supposed to be rare, and they would certainly have to meet stringent conditions, similar to the conditions for the withdrawal of life-saving treatment from such individuals. The burdens of such a life would have to vastly outweigh its benefits, and the patient would have to have no capacity for recognizing or assessing the nature of the imbalance. Whether Tracy Latimer met these conditions I leave as an open question, my point here being that the line of argument for nonvoluntary euthanasia that we are now considering is logically independent of the argument for voluntary euthanasia based on unbearable suffering. Among other things, the argument for nonvoluntary euthanasia would likely require us to completely reevaluate our moral relationships to non-human but otherwise sentient animals, as well as to those members of our own species whose cognitive capacities are similarly limited.[1] For example, why must we do everything within our power to keep severely limited human beings alive, while we are fully prepared to kill, for the most trivial of reasons (e.g., we like the way they taste when cooked in just the right sort of way) members of other species who are far more cognitively and emotionally sophisticated? These are far deeper moral issues, and as such they have nothing to do with the logic of the argument from unbearable suffering, a simple and straightforward argument regarding the moral importance of autonomy that has nothing to do with the case of Tracy Latimer.

4. THE LOGICAL LIMITS OF VOLUNTARY EUTHANASIA

But what about patients who were once competent, but now are not? So far, my argument has said nothing directly about them. At this point in its development, the logical independence claim must cross paths with

---

[1]   Singer, *Rethinking Life and Death*, 159-83.

two venerable lines of thought about end-of-life decision making, one moral and one legal.

In an article in the *Journal of the American Medical Association*, Lawrence Gostin puts the point well that according to US courts, there is no logical distinction to be made between competent and noncompetent patients regarding the withdrawal of life-saving treatments.[1] Competent patients have the right to have withdrawn any treatments they do not want to receive. Similarly, for patients who were at one time competent, the courts have found it allowable for treatment to be withdrawn on the condition that evidence can be produced to show that this is what the patient would have wanted, were he or she competent and able to tell us. But so too for patients who were never competent: treatment may be withdrawn, if this is what the patient would tell us to do, were he or she supposed to be competent. According to the courts, then, the withdrawal of treatment is always a matter of personal autonomy, whether patients are competent, were competent or, indeed, were never competent.

In an argument that these cases are not at all alike, Beauchamp and Childress, in their *Principles of Biomedical Ethics*, turn to the *Conroy* case decided by the New Jersey Supreme Court and its three-way distinction between the subjective interests test, the limited-objective interests test, and the pure-objective interests test.[2] According to the subjective interests test, if a once-competent patient's wishes are clearly known, it may be appropriate to withdraw live-saving treatment. According to the limited-objective interests test, treatment may be withdrawn from a once-competent patient if there is some trustworthy evidence that this is what that patient would have wanted and, secondly, if it is the decision-maker's conviction that the burdens of the patient's continued life outweigh its benefits. According to the pure-objective interests test, treatment may be withdrawn if the following two conditions are met: "The net burdens of the patient's life with the treatment should clearly and markedly outweigh the benefits that the patient derives from life" and "the recurring, unavoidable and severe pain of the patient's life with the treatment should be such that the effect of administering life-sustaining treatment would be inhumane."[3] This last test is intended to apply to patients who were never competent.

---

[1] Gostin, "Deciding Life and Death in the Courtroom."
[2] Beauchamp and Childress, *Principles of Biomedical Ethics*, 170-77.
[3] Quoted in Beauchamp and Childress, *Principles*, 175-76.

Beauchamp and Childress argue that the second two tests are normatively and conceptually distinct from the first test, in which there is a clear advance directive from the once-competent patient. In the second two cases, we simply do not know what the patient would have wanted, were the patient to have wanted anything at all; hence, the only appropriate test in either of the second two kinds of case is the pure-object interests test, a test that in no way concerns itself with considerations of autonomy or personal values and beliefs. Supposing Beauchamp and Childress are right and the US courts are wrong, how would the argument of the former affect the logical independence claim I have been urging against the slippery slope argument from voluntary to nonvoluntary euthanasia?

According to the logic of unbearable suffering, voluntary euthanasia requires the judgment of a competent patient that, under certain conditions, his or her life is not worth living. This requirement can obviously be met whether, in those conditions, the patient is competent or not. Thus, advance directives may clearly count as cases of voluntary euthanasia, and there are good reasons for allowing them to do so. First, a patient may not want to have his or her life ended sooner rather than later; that is, the patient may want to live out his or her life as fully as possible, ending it only after the threshold of loss of competence has been passed. This parallels Sue Rodriguez's argument that in denying her the constitutional right to assistance with her death, the Canadian Supreme Court put her in the position of having to end her life before she would otherwise want to, that is, while she was still in a position to be able to commit suicide on her own, and before her condition had actually worsened to the point at which she judged it unbearable. Second, a patient may want to risk a potentially life-prolonging treatment option only on the condition that if the risk fails, and he or she is rendered incompetent, a prolonged life in the resulting condition will be ruled out by his or her advance directive.

Insofar as they are based on the argument of unbearable suffering developed above, these reasons do not extend to once-competent patients without advance directives, or to patients who were never competent. Making euthanasia an option for these patients would require a logically independent line of argument, one based on something like the pure-objective interests test, but with a much stronger second clause: e.g., the recurring, unavoidable and severe pain of the patient's life with treatment should be such that the effect of administering even palliative treatment would itself be inhumane.

So where does this leave us? If we follow the argument of Beauchamp and Childress, our reasons for allowing voluntary euthanasia stretch far enough to allow for euthanasia in cases of advance directives, but no further. Although such cases will involve patients who are noncompetent at the time of death, thus suggesting nonvoluntary euthanasia, there are good reasons for focusing on the direct connection between advance directives and individual autonomy in these sorts of cases, making them best understood as an important sub-class of cases of voluntary euthanasia. On the other hand, if we follow the reasoning of the US courts, there seems to be no logical reason to draw our limits with patients who have left clear advance directives, and hence no logical reason not to slide from voluntary to nonvoluntary euthanasia on anyone's understanding of the term. What we are left with, then, are two different arguments, and two different results regarding a logical slippery slope from voluntary to nonvoluntary euthanasia. But our original question was this: If we were to allow voluntary euthanasia, would we then, logically, have to allow for nonvoluntary euthanasia as well? The answer to this question is clearly no, if we are careful to choose the right argument for voluntary euthanasia, i.e., the one suggested by the response of Beauchamp and Childress to the three tests of the New Jersey Supreme Court for the withdrawal of life-saving treatment. Logic alone does not lead to a slide from voluntary to nonvoluntary euthanasia, if the logical line is drawn in the right place.

5. CAN LOGIC HOLD THE LINE AGAINST THE SLIPPERINESS OF PUBLIC OPINION?

The conclusion of the last section invites an obvious question. If the US courts have missed the slalom gate of competence and noncompetence, can a logically clear line like the one suggested above between voluntary and nonvoluntary euthanasia be made clear enough in the public mind to result in a workable euthanasia policy, i.e., one that allows voluntary euthanasia but does not automatically lead to nonvoluntary euthanasia? Two possibilities arise here: the first, which we already have some evidence of, is conceptual confusion; the second is a deep shift in underlying values. If we give up or modify the current set of moral and legal distinctions that define appropriate end-of-life medical care, will the corresponding shift in our thinking about the values inherent in life and death lead us to accept arguments with regard to nonvoluntary euthanasia that we otherwise would not? In the remainder of this section I argue that neither worry is well founded, whatever one might want to say about the conservative point of the second. The shift in values, if indeed it is a shift, is not as large as it might initially seem, and the logical distinction based on unbearable suffering is no more complicated than other distinctions that have until now been well enough understood to make for workable end-of-life medical care, policy, and law.

With regard to putatively clear medical lines and the potential slipperiness of public opinion, the concept of brain death is an important example for several reasons. Back when it was first introduced by an ad hoc committee at Harvard Medical School in 1968, the idea of brain death ran counter to a long-accepted definition of death, one that required the heart and lungs to have irreversibly stopped functioning.[1] What the public was asked to believe was that even though a patient might still be breathing, and even though the patient's heart might still be pumping blood, the patient was in fact dead. It was a lot to believe, and yet the public believed it. The medical establishment, of course, had much at stake in gaining acceptance for this definition, and did a great deal to influence public thinking in its favor.[2] So the question we might ask with regard to the unbearable suffering criterion for voluntary euthanasia is whether the medical establishment might be convinced to have an important stake in promulgating it to the public. For unlike brain death, voluntary euthanasia unavoidably crosses two other putatively clear lines that have traditionally governed medical decision making at the end of life.

Before examining these principles, however, we should pause to consider the second way in which the example of brain death is instructive. There is growing concern that both the criteria and the concept of brain death are unworkable. Perhaps the strongest and most sustained attack comes from Peter Singer, who argues that many patients who have been thought to have met the criteria for whole brain death probably didn't; and as regards the concept of brain death itself, if we really believe that brain-dead patients are already biologically dead organisms, why then do we seem to have so much trouble actually thinking of them in that way, before we turn their respirators off?[3] If attacks like Singer's are ultimately successful, the medical establishment will have powerful reasons

---

[1] See "A Definition of Irreversible Coma: Report of the Ad Hoc Committee of the Harvard Medical School to Examine the Definition of Brain Death," *Journal of the American Medical Association* 205 (1968): 337-40.

[2] Singer, *Rethinking Life and Death*, 20-37.

[3] Singer, *Rethinking Life and Death*, 32-37. See also Truog, "Is it Time?"

for allowing advance directives requesting euthanasia under exactly those conditions under which vital organs are now removed. For if we recognize that many such patients are not completely dead, removing their organs will certainly kill them, and for this to be justifiable, we will at a minimum need some form of consent. Advanced directives would be the clearest indicator that this is indeed what such patients would want done at the end of their lives, as their brains are irreversibly shutting down with no hope of recovery.

On the other hand, hindering all discussion of euthanasia within the medical community are two other allegedly clear lines that are drawn in the context of end-of-life medical decision making. The first line is drawn by a distinction between acts and omissions, the second by the doctrine of the double effect. The distinction between acts and omissions holds that it is allowable, in certain circumstances, to omit treatment that would save a patient's life, but that it is not allowable, in these same circumstances, to directly cause the patient's death through an act of euthanasia. With an omission, it is the disease that causes the patient's death; with an act, it is the physician who causes the patient's death. The doctrine of the double effect, on the other hand, allows the physician to act in a manner that results in the patient's dying sooner than he or she otherwise might have, but does not allow the physician to act with this particular end as his or her ultimate goal, in effect doing evil that good may come of it. In acting according to the doctrine of the double effect, the physician must intend to treat the patient's pain and must use only as much pain medication as is needed to achieve this goal. If, of course, that same amount of pain medication also hastens the patient's death, that is not what the physician ultimately intended to do, and so it is not part of what he or she did do, which was simply to treat the patient's pain.

Both the distinction of acts and omissions and the doctrine of the double effect allow physicians, in point of fact, to hasten the deaths of their patients. Neither line, however, requires the consent of the patient whose death is brought about. Both lines are the last vestiges of a paternalistic tradition in medicine that allowed physicians to act in the best medical interests of their patients, whether the patients acknowledged these interests or not. In the case of competent patients who find their situations to be ones of intolerable suffering, both lines enable physicians to do what their patients request of them: to end their suffering by hastening their death. But whether patients' requests will be honored depends on the aims of medicine, not their own. For the aims of medicine, according to many doctors, are to heal and not to kill; and so, while the practice of medicine may enable physicians to omit a life-saving treatment or to act according to the doctrine of the double effect, it may not allow them to act in a way that causes a patient to die. But such medical paternalism has two unwelcome effects: first, it doesn't allow competent patients to be treated in accord with their best medical interests, as they see them, and second, it allows noncompetent patients to be hastened toward their deaths by either the omission of treatment or the lethal use of pain medication. Sometimes, perhaps, this is appropriate, but sometimes it is surely not. Deciding when it is appropriate and when it is not is not just a medical decision, but a moral decision as well. Adopting the unbearable suffering argument for voluntary euthanasia makes this point crystal clear. Medical paternalism in end-of-life care is inappropriate for competent and noncompetent patients alike.

Aside from their latent paternalism, both doctrines suffer from internal sources of logical tension. The main internal problem with the distinction between killing and letting die is that given medicine's current control of the dying practice, there is no difference in point of fact as to what the cause of the death is for patients from whom life-saving treatment has been withdrawn. This point is well argued by Dan Brock, who points out that for any event, any number of causal factors is such that had that particular factor not been present, the event would not have occurred.[1] The one factor that we humans pick out as the cause of the event thus depends on our interest in the event in question, rather than on a simple empirical connection of one event and one single cause.

To construct a simple example of this point, suppose that I hold my keys out in front of me and, with a flourish, drop them at your feet. What caused the keys to fall to the ground? If we are physicists, of course, we will say that it was gravity, and provide an appropriate equation. If, on the other hand, we are biomechanists, we will say that what caused the keys to fall was the flexing of the muscles in my arm and hand, which led to the fingers' release of the key ring. But if we are neurophysiologists, we will say that what caused the muscles to flex was the neural signal from my brain, which led the muscles to flex and the fingers to release and the keys to drop. Social psychologists, of course, will insist on looking for quite another kind of cause: perhaps I wanted to insult you? Or perhaps my point was pedagogical? Maybe all I wanted to do was to make a simple point about the causal structure of the

---

[1]   Brock, "Forgoing Life-Sustaining Food and Water."

world, namely, that while the world produces a host of causal factors for any given event, which of those factors is *the cause* of the event is something that no amount of empirical research will ever determine. The empirical world deals out causal factors, and we humans are interested, for the most part, in deciding which card, or factor, to pick as the cause of this or that particular event that is in some way important to us.

There are three interesting lines of response to this argument. In "Assisted Suicide, Causality and the Supreme Court of Canada," Edward Keyserlingk accepts the argument, but argues that in identifying the appropriate cause of death in medical contexts—in deciding, that is, which card to pick—the most important human interest at stake is that of promoting the best consequences for all patients.[1] Whether or not physicians' acts or omissions count as the cause of death, and hence count as wrong, is something that depends on the moral consequences of drawing the line wherever we choose as a society to draw it. The main premise of Keyserlingk's argument is that by drawing the line where we currently do, and by allowing death by omission but not by act, we in fact produce the best possible consequences; in particular, were we to allow active death at the patient's request, we would slide down the slope to nonvoluntary euthanasia, which would be a morally terrible consequence. To make the slippery slope argument work, of course, Keyserlingk needs to suppose one of two things. Either there is no deep logical divide between voluntary and nonvoluntary euthanasia, or if there is such a divide, the public cannot be expected to understand it. But as we have seen above, there is good reason to suppose that the first of these claims is false. Whether the second claim is likewise false, or at least unpersuasive as it stands, is the focus of our current discussion.

A second argument that needs to be considered here is the US Supreme Court's argument in *Vacco*. The Court begins with the legal point that a clear line between acts and omissions can be drawn in cases of voluntary euthanasia or, more specifically, physician-assisted suicide, the matter before the court in *Vacco*, because it has been drawn in law in a number of past cases having to do with the right of competent patients to refuse treatment. Unwanted interference with our bodies is a battery, and it is a battery regardless of whether it is performed by a physician as a form of medical treatment.

As far as refusal of treatment and battery are concerned, there is nothing morally wrong with this argument. But the deeper question, as

---

[1] Keyserlingk, "Assisted Suicide."

Gostin makes clear in his own discussion of the case,[1] is how we are to understand patients desiring to die but with no life-saving treatment to be withdrawn to be receiving equal protection of the law, when the law allows other patients, desiring to die and, luckily for them, receiving life-saving treatment, to have that treatment withdrawn. In distinguishing between patients in these two sorts of situation, the court relies on the differences of causation and intent: when life-saving treatment is appropriately withdrawn, the patient's death is neither the causal consequence nor the intended result of that medical action. With voluntary euthanasia, the patient's death is both caused and intended by the physician who acts to end the patient's life. Against this aspect of the court's reasoning, Gostin makes the point that both of these alleged differences are hard to accept philosophically. Against the difference in causation, there is Brock's argument, which distinguishes between the causal factors and "the cause" of any event, as well as other similar arguments. Against the difference in intent, Gostin gives the standard objection that whether a physician withdraws treatment or gives a lethal injection, the physician's intention may well be the same: to end the patient's suffering.

I will return to the question of intent in a moment. What is new and interesting in Gostin's discussion of *Vacco* is his proposal of an argument that the court could have used in place of causation and intent. According to Gostin, what the Court could have distinguished between is negative and positive rights. A negative right is a right not to receive something (say, governmental interference in one's life through taxation), while a positive right is a right to receive something (say, a welfare check). Generally speaking, this sort of moral distinction will likely find its broadest appeal in the US, where positive rights to health care are already significantly limited, at least relative to other developed nations. But even in the US it is generally believed that physicians have a duty not to abandon their patients to unbearable suffering. Unless there is a difference between causation and intent, it is hard to see why it should matter to the discharge of this duty how exactly it is carried out, actively or passively, when ending the patient's life is the only way of ending the patient's unbearable suffering.

Here it might be argued that physicians abandon no one to unbearable suffering if they make available completely effective palliative care. But again, even assuming palliative care can be made entirely effective

---

[1]   Gostin, "Deciding Life and Death in the Courtroom."

from a purely medical point of view, palliative treatments, like any treatments, can be refused by the patient. And even apart from such a refusal, the patient's condition, with the treatments, might still be unbearable from the patient's own point of view. If the patient's condition of unbearable suffering is directly linked to his or her medical condition, including past medical interventions, it seems inappropriately paternalistic to say that the aims of medicine cannot be stretched to include the one treatment choice that would end the patient's suffering. It is also hard to see why in such a situation palliative care would not itself be a battery against the patient, were the patient to sincerely want euthanasia and nothing else.

The third objection to Brock's argument that I want to consider here is based on the doctrine of the double effect. My response to this objection trades on points made by Keyserlingk and the US Supreme Court in the *Vacco* decision, to the detriment of both. In an example constructed to convince us that there is no deep moral difference between killing and letting die, Brock asks us to consider an evil nephew and a benevolent doctor.[1] The nephew, to gain his inheritance, sneaks into his aunt's room and turns off her respirator, while the doctor, at his patient's sincere request, turns off her respirator too. Both patients die. According to Brock, in turning off the respirator, both the nephew and the doctor *do the same thing*, so if the nephew kills, then so too does the doctor. Brock's point is that while the one kills unjustifiably, the other does not. But if we accept the doctrine of the double effect, it seems clear that the nephew and the doctor do not do the same thing. One aims directly at death as a necessary means to gaining his inheritance, while the other aims at relieving his patient's suffering, with, of course, the unintended side effect that the patient dies. So while the nephew kills, the doctor does not.

The problem with this move is that if it succeeds, there is no deep moral difference between killing and letting die. In settling the question of who kills and who lets die, intent also settles the question of cause of death. In the doctor's case it is the disease that is the cause of death, but in the nephew's case, it is the nephew's pulling of the plug. But then there are not two differences distinguishing withdrawal of treatment from euthanasia, i.e., causation and intent, but only one, intent, and it is surely the less plausible of the two. On the other hand, if we reject such an appeal to the doctrine of the double effect, we are left with

---

[1] Brock, "Forgoing Life-Sustaining Food and Water."

Brock's original claim, that in turning off the respirator both the nephew and the doctor do the same thing; and so there must be something else that morally distinguishes their actions, other than killing and letting die. Causation will not stand by itself, and if we marshal intent in its defense, the second distinction extinguishes the first as an independent source of moral suasion.

6. CONCLUSION

There are a number of slippery slope concerns I have not addressed in this paper, such as those occasioned by cuts to the health-care system and the unavailability of treatment options that might make continued life bearable for those who, unlike Sue Rodriguez, wished to pursue such a course. My argument has instead focused on the potential slippery slope from voluntary to nonvoluntary euthanasia. Its conclusion is that, drawn in the right place, there is a logically clear line separating the two forms of euthanasia. Moreover, there is good reason to draw the line precisely where it is required, for competent patients facing a condition of unbearable suffering, and to draw it in a fully public way, in the same way, that is, that the new definition of death was publicly promulgated. Current lines that allow physicians to hasten death and to declare patients dead for the purposes of transplantation are coming under increasing challenge, and it is not unreasonable to suppose that their logical infirmities in responding to these challenges are partly responsible for the current slippery situation of public opinion.

In the future, it is not unthinkable that we will also come to allow nonvoluntary euthanasia, subject to stringent requirements regarding what is objectively best for the patient in question. Be that as it may, it has been my argument in this paper that whether or not we do come to allow nonvoluntary euthanasia, our prior allowance of voluntary euthanasia will have nothing logically to do with the issue. If we justify voluntary euthanasia on the basis of the unbearable suffering of competent patients, that justification commits us to nothing with regard to those patients who are not suffering in this way.

REFERENCES

Beauchamp, Tom L., and James F. Childress. *Principles of Biomedical Ethics.* 3rd ed. Oxford: Oxford UP, 1989.

Brock, Dan W. "Forgoing Life-Sustaining Food and Water: Is It Killing?" *By*

No Extraordinary Means: The Choice to Forgo Life-Sustaining Food and Water. Ed. J. Lynn. Bloomington: Indiana UP, 1986.

Gostin, Lawrence O. "Deciding Life and Death in the Courtroom: From *Quinlan* to *Cruzan, Glucksberg,* and *Vacco*—A Brief History and Analysis of the Constitutional Protection of the 'Right to Die.'" *Journal of the American Medical Association* 278.18 (1997): 1523-28.

Keyserlingk, E.W. "Assisted Suicide, Causality and the Supreme Court of Canada." *McGill Law Journal* 39 (1994): 708-18.

Marquet, R.L., A. Bartelds, G.J. Visser, P. Spreeuwenberg, and L. Peters. "Twenty-Five Years of Requests for Euthanasia and Physician Assisted Suicide in Dutch General Practice: Trend Analysis." *British Medical Journal* 327 (2003): 201-02.

Onwuteaka-Philipsen, Bregje D., Agnes van der Heide, Dirk Koper, Ingeborg Keij-Deerenberg, Judith A. Rietjens, Mette L. Rurup, Astrid M. Vrakking, Jean Jacques Georges, Martien T. Muller, Gerrit van der Wal, and Paul J. van der Maas. "Euthanasia and other End-of-Life Decisions in the Netherlands in 1990, 1995, and 2001." *The Lancet* 362 (August 2003): 395-99.

Singer, Peter. *Rethinking Life and Death: The Collapse of Our Traditional Ethics.* New York: St. Martin's, 1994.

Truog, Robert D. "Is it Time to Abandon Brain Death?" *Hastings Center Report* 27.1 (1997): 29-38.

van der Maas, Paul J., Johannes J.M. van Delden, Lois Pijnenborg, and Caspar W.N. Looman. "Euthanasia and Other Medical Decisions Concerning the End of Life." *The Lancet* 338 (August 1991): 669-74.

van der Maas, Paul J., Gerrit van der Wal, Ilinka Haverkate, Carmen L.M. de Graaf, John G. Kester, Bregje D. Onwuteaka-Philipsen, Agnes van der Heide, Jacqueline M. Bosma, and Dick Willems. "Euthanasia, Physician-Assisted Suicide, and Other Medical Practices Involving the End of Life in the Netherlands, 1990-1995." *The New England Journal of Medicine* 335 (1996): 1699-1705.

PART III

INDIVIDUAL AND SOCIAL ASPECTS OF VOLUNTARY AND NONVOLUNTARY EUTHANASIA

Chapter 9

ROBERT LATIMER'S CHOICE[1]

Bryson Brown

Tracy Latimer was born on 23 November 1980; the birth was difficult, and she had to be resuscitated. Within 20 hours she was sent to an intensive neo-natal care unit and placed on drugs to try to reduce the brain damage she had suffered. She was diagnosed with severe cerebral palsy, her brain damaged in multiple sites. As a result of her brain damage, she had life-threatening epileptic seizures. And as she grew older, her spine and hips deteriorated as her spastic muscles pulled them out of place. She went through drastic operations aimed at controlling the growing distortion of her skeleton, severing muscles to relieve tension. The operations culminated with the insertion of two stainless-steel rods running the length of her back in order to straighten it. Tracy faced still more operations to come. Doctors hoped next to reduce the pain of her dislocated hip by amputating the upper part of her femur. Through all this, Tracy could not take most pain-control medications: they were incompatible with the drugs that controlled her seizures. Her suffering was terrible, and it would continue for as long as she lived.

In this paper I will examine the choice Robert Latimer made for his daughter—the choice of active, nonvoluntary euthanasia. Tracy could not express herself clearly enough to refuse treatment or to indicate a desire to end her life. Nor was she competent to make such a choice. What should we do, and what *may* we do, for people in such dreadful circumstances? Even if we believe that a competent adult who faces such prospects could reasonably choose to die, and that it would be

[1] I want to thank the Social Sciences and Humanities Research Council of Canada for support of my research; thanks go also to Professor Sue Sherwin, for corrections, helpful suggestions, and especially for her careful and sympathetic reading of the paper, and to the Centre for Applied Philosophy and Public Ethics at the University of Melbourne for the opportunity to present the paper there. Responsibility for any remaining errors, of course, rests solely with me.

acceptable for us to help that person die if she could not kill herself, we may still wonder whether we can justify making such a choice for another individual.

My view is that if passive euthanasia is justified,[1] then so is active euthanasia. And if active, voluntary euthanasia is justified, then so, in a few, truly dreadful cases,[2] is nonvoluntary euthanasia. Further, I am persuaded that passive euthanasia, as now practiced, is generally justified, though in some cases active euthanasia would be preferable.[3] To make an effective case for this, I will have to examine the constraints that credible ethical considerations might impose on such drastic actions, in such dreadful circumstances. I will begin with a few important points that will help clear the way. Then I will turn to the circumstances of Tracy Latimer's death, taking up more fundamental questions as they arise.

1. CLEARING THE WAY

Before we turn to the initial arguments, I want to briefly distinguish two general approaches to ethical questions: the *consequentialist* and *deontic* views. Consequentialists hold that the question "Are the consequences of this action good or bad?" is the central question in ethics. What makes consequences good (or bad) can vary; the greater happiness of the greater number is the utilitarian answer, while others have offered different, and sometimes richer, conceptions of human needs and their satisfaction. For deontic ethicists, "Is this action right or wrong?" is the fundamental ethical question; what makes actions right or wrong is whether they accord with the *rules* determining what kinds of actions are permissible. These rules impose duties, specify rights, for-

---

[1] In the sorts of conditions widely taken to justify it, i.e., when pain and other suffering cannot be adequately controlled, there is no evidence that an improvement can be expected, and the patient judges that it would be better to die rather than continue to suffer.

[2] I think we have to be fairly conservative here and require convincing evidence of severe, ongoing, and uncontrolled pain that cannot be expected to improve. Other forms of suffering that might lead a competent patient to choose euthanasia are much more difficult to evaluate the significance of for another person. Thus I believe we can confidently judge that someone in extreme and unrelenting pain would have an extremely low quality of life, but we cannot confidently make the same judgment of someone who is severely mentally and/or physically disabled, but not in pain.

[3] Because it is quick, and so prevents further suffering better than passive methods, which often take more time, and because it can be done in ways that cause no additional suffering (imagine struggling for breath as you endure slow respiratory failure in the final stages of passive euthanasia).

bid some kinds of actions, and require others. Perhaps the most strik-ing difference between deontic and consequentialist evaluations of actions is that deontic rules turn on features of actions that can be seen to hold (or fail) at the time of the action, while the full consequences of our actions, good or bad, are generally not apparent when we act, and often cannot be predicted with confidence.

Of course neither group regards the other's concerns as irrelevant — for many consequentialists, intuitions about right or wrong (when they aren't misguided) can be traced to the typical consequences of various kinds of actions. So deontic intuitions are often reliable guides to the consequentialist evaluation of actions. And deontic ethicists generally recognize that when a rule requires us to do something with disastrous consequences, we need to carefully (and critically) examine the rule before we act on it: the threat of disaster cannot just be dismissed with an airy "Yes, but it's still the right thing to do." Often such examinations will lead to new and subtler rules, while the original rule becomes a mere "rule of thumb." Violating a good rule of thumb, of course, is often permissible, and so we can avoid the threatened disaster.

Now I turn to my arguments. First, many have argued against euthana-sia by proposing an alternative: improved palliative care (and especially pain control). I certainly support research on and improvements in pain control and palliative care in general. But we are obliged to con-sider the real circumstances of actual patients, not the circumstances they would be in if ideal palliative care were in place. It is unacceptable to put individuals through dreadful suffering now simply because we might, at some point in the future, be able to reduce the suffering of others in a similar plight to a bearable level.

For a consequentialist, the point is obvious. But even from a deontic perspective, to impose suffering on present patients in the pursuit of an unattained ideal of palliative care treats these patients as mere means to an end, just as killing terminal patients because of the costs of good pal-liative care would. So whether we approach the question in a conse-quentialist way, or from a deontic, rights-centered point of view, the policy of refusing euthanasia now because we could improve palliative care in the future is unjustifiable. Denying the best available treatment to patients today, on the grounds that we might be able to do better by similar patients in the future, is perverse at best. We need to do the best we can by today's patients *while* we work to do better still in the future.

There is a related, pragmatic concern worth examining here: some have urged that accepting euthanasia may reduce the strength of the imperative to improve palliative care and pain control. The "problem," they suggest, may seem to go away once those who can't cope with their suffering (or the suffering of their loved ones) are allowed to end it. I think this point is an important caveat but that it fails as an objection to euthanasia. Rather than show that euthanasia is wrong for real individuals in their actual circumstances, it changes the subject, invoking a possible side-effect of accepting euthanasia.

Of course if the worry is real, then accepting euthanasia will have a bad side-effect. So a consequentialist would have to say that unless there is some way to avoid the side-effect, the worry is relevant to the debate over euthanasia. But this sort of worry needs substantial evidential support. We know that suffering will result if euthanasia is not allowed; it would be strange to reject euthanasia merely on the grounds of a hypothetical worry about an indirect consequence of allowing it. We don't usually give such hypothetical possibilities much weight in practical or moral reasoning, for the very good reason that the indirect consequences of policies in complex social systems are very difficult to predict reliably. Moreover, there are many strong motives for improving pain control that will persist even if euthanasia is available and chosen by some patients.[1]

On the other hand, if the objection is meant to appeal to a non-consequentialist concern about this risk, then the appeal to side-effects puts the blame in the wrong place. What has gone wrong if the implementation of euthanasia has this bad consequence? It seems clear that the blame should not be laid at the doorstep of euthanasia, if allowing euthanasia is otherwise justified. The moral failing would lie, not in allowing euthanasia, but in whatever weakness of will or loss of purpose leads us to subsequently give up seeking improvements to palliative care. The deontologically inclined must make a very strong case to overcome the *prima facie* evidence that allowing euthanasia is not the real problem in such cases.

2. KILLING AND ALLOWING TO DIE

Another point that I want to settle early is the supposed distinction between active and passive euthanasia. Some philosophers draw a sharp

---

[1] I think there is another problem that has been historically important, and continues to have a real impact on pain treatment: pain, in a sense, is the *patient's* problem, not the physician's. To a large degree, medical outcomes are evaluated not by how much the patient suffers along the way, but by the final result. This is particularly significant when the patient is unable to complain (hence the tendency to dismiss and ignore pain in infants) or has low social status.

line between passively allowing someone to die and actively bringing about their death. Robert Latimer did not merely withdraw the seizure medications that Tracy had been receiving, and allow her to die as a result. He actively and deliberately took steps that brought about her death. If there is an important moral distinction between passive and active euthanasia, then we might be prepared to accept the withdrawal of life-sustaining medications or treatments, while condemning any active killing of patients. But this distinction is, in principle, empty, though it remains pragmatically interesting.

The reason for this is not complex, but it is rather deep: there is no principled distinction between action and non-action. We can distinguish between doing an action of some kind or other, and not doing something of that kind. But we are always acting in one way or another. I never have a choice between doing something and not doing something. What I sometimes *do* have is the choice between doing something of one kind, and doing something of an incompatible kind. But in case this rather abstract point is not convincing by itself, I will discuss some examples that illustrate it and try to explain why there is some intuitive force in the distinction, despite its fundamental emptiness.

Consider two possible cases of euthanasia. In the first, a doctor administers a painless but lethal injection. In the second, a physician withholds a life-saving procedure (for the sake of symmetry, another injection). We are intuitively inclined to categorize the first as active euthanasia, and the second as passive. If the active-passive distinction is to mark an important difference between these cases, it must tell us that, in the first case, death was brought about in some substantial sense that does not apply to the second, where death results but does so only passively. Further, this passivity must make a substantial moral difference, perhaps even the difference between a morally acceptable act that results in the patient's death and a morally unacceptable one.

In this symmetrical pair of examples, the first involves doing an action of a certain kind (administering an injection), while the second involves not doing something of that kind. But in both cases, what is done has the same (salient) consequence: the patient dies. And the notion that "nothing is done" in the second case results from our presenting it according to a particular classification scheme for actions. Certainly many things *are* done in the second case—and these things, taken all together, are incompatible with an action kind required for the patient to go on living, i.e., administering the injection at the necessary time. Equally, there are things that are not done in the first case, including all the action kinds that are incompatible with the kind of action that kills the patient, i.e., administering the injection. So we cannot truly say that something is done in the first case while nothing is done in the second. In both cases, some sorts of things are done and other sorts of things are not. In both cases, the things that are not done include things that would have extended the patient's life, and the things that are done include (by being incompatible with these) things that have shortened the patient's life.[1]

This position is controversial, but it is also widely held. Rather than review the entire body of literature on the issue, I will address some recent efforts to defend the active/passive distinction and explain why they fail.

In "A Question of Balance," Linda Emanuel cites a religious account of the distinction made by Childress[2] and proposes to extend it to a parallel secular account: "Nonreligious arguments can use similar logic and aspirations for a natural death." She concludes, "*A balance of deliberation suggests that the act/omission distinction in some specific and rather theoretical circumstances may not matter, but that in most cases the distinction is morally relevant.*"[3] But this is clearly a confusion on Emanuel's part. The "theoretical" nature of the cases invoked to argue against the act/omission (active/passive) distinction is meant to *isolate* this distinction from other differences in the circumstances, so that we can tell whether the distinction is really doing any moral work, or whether it is other features of the actions and circumstances that matter. When we carry out such thought experiments, the point is not to show that there is no moral difference *ever* between *any* particular cases of action or omission. (To claim this would be absurd!) Instead, the point is to show that the moral difference is not *due to the difference* between act and omission, but to other features of the cases. This is just what it means for the act/omission distinction to be morally irrelevant. Further, and perhaps toward a reconciliation on this issue, this point is a very small one. The ordinary cases in which acts and omissions occur are indeed usually different in ways that can be morally important. The point is only that we misconstrue these moral differences when we attribute them to the mere difference between act and omission; they are due to other differences, which need to be better examined before general conclusions are drawn from them.

---

[1] For a closely related argument against the supposed distinction between active and passive euthanasia, see Rachels, "Active and Passive Euthanasia."

[2] Childress, "Religious Viewpoints."

[3] Emanuel, "A Question of Balance," 239; italics in original.

Similarly, Annas argues (in criticizing the two US Supreme Court decisions in Part I of this book) that there is a clear distinction between the refusal of life-saving treatment and suicide.[1] But this does not establish either the importance of a general distinction between action and inaction or the *moral* significance of distinguishing what physicians do when they withhold treatment under certain circumstances from what they do when they assist someone to commit suicide in similar circumstances. Annas's own inclinations on these questions are clear, for example, when he remarks without further ado, "And the state has a compelling interest in protecting the lives of all persons, including those who are suffering and near the end of life."[2] But the question cannot be avoided: what interest *does* the state have in protecting the lives of "those who are suffering and near the end of life"? And what makes this interest so compelling as to rule out assisted suicide and euthanasia? In fact, though the Supreme Court's reversal of these two decisions does find some important interests are at stake, its decision does not take a moral stand at all, leaving the final answer on the permissibility of assisted suicide and euthanasia to public debate and the political process. Annas seems irritated by "abstract" philosophical claims about the insignificance of intent and the role of the doctrine of double effect in these contexts.[3] But, like Emanuel, he misses the point. The abstract point that the active/passive distinction is empty is compatible with its use, in particular cases, marking real distinctions between different kinds of action. And the bare distinction between intended and unintended consequences is equally as empty when it is considered separately from the implications of different intentions for a wider range of actions. Finally, the distinction Annas endorses between a natural death that "results from some underlying disease or pathology" and a death that results from ingesting a lethal dose of medication[4] invokes a line that gets progressively harder to draw. When life-sustaining treatments such as nasogastric (NG) feeding tubes are withdrawn, the claim that the underlying disease or pathology is the cause of death seems outright disingenuous—starvation is normally quite separate from the disease process in such cases. And when a lethal dose of medication is provided because of pain, suffering, and the terminal nature of the illness, the

---

[1] Annas, "The Bell Tolls for the Right to Suicide."
[2] Annas, "The Bell Tolls for the Right to Suicide," 212.
[3] Annas, "The Bell Tolls for the Right to Suicide," 221.
[4] Annas, "The Bell Tolls for the Right to Suicide," 221-22.

pain and suffering constitute an INUS condition[1] (and so at least a distal cause) for the death.

Further, if we set the philosophical argument over fundamentals aside, it is clear that the active/passive distinction can be morally significant with respect to euthanasia only if we can mark a real, *general* moral difference between acting and not acting, where both the action and the inaction have the same result, i.e., that someone dies. But this is a very hard row to hoe. In both cases, the consequence is the same. Let's suppose further that the consequence is just as foreseeable in both cases (as is likely when euthanasia is the issue before us). Let's also suppose that the pragmatic or contextual conditions that might diminish responsibility in passive cases are ruled out (such as the fact that, if I don't feed the patient, or give a life-saving injection, someone else still could). Then what basis could we have for regarding the "passive" form of euthanasia as somehow producing a diminished responsibility for the patient's death? The outcome is equally as certain in both cases, the alternative action not leading to the patient's (immediate) death is equally as available, and the possibility of someone else's intervening (to prevent the injection in the first case, or to give it in the second) is ruled out by the circumstances, or is symmetrically present in both. How could we ever motivate or explain a moral distinction that makes so little difference? Founding a position on such a raw appeal to controversial intuitions is not a constructive way to approach philosophical issues.

Lastly, a recent decision of the US Supreme Court[2] presents us with an effort to draw a similar sort of line between action and inaction. The Court ruled that there is a right to refuse unwanted interference with one's body, but there are no positive duties for people to do anything for someone else. The administration of a life-saving drug, it concluded, could be refused as an unwanted interference, while the administration of a lethal drug could not be demanded. Rather than endorse passive euthanasia as something done by medical personnel, the court assimilates such cases to other cases where patients refuse treatment, and holds that deferring to such wishes is justified by a general right to refuse interference with one's body.

My first concern about this position is with the claim that there are no positive duties for people to do things for others. I accept for argu-

---

[1]   That is, an insufficient but *necessary* part of an *unnecessary* but sufficient condition—a key concept in Mackie's account of causation. See Mackie, *The Cement of the Universe*, Oxford, Clarendon P, 1974.

[2]   *Washington v. Glucksberg*, 117 S. Ct. 2302 (1997). See Chapter 1, above.

ment's sake that there are no such general duties, i.e., none that apply independently of some relationship holding between those involved. But within various relationships, positive duties clearly do arise. For example, parents have a positive duty to provide for their children. And— more to the point here—physicians, nurses, and other health-care personnel have positive duties to give appropriate medical care to their patients. The Court holds that this duty can be trumped by a more fundamental duty to accept a patient's considered refusal of treatment. But, while this provides legal room for some of the practices falling under the rubric of "passive euthanasia," it leaves the limits of *appropriate medical treatment* unaddressed. There are two possibilities here: either the Court has implicitly begged the question by assuming that appropriate medical treatment can never aim at the patient's death, or it has not addressed the question at all, in which case its argument is drastically incomplete. Either way, the Court's invocation of "refusal of treatment" to defend some forms of euthanasia evades the question rather than answers it.

Moreover, the distinction the Court assumes between interference and non-interference is just a variation on the active-passive distinction. There are many actions people can take (especially in a medical context) that have effects on someone else's body. Some of these we regard, intuitively, as "interference" (whether wanted or unwanted), while others we regard as "non-interference." Beginning from common-sense cases, we regard a punch in the nose as interference, and not blocking a punch in the nose as non-interference. But both have the same result: a punch in the nose occurs. We'll consider below how and why such distinctions arise, and why they are rightly relegated to a *secondary* role in ethical reasoning.

3. MORAL RESPONSIBILITY

Why are so many people inclined to believe that passive euthanasia (such as death produced by withholding food, water, by turning off a respirator, or by ending some medical treatment essential to the patient's continued life) leaves those who carry it out with a diminished responsibility for the patient's death, while active euthanasia makes them outright killers? There are pragmatic facts about these sorts of actions that provide some account of this intuition. First, we might ask, *who* is responsible for the actions that lead to the patient's death in a case of passive euthanasia? Who *doesn't* give the necessary injection, or provide IV fluids or food? In most cases, a number of people are in a position, or could be in a position, to do these things. Only when they *all* fail to do them does the patient die. So health workers (and others) may well feel less *personally* responsible for such a death.

Contrast this with actively giving a lethal injection. No one doubts who the agent of the patient's death is in that case, and whoever gives the injection will accordingly feel personally responsible for the death. But the contrast is a pragmatic one, since specifying the circumstances so as to remove these asymmetries makes the significance of the active-passive distinction fade away: if only one person is in a position to give a life-saving injection, and she is in a position where giving it is a simple and straightforward action (and she knows this), then her failure to give it makes her just as individually responsible for the patient's death as someone who administers a fatal injection. Similarly, if someone gives a fatal injection, but does so in a context where many others are in a position to prevent the injection, or to ensure it does not kill the patient, then the giver of the injection may be responsible for the death, but only in the same sort of diluted way as those who fail to feed, or give a life-saving injection, when others could also have done so but did not. In both cases others were in a position to ensure that the agent's action did not bring about the patient's death. As a result, responsibility for the outcome is shared. In neither case is the difference between action and passivity significant.[1]

This sort of concern, of course, has little or no role to play in the Latimer case. Robert Latimer is clearly responsible for his daughter's death, as responsible as any of us is ever likely to be for a consequence of our actions. But anyone who, by failing to perform an action of a kind they are perfectly capable of doing, deliberately allows someone to die is equally responsible for that death. Intervening actions of others may produce shared and/or diminished responsibility. But nothing can rescue the active/passive distinction.

4. INFORMED CONSENT

The status of informed consent as a criterion for ethical medical treatment is at the heart of the issue before us. It's worth asking at the out-

---

[1] See Greene et al., "An fMRI Investigation of Emotional Engagement." Studies like this help to illuminate how context and circumstance affect our moral and emotional responses; my suspicion is that different responses to very similar (and symmetrically posed) cases typically arise from contextually sound rules of thumb, not fundamental moral principles.

set why we talk of *informed* consent, rather than just consent. Surely, if the only value at stake were some sort of respect for the patient's own wishes in regard to her medical treatment, the patient's voluntary participation would suffice. We could leave it to the patient to decide on what basis she will make her choice, as we already do in so many other areas of life. So the emphasis on "informed" here must be motivated by some special concern.[1]

There seem to be two possible reasons for this. The first is fear that patients' choices may be manipulated by health-care providers who distort or withhold information. Thus the patient must be properly informed, because without this requirement physicians, hospitals, insurers, and others might try to direct her choice to their advantage by providing only limited or misleading information. This is an interesting reason, closely related to the aims of truth in advertising legislation and the public provision of health information. But it is particularly interesting here, since it seems insufficient to explain the force of the informed consent requirement in medical decision making. After all, we allow extensive and very deliberate manipulation of people's choices as consumers by advertisers, and truth-in-advertising legislation rarely requires the dissemination of specific information.[2] Why do we make medical treatment an exception to the more free-wheeling approach typical in advertising?

One answer to this question is that it is because we think, in some types of decisions, that a *reasonable* choice can be made only with the help of certain information, and that it is sufficiently important to make a reasonable choice that we must provide people with at least that much to base it on. Patients, after all, are usually ill, and often anxious and even desperate about their condition. They are, therefore, vulnerable, in ways in which someone sitting comfortably in their living room watching TV is not, to the suggestions, pressures, or marketing efforts that might be brought to bear on them. This brings us to the second motive for invoking informed consent, rather than mere voluntariness,

---

[1] The discussion to follow ignores the legal history of this doctrine, which is of interest in its own right. But my concern here is to develop an account of the principles underlying its ethical standing, rather than the historical sources of its role in jurisprudence.

[2] There are interesting exceptions to this: labeling requirements for various sorts of products such as mileage information on cars, power-consumption information on appliances, nutritional information on food, side-effect information in advertising for prescription drugs, and health warnings in tobacco ads and packaging. It seems to me that these all fall under the rubric of information considered essential for consumers to make rational choices, as I suggest below.

as a criterion for medically acceptable practice. This motive is founded in a kind of idealization regarding choices, where an ideal choice must be based on all the relevant evidence about risks, benefits, and other possible effects of making the choice one way or another. Broadly, we think that a rational choice is one we would make if we were well informed and thinking straight. The notion of informed consent invokes objective standards for determining the kinds of information that are relevant to such choices, standards that determine the grounds on which an ideal rational agent would make such choices.[1]

We move toward this ideal (though only a little way, really) by ensuring that all patients have such information at their disposal. Similarly, we move toward this ideal in nutritional issues by providing information about the nutritional contents of various foods, and in the issue of smoking by making sure that smokers are confronted with clear information about the risks of smoking whenever they look at a package of cigarettes. Nothing ensures that people will respond rationally to this information. But if we are optimistic enough to believe that the likelihood of a rational choice is higher if they have certain information at the time of the decision, we may come to believe it is worth the trouble to require the information be presented.

Of course, if actual informed consent is a necessary condition in all cases of medical decision making, we are in serious trouble. Standard procedures must often be performed under conditions that make it impossible to get informed consent. Worse, if the point of informed consent is simply to provide conditions under which a certain kind of ideal, rational decision making is possible, at least in principle, then even when the necessary information is given, we have not done all that we might. The notion of a rational choice is very highly idealized. It requires rational assessment, by the patient, of the relevant available information about her condition, possible treatments, and their likely outcomes. Consent that results from irrational thinking (gambler's fallacy, wishful thinking, etc.) may be informed consent, in the legal sense. But it does not accurately reflect what a reasonable person would choose

---

[1] Suppose otherwise—that is, suppose that the standards of information are not objective. How could the courts apply such a standard in, for example, malpractice cases? The patient could retroactively find some aspect of the procedure that she was not told about (say, the precise room temperature at which the procedure was to be conducted), and then sue because she had not been informed of this fact, and she finds it horrific (for some idiosyncratic, possibly religious, reason) that the procedure was performed at that temperature: "I would never have consented," she declares, "had I known the room would be at 22°C."

on the basis of the information given (holding the patient's preferences fixed). We would be remiss if we did not at least attempt to correct these fallacies when patients seem to be committing them, and it would be positively monstrous to deliberately encourage such bad reasoning.[1]

Moreover, if the patient's preferences themselves are irrational (for example, if they assign high disvalue to slight present discomfort and low disvalue to serious pain and disability in the future), again we must have serious concerns about the validity of the consent given. In fact, when a patient's choices seem to be clearly irrational, efforts are made to explain the issues again, to ensure the patient is aware of the consequences of her choice, and that she is carefully and reasonably weighing the various values at stake. In the end, then, the principle of informed consent comes down to giving the patient's own choice the benefit of the doubt, once all these questions and concerns have been addressed as well as the circumstances allow.

So why do we give such weight to the notion of informed consent in medical ethics? What I want to suggest is that it is a matter of respect (on the part of physicians) and a matter of trust (on the part of patients): we show respect for the individual by making her choice decisive, *after* doing our best to ensure the choice has been made based on the best available information, reasonably considered. Our reasons for showing such respect, I think, are founded in the fact that she is the person most closely concerned, and in the best position to make a choice for herself, where the *right* choice is at all in question. But most importantly of all, I know that I would not want someone else to make such choices for me, however well-intentioned they were—I simply would not trust others to accurately grasp what matters to me or to weigh the various considerations I would think important.

This means that when the right choice is obvious (and I can trust others to see this) there is not much of an issue. We will operate on an unconscious accident victim to save her life or preserve a limb, even without consulting a close relation. But whenever there is doubt as to

---

[1]   Moreover, in my experience, it's clear that health-care professionals recognize this. I have had doctors point out that information in a given case must guide the conclusions we draw from otherwise inconclusive diagnostic tests, insist vigorously on the grim prognosis of our son's illness when we showed signs of hope that a new treatment might help him, and in general take responsibility not just for giving us information, but for guiding us in how to reason about it. In the case of our hopes for our son, I think they were confusing hope with unreasonable *expectations*, which we did not have. But in other cases it seems to me that this sort of effort is precisely in the spirit of the doctrine of informed consent.

how best to proceed, we show respect for patients by giving them a generous benefit of the doubt when it comes to making such decisions for themselves, once we have done our best to give them the means to make a rational choice. And even when there is little or no doubt, we present the choice to them for confirmation if we can. What I want to emphasize is that this view of informed consent makes it a limited and pragmatic sort of thing. Consider the choice that is actually presented to the patient—a choice between some treatment or treatments and none at all. I'm sure I'm not the only parent or patient who has felt that the circumstances left no real choice at all. The patient's informed consent is either informed consent to (one of) the treatment options offered by her physicians, or informed refusal of all treatment. Of these options, at least the treatment options offered by physicians will be ones the physicians consider rationally tenable choices in the circumstances. As to the option of refusing all treatment, there is a real and well-founded reluctance to force treatment, but even this reluctance can fade when the patient's choice is perceived as clearly irrational. At the very least, the circumstances, probable outcomes, and risks will be re-explained, with emphasis on the physician's recommendations. Few patients can resist this sort of persuasion, at least with respect to treatments that can be carried out straightforwardly (stopping smoking, or changing one's diet, is another matter). As a general rule, only a strongly rooted objection to the treatment(s) proposed, or outright rejection of the physician's judgment, will do the job. So any choice a patient makes will be acceptable to physicians, unless she refuses treatment that they regard as very clearly and definitely in her best interest.

The point of this discussion has been to examine why informed consent has become a central criterion for ethical medical treatment; by implication, we have also gained an understanding of the limits of informed consent. Since on my view it is founded in the ideal of rational choice, made by the person most directly concerned and in the best position to take account of the values at stake, I believe that it does indeed have limits. There are good reasons to give the benefit of the doubt to the patient's choice, but these reasons can sometimes be morally overridden in circumstances where the patient's choice is clearly and persistently irrational, and poses a significant threat to her well-being.[1]

---

[1] This has implications for the issue of forced treatment in psychiatric illnesses. It is also worth thinking about how rarely this sort of extreme case really arises outside of that category. Blood transfusions for Jehovah's Witnesses are an interesting example. Here, of course, the general policy is not to force transfusions on adults, but to insist that children be given the

Informed consent is not always necessary for morally acceptable medical care. It is an effective practical means to ensure that some moral concerns we have about medical care (including its importance and its personal nature) are addressed. But it is not, and cannot be, the only way to address these concerns. When these idealizations regarding individual rational choice cease even to approximate the choice processes in the patient or her guardians, informed consent needs to be supplemented (and even, in the worst case, replaced) by other ways of ensuring ethical medical practice.

5. THE CONSEQUENTIALIST VIEW OF THE LATIMER CASE

With all this in mind, let's turn back to the Latimer case and nonvoluntary euthanasia, i.e., euthanasia in the absence of informed consent. This is (I pause to emphasize) a completely separate issue from forced or *in*voluntary euthanasia, i.e., euthanasia performed either without the consent of a competent patient, or against the express wishes of such a patient.[1] I will argue that, given the conditions that Tracy Latimer faced, nonvoluntary euthanasia is a reasonable response. But I also hold that the decision to perform such a procedure should not be made solely by parents or guardians, or even by parents together with the patient's primary-care physician—some sort of quasi-judicial proceeding, involving physicians and an independent representative of the patient's interests, should be the standard for such grave decisions.

---

treatment, whether they or their parents consent. This is a kind of case in which the standard of informed consent really has substantial force, since straightforward and reliable life-saving treatment can be blocked by the patient's refusal. But the patients in such cases expressly value their obedience to religious strictures above their lives. And if they continue to do so after discussion and careful explanation, then we may reasonably accept their decision as rational given their preferences. The exception made in the case of children is interesting, since their preferences often match those of their elders, yet we insist on treating them without consent. We can rationalize this by claiming that the preferences children have are strongly influenced by their parents' preferences (and those of other influential adults) and that they have had, as yet, insufficient opportunity to reflect on and choose for themselves the religious views that underlie their expressed preferences. But this is pretty rough and ready stuff. It's obvious that similar deficiencies will often explain the preferences of adults, yet in the case of adults, and especially in the case of adults' religious beliefs, we do not press the point. This rather arbitrary line between our treatment of children and of adults bears a family resemblance to other such lines, such as the age of majority.

[1] I only mention this because some have claimed that allowing euthanasia for patients like Tracy Latimer would threaten other disabled people—people perfectly capable of expressing their own wishes—with forced euthanasia.

In our present legal system, parents are the decision-makers for young children. Up until her death, Tracy's parents made all decisions regarding her medical treatment. In particular, it was Mr. and Mrs. Latimer who decided to go ahead with an operation that tied Tracy's spine to two steel rods embedded in her hips, preventing it from curving further as her disease progressed, and who consented to (and often administered) the drugs and other treatments that kept Tracy from dying of epileptic seizures. And it was Mr. and Mrs. Latimer who witnessed Tracy's suffering and the deterioration of her condition that preceded her death.

From a consequentialist point of view, it is easy to see how to justify nonvoluntary euthanasia in such a case. All we need are two conditions. First, Tracy's suffering must be such that her death is better, with respect to whatever morally significant goals our consequentialist approach recognizes, than her continued life.[1] Second, the effects of allowing her and others like her to be killed (given substantial safeguards and high standards of evidence) must not outweigh this evaluation of her particular case. The first condition is arguably met, on the grounds of consequentialist concerns including pain and suffering and the lack of either prospects for improvement or opportunity for enjoyments sufficient to outweigh that suffering.[2] Further, even if it was not met in Tracy's case, it can and will be met in other cases. I leave the second aside for now, to be taken up when I address the issue of how institutions allowing for nonvoluntary euthanasia while preventing abuses could be developed.

6. DEONTOLOGICAL WORRIES

Of course many object to an ethics founded on consequences alone. There are several familiar arguments that aim to show that ethics cannot simply be a matter of pursuing the best consequences, however

---

[1]   The Supreme Court of Canada seems to have concluded that the consequentialist case fails on this point, when they declared that what Tracy suffered at the hands of her father was far worse than anything she would have suffered if she had continued to live. But this declaration sounds more like a desperate effort to justify Latimer's extremely harsh sentence than a serious claim about Tracy's prospects for a bearable life.

[2]   It is all too easy to avoid recognizing this fact—hope for improvements in treatment and better outcomes than a reasonable prognosis would support is almost irresistible, even for parents confronted with the real situation on a daily basis. And others who know less severely ill children with the same condition may tend to substitute those children for Tracy when they try to think about the case, forgetting just how dreadful her situation really was. Looking at Tracy's circumstances through rose-coloured glasses will certainly mislead us when we come to evaluate what Robert Latimer did.

high-minded and laudable those consequences may be. Other constraints, including prominently the notion of respect for individuals, are urged as at least supplementing what consequentialism has to tell us about ethics. It would be absurd of me to attempt to resolve this long-standing and complex debate here.[1] But I will examine briefly some of the main considerations that might be held to count against the result we have arrived at on consequentialist grounds. I believe that an adequate response to these concerns can be arrived at in the same way I propose that we deal with our deferred worries about the broader consequences of allowing nonvoluntary euthanasia, i.e., through the careful construction of institutions that will ensure (as far as possible) that the practice will be carefully limited, and shaped as much as possible by respect for individuals and their values and preferences. For our purposes, the exact role and status of such deontic constraints in ethics need not be settled, so long as we are prepared to recognize that they cannot credibly be taken to be so fundamental and so unquestionable as to overrule strong consequentialist considerations, where measures are taken to ensure respect for individuals and other characteristic deontic concerns.

Consider how you would feel knowing someone is about to make a decision that affects your interests, using a consequentialist system of ethics. There are two broad concerns you may reasonably have about the situation:

1. What if your interests are sacrificed, in the final choice, for some greater benefit to others?
2. How can you be sure the person making the choice is really getting things right?

The first concern provides grounds for individuals to resist consequentialist systems, since their individual interests may suffer as a result. The second provides further grounds, linked to psychological limits and concerns about error. The two reinforce each other, since the special regard we each have for our own interests casts doubt on the concern one

---

[1] Some claim that any purely consequentialist approach to ethics must fall afoul of scapegoating and other standard counterexamples to utilitarianism. But there are real reasons a consequentialist thinker can give for avoiding scapegoating, including mistrust of others' ability to judge fairly and accurately when such a procedure would be consequentially justified. Human limitations and biases, and the special concern that each person has for his/her own welfare, provide plenty of consequential reasons for binding ourselves with rules that respect individuals in certain ways, as well as *some* other typically deontic ethical intuitions.

person might have about a sacrifice of another's interests. Together they provide consequentialist reasons for concern about a too-direct application of purely consequentialist considerations in decision making. Anxiety about the prospect of being scapegoated, or otherwise harmed in the interest of others, and worries about whether decision-makers (with their moral and epistemic limitations) can really be trusted to do such things only when they really do maximize achievement of our goals, represent a considerable cost. And security in one's person, and confidence that others' choices are constrained in ways that forbid them to harm you in certain ways, are of considerable *consequential* value.

The over-demanding character of consequentialist ethics also shows up clearly here. One way to explain why we aren't required to do whatever is best for all is to say that we are each entitled to have (and act on) a special regard for our own welfare. But in fact, such a "protected" range of actions may well be consequentially justified, since its existence may contribute (in the end) to a consequentially better result than a simple and direct attempt, at each moment, to maximize the value of our actions' consequences.[1] The need for a simple procedure by which to calculate the moral constraints on our actions is important here. There is no straightforward way to identify the kind of action that is optimizing for any plausible consequentialist system. *Any* sort of action (as described in terms of its locally discernable features) might be optimal, depending on the circumstances. This implies that the epistemic/calculational burden of consequentialist reasoning is immense—in fact, it is utterly overwhelming. By contrast, deontological approaches focus on action kinds described in more epistemically accessible terms. And this is very helpful—it allows us to produce rules for action that we can actually follow with some confidence of success. Of course they will occasionally lead us to make the wrong move from a consequentialist point of view. But our epistemic limitations and our selfishness combine to suggest we should be modest and restrained in invoking such consequentialist considerations to defend rule breaking.

That said, it is also important to recognize that these rules get their justification from the consequences of our adopting them. And that brings the role of empirical evidence to the fore. As evidence accumulates, we are often in a position to improve on the rules we have in place,

---

[1]   See, e.g., Railton, "Alienation, Consequentialism and the Demands of Morality."

i. By rejecting rules whose overall costs exceed their benefits.

ii. By adding new rules that promise, on the evidence, to help us prevent some bad outcomes or achieve some good ones at acceptable cost.

iii. By making the rules we have more richly conditional on *epistemically accessible* features of the circumstances that can be used to guide more consequentially successful behavior.

Deontic constraints, on such a view, do not stand prior to or independent of consequentialist questions. They represent our best present solution to the problems of deliberation, while respecting both our special concern for (and knowledge of) ourselves, and the constraints on sacrificing others that are essential to preventing some important kinds of abuse.

Let's return to the case at hand with these thoughts in mind. Some deontological thinkers may be prepared to defend a blanket prohibition against nonvoluntary euthanasia despite the consequentialist case in its favor. But this stand looks more than a little odd in the circumstances of the Latimer case. Here there were certainly conditions that could justify a rational, self-aware, and competent person choosing death over continued suffering. The available evidence, both for Robert Latimer and for the courts, included extensive information regarding Tracy's condition, her suffering, the ongoing inadequacy of her pain control, and her unhappy prognosis.

It is possible, I believe, to frame reasonable and enforceable rules allowing, given this kind of evidence and in this extremity, that Tracy be killed—a harsh-sounding word, but a merciful act. We must still ask whether such rules would lead to worse results than those that Tracy and others face without them. But these rules can be written to prevent a slippery-slope broadening of euthanasia to cases where extreme and uncontrolled suffering does not exist. And a publicly accessible process of judgment, with these standards clearly applied, would protect against abuses that might well pass unnoticed without such a system, and may well be occurring *now*. So the level of protection for other disabled people might well increase with such a system.

The law is a blunt instrument, and it is hard to be sure that every case that goes through such a process will be treated as we ideally would like it to be. But it is also important here to recognize that important risks arise in both directions. Allowing people to be killed raises the concern that some who should not be killed will be. However, the suffering of people whose pain is uncontrolled and incurable is an important moral concern as well. Rules allowing nonvoluntary euthanasia should be very conservative, to ensure that the first risk is minimized. But as the law stands, the second type of concern — concern for those like Tracy, trapped in a hopeless and painful existence — is completely ignored. This, I think, can only be justified if the harm done by mistakenly killing someone — someone in severe pain, but whose suffering is not irremediably or unbearably bad — is incommensurably worse than the harm done by not ending the pain of someone whose suffering is irremediable and unbearable. However, this incommensurability claim is extremely hard to justify.

First, it seems to imply that any form of euthanasia, active or passive, must be rejected, since the risk of allowing a death that is wrong is immeasurably more important than the risk of imposing unnecessary suffering. This implication might be dodged by claiming that a patient can make such a choice, accepting the risk for herself, but it is unacceptable for anyone else to ever make such a choice for another. This is an interesting way of trying to sharply distinguish voluntary from nonvoluntary euthanasia. But it is unconvincing. First of all, our examination of informed consent does not suggest that it could justify procedures that could never be justified on independent evidence. The reasons we found for making informed consent an important part of ethical medical practice had to do with the importance of medical decisions, the ideal of rational choice as a process involving correct reasoning based on all the relevant evidence, and respect for the individual's own preferences. Only the last of these can help here. And it can't help much, since we have assumed here that any individual who chooses to die must be making a mistake. Respect for the individual might extend far enough for us to reject laws forbidding suicide. But it would not extend so far as to force cooperation with a patient's necessarily irrational desire to die.[1]

---

[1] This line of attack against euthanasia is surprisingly popular — see, for example, Pellegrino, "The False Promise of Beneficent Killing," 83, where he insists that "the plea for assistance in suicide is a desperate appeal for another kind of help — for support, for reassurance of love...." It strikes me as odd that someone who insists on the moral requirement not to ignore patient preferences (p. 78) can be so cavalier about the express preferences of patients whose choice he wishes to reject. Surely part of respect for others' preferences is being willing to hear them and take them seriously even when they don't accord with one's own. No doubt this absolutism on Pellegrino's part is related to his views on human dignity as a value; he claims that real human dignity simply cannot be lost; the loss patients experience is "a loss of worth they perceive in the way those about them see them" (p. 84) The obvious reply here is to point out that this view of human dignity is not universally shared, and those who do not share it should not be bound by Pellegrino's opinion on such a personal question.

Second, and far worse, is the fact that this incommensurability claim is clearly false, at least in the judgment of many. In terminal cases where there is severe pain and a strong expectation of death in a short time (days or perhaps weeks) regardless of intervention, there is a widespread acceptance that passive euthanasia, up to and including pain-control measures that ultimately suppress respiration, is justified. How could this be justified if the risk that this death is premature is incommensurably worse than any risk of suffering? Given this absolute principle, it seems we would be required to withhold any and all pain-control measures that carried a significant risk of death, since the suffering this would impose is unimportant compared to the risk of (premature) death that effective pain control involves.

Finally, it is clear that many do not accept this strong incommensurability claim. The fact that some clearly and articulately prefer an earlier death to enduring pointless suffering places a weighty burden of proof on those who claim that the risk of unnecessarily choosing an early death is so much worse than that of facing "mere" ongoing suffering. Drawing a sharp line between voluntary and nonvoluntary euthanasia here would impose this incommensurability thesis on all but those who can speak for themselves. I can't see any way to defend such an absolute position. It requires that we accept the incommensurability thesis as a default position that can only be defeated by the express contrary wishes of the patient. But there is no reason why those who reject this incommensurability for themselves should meekly accept its imposition on others; there is no reason to concede the moral high ground to the opponents of euthanasia and tie the defense of euthanasia exclusively to a "right of self-determination." The consequentialist approach to justifying rules presented here gives a much more general account of how a system of rules permitting euthanasia can be justified without such a narrow appeal to individual rights.

7. INSISTING ON INFORMED CONSENT

Suppose someone simply insists that without informed consent nothing so extreme as euthanasia can ever be justified. This seems peculiar right at the start: all other medical choices are assigned to the parents of children. Once we recognize active euthanasia as a permissible medical response in some circumstances, how can we justify ignoring the fact that these circumstances obtain in a case, just because the patient herself is not in a position to make the choice? Further, informed consent has a derivative status here—it is not an unexaminable, primitive ethical constraint, but a substantial and interesting rule whose grounds need to be worked out. On the view I have outlined above, the bar cannot be set so high. Perhaps some other views will allow the bar to go higher. But respect for the individual cuts both ways here: respect for life and autonomy, reflected in the requirement of informed consent, must compete with respect for suffering. We don't show much respect for a *person* if their being alive is all that we value about them. That narrow a "respect" is perfectly compatible, for example, with the practice of torture. So it is hard to see how respect for individuals can lead to an absolute constraint on euthanasia.

Further, if we insist on informed consent as a sine qua non for euthanasia, we must be prepared to face the consequences. The consequences don't go away just because we think palliative care could be better than it is, or because we don't like to think of the real, horrific, crushing pain and suffering that some among us are subjected to. The consequence of a blanket prohibition on nonvoluntary euthanasia is that some people, including some children, will be forced to suffer horribly, far more horribly than anyone who accepts voluntary euthanasia would ever force those with the ability to cry "hold, enough" to suffer. If we accept that it can be rational to prefer death to life (and I believe we implicitly do this if we offer it as an option to patients in a position to make their own choice), then we must recognize that even those who are not competent to make such a choice can find themselves in such a predicament. If we then deny the obvious remedy to those individuals, we have a high justificatory burden to carry.

The notion that this is such a unique sort of intervention flies in the face of our discussion of action and "inaction" above—it pretends that there is a very special ethical character that belongs to these particular actions simply because they aim to bring death about. But in the absence of a convincing theory of what that difference is, and why it has such paramount ethical status as to *require* that the unfortunate noncompetent be forced to suffer indefinitely, this is unpersuasive. It implies that our only obligation to a noncompetent person in uncontrollable pain is to accept their suffering for as long as they (can be made to) live. I suspect this is easier for caregivers than for their patients, and easier for caregivers who do not love their charges than for those who do. It is far easier still for the distant observer who can avoid coming face to face with the patient's suffering. But it cannot be regarded as a way of protecting patients at all, unless we are so confused as to believe that the sort of life that is not worthwhile for a rational and competent person *must* still be worthwhile for the noncompetent.

Tracy's euthanasia was not voluntary. But neither was her ongoing treatment, including the drastic operations, the anti-seizure medications that ruled out strong pain-control drugs for her, and all the rest. Robert Latimer did not impose on his daughter any more when he killed her than he did when he and his wife decided in favour of all the various treatments Tracy underwent during her life. In both cases, the Latimers made decisions that Tracy, had she been competent, might well have rejected. A competent Tracy (if we could separate that competence from the entangled capabilities for other, possibly compensating enjoyments in life) might well have preferred to die of her seizures while taking morphine than go on living without adequate pain control. And she might (though in truth I think this is harder to imagine) have preferred to go on living despite her pain. But in both cases, Tracy's preferences (if she had any) were inaccessible; the decision had to be made by others. In such circumstances, we are not absolved of responsibility for the consequences of our choices, and no loving parent could ever accept such absolution anyway. If we choose not to act to prevent suffering like Tracy's, we accept something horrible, something I believe is far more horrible than the death that Robert Latimer gave his daughter.

The point here is reinforced by the fact that we have rejected the usual distinction between passive and active euthanasia. Other things being equal, there is no morally significant difference between the imposition of suffering by "inaction" and its imposition by deliberate action. And the reason for this is fundamental, not a matter for casuistic debate about intuitions and examples. There is no real distinction between action and inaction except relative to a given categorization of action kinds. A full categorization—as opposed to a gappy one—will ensure that whatever choice is made is a selection to perform an action of some recognized kind. If we do not act to end suffering when we could, we have *chosen* that suffering over the alternative. When the alternative is clearly better, we have not chosen as we should, whatever excuses we may try to make for ourselves.

Some still worry about the risks of a slippery slope that will lead to far more killings than those we can accept as justifiable. This position argues that Tracy Latimer and others like her must suffer, because the alternative will put others who clearly should not be killed at risk. I've raised the issue of safeguards briefly above; responding to this position requires a more careful examination of what we can do to avoid this slippery slope while allowing for nonvoluntary euthanasia in circum-stances like Tracy's. Reasonable safeguards can keep what risk there is at bay by imposing checks and balances on the decision-making process. These would include the involvement of other medical personnel, including—as is already done in other treatment decisions for some patients—a committee of professionals charged with examining the patient's condition, prognosis, etc., before approving the option of euthanasia. Pellegrino rejects this approach[1] on the grounds that it medicalizes the decision-making process, placing the patient in a pas-sive role that encourages acceptance of what the doctors recommend. He also suggests that such committees could not be trusted because only those who favor euthanasia would agree to serve on them. The first point is not particularly convincing; if the patient or her representative (in nonvoluntary cases) must initiate the process, then the role of the committee would surely be to assess the patient's condition and treat-ment options and determine whether the patient's preferences are gen-uine and reasonable (not the product of pressure, depression, or other pathology), and whether there is a medical alternative that will address the patient's concerns. The second point strikes me as quite unfair. No one *favors* euthanasia in the sense of thinking it appropriate for every-one, and someone serving on such a committee might well apply very conservative standards for when euthanasia is legitimate. In fact, the only sort of person "ruled out" here would presumably be someone like Pellegrino, who rejects the sincerity or rationality of *all* requests for euthanasia. And Pellegrino's blanket insistence on pathologizing all such requests simply begs the question against those like myself, who find such requests perfectly reasonable *in some cases*, in the light of their sincerely held values.

It might also be proposed that active euthanasia is an extreme (and literally desperate) form of medical intervention, and so must pass an unusually high standard of consent. But this does little to differentiate voluntary from nonvoluntary euthanasia. In either case we proceed in a way that will predictably kill the patient, because we judge that in the circumstances they are better off dead than alive, from their own point of view. If we want to raise the standards of consent, we need to inves-tigate and rule out factors that could (irrationally) influence a patient's consent for her own case just as much as we need to investigate and rule out factors that could (irrationally or otherwise unjustifiably)

---

[1] Pellegrino, "The False Promise," 88n.

influence a patient's decision-makers when the patient is not competent. Further, very high standards can be set—standards regarding the patient's condition, level of pain, prospects for improvement (short and long term), etc. All the reasons that would justify offering euthanasia to a competent person will apply to the noncompetent as well—the only difference is who will make the decision. And at this point I believe that good evidence of the decision-maker's care for the patient's welfare, together with well-designed procedural checks of the evidence and the patient's circumstances, is sufficient.[1] In general, I believe there are as many reasons why someone might make the wrong choice for themselves as there are why a caring decision maker might make the wrong choice for her charge; but as these reasons are different, I think it important to impose careful procedural constraints to ensure high standards of evidence are met.

If physicians would consider the option of active euthanasia a reasonable choice for a competent patient in certain circumstances, then they should consider the same option a reasonable choice for a medically similar incompetent patient. Just as physicians must carefully consider whether a competent patient is in position to make a well-grounded choice in the matter, they must also carefully consider whether an incompetent patient's decision-makers are in such a position. Just as they would have to examine the circumstances carefully before agreeing with a competent patient's request for euthanasia, they would have to do the same for the noncompetent. And these considerations should be examined within a carefully designed institutional structure considering each case, charged with deciding whether the euthanasia option is acceptable on the grounds of the patient's prognosis, level of suffering, and the options for pain control and other ameliorating treatments.[2] No such system can ever be perfect. But it is important here, as elsewhere, not to make the perfect into an enemy of

---

[1] Of course this assumes that we can understand and evaluate the suffering (and enjoyments) of others. But this is not such a strange idea—in fact, rejecting this view demands an extreme skepticism about others' feelings. And the upshot of such skepticism is to render all moral evaluation of actions based on those feelings epistemically indefensible. For example, I couldn't have adequate evidence that torturing you is wrong, since I couldn't be sure that your apparent signs of pain really indicate pain rather than enjoyment of what is being done to you. It is far better for ethical purposes to accept that we have a pretty good idea of how others feel about such things.

[2] These further checks are meant to ensure that the choice is not made lightly or behind closed doors; these sorts of check are important for any form of euthanasia, to assure us that what is done bears scrutiny.

the good. It is far better, I think, to adopt the best system we can devise, and watch it carefully.

REFERENCES

Annas, George J. "The Bell Tolls for the Right to Suicide." *Regulating How We Die: The Ethical, Medical, and Legal Issues Surrounding Physician-Assisted Suicide.* Ed. Linda L. Emanuel. Cambridge, MA: Harvard UP, 1998. 203-33.

Childress, James F. "Religious Viewpoints." *Regulating How We Die: The Ethical, Medical, and Legal Issues Surrounding Physician-Assisted Suicide.* Ed. Linda L. Emanuel. Cambridge, MA: Harvard UP, 1998. 120-47.

Emanuel, Linda. "A Question of Balance." *Regulating How We Die: The Ethical, Medical, and Legal Issues Surrounding Physician-Assisted Suicide.* Ed. Linda L. Emanuel. Cambridge, MA: Harvard UP, 1998. 234-60.

Greene, Joshua D., R. Brian Sommerville, Leigh E. Nystrom, John M. Darley, and Jonathan D. Cohen. "An fMRI Investigation of Emotional Engagement in Moral Judgment." *Science* 293 (2001): 2105-08.

Mackie, J.L. *The Cement of the Universe.* Oxford: Clarendon P, 1974.

Pellegrino, Edmund D. "The False Promise of Beneficent Killing." *Regulating How We Die: The Ethical, Medical, and Legal Issues Surrounding Physician-Assisted Suicide.* Ed. Linda L. Emanuel. Cambridge, MA: Harvard UP, 1998.

Rachels, James. "Active and Passive Euthanasia." *The New England Journal of Medicine* 292 (1975): 78-80.

Railton, Peter. "Alienation, Consequentialism and the Demands of Morality." *Consequentialism and its Critics.* Ed. S. Scheffler. Oxford: Oxford UP, 1988.

Chapter 10

HARD END-OF-LIFE DECISIONS FOR PHYSICIANS AND FAMILY MEMBERS

John A. Baker

1. SETTING OUT THE ISSUES

Much of the literature examining the ethical and moral issues involved in end-of-life decisions[1] poses questions in a way that leaves unspecified whether the person making the decisions is a lay person or a member of what I will refer to as a *regulated* profession—a nurse, a physician, and so on. Thus, for example, there are many articles devoted completely generally to the questions of whether euthanasia is morally permissible, of whether the distinctions between acts and omissions and between letting die and killing are morally significant, of whether death is always a harm, and so on. These are important issues, of course, and they are issues of great significance *both* for lay people *and* for professionals, but this fact does not entail that the issues should play out in exactly the same way in both lay and professional settings. The primary goal of this paper is to explore these differences.

To help focus the issues, I will use the adverbs "morally" and "ethically" (and the related adjectives) exclusively for classifying (as opposed to evaluating) the *reasons why* a certain person *ought* to do a certain action in a certain context. To say of a certain person that he or she *morally*

---

[1] In this paper I want the phrase "end-of-life decisions" to include not only decisions where, whatever decision is made, the life will anyway end in the near future, but also decisions where the life will end *only if certain decisions are made*. There is a tendency in the literature to avoid some of the moral issues by limiting discussions of end-of-life decisions to cases where death will occur whatever is done: sometimes that is not so, and in the cases I want to discuss it will not necessarily be so.

ought to do that action in that context will be to say that there are *moral* rather than *legal* or *religious* or *prudential* reasons for doing that act. To say of a person that he or she *ethically* ought so to act will be to say more narrowly that the reasons for doing the act have the following structure: (i) that person is a member of some regulated profession, (ii) that person is functioning in this context as a member of that regulated profession, and (iii) the laws, codes, and practices governing that profession require that action of that person in this context. It will emerge from my discussion of regulated professions that, though the fact that one occupies a certain rôle can in certain circumstances be the source of *moral* reasons for doing certain acts, a rôle can only be a source of *ethical* reasons when the rôle in question counts as a profession.[1]

This terminological fiat will help make clear that two questions about end-of-life decisions by members of regulated professions are non-trivial. First, is the fact that, in the above-defined sense, one *ethically* ought to do a certain action enough to establish that one (also) has a *moral* reason to do the action? Second, should *ethical* reasons for acting be viewed as being especially stringent in comparison with other kinds of reasons for action?

The goals of this paper can now be stated in more detail.

First, I want to offer in some detail an account of the sources of the rights and duties that members of regulated professions, as members of their profession, have, that is, the sources of their ethical duties: I will focus on the situation of physicians. These ethical duties, I will argue, are to be distinguished from their moral duties. Second, in relation to end-of-life decisions, I want to bring out as clearly as I can the fact that the kinds of choices that physicians ethically and morally need to consider are a function of the sources of their rights and duties and that there is a range of ethical and moral choices available to physicians, a range not, as far as I know, considered in the literature. It will not be possible in this paper to spell out the conditions under which physicians in the end should opt for one or other of the various actions in the range: for the purposes of this paper it is enough if I set out the main options. Third, I want to offer some explanation of why physicians, as physicians, need to consider different decisions and indeed different kinds of decisions in end-of-life situations from those which lay people and especially family members need to consider. My fourth and final

---

[1]   For important discussions of the moral functioning of rôles, see Hardimon, "Rôle Obligations," and Simmons, "External Justifications and Institutional Rôles."

goal in the paper is to contrast the range of moral choices facing physicians with the range of moral choices facing family members in end-of-life situations and to provide some exploration of these contrasts. A large part of the explanation of the contrasts is revealed by my terminological fiats above, which entail that, although lay people may have *moral* duties in end-of-life decisions, they cannot, as lay people, have *ethical* duties, and so their moral choices should not be viewed as being at all constrained by such duties or by the reasons for assigning such duties. It is my view that, even though the current legal structures forbid, for example, hastening the death of a sick spouse or a sick child, a family member's moral duties may permit, even require, this in certain circumstances. However, in this paper I cannot hope to spell out all of the reasoning to such a conclusion, so my goal is a more limited one: I will make some modest proposals about the range of options available to family members in end-of-life situations and about how to think about the way in which such moral decisions should be construed.

It is worth noting right from the start that a sub-text of this paper is that in making hard moral decisions it is rarely if ever enough simply to apply to the particular situation that set of moral principles which one holds are correct: one has to take into account the realities of the *social* situation[1] and do the best one can in the circumstances. If only for that reason it is vital, when thinking through complex moral and ethical issues, to have in mind some detailed real life examples. I therefore begin by describing in detail two cases famous in Canadian experience.

2. TWO CASES: SUE RODRIGUEZ AND TRACY LATIMER

Sue Rodriguez

In mid-1993 Sue Rodriguez[2] was a 42-year-old mother, suffering from amyotrophic lateral sclerosis (ALS). Her condition was deteriorating rapidly and her prognosis was not good: she expected soon to lose the ability to swallow, speak, walk, and move her body without assistance, and thereafter to lose the capacity to breathe without a respirator and to

---

[1] I argue some of the theoretical background to this claim in my paper "Rights, Obligations and Duties in the Intersection between Law and Morals."

[2] The following account of Sue Rodriguez's situation for the most part uses the words of Justice Lamer of the Supreme Court of Canada. See *Rodriguez v. British Columbia* (Attorney General), SCC [1993] 3 S.C.R. 519.

eat without a gastrotomy. Her life expectancy was between 2 and 14 months. Importantly, she did not wish to die so long as she still had the capacity to enjoy life, but wished, instead, that a qualified physician be permitted to set up technological means by which she might, when she was no longer able to enjoy life, by her own hand, at the time of her choosing, end her life. To this end, she had requested that the Supreme Court of British Columbia rule that s. 241(*b*) of the Criminal Code (the section prohibiting assisting a suicide) be declared invalid.[1] The Supreme Court of British Columbia dismissed her application, and the majority of the Court of Appeal affirmed the judgment. She appealed these decisions to the Supreme Court of Canada, which in turn denied her appeal.

Consider now the following two imaginary scenarios.

First, imagine that you are the attending physician of someone in Sue Rodriguez's situation—the physician of someone who has been diagnosed as having ALS, someone who wants her life to last as long as possible, probably beyond the point where she would have the physical capacity to kill herself, who asks you, her physician, to promise that, when she decides that the time has come to administer to her or help her to take some medication—a barbiturate, for example—which will cause her death, you will do so. Imagine, however, that the Supreme Court has *already* denied Sue Rodriguez's request that s. 241(*b*) of the Criminal Code be set aside in situations like this. If you accede to your patient's request, you will arguably be guilty of a criminal act.

As a second scenario, imagine that you are the husband of someone in Sue Rodriguez's situation and that she asks you to administer or help her take a medication which she has already got hold of—a bottle of some strong barbiturate, for example.

In the first imaginary scenario there are both ethical and moral questions facing you as a physician, and these questions involve several subordinate questions, specifically: (i) *how* you should figure out whether ethically—that is, as a physician—you should accede to her request; (ii) *whether* ethically you should accede to her request; (iii) *whether*, if acceding to her request would not be ethically impermissible, it would be morally permissible for you to accede to her request and in so acting to act contrary to your ethical duties; (iv) if it would be morally permis-

---

[1]   The ground argued was, in the word of Justice Lamer, that this section "violates her rights under ss. 7, 12 and 15(1) of the *Canadian Charter of Rights and Freedoms,* and is therefore, to the extent it precludes a terminally ill person from committing 'physician-assisted' suicide, of no force and effect by virtue of s. 52(1) of the *Constitution Act, 1982."*

sible for you to accede to her request, *how* you should morally go about doing so (as we will see, there are clearly a variety of ways of doing so); and (v) *what pattern of reasoning* you should use in deciding whether and, if so, how you morally should accede to her request.

Note the obvious but important point that, if indeed it emerges that it is ethically wrong to accede to her request, and if that issue is, as I have suggested and will argue further below, decided by examining the laws, codes, and practices in force for the medical profession, then it obviously cannot be by a consultation of these laws, codes, and practices that you decide whether it is morally right to act contrary to your ethical duties—the method of answering the moral question will of necessity be different from the method for answering the ethical question.

Given my terminological fiats above, there are, in the second imaginary scenario, no ethical questions facing you as a husband, but you do face the following moral questions: (a) *whether* morally you ought to accede to her request; (b) if so, *how* you should do so; and (c) *what pattern of reasoning* you should use in deciding the answers to these questions.

To make the two "how" questions above—questions (iv) and (b)—a little clearer and because these questions will be important in the later discussions, here are some examples of the kinds of ways in which you might morally go about acceding to your patient's or wife's request:

a. You might administer the barbiturate to her and do so without any attempt at secrecy—you might, for example, when she was dead, report what you had done to the police. Indeed, you might even invite the media to view you administering the barbiturate and causing her death. You might in so doing be calling on the government to take seriously what the Supreme Court has said about the possible need for legislation in the area—clearly various scenarios are possible here.

b. You might try to find a way of securing the administration of the barbiturate in a way that would, perhaps by a stretch, count as legal administration of the barbiturate—see, for example, the use of "terminal sedation": again various scenarios would be possible, with a little inventiveness.[1]

---

[1] For a helpful survey of practices of this kind in the US, together with some useful citations, see Dworkin et al., "Assisted Suicide: The Philosophers' Brief," which appears together with a very useful introduction by Dworkin.

c. You might administer the barbiturate secretly and try in some way to cover up the fact that you had administered the barbiturate and thereby caused her death — again with a little inventiveness, various scenarios are possible.

Assume that in thinking through the three ways of acceding to your patient's or wife's request you are fully informed about the legal status of the three acts listed above. In Canada it is clear that it is legally impermissible either to assist a suicide, though whether the Crown would prosecute is less than completely clear; Crown discretion is extensive. Similarly, it is legally impermissible to administer so-called "active euthanasia" even when requested to do so by a competent adult: a wide variety of clauses in the Criminal Code are relevant here, including Article 245 (Administration of a Noxious Thing), though again Crown discretion is extensive.

Clearly the legal situation is such that if you do accede to your patient's or wife's request you may avoid prosecution, but it is also possible that you may not — and, if prosecuted, you may or may not suffer severe penalty. The first (and, if caught, the third) way of acceding to your wife's or your patient's request would almost certainly tie the hands of the Crown, who might otherwise have considered the possibility of exercising its discretion either not to prosecute or simply to lay some low-level charges.

Tracy Latimer

Consider now the situation of Robert and Laura Latimer,[1] living and farming in rural Saskatchewan. They had four children, of whom Tracy, born in 1980, was the oldest. The physical condition of Tracy in 1993 was briefly as follows. She suffered from a severe form of cerebral palsy and was quadriplegic. Her condition had been caused by neurological damage at the time of her birth and was permanent. Despite attempts to control her condition with medication, five or six times daily she suffered muscle spasms, some of which were severe enough to shake her

---

[1]   The following account of Tracy Latimer's situation is primarily drawn from the text of the Supreme Court of Canada ruling in the case *R. v. Latimer* [2001] 1 S.C.R. 3, 2001, SCC1, supplemented by an examination of some of the lower (Saskatchewan) court records. For the latter, see "the statement of reasons" by Justice Tallis in the Saskatchewan Court of Appeal, in *R. v. Latimer*, (1995), 99 C.C.C. (3rd.) 481, July 18, 1995, and the further, different, "statement of reasons" by Justice Bayda, in the same case.

whole body: on occasion the spasms had apparently dislocated various joints. She had difficulty breathing. She had to be spoon-fed. She also suffered from scoliosis, which had earlier required surgery (metal rods had been implanted to support her spine) and would apparently require further surgery on her right hip: it had become dislocated and was causing her considerable pain. Taking food was so difficult for her that she could not consume a sufficient amount of nutrients, though this was not (yet) a life-threatening problem. It was further apparently accepted by all of the courts and believed both by the attending physician and by Mr. and Mrs. Latimer that she experienced a good deal of pain, and that the pain could not be reduced by medication because this medication tended to interfere with the medication taken to control the muscle spasms — itself a source of pain. And finally it was believed by her physician that further surgery was necessary because of her scoliosis — the procedure involved removing her upper thigh bone, a procedure that would leave her lower leg loose without any connecting bone; it would be held in place only by muscle and tissue. The anticipated recovery period for this surgery was one year. Her situation was truly miserable and she had a serious disability, but she was not terminally ill and her life was not in its final stages.

I will focus on the moral question of what Mr. and Mrs. Latimer morally ought to have done in their situation: clearly there is no ethical issue here, since neither Robert nor Laura Latimer was acting as a member of a regulated profession.

It is crucial to recognize that Tracy was vulnerable in four importantly different ways. First, she was, like Sue Rodriguez, physically incapable of seeking relief from her pain and misery by ending her own life. Second, Tracy was, unlike Sue Rodriguez, a minor, not legally competent to consent to or to refuse treatment in her own right. Third, again unlike Sue Rodriguez, Tracy was so severely mentally undeveloped that she could not understand the nature of her situation, she could not form conceptions of what might count as relief of her situation,[1] and she did not have the conceptual resources needed for someone to have wishes or preferences about possible ways of dealing with her situation: she was at most capable of *manifesting* her misery or pain. This third point entails that, fourth, she was dependent on, and hence vulnerable to, the limitations of the moral strength[2] and the good will of others

---

[1] For example, she was incapable of forming a conception of death, let alone of her own death.

[2] By "moral strength" here I mean both the capacity to think through the moral complexities of the situation and the courage to act on certain moral choices.

much more than Sue Rodriguez was. In summary, Tracy was physically, legally, and psychologically entirely dependent on others to make decisions on her behalf, not only decisions about treatment, but also decisions about prolongation of life.

The import of these four points is that it is vital to remember that those who are as vulnerable as Tracy are not only vulnerable to being wrongly killed, but are also vulnerable to being wrongly kept alive.[1] I have been deeply saddened by the willingness of those speaking for people with disabilities to talk in ways which suggest strongly that, in order to protect some people from wrongful killing they are willing to countenance *sacrificing* the Tracy Latimers of this world by forcing them to continue living unbearable lives, excluding them from the possibility of relief from such lives. There are problems here, of course, but the problems are not to be addressed by simply sacrificing the vulnerable for the benefit of those less vulnerable. Minimally, the moral issues need to be faced squarely.

So let us face the issues squarely. To focus ideas it will be useful to mention just the three alternatives that apparently faced Robert and Laura Latimer on 12 October 1993. According to Chief Justice Bayda, on that day, Robert Latimer heard that in the orthopaedic surgeon's opinion, Tracy needed further surgery to lessen the damage being done by her uncontrolled muscle spasms, surgery that would involve further pain for her and a recovery period of up to a year, and that yet further surgery would probably be required. He also received a phone call from the social worker who had been working on Tracy's case and who was, in effect, offering to place her in a nursing home. So the three alternatives that Robert and Laura Latimer seemed to face were these:

1. They could follow the surgeon's suggestion on how to deal with the scoliosis — major surgery followed by a year of painful recovery. But this surgery would in no way address the other problems Tracy was facing: the fact that she would continue to have regular body-wracking spasms several times a day, spasms severe enough to have dislocated her spine and her hip several times in the past; that she would not be able to move herself at all; that eating and chewing her food would remain so difficult

---

[1]   Important discussions to be consulted here include Engelhardt, Jr., "Infanticide in a Post-Christian Age" and "Ethical Issues in Aiding the Death of Young Children."

for her that she regularly vomited what she did manage to swallow; that she would continue to be unable to control her bowels at all and would therefore have to continue to wear a diaper; that although maybe on occasion she would have some pleasurable experiences ("listening" to music, being with her family, being "rocked gently by her parents"), much of the time she would be in pain, pain that would—for up to a year after her surgery—be worse; and finally that the rest of her life would continue in this way or worse.

2. They could perhaps make arrangements to place her in a "group home," as they had done in 1993 when, to provide respite for the family, Tracy had spent some time in such a home in North Battleford. This would relieve the Latimer *family* of the daily caring duties they had been providing for Tracy, but *her* life would otherwise not be any better than the life she would have if the first option were chosen; in fact, it would in one way be worse, since in the group home she would not be with her family and have the small and intermittent joys which that brought her.

3. They could attempt to find a way to end Tracy's life in a way that would not frighten her and that would be as painless as possible. They could try to do this in a way that would not have legal consequences for them, or they could do it openly.

Now, if Tracy had not been so brain damaged, her parents might have been able to consult her wishes. But Tracy's parents could not do this: indeed, as noted above, it is doubtful if she could be said to *have* wishes or preferences in anything other than a very attenuated sense: she was in pain, she was afraid, and she wanted the pain to end. So Robert and Laura Latimer would have to proceed in very different ways. But the Latimers still faced problems similar to those facing the imaginary husband in the Sue Rodriguez case: they needed to figure out (i) *which of the three alternatives* that I have described above to choose; (ii) if they decide on the third alternative, *how* they should morally proceed— by publicly defying the law, by finding a near legal way of securing her death, or secretly—for again there are clearly a variety of ways of doing so; and (iii) *what pattern of reasoning* they should use in deciding whether and, if so, how they morally should end her life.

3. THE DUTY OF RESCUE

From the above descriptions it is, I am sure, clear that the situations of both Sue Rodriguez and Tracy Latimer were full of terrible discomfort, pain, and misery, that their situations were not tolerable, and that there was no possibility of any significant amelioration of their situations. They clearly needed help, and, because their situations were both intolerable and could not be ameliorated, I will assume, for the purposes of this paper, what they needed was the relief that only death would bring.[1] At issue, therefore, is whether it could be morally or ethically permissible for anyone to address this need by providing help of this kind. Also at issue is whether we ought to say more strongly that there was someone who had an ethical or moral *duty* to provide this help.

A natural place to begin investigation of the possibility of a duty here would be to look at the way the familiar Duty of Rescue might play out in the context of these relationships. The principle affirming such a duty is also called by some the "Good Samaritan Principle" and in one place the "Kew Gardens Principle."[2] As a first approximation the principle can be taken as stating:

If (i) a person B is suffering grave physical or mental harm, pain or distress [the need condition], and

(ii) a person A knows that B is receiving that harm, pain or distress [the knowledge condition], and

(iii) A is capable of acting in some way to help B [the capacity condition], and

(iv) A is in the proximity of B at the time [the proximity condition], and

(v) if A does not help B, then (it may be that) no one else will help [the last resort condition],

then, other things being equal, A has a moral obligation to help B, if B consents to the help or would consent if she were able to consent [the consent condition].[3]

---

[1] Obviously this statement is philosophically contentious on various fronts, but for the stated purposes of this paper it will be worth setting these issues on one side.

[2] See Simon, Powers and Gunneman, *The Ethical Investor*. They refer to the principle as the Kew Gardens Principle after the stabbing and slow death of Kitty Genovese in Kew Gardens, New York: her death was watched by 38 bystanders who did nothing. See further Rosenthal, *Thirty-Eight Witnesses*.

[3] The handy names for the need, proximity, and capacity conditions were, as far as I know, first suggested in Simon, Powers and Gunneman, *The Ethical Investor*.

This statement of the principle needs some refinement, but none of the refinements that I will suggest will alter the important point that the principle imposes a duty to help on *anyone* to whom the stated conditions apply: it is not necessary that the person with the duty to help be in some special relationship to the person in need.[1] This said, refinements to the principle are indeed necessary if the principle is to be applicable to the cases before us.

First, sometimes the person in need cannot consent: she is unconscious, or there is no time to get the consent (e.g., the person is drowning), and sometimes—and for our purposes more notably—the person is not competent to give consent. Clearly an account is needed of the conditions under which a prospective Good Samaritan can conclude that indeed the person needing the help, or her surrogate, "would have consented." A familiar way of dealing with these situations is by the substituted judgement test, which would say here that help is to be provided (and in a certain form) only if the Good Samaritan would infer that the person to receive the help would have consented, *ceteris paribus*, to such help if she had been able to express her wishes.

The test is attractive for all of the kinds of reasons that make George Bernard Shaw's version of the golden rule attractive: "Do unto others as *they* would be done by." Clearly, Jesus' version is not the one suited to the substituted judgement test, for that says not "Do what *they*, as far as you can infer, would wish," but "Do what *you* would wish if you were in their position," and that is obviously very different. And it is clearly attractive in the case of those who are not now capable of consenting but who once were capable, for in those cases we do at least stand a chance of making sense of the question "what *would* they have said if they had now been capable?" It is even attractive for cases where, though the person in need cannot consent, she or he can at least indicate her or his wishes or preferences.

But the test is clearly neither attractive nor indeed usable when the person to be helped is an infant or someone who, like Tracy Latimer, has (for whatever reason) never developed to the stage where she can formulate wishes or preferences. Indeed, if proxy decision-makers think they are using that test in such cases, then it is tempting to accuse them of self-deception, for it is completely unclear what would be involved at

---

[1]   It will be remembered that Jesus' story about the Good Samaritan in Luke 10: 29ff is offered as part of a discussion of the Jewish law requiring love of neighbour (*plèsion* in the demotic Greek). Jesus was asked who is one's neighbour and he replied with the story of the Good Samaritan.

all in inferring what an infant "would wish or prefer if she were capable of expressing her wishes or preferences." Let me be a bit more precise. I am talking here only about those who (i) are not now capable of consenting and (ii) have never been capable of consenting: hence, the cases I am talking about are not people of whom we can ask "What would they say if they were now capable of saying something?" In Tracy's case, of course, she would never have become capable even if she had lived longer.[1]

In such cases, it might be worth noticing that the Supreme Court of Canada has espoused a rather different test, at least for certain settings, namely the "best interests" test.[2] According to this test, the proxy decision-maker is to ask what would be in the best interests of the recipient of the help. The problem with this test is that without supplementation it offers no way of judging what *are* the best interests of the prospective recipient of the help. It is tempting here to think of using Jesus' version of the golden rule: that is, imagine yourself with your own values, wishes, and preferences in the situation of the incapable person and ask what you would choose in that situation. This at least gives one a handle on the situation. But it is clearly not the right handle, at least not in the case of those who are not capable of having wishes and preferences: it is worth reminding ourselves that those who are incapable of conceiving wishes and preferences can nevertheless be capable of feeling pain and discomfort and probably in some cases capable of feeling unease and fear, and in most circumstances anyone would want pain, discomfort, unease, and fear to end, especially if they do not know its cause or the prospects for its ending. This thought perhaps might suggest that the absence of the ability to formulate wishes and preferences in relation to the nature of the help is not quite the source of overriding concern that we might otherwise expect it to be, but it is clearly very difficult, and that should not be forgotten.

The second problem with the Duty of Rescue concerns the kinds of help that it would be morally acceptable for Good Samaritans to give. There are good reasons to say that, as a society, we want to reserve certain kinds of activities not merely to people who as a matter of fact do have the needed skill: as a society we have reasons of policy to reserve such kinds of activities to people who have demonstrated that they have

---

[1] Different again are cases where the person in need is a person who cannot now consent and will never be capable of consenting but who was once capable of consenting. For these kinds of cases see the very important article by Agnieszka Jaworska, "Respecting the Margins of Agency."

[2] See *Mrs. E. v. Eve* SCC [1986] 2 S.C.R. 388.

the needed skill, and demonstrated it before some accredited testing agency. I call this the problem of reserved behaviour. The need to designate certain activities as reserved and certain people as qualified to provide this help is what gives rise to our society's decision to introduce the institutions called accredited or registered or, as I am calling them, regulated professions. Examination of this issue will reveal that, at least for physicians, the Duty of Rescue cannot be the whole story, and it may not even be the right story.

4. THE ETHICAL POSITION OF PHYSICIANS

The duty of physicians to help people in need may derive perhaps in part from the Duty of Rescue,[1] but it derives more importantly from, and it is at least constrained by, the fact that physicians are, and for good social policy reasons should be counted as, members of regulated professions. This fact structures the very nature of the ethical and moral rôle occupied by physicians, and it also fixes the methods that physicians need to use when deciding what medically and ethically they *may* do and what medically and ethically they have a *duty* to do. This claim needs to be spelled out in detail, for it is here that the differences between the duties of family members and the duties of physicians emerge clearly. I begin by outlining what is clearly the best theory of the grounding of those rights and duties that members of regulated professions have as members of their professions.

The Best Theory of Professional Rights and Duties

Professions fall into a variety of categories: journalism, the priesthood, and academe fall into one category, while the law, medicine, nursing, and clinical psychology fall into a different category. The latter are and

---

[1] In the literature various suggestions about the sources of the rights and duties of physicians have been discussed or assumed. But, for reasons that emerge in the coming section, none of them could provide an acceptable basis for the ascription of the ethically special status of physicians, and for reasons very similar to those that make the Duty of Rescue inadequate for this rôle. To fix ideas I will mention just a few of these mistaken views: it will emerge that the special status of physicians cannot derive from the facts (if they are facts) that physicians typically have (i) more specialized knowledge, skills, and experience or (ii) a stronger desire to help people who are in need of help than does the average citizen; nor does it derive from the fact (if it is a fact) that they (iii) care more for the sick and needy than does the average citizen; nor does it derive from the facts (if indeed they are facts) that (iv) physicians count themselves as having a calling to help those in need or that (v) they have committed themselves to helping those in need.

—I would argue for public policy reasons—should be regulated by state action: I will refer to them as regulated professions, intending this as a normative/descriptive categorization—they either *are*, or if they are not, they *ought* for public policy reasons to be regulated in the way I will describe. The former are typically better not so regulated: to regulate journalists, priests, and academics in the way I will describe shortly would be to endanger the great social goods, respectively, of a free press, religious freedom, and academic freedom.

The reason why regulated professions should be—and in Canada are—regulated by state[1] action emerges from the following account of their status:[2]

Let R be a rôle of some sort. Then R can be viewed as a regulated profession if and only if:

1. The state believes
   a. that the adequate fulfilment of duties attached to R could serve some goal or complex of goals G,
   b. that G will be of great value either to specific members of society or to society at large,
   c. that failure to fulfil the duties of R will have serious deleterious effects either on specific members of society or on society at large,
   d. that G is best or most safely accessible if the only people permitted by the state to occupy the rôle have acquired a certain level of skill in the tasks required for the fulfillment of the duties attached to the rôle, and if the performance of those permitted to fulfil the rôle is in some way monitored, but
   e. that G is best, or most safely, accessible if in the fulfilment of their duties those occupying the rôle R can be and are trusted to exercise discretionary authority to decide for themselves, subject to certain constraints, what would be the best thing to

---

[1] In Canada, regulated professions are designated as such by federal or provincial legislation or regulation. It will not matter to my paper that in different jurisdictions, professions become regulated in different ways. To keep things generic and simple I will talk of "state regulation."

[2] The analysis that follows is of necessity rather schematic and is therefore best thought of as providing a rational reconstruction of what is in reality the product of many historical, political, and accidental factors. The basic idea for the following account was first, as far as I know, adumbrated by Michael Bayles, though not in quite these terms and without the emphasis on what I will call "discretionary authority," a notion central to my analysis. See his *Professional Ethics*, especially pp. 7-11.

do in the circumstances, without necessarily needing to consult a superior or to consult a "rule book."

2. The state believes that the best or the only way in which the points mentioned in 1 can be implemented is to create a "professional association" to serve as a regulatory body for those who will occupy the rôle, assigning to this regulatory body

  a. the right and the duty to lay down modes of training and standards of skill for prospective practitioners of the rôle,[1]

  b. the right and the duty to grant to certain people licence to exercise the rôle R,

  c. the right and the duty to lay down for the rôle both (i) rules of standard practice, rules of correct behaviour, and, where appropriate, such other constraints on any discretionary authority granted to practitioners as are needed, and (ii) the authority to enforce these rules,

  d. the right and the duty to take steps to ensure that those licensed to practise fulfil their duties with competence and in ways suited to the goals G.

3. A particular person becomes a practitioner of the professional rôle R

  a. by completing successfully the training required by the association, and

  b. by being licensed by the association to practice in that professional rôle.

4. In becoming a practitioner of the professional rôle R, a person implicitly promises or explicitly contracts to fulfil the duties assigned by the association in accordance with the rules set by the regulatory body of the profession.

Applying all this to the situation of physicians, we could say (i) that the bases of the rights and duties which physicians have lie both in the fact that physicians have or should have the knowledge and skills to provide these socially valuable services and in the fact that society counts it worthwhile to "institutionalize" the rôle played by the people who will be providing these services, and (ii) that a particular physician acquires the rights and duties of a physician by virtue of having voluntarily received the requisite training and joined that profession.

---

[1] Typically, though not always, the professional association limits entry to those who have completed some extended and advanced courses of training at an institution accredited by the association as qualified to train prospective members of the association.

Conscience and the Discretionary Authority of Professionals

Fundamental to the above account is the idea (expressed in point 1(c) above) that in setting up a profession the state believes that the complex of goals is accessible or best secured only if the accredited members of the profession are trusted both by their clients and by society at large to exercise discretionary authority to decide for themselves, within certain constraints, what to do, without consulting superiors or text books. Trust here is fundamental. Most people in the health-care professions and in the philosophical community would agree, I expect, that there is a need to steer a path between, on the one hand, an inflexible, rule-bound profession, and, on the other, an "unregulated" profession, as we might call it.[1] The solution to this problem has been the development of a complex system of quite generally worded and variously interpretable goals, values, and principles,[2] together with a large number of often much more specific rules, regulations and "standards of care," *all* of which prospective members of the profession are expected to internalize, and practicing members of professions are expected to use to guide and in some cases constrain the exercise of their discretionary authority. Some of these are explicitly or implicitly adopted either by the state or the profession, though some are traditional to the profession. I will, for brevity, refer to these as the laws, codes, and practices of the relevant profession. These may be viewed as providing in outline form a specification of the grounds for ascribing ethical rights and duties to the members of the profession, but they are better viewed as providing constraints on their decision making, though the constraints are really quite loose in practice. Indeed the constraints are in most jurisdictions made even looser by the inclusion in the laws, codes, and practices, either explicitly or implicitly, of some sort of freedom of conscience clause. In their classic form, such conscience clauses free the physician from a duty he or she would otherwise need to fulfil, a duty that the laws, codes, and practices impose generally, but from which the conscience clause frees the physician—for "reasons of conscience." The rôle of conscience in the exercise of discretionary authority which espe-

---

[1] Clearly deregulation is a historical concept—something can only be deregulated if it was once regulated.

[2] A now classic discussion of a way in which principles should be felt to guide decision making by physicians is Beauchamp and Childress, *Principles of Biomedical Ethics*. The changing views of the ways the principles discussed there might be interpreted can in part be tracked by comparing their treatment in the successive editions of the book.

cially physicians are granted is fundamental and needs our attention for the argument to come.

It is important that freedom of conscience clauses are, as far as I know, always articulated in one logical direction. They all cover scenarios with the following structure:

a. some act is required by the laws, codes, and practices of the profession in such and such circumstances;

b. a physician on some moral or religious ground disapproves of doing that kind of act or at least of doing the act in some particular circumstances;

c. in such a situation the conscience clause licenses not doing the act in those circumstances.

For present purposes, the existence of such conscience clauses in the laws, codes, and practices of professions is very important, for what they signal is that it is viewed as being part of the discretionary authority of physicians that they are permitted to bring *moral* or other kinds of assessment to bear on the *ethical* duties that they have as physicians, and even more importantly that they are permitted to refuse to fulfil their ethical duties if in their personal opinion these ethical duties conflict with what they view as their moral duties. Crucially, the physician is permitted or even required[1] to assess the moral permissibility of what ethically they are required to do.

But consider now the following very different kind of scenario:

a*. some act is forbidden by the laws, codes, and practices of the profession in such and such circumstances;

b*. a physician who is in those circumstances believes on moral or religious grounds that failing to do that act in those circumstances would be wrong.

---

[1] For the kinds of grounds for saying that they are required, see the literature devoted to the so-called Nuremberg "Doctors' Trials." See, for example, Edmund D. Pellegrino, "The Nazi Doctors and Nuremberg: Some Moral Lessons Revisited," *Annals of Internal Medicine* 127.4 (1997): 307-08, for a very brief but useful bibliography of relevant materials. Two crucial lessons are to be learned from the Nuremberg trials of the Nazi doctors. The first is the lesson usually mentioned in discussions of these trials, that the demand for informed consent, whether proxy or not, before the implementation of medical procedures is morally and should be ethically essential. But it is the second lesson that is as important for our present purposes, namely that even if a certain procedure could (by some stretch of the imagination) be viewed as permitted by the laws, codes, and practices in force in a certain jurisdiction, a physician working in that jurisdiction cannot escape moral criticism simply by citing the fact of this supposed legality.

If, for obvious reasons, we call cases where (a) and (b) hold "Nuremberg cases," then we might call cases where (a*) and (b*) hold "*Reverse Nuremberg cases*."[1] The laws, codes, and practices of many—maybe most—professions contain conscience clauses to cover Nuremberg cases, but, as far as I know, the laws, codes and practices of *no* profession include a conscience clause to cover Reverse Nuremberg cases.

Clearly, in both Nuremberg and Reverse Nuremberg situations the physician faces a moral problem. In the Nuremberg situation, the laws, codes, and practices of the profession usually explicitly authorize the professional's setting her moral duties above what would otherwise be her ethical duties. In Reverse Nuremberg situations, the laws, codes, and practices of the profession do *not* authorize this. In Reverse Nuremberg situations, therefore, a physician will seemingly need to ask whether it could be morally permissible to act in ways forbidden by the laws, codes, and practices of one's profession. This is the moral situation facing the physician in the first imaginary Sue Rodriguez case. It is the situation faced by physicians whether they are countenancing terminal sedation of their patient or countenancing any kind of stronger action. It is a situation that physicians face on a regular basis in both Canada and the US,[2] and presumably elsewhere.

It was also the issue facing the obstetrician Dr. Henry Morgentaler in the 1970s and 1980s: Morgentaler concluded that the laws, codes, and practices in force in Canada at the time were morally unacceptable in that they forced women to go to term with unwanted pregnancies. He decided for that reason to give women abortions even when apparently the law, and the codes and practices of his profession, said he should not do so. He did so at first secretly, and then very publicly reported that he was doing so. He was prosecuted several times, but he was acquitted at jury trials, insisting throughout that he was doing the right thing; indeed, he insisted not only that what he was doing was *morally right*, but also that, even though his professional association counted what he was doing ethically wrong, "at a deeper level" his actions were *ethically right*. In the end, the Supreme Court of Canada agreed with much of what Dr. Morgentaler had been saying about the abortion law and struck it down as being unconstitutional and as violating the security of

---

[1] I acknowledge feeling some discomfort with the name, but I hope that the fact that the name is so striking will help the reader to keep the idea straight.

[2] See Dworkin et al., "Assisted Suicide," for a concise and useful report of the experiences of physicians in the US in end-of-life decision situations.

the person of women who were refused abortions under the law, a security guaranteed under the Charter of Rights and Freedoms.[1]

In facing Reverse Nuremberg situations, what becomes crucial is the question of the relative stringency of one's moral and ethical duties *in the particular situation*: I add the italicized phrase to warn against the error of thinking that we can in global ways assert either that moral duties have greater stringency than ethical duties or vice versa; I would argue, in fact, that the issue of stringency needs to be decided in particular specific contexts in a case-by-case fashion.[2] Clearly, if we think of applying the reverse Nuremberg idea to the case of assisted death, the big questions would be how stringent we should count the duty to assist the death of someone who is suffering endlessly and futilely. More briefly and perhaps simply, the question is whether the duty *not* to assist a death is more stringent than is the duty to ease suffering if the only way to do so is by assisting a death.

To come to grips with the Reverse Nuremberg issues in this context I will introduce the phrase rôle differentiation, a semi-technical phrase coined by Richard Wasserstrom.[3] A right or a duty is *rôle differentiated* if the right or duty is acquired by virtue of the fact that the right- or duty-holder comes to occupy or occupies some rôle. I will say that a rôle-differentiated right or duty is strongly[4] rôle differentiated if the stringency of that duty or the strength of that right is such that it is appropriate for the person in the rôle always "to put on one side" (that is, to override) considerations such as prudence and morality, which would otherwise be relevant in determinations as to what ought to be done. Clearly, on the account I have offered above, the duties and rights that physicians, *qua* physicians, have are rôle differentiated. Equally clearly, what is at issue in the question about stringency I raised in the last paragraph could be addressed by asking whether we should ever, or perhaps always, count physicians' duties as strongly rôle differentiated.

---

[1] See *R. v. Morgentaler* [1988] 1 S.C.R. 30, 63 O.R.(2d)281.

[2] See Baker, "Rights, Obligations and Duties."

[3] See Wasserstrom, "Lawyers as Professionals." This has been variously reprinted; see, for example, Callahan, ed., *Ethical Issues in Professional Life*. I will use the phrase in a slightly different way from Wasserstrom's usage. For example, it is *behaviour* that in Wasserstrom's usage is or is not rôle differentiated; I will talk of *duties* as being rôle differentiated.

[4] The term "strong differentiation" comes from Alan Goldman. See his "Business Ethics" and *The Moral Foundations of Professional Ethics*. Note that it is very odd that Goldman uses the terminology of rôle differentiation without acknowledgement to Wasserstrom.

5. THE PHYSICIAN AND THE MORAL DUTY OF RESCUE

The discussion so far strongly suggests not only that *ethically* the physician ought *not* to provide to the patient in the hypothetical Sue Rodriguez case the help she requested, for the laws, codes, and practices (at least the public practices) of the profession in Canada are unambiguous on that question,[1] but also that this is not the end of the matter, for the physician still has to face the fact that he might well be in a Reverse Nuremberg situation, that is, a situation in which he needs to ask himself whether he *morally* ought to ignore or defy these laws, codes, and practices and grant the painless death requested or perhaps needed.

I will explore an argument for saying that we should view the Reverse Nuremberg choice the physician faces as requiring that he comply with the laws, codes, and practices of his profession — in other words, an argument for saying that the duty not to help her in the way requested is a strongly rôle differentiated duty. But I will also argue that the details of the account I provided earlier of the ethical situation of physicians suggest strongly that there are complications that need to be addressed. The argument is in two stages:

First Stage

In this first stage I review the reasoning of the Supreme Court of Canada in the Sue Rodriguez case. We may note that the Supreme Court considered three main options:

a. it could uphold the present law on assisted death;
b. it could offer some interpretation of that law which would permit assisted death;
c. it could, as it did in the Morgentaler ruling, simply strike the law down and leave decisions about assisted death to health-care professionals in consultation with the family and, if possible, the patient.

We may also note that, persuasively, the Court stated that option (c) would be worse than option (a) (because of the appalling danger of abuse of the absence of law that might ensue), that, though option (b)

---

[1] See, for example, the *Policy Statement*, "Euthanasia and Assisted Suicide" (update 1998), approved by the Canadian Medical Association Board of Directors on 9 May 1998.

might be attractive to reasonable people and certainly consistent with the majority of people's opinion on this matter, the option would encroach on what the Court viewed as the prerogative of Parliament, and so, they concluded, they should uphold the current law and invite Parliament and the country to address the issues.

Now a lot more could and should be said about this first stage of my argument,[1] but I want to move on to the second stage of the argument.

Second Stage

In this stage we may note that the reasons for counting medicine as a regulated profession in effect could equally serve as an argument for counting at least some of the duties of physicians as strongly rôle differentiated, notably when the duties in question are of a kind where professionals' failure to comply with such rules will put in jeopardy the trust that is needed if society is to be justified in allowing the professional the discretionary authority needed if the professional is to be able to serve the rôle society assigns to him or her. It is next noted that end-of-life decision making is an area where, as noted by the Supreme Court, society needs to ensure that the trust lodged in physicians is not abused, as it so easily could be.

This completes the argument for saying that end-of-life decisions by physicians should be counted (at least *prima facie*) as governed by strongly rôle differentiated duties. Clearly again, much more could be said about this stage of the argument, but I will say only that it will not do to object to the argument that physicians across North America have found the moral strength—and that is what it seems to be—to move beyond the letter of the laws, codes, and practices governing their behavior and find ways of helping those suffering in end-of-life situations of the kind I have been discussing. Moving though this objection is, it does not seem to go to the point of the argument I have offered, for the obvious reason that the fact that they *do* so act and that the act requires bravery does not prove that they are morally *right* in so acting.

The Complications

I now turn to the complications which I said earlier derive from my account of the ethical situation of physicians.

---

[1] See, for example, again the very important attack by Dworkin et al., "Assisted Suicide," on views that might be held to be *like* the Supreme Court's view that option (b) should be rejected to protect the prerogative of Parliament.

It is important to be clear from the start that the most the argument above shows is that we have reason to view physicians' duties as strongly rôle differentiated in situations like those of Sue Rodriguez's physician: their ethical duties are to be viewed as overriding any other duties they may have. It does not show that the laws, codes, and practices governing the practice of medicine in situations like this are not in need of change. Nor does it show that physicians should not work hard to change these laws, codes, and practices: in fact, it does not even show that they should not use civil disobedience methods to secure these changes. All it does is suggest that, until these changes are put in place, duties that physicians *as physicians* have should be viewed as being strongly rôle differentiated in the sense I have described. But this leaves open various other possible ways of acting, all of which can intelligibly be interpreted as being consistent with the laws, codes, and practices governing the actions of physicians. Given the stated goals of my article, it is important to review these alternatives.

First, though more by way of contrast than anything else, the physician may indeed take the following approach:

(a) *The professional integrity approach*: He might decide that, since the laws, codes, and practices of his profession and the laws of the land forbid assisting a death in this case, and since to assist a death would be to act as part of his rôle as a health-care professional, that must indeed be viewed as being the end of the matter, no matter that the refusal will lead to one or other of the following sequelae:

either (i) the patient will acquiesce in the decision and take no further steps—the patient will then of course suffer interminably and futilely,

or (ii) the patient will try to find someone else who knows how to induce a relatively painless and quick death and who will help her to die—the need to do this itself becoming a source of further distress,

or (iii) the patient will try to find someone to help as in (ii), but this other person will not have the expertise to create a relatively painless and quick death and the patient might die in a more painful way than might have been otherwise possible.

Clearly a danger of the approach is that it can slide into what might well be called the professionally rigid approach or even, in some cases, the professionally cowardly approach.

Now contrast this approach with the following approaches, all of which, I would suggest, could be viewed as being compatible with the view that the person making the decision is still a physician, and even with the view that he is indeed in a strongly differentiated rôle:

(b) *The evasive approach*: He might decide that, although the laws, codes, and practices of his profession forbid assisting a death in this case, he will hasten the death anyway, but he will try to find ways of interpreting the laws, codes, and practices of the profession in such a way as to allow him to argue that he is acting ethically after all.[1] This is, of course, what many physicians are doing now. They increase the pain-control medications as far as they can under the rules, predicting that this will ease the patient's suffering, predicting also that this will hasten the patient's death, but carefully not saying that they are doing so *in order to* hasten the death—they invoke sometimes either sincerely or hypocritically the doctrine of double effect.[2] Alternatively, and this is done in the case of infants, they post "no treatment" or "do not resuscitate" or "no code" codes on the patient's chart, or, as in the case of nurses, they use the technique of "slow code."[3]

---

[1] On this approach a possible side benefit for the physician will be that he may escape the full wrath of the law and his profession. Notice, however, that this is only a *side* benefit and is not intended to be integral to the approach.

[2] The report by Dworkin et al., "Assisted Suicide," of recent research on the end-of-life decision-making practice of physicians in the US provides a basis for my empirical comments above. They report (citing Anthony L. Back et al., "Physician Assisted Suicide and Euthanasia in Washington State," *Journal of the American Medical Association* 275.12 [1996]: 919, 920, 922) that "in a recent study in the state of Washington, which guaranteed respondents anonymity, 26 percent of doctors surveyed said they had received explicit requests for help in dying, and had provided, overall, lethal prescriptions to 24 per cent of patients requesting them," and continues (citing David J. Doukas et al., "Attitudes and Behaviors on Physician Assisted Death: A Study of Michigan Oncologists," *Clinical Oncology* 13 [1995]: 1055, and L. Slome et al., "Attitudes Toward Assisted Suicide in AIDS: A Five Year Comparison Study," <http:// gateway.nlm.nih.gov/MeetingAbstracts/ma?f=102219213.html>) that in other studies, 40% of Michigan oncologists surveyed reported that patients had initiated requests for death, 18% said they had participated in assisted suicide, and 4% in "active euthanasia"—injecting lethal drugs themselves. In San Francisco, 53% of the 1,995 responding physicians said they had granted an AIDS patient's request for suicide assistance at least once. He comments that "These statistics approach the rates at which doctors help patients die in Holland, where assisted suicide is in effect legal!"

[3] See the now perhaps rather dated (1985) examination by Magnet and Kluge, *Withholding Treatment from Defective Newborn Children*. Particularly interesting for our purposes is their further report that in fact physicians, at least in Canada, are strikingly ignorant of what their ethical and legal duties are in relation to end-of-life decisions.

(c) *The public protest approach*: He might however decide that, even though the laws, codes, and practices of his profession and the laws of the land forbid assisting a death in this case, nevertheless, as a physician, he has a duty to work to make the laws, codes, and practices under which he works as sensitive to complex moral and personal issues as they can be made,[1] and that therefore he will assist the death anyway, but do so in a way calculated to draw the death and its manner to the attention of the authorities—he might view such an act as a form of civil disobedience. Clearly, going public may itself have consequences for the patient and, of course, for the physician, but it is important that it seems equally clear that in so acting he is still acting as a physician, for, notice, he will be liable to consequential discipline by disciplinary bodies of the profession and, notice, only a physician could make this sort of protest.

It is important to be clear that even the public protest approach can be interpreted as being compatible with the view that the physician is in a strongly differentiated rôle: the physician continues to act as a physician and may well view himself as complying with what "at a deeper level" the laws, codes, and practices of the profession demand. He may argue indeed that his ethical duties as a physician require that he use his authority as a physician to try to change the laws, codes, and practices governing the profession: he has an ethical duty to work from within the profession. This was the approach taken by Morgentaler on abortion, and it is the approach that has been taken by Jack Kevorkian in the US (though Kevorkian tried unsuccessfully to devise a way of inducing death that might possibly have saved him from successful *legal* action). The point is that a physician can take the public protest approach without ceasing to be a physician, though of course a consequence of his taking this approach may well be that he is losing his licence to practice as a physician, a clearly different matter. In this respect the next approach is significantly different from the first three, since arguably in this approach the person in the physician's rôle does not act as a physician but instead steps outside that rôle and its duties.

(d) *The* sub rosa *approach*: He might decide that, though the laws, codes, and practices of his profession and the laws of the land forbid assisting a death in this case, he will hasten the death anyway but, unlike

---

[1]   In the Canadian Medical Association's *Code of Ethics*, for example, there appears the statement that an ethical physician "will accept his share of the profession's responsibility to society in matters relating to public health, health education, and legislation affecting the health or well-being of the community," a sentence open to a wide variety of interpretations.

with options (b) and (c), he will neither do so defiantly nor do it under some pretext with some piece of sincere or otherwise legal legerdemain: he will instead just secure the death *sub rosa*, secretly, covering his tracks as best he can and hoping that no questions will be asked.

In many cases it will be hard to distinguish this approach from the evasive approach, of course, but there are differences.[1]

Now the task of choosing between these approaches is not something to which the literature has given much attention.[2] I refer to the absence of an account of how such choices are to be made as the problem of "interim decision making" — the problem of spelling out an account of the mode of reasoning to be followed by someone when the laws, codes, and practices in force in a society are significantly less than morally ideal — a very common situation, of course.[3] In this paper I do not have space to address this problem; indeed, I do not even have space to spell out the conditions under which physicians in the end should opt for one or other of the various actions in the range — that would require a series of further papers. But I will mention one very useful, but clearly incomplete, suggestion that was made many years ago by David Lyons,[4] though in a rather different context. In part, his suggestion was that in choosing how to proceed we should bring to bear what he called a "minimizing condition." A minimizing condition states that in less than utopian situations one should neither comply with the laws, codes, and practices in force nor do what some ideal laws, codes, and practices would require, but instead choose that action which, taking all relevant considerations into account, will minimize those bad effects that compliance with the laws, codes, and practices in force would, in the circumstances at hand, create. This might seem to suggest a strategy for dealing with such situations — the strategy of thinking globally (asking globally whether the laws, codes, and practices in force seem to be acceptable) but acting locally (concentrating on minimizing any bad

---

1   The empirical evidence about physicians' practices in the US and Canada reported in the footnotes attached to the evasive approach could well be cited here too, for the reports of their practices do not distinguish the two approaches.

2   The literature addressed to what is often called the problem of political obligation — the problem of why, if at all, people have a moral duty to obey the law in general — is perhaps relevant, as is the literature addressed to the question of whether civil disobedience is ever permissible, and if so, when. On these issues see Edmundson's excellent *The Duty to Obey the Law*.

3   I discuss the issues in my "Rights, Obligations and Duties."

4   Lyons, *Forms and Limits of Utilitarianism*, pp. 128 ff. Lyons's development of his idea of a minimizing condition is rather different from that here, but the idea is similar enough to warrant the use of his phrase.

effects on the people with whom one is dealing directly), but whether in doing that one should take the public protest, the evasive or the *sub rosa* approach is obviously not determined by the minimizing condition. This said, I have at least done what I said I would try to do: I have spelled out the *kinds* of options available to a physician in end-of-life decision contexts. I am thus in a position to turn to what are, I will suggest, the very *different* end-of-life moral issues to be faced by family members, and specifically to the decisions facing Sue Rodriguez's husband and Tracy Latimer's father.

6. THE HUSBAND, THE PARENT, AND THE MORAL DUTY OF RESCUE

I begin with some very general and, I hope, reasonably uncontentious comments about the moral rights and duties of husbands and parents.

To become a biological or an adoptive parent or a husband is to enter a rôle.[1] There are in Canada and most countries legal procedures by which parenthood, whether biological or adoptive, and marriage can be registered or otherwise acknowledged, so that these statuses have legal recognition. The situation is very similar for husbands. Moreover, attached to the rôles of parent and husband are certain rights and duties. Some of these rights and duties are recognized in the legal structures of society, which include provisions for actions to be taken if the parents or the husband fail to fulfil their duties. In addition, there are very strong social conventions in force, which also assign both rights and duties. For parents, a fundamental duty, recognized both in law and in the conventions in force, is to serve as the *primary* provider of care for their children. The situation for the spousal relationship is more complex, but most would agree that a fundamental part of the spousal relationship is defined through a "special" duty to provide care if the spouse is in need.

I turn now to the moral choices facing Sue Rodriguez's husband. Imagine that Sue Rodriguez's physician, for whatever reason,[2] refused

---

1   Sometimes people become biological parents "involuntarily," as my colleague Elizabeth Brake put it in her interesting paper "Abortion Rights and Child Support Law," delivered at the World Congress of the International Association for Philosophy of Law and Social Philosophy [Internationale Vereinigung für Rechts und Sozialphilosophie (IVR)], Lund, Sweden, August 2003. This introduces complexities into the situation that I will not have space to address.

2   Perhaps he would have been persuaded in one direction or another by my argument in the last section!

to assist Sue Rodriguez to die. Imagine further that no physician could be found willing to assist her to die. Sue Rodriguez wants to die, and indeed needs death as a relief. Two kinds of factors become relevant here.

First, obviously the Duty of Rescue is relevant. The need, knowledge, proximity, and consent conditions are clearly satisfied in this case, and given the special duty of caring owed by a husband, the last-resort condition is especially clearly satisfied. Of course, the physician fulfills the capacity condition of the Duty of Rescue in a way that a lay person like Sue Rodriguez's husband cannot hope to fulfill: the husband will probably need to do a lot of background work before setting out to give his wife a painless death, work that a physician would not need to do. This difficulty is, of course, not insurmountable. There are also very serious risks to the husband if he does attempt to fulfil what he sees is his duty of rescue. In some versions of the Duty of Rescue, an escape clause is included which says that the prospective Good Samaritan is excused from the duty to help, if helping would involve accepting serious cost: it is then referred to as the duty of easy rescue. If we were working with the duty of easy rescue, then the risk of helping might have released Sue Rodriguez's husband from the duty of rescue he would otherwise have. The question is whether in the situation in which the husband finds himself this exclusion is applicable. My view is that it is not obvious that it is and that we should say he has a duty to help here, though if fear for himself causes him to refuse to help, then clearly so serious would the consequences of being caught be that we could not but forgive the lapse— but a lapse, I want to suggest, it is. I want to suggest that the reason why risk to himself should not be counted as an exclusion reason in this case is that Sue Rodriguez's husband is her husband—and thus in a special relation to her: he is not a "mere" Good Samaritan. Let us look at this point.

As I argued above, both the law and the social conventions in force in our society impose special duties on the husband, duties of support and caring in various ways, some recognized in the law and some merely recognized in the social conventions. Moreover, in voluntarily becoming a husband, Sue Rodriguez's husband can plausibly be said to have voluntarily taken on these duties. Third, the duties of support and caring imposed in these laws and in the social conventions can plausibly be said to be of a kind that would survive moral criticism.

Therefore, Sue Rodriguez's husband, on two kinds of morally acceptable grounds, owes a duty to help her in some way or another.

But assistance to die is the form of help she wants and needs, and assisting her to die in the way countenanced is contrary to the law.

Thus, although the principles affirming the Duty of Rescue and a duty to provide support and care to one's spouse would probably survive examination by standard methods of assessment, in their application here they would call for illegal acts. This gives us the result that specific laws, codes, and practices can belong in the list of satisfactory, optimal or ideal laws, codes, and practices even though problems can be imagined about whether in a particular situation they should be acted on. In an ideal society, the laws, codes, and practices of the society and of medicine would have made provision for physician-assisted death with safeguards against abuse: but in our society those laws, codes, and practices are not in place. The consequence is that a great evil can occur — a woman is left wanting to die and needing to die in order to get relief from her misery, but the laws, codes, and practices that are in force forbid the help needed.

It is not at all clear where we should go at this point, but I have one small, modest suggestion.

Remember, first, the obvious point that Sue Rodriguez's husband's moral situation is very different from her physician's moral and ethical situation in one important and perhaps decisive way. The physician occupies a professional rôle, a rôle that the state counts as sufficiently important that it sets up a complex administrative apparatus, rightly I would add, and a rôle that, it has often been argued, can be fulfilled only if the person occupying the rôle is believed quite generally to be a person who complies with the laws, codes, and practices that define her or his professional duties — a person to be trusted to exercise his discretionary authority in ways compatible with the laws, codes, and practices in force. Fulfillment by the husband of his rôle duties does not require this kind of general public trust. These comments about the physician's situation square very much with my suggestions about the kinds of things that Sue Rodriguez's physician needs to take into account in figuring out what morally he ought to do. From this it follows that the kind of argument I offered in the last section when examining the moral situation of Sue Rodriguez's physician seems not to be available here: there is no reason to view the husband's rôle as being in any sense a strongly differentiated rôle.

The second part of my modest suggestion about how to go about making the interim decision Sue Rodriguez's husband faces is also a consequence of the point I made in the last section — that interim decisions are not about what might be called the society-wide, "global." issue of what laws, codes, and practices we should have in force; they are about local issues. In the cases we are looking at, what is at stake is the fact that compliance with the kinds of laws, codes, and practices that we would want to put in the public domain can leave unaddressed situations in which people suffer terribly. Maybe again what is needed is David Lyons's "minimizing condition."

Imagine that we say this. Then we would have at least in outline a way of addressing the problem of the need for "interim decisions," especially in non-utopian settings where a non-utopian setting is a social and historical context in which the laws, codes, and practices that *ought* to be in force are *not* in force. What we should do in such contexts is to apply those moral laws, codes, and practices that would survive examination in the usual ways, i.e., that would count as at least minimally morally acceptable, but apply them in a way modulated by a minimizing condition of the kind described above. In this case, it would seem we could conclude that Sue Rodriguez's husband ought morally to assist her in the way she asked, or in some equivalent way. The minimizing condition might also suggest at least here that he ought to do this secretly—after all, as a husband he does not owe any duty of the kind that physicians as physicians owe, i.e., to work to ensure that acceptable laws, codes, and practices are in force in the society.

We must, of course, recognize that society and the law may well, indeed probably will, react very negatively to such actions in some cases, and we need to factor this reaction into the decision, but we factor it in only as a circumstantial consideration, not as an integral feature of the choice situation. Sue Rodriguez's husband maybe will recognize that he will be prosecuted by the law and reviled by some of his fellow citizens, but these are merely facts that structure the context in which the action will be done; they are costs, but not moral costs. Although in familiar kinds of reasoning about our moral rules we need to think globally, with interim decision making we need to narrow our focus and think and then act locally, in some cases *very* locally, the bounds of the thought and the action sometimes being limited to the family or the friend. We decide what we should do as friend or parent, setting aside global or public considerations and addressing only the nature and the effects of our action on the narrow family or friend relationship.

Robert Latimer's situation is in many ways identical to that of Sue Rodriguez's husband, though in some very important ways his situation is different. Again, first, he is in a special relation to Tracy: she is his daughter. The laws governing parenthood impose legal duties on him as a parent. He clearly also assents to a very demanding interpretation of the social conventions that impose on parents a duty to care for and promote the well-being of their children: the courts all affirmed that for all of his life he was a model father. Second, and again in a very clear way, the Duty of Rescue applies in his situation — Tracy needs death as a relief, and clearly the knowledge and proximity conditions are satisfied. From the court records it seems that Robert Latimer's understanding of how to kill his daughter painlessly was not great, but, apart from that, he clearly had the capacity to kill her, though using his truck exhaust gases was not perhaps the most effective way to do so, especially if he wanted to avoid it being noticed that he had killed her.

The crucial differences between the interim moral decision that Robert Latimer needed to make and the interim decision that Sue Rodriguez's husband had to make are these. First, and most important of all, Tracy Latimer was not only vulnerable in the way Sue Rodriguez was vulnerable, but she was also vulnerable in each of the four ways I listed in my long description of her situation: she was both physically and mentally so incapacitated that not only was she physically unable to seek her own death as a relief, she could not even form a conception of this kind of relief and she could not ask someone else for this kind of relief. As I pointed out earlier, what this meant was that Tracy Latimer depended for relief on her father even more than Sue Rodriguez depended on her husband. If Sue Rodriguez's husband had failed her, then Sue Rodriguez could ask someone else — a friend or another relative perhaps. But Tracy Latimer could not do that. Notice that, far from Tracy's dependence on her father in the ways I have described being a reason for Robert Latimer not to kill his daughter, these factors increase the stringency of the duty Latimer has to secure in one way or another this death. When all is said and done, there were only two morally possible sources of relief for Tracy: her mother or her father. Earlier that very year, 1993, her mother, Laura, had given birth to one of Tracy's sisters, and there were two other young siblings to be cared for as well. It would not be unreasonable to view the duty to help Tracy as falling more on Robert than on Laura.

So our question is what, then, with his fatherly duties, Robert Latimer morally should do. He clearly faces an interim decision problem. Common morality gives him no unambiguous answers to his questions — people are confused on these matters. Even though there is very considerable Crown discretion about whether to act on these matters, the letter of the Criminal Code as it stands is, however, very clear: he is forbidden to kill his daughter, even in this situation. Asking what public laws, codes, and practices we should have will surely reveal that as a society we would not want as a public rule that parents be left so much discretion that it would be up to them to decide on life-or-death matters for their children. A variety of arguments are readily available, I would argue, for saying that parental rights in these matters need to be very carefully circumscribed. But, and this is again my point about interim decisions, I do not think that this is the end of the matter. I agree that the public laws, codes, and practices should not allow discretion to individuals on such matters, discretion about whether to comply with the rules in force. I agree, in other words, that we should not have an understanding of such public laws, codes, and practices that says that when they require or forbid certain acts, parents should be counted as having the discretionary authority to decide whether or not to comply. But I also think that there is more to be said.

What needs to be said is surely clear from the discussion so far. Again for a situation like Tracy and Robert Latimer's we need minimizing conditions of the kind I outlined when discussing the interim decision that Sue Rodriguez's husband needed to make — conditions that would make morally right the act of granting to Tracy the gift of death.*

REFERENCES

Baker, John A. "Rights, Obligations and Duties in the Intersection between Law and Morals." *Law, Morality and Legal Positivism: Proceedings of the 21st World Congress for Philosophy of Law and Social Philosophy.* Ed. Kenneth Einar Himma. Wiesbaden: Franz Steiner Verlag, 2004. 147-56.

Bayles, Michael. *Professional Ethics.* Belmont, CA: Wadsworth, 1981.

Beauchamp, Tom L., and James F. Childress. *Principles of Biomedical Ethics.* 5th ed. Oxford: Oxford UP, 2001.

Callahan, Joan C., ed. *Ethical Issues in Professional Life.* Oxford: Oxford UP, 1988.

Dworkin, Ronald, Thomas Nagel, Robert Nozick, John Rawls, Thomas Scanlon, and Judith Jarvis Thomson. "Assisted Suicide: The Philosophers' Brief." *New York Review* 27 March 1997: 41-47.

Edmundson, William A., ed. *The Duty to Obey the Law: Selected Philosophical Readings.* Lanham, MD: Rowman & Littlefield, 1999.

---

* My thanks to Elizabeth Boetzkes, Michael Stingl, John Woods, Lorraine Hardingham, and Jay Odenbaugh, and to the members of the University of Calgary Ethics Research Group — Brenda Baker, Shadia Drury, Trudy Govier, Tom Hurka, Ann Levey, and Dennis Mckerlie — for their helpful comments on earlier versions of this paper.

Engelhardt, H. Tristram, Jr. "Infanticide in a Post-Christian Age." *Euthanasia and the Newborn*. Ed. R.C. McMillan, H.T. Engelhardt, Jr., and S.F. Spicker. Dordrecht: D. Reidel, 1987. 81-86.

———. "Ethical Issues In Aiding The Death Of Young Children." *Beneficent Euthanasia*. Ed. Marvin Kohl. Amherst: Prometheus Books, 1975. 81-89.

Goldman, Alan. "Business Ethics: Profits, Utilities, and Moral Rights." *Philosophy and Public Affairs* 9 (1980): 260-86.

———. *The Moral Foundations of Professional Ethics*. Lanham, MD: Rowman and Littlefield, 1980.

Hardimon, Michael O. "Rôle Obligations." *Journal of Philosophy* 91.7 (1994): 333-63.

Jaworska, Agnieszka. "Respecting the Margins of Agency: Alzheimer's Patients and the Capacity to Value." *Philosophy & Public Affairs* 28.2 (1999): 105-38.

Lyons, David. *Forms and Limits of Utilitarianism*. Oxford: Clarendon P, 1965.

Magnet, Joseph E., and Eike-Henner W. Kluge. *Withholding Treatment from Defective Newborn Children*. Cowansville, QC: Brown Legal Publications, 1985.

Rosenthal, A.W. *Thirty-Eight Witnesses*. New York: McGraw-Hill, 1964.

Simmons, A. John. "External Justifications and Institutional Rôles." *Journal of Philosophy* Volume 93.1 (1996): 28-36.

Simon, John G., Charles W. Powers, and Jon P. Gunneman. *The Ethical Investor: Universities and Corporate Responsibility*. New Haven, CT: Yale UP, 1972. Reprinted as "The Responsibilities and their Owners." *Ethical Theory and Business*. Ed. Tom L. Beauchamp and David E. Bowie. 1st ed. Upper Saddle River, NJ: Prentice-Hall, 1979.

Wasserstrom, Richard A. "Lawyers as Professionals: Some Moral Issues." *Human Rights* 5.1 (1975): 1-24.

Chapter 11

FEMINIST REFLECTIONS ON TRACY LATIMER AND SUE RODRIGUEZ

Kira Tomsons and Susan Sherwin

1. INTRODUCTION

We approach the exploration of the issues raised by the deaths of Sue Rodriguez and Tracy Latimer from a feminist perspective. In so doing, we do not attempt to speak for all feminists: there are many different approaches to feminism, and there is room for much disagreement among feminists on the complex matters that arise in these cases. Rather, we shall lay out some of the important concerns associated with end-of-life decision making that we believe are generated by an oppression-based approach to feminism.

It should be noted that, like most of our fellow Canadians, we have a great deal of sympathy for the principal arguments offered by Sue Rodriguez (that her choice of assisted death should be respected as a matter of autonomy) and by Robert Latimer (that he acted out of loving compassion for his daughter, Tracy). In these cases, and in many other discussions of assisted death, proponents of permissive policies appeal to widely held moral principles: promote autonomy, prevent suffering, and build solid guidelines and procedures to prevent possible abuse. We endorse these principles and acknowledge that they figure prominently in many feminists' analyses of assisted suicide and euthanasia. We believe, however, that each of these principles must be interpreted through a feminist lens. Moreover, there are additional concerns generated by a feminist ethics perspective that tend to be overlooked in most debates about assisted suicide and euthanasia. It is our intention to make some of these concerns visible so that they can be addressed within the national debate.

In this paper we examine two feminist approaches to the issue of assisted death, both of which rely on an understanding of how oppression is created and sustained by social and political institutions and practices. The first approach focuses primarily on the ways in which particular state policies toward assisted suicide and euthanasia may affect existing oppressive relations between dominant and vulnerable groups. The second approach is grounded in a feminist ethics of care. Both of these approaches raise concerns about how vulnerable groups and interpersonal relationships will fare if permissive policies toward euthanasia and assisted suicide are endorsed. In our view, these concerns make decisions about practices of assisted death even more complex than they appear in non-feminist discussions. Hence, we shall not attempt to offer a definitive policy recommendation on euthanasia or assisted suicide. Our goal is more modest: to make visible some of the complexities that an oppression-based analysis adds to moral deliberations in pursuit of such policies.

2. OPPRESSION

Because oppression is a central concept in our discussion, we shall begin by sketching out an account of it.[1] Key to understanding oppression is the recognition that it is a phenomenon that exists between social groups. Specifically, membership in one or more oppressed groups makes one more likely to encounter restriction and dangerous hostility in one's life. In other words, people have oppressive experiences because of their membership in certain social groups. Marilyn Frye makes this explicit when she writes, "One is marked for application of oppressive pressures by one's membership in some group or category."[2] For example, women are much more likely to encounter sexual harassment, to be raped, and to experience domestic violence than men are. Blacks are more likely to be harassed, wrongly arrested, and discriminated against than whites. Gays and lesbians have, until very recently, been prohibited from marrying and they frequently face public condemnation regarding their sexuality.

---

[1] A much fuller account of oppression can be found in Tomsons, "Oppression: A Conceptual Analysis."

[2] Frye, The Politics of Reality, 15.

Oppression is not the simple matter of restricting an individual's liberty, however. We all experience limitations to our activities: for example, we are required to wear seatbelts and pay taxes. We even experience limitations as a result of biological differences: for example, men (and some women) cannot bear children, and some of us are required to wear glasses when we drive. But to call these limitations oppressive is to have "stretched [the concept of oppression] to meaninglessness."[1] What makes the limitations oppressed groups face actually oppressive is their systematic nature. Frye uses the analogy of a bird cage to illustrate this point. Single bars on a cage do not imprison. It is only through the use of multiple, inter-connected bars that one is successfully contained. When one focuses solely on the individual bars of a cage, one merely sees individual harms that can, perhaps, be corrected. But once we see the entire cage and the interactions among the multiple bars, we can see how completely the cage contains and imprisons. Similarly, looking at individually disconnected incidents and attitudes often masks the systematic way in which certain groups experience oppression. Hence, oppression can sometimes only be recognized when the multiple ways in which people experience limitations and restrictions are seen. It is also important to note that different categories of oppression can intersect such that people experience oppression (and privilege) differently depending on the various types of social groups to which they belong. A white woman, for example, experiences oppression differently than an Aboriginal woman; she also experiences white privilege differently than does a white man. As well, oppression is not a single sort of experience but rather diverse kinds of experiences.

Put simply, oppression is an unjust state of affairs that exists between members of different social groups and that is (a) harmful to members of some social groups while being beneficial to others, (b) perpetuated by social institutions and structures, and (c) deeply rooted in the history of relations between the social groups in question. In her book *Justice and the Politics of Difference*, Iris Young identifies five different types (or "faces") of oppression that may characterize the experiences of members of oppressed groups: cultural imperialism, violence, exploitation, powerlessness, and marginalization.[2] These five faces of oppression provide a lens through which we can examine and understand the experiences of those who face oppression. We propose a somewhat different

---

[1] Frye, *The Politics of Reality*, 1.
[2] Young, *Justice and The Politics of Difference*, 40.

list of elements to capture the various dimensions of oppression in all aspects of life: physical harm (including violence and poor health resulting from oppressive practices), economic harm (material deprivation associated with belonging to a disadvantaged group), psychological harm (often manifested as depression or self-hating), cultural harm (where one culture dominates or annihilates another), and moral harm (where members of an oppressed group are denied full moral status or have reduced opportunities for exercising autonomy). In addition, it is essential to pay attention to the historical context in which the harms in question occur, for mechanisms of oppression are created over time in quite specific ways. Institutions and social patterns are developed through time, rooted in religious and cultural traditions that embed themselves in society. Patricia Monture-Angus vividly illuminates this point as she argues for the importance of coming to grips with history in order to understand and effectively respond to the current needs of Aboriginals, and in particular Aboriginal women.[1]

Using the framework of oppression makes clear the necessity of looking beyond the level of individuals when examining social policies. It requires us also to explore questions of justice between different groups. It directs us to look at how different groups are likely to be affected by each policy option and by prevailing attitudes toward them, paying particular attention to the situation of members of currently oppressed groups. It is with this understanding of oppression that we now reflect on the question of appropriate policies regarding assisted suicide and euthanasia.

3. EXAMINING POLICIES THROUGH AN OPPRESSION LENS

In this section, we explore the role of oppression in examining the arguments put forward in support of permissive policies in the area of assisted death. Traditionally, within secular discussions, questions about the moral legitimacy of the practices of euthanasia and assisted suicide have focused on examining their impact on individuals with respect to matters of autonomy and beneficence. We will look at the ways arguments based on each of these key principles play out when we explicitly attend to considerations of oppression.

---

[1]   Monture-Angus, *Thunder in My Soul*.

Autonomy

If we look at the case of Sue Rodriguez in the usual (non-feminist) way, the principles of autonomy and beneficence seem to offer straightforward support of a permissive policy of assisted suicide. Indeed, her case illuminates these elements particularly clearly. Rodriguez was an adult who was clearly competent, able to reason intelligently and make her demands known through both the media and the court system. Her request for assisted suicide seems to be a clear example of someone seeking to exercise her autonomy. Faced with a debilitating disease that was leading to an inevitable (and frightening) death, Rodriguez was surely the best judge of when would be the right time to end her life. Furthermore, the fact that her disease physically prevented her from exercising a choice that a healthy person could (as suicide itself is no longer illegal) suggests that society was actually obligated to help her as a matter of equality. Many feminists who adopt a liberal stance would readily support her right to exercise her autonomy in this important area.

However, this approach—grounded as it is in individual rights— masks the nature of oppression. When we begin with a concern about pervasive patterns of oppression, we realize the importance of looking beyond the situation of an individual and asking what impact each policy option is likely to have on members of oppressed groups. Starting with an understanding of oppression reshapes how we interpret the core concepts of autonomy and beneficence, and it reorients our thinking on the practical problem of ensuring that abuses are prevented. It also generates different moral questions. For example, should we attach any significance to the fact that both of the "patients" were female, since women and girls are members of an oppressed group? What effect will our moral and legal decisions in these two cases have on other people with disabilities, many of whom are already vulnerable to oppressive attitudes and decisions? How do the hidden assumptions that already permeate medicine and society about the worth and value of those in oppressed groups affect the sorts of policies and decisions that are made, both in the medical sphere and in the larger political realm? And how will different policy decisions alter the social positions of those who are oppressed? With these questions in mind, we take on the question of whether the Rodriguez case is really as easy as it appears and highlight the ways in which the case of Tracy Latimer adds further levels of complexity to the issue of setting policy on assisted death.

We see no need to reject the important principles of patient autonomy or beneficence. We think that they are properly at the centre of the debate surrounding euthanasia and assisted suicide and can inform efforts to prevent abuse of whatever policies are adopted. We propose, however, that we revisit these concepts through a feminist lens, and we begin with the conception of autonomy that has been assumed throughout much of the discourse on end-of-life decision making. The familiar liberal conception of autonomy presumes an atomistic conception of the self, where the only relevant external influence to be considered is the absence of explicit coercion. Diana Meyers points out that "self governance has been taken to presuppose unfettered independence from other individuals as well as from the larger society."[1] Like Meyers (and several other feminists), we propose that a more accurate account of autonomy makes clear that it is relational in nature; in particular, people are recognized as being embedded within webs of relations which affect our decisions in both positive and negative ways.[2] A feminist relational conception of autonomy recognizes the impact of patterns of dominance and oppression on the options and the decision-making resources available to individual agents. Typically, oppression limits available options such that the most attractive ones are those that are compatible with ongoing patterns of oppression; at the same time, high penalties are commonly attached to choices that challenge prevailing norms. For example, women are rewarded for complying with prevailing beauty norms despite the expense and risk that may be involved in pursuing these norms, and they are frequently devalued if they flout those norms. As well, oppression often inhibits the decision-making capacities of individual members of oppressed groups when their relative powerlessness has failed to provide them with sufficient opportunities to develop the necessary skills of autonomous decision making.

Therefore, oppression can have a serious impact on people's ability to make decisions that further their own well-being; this problem is especially acute when part of the oppression they face is the subsuming of self-interest into the interest of others. In her feminist critique of permissive policies governing assisted death, Susan Wolf raises a number of serious concerns about the likely impact of such policies on

---

[1] Meyers, "Intersectional Identity," 152.

[2] A number of other feminists have also recommended movement from an individualistic notion of autonomy, evaluated in isolation from the larger social context, to a relational concept. See, for example, Jennifer Nedelsky, Lorraine Code, Marilyn Friedman, Susan Sherwin, and the authors within Mackenzie and Stoljar's *Relational Autonomy*.

women.[1] She observes that the virtue of self-sacrifice has been traditionally placed upon women and notes that this emphasis on the sacri-
ficial nature of women's "virtue" may mean that the availability of an
option of assisted suicide will increase the pressure on many women to
choose it in order to lessen the burdens on their family. This pressure
may not be overt—it may be that no one sets out to deliberately coerce
women to choose early death; it is often subconscious and rooted in the
commonplace values that valorize feminine virtues of self-sacrifice.
Thus, to appeal to a traditional sense of autonomy (understood as the
ability to make choices independent of explicit external coercion)
masks the myriad ways in which the desires and preferences of the
oppressed are distorted by oppressive values.

There are two issues at stake. The first is that in many cases, what
appear to be "autonomous" decisions on the part of women are not
really autonomous because they enact internalized cultural norms that
discourage full autonomy for women. In particular, we have reason for
concern about decisions made within oppressive contexts in which
women have internalized oppressive attitudes and values; in some contexts, the dominant values (e.g., regarding the importance of women
being self-sacrificing in family matters) are so well entrenched and
widely accepted that they preclude meaningful access to outcomes that
conflict with those values. Hence, determining whether a decision is
autonomous requires more than an evaluation of the decision-making
capacity of the individual agent and a search for immoral actors
engaged in applying coercive force. It also requires an evaluation of the
prevailing social values and their role in shaping each patient's understanding of her own interests.

The situation is made even more complicated by the fact that the
actions of some members of an oppressed group may reinforce the
oppression of other members of that group by serving as examples of
the appropriateness and pervasiveness of these coercive values (e.g.,
self-sacrifice). Hence, relational autonomy also requires us to consider
whether the choices of the individual in question will likely contribute
to ongoing oppressive values and attitudes; if it will, then the morality
of the decision must be cast into doubt. Ann Cudd writes,

> …women are oppressed by the vicious cycle phenomenon, and
> thus, by means of their own individually rational choices. Because

---

[1] Wolf, "Gender, Feminism and Death."

their individually rational choices reinforce the oppressive institutions and so harm other women, one might question the morality of those choices.[1]

The second issue, then, is whether respecting the autonomous rational choice of one member of an oppressed group may lead to less autonomy for other members of that group. It may be that Sue Rodriguez's decision was, from an individualistic standpoint, perfectly rational, clearly competent, and autonomous; it may even be autonomous from a relational perspective (reflecting her best interests despite the distortion that oppression might produce in shaping them). Yet, policies supporting such decisions might still harm other women if the decision were taken as valorizing women's self-sacrifice. For example, while Rodriguez might very well be acting from selfish motives, forgoing any appeal to the virtue of self-sacrifice, her actions may be read by others in different ways. Other women, who are more vulnerable to the forces of oppression, may interpret her decision as setting a standard that they should follow. They may lack the education and opportunity to be able to articulate their desires and motivations as clearly as she did; moreover, as Wolf argues, their motivations for seeking death may be suspect if they are making decisions within oppressive contexts.[2] Attention must move from analysis of individual choices to examining patterns across groups. In recognizing that our individual choices affect others, the question of whether assisted suicide and euthanasia can be permitted must be answered with an understanding of the oppressive context in which such individual decisions will be made.

To conclude that the complexity inherent in a relational understanding of oppression prohibits permissive policies for assisted suicide and euthanasia would be moving too quickly, however. We are committed to identifying and eliminating systems of oppression. What is unclear is where this commitment leads. We have shown how such a commitment may require restricting some choices of particular individuals to prevent the oppression of others, but the analysis of oppression cuts (at least) two ways.

There is a long history in which women and members of other oppressed groups have been judged as deficient with respect to the competency criteria for autonomy. Women are perceived as being

---

[1] Cudd, "Oppression," 41.
[2] Wolf, "Gender, Feminism and Death."

affected strongly by others (women's tendency to attend to relations when making moral decisions), and people with disabilities are perceived as dependent (incapable of caring for themselves). In fact, our own analysis suggests that there may be some truth underlying such stereotypes, since women are commonly expected to put the interests of others first, and people with disabilities do rely more than most on the support of others. Members of these oppressed groups thus fail to meet traditional standards of competence that presume independence, self-sufficiency, and rationality. As a result, they are often targeted for paternalistic interventions, where decisions are made in their supposed best interest, rather than in accordance with their desires (i.e., their autonomous wishes). Thus, when a woman requests assisted suicide or euthanasia, her request might very well be denied because it is seen as the request of a "hysterical" woman, or someone who is not acting rationally and competently. The difficulty with this response is that paternalism is not an adequate solution to the problem of distorting socialization, since there is little reason to believe that the others who make decisions on behalf of members of oppressed groups will know the true interests of those individuals better than do the specific patients themselves.[1]

Moreover, paternalistic attitudes may be exacerbated by other categories of oppression, such as race and class. In other words, under permissive policies, an individual like Rodriguez (who stands in a position of privilege in some dimensions) may be more likely to have her voice heard and acknowledged than those who have less education, are poor, black, or are cognitively disabled. Refusing to allow the option of assisted suicide or euthanasia may further restrict the options and autonomy of members of such disadvantaged groups, thus furthering the oppression they face. For society to refuse to allow them the options they seek reinforces the paternalistic perception that oppressed groups are unable to make their own choices. This amounts to denying members of oppressed groups moral agency and the ability to make those kinds of decisions on their own.

Adopting a feminist relational interpretation of autonomy adds complexity to the role of the principle of autonomy in deliberations about social policy regarding assisted death. It does not provide a straightforward, simple answer. We turn, next, to reflections on beneficence, the second moral principle commonly invoked in debates about assisted death.

---

[1] See Sherwin, *No Longer Patient.*

Beneficence

Appeals to autonomy, however it is interpreted, are of little value in cases where the possibility of patient autonomy is absent, as it was in the case of Tracy Latimer. Her brain was damaged to a point where, it appears, she would never develop the competency to exercise her autonomy. This is a more complex situation for liberals who base their support for permissive policies of assisted death on patient choice (autonomy). Such cases move us from Rodriguez's quest for assisted suicide (which is patient-driven) to nonvoluntary euthanasia (where the choice is in the hands of another). Those who argue in support of permissive policies for nonvoluntary euthanasia rely primarily on principles of beneficence. No one seriously proposes tolerating involuntary euthanasia (where the killing is done against the will of the patient), but many people believe that compassion requires that we be able to terminate the lives of people who lack the capacity for autonomous deliberation but who are afflicted with uncontrollable suffering.

It certainly seems to be the case that Robert Latimer was acting out of a principle of beneficence. He was, we believe, responding to the pain that he saw his daughter to be suffering. We urge caution, however, in moving from a recognition that he acted from love—in accordance with his understanding of what would be best for his daughter—to the conclusion that his actions were morally proper. For even if he did act out of beneficence, evaluations of the pain and suffering of persons with limited communicative skills like Tracy are problematic, since they are strongly informed by personal perceptions of what it means to be sick or disabled. Such perceptions are generally skewed by oppressive forces.

People with disabilities are already oppressed, and the worry on the part of many disability activists is that permissive policies and societal support of Robert Latimer's actions increase the vulnerability of people with disabilities. Among the able-bodied majority, disability is almost universally seen as negative, even though many of the limitations people with disabilities experience are artefacts of our society. These limitations arise because our society has been structured to accommodate the needs of those without disabilities and has, until very recently, been unresponsive to the needs of people with disabilities. Being blind is disabling in a society that is vision-oriented, and being in a wheelchair is disabling when sidewalk curbs are too high and door jambs too narrow, but things could easily be arranged so that these conditions are not seriously limiting. As well, the healthy tend to fear illness and assume its effects are intolerable, when many people living with illness do not judge their lives to be unbearable. When a narrow conception of health is highly valued, the sick and disabled are often expected to see their conditions as others do—that is, as negative.[1]

We must keep in mind that those who are involved in developing policies, as well as those who would be involved in the actual processes of enacting assisted suicide and euthanasia, are likely to belong to privileged groups. In Canada, doctors, for instance, are mostly white, middle and upper class, and not disabled. They are unlikely to have direct experience with disability but are very likely to share dominant cultural prejudices regarding its extreme disadvantage. It is appropriate, then, to worry that their exaggerated ascriptions of the negative value of disability will affect end-of-life decisions, particularly when those decisions are nonvoluntary, as in the case of Tracy Latimer. If the people making decisions regarding end-of-life decision are not themselves disabled, then the value judgments that go into the endorsed policies are unlikely to be the same as those of the disabled.[2] Feminists should thus be concerned that decisions and policies made by the able-bodied (and those who are cognitively normal) might well reflect values that misrepresent the lives of those who experience disability. If those who are the targets of such practices do not agree that their lives are not worth living, then nonvoluntary euthanasia is not an expression of beneficence at all, but rather a serious violation of the interests of those whose lives are being terminated. Far from being paternalism, it would constitute unacceptable involuntary euthanasia, despite the good intentions of its supporters. The situation is complex, however, since here, too, we must recognize that oppression can cut in more than one way when interpreting the principle of beneficence. The difficulty in the case of Tracy Latimer is that she was unable to speak for herself. We cannot assume that the perspectives and life experiences of people with lesser disabilities are any more reliable predictors of her actual experiences than those of people without disability. There is enormous variation among the many people who live with disabilities, and it is not sufficient to allow the most articulate among this group to determine the situation for all others. There remains the possibility that Tracy Latimer, or others with severe disabilities, do live with unremitting suffering and would prefer

---

[1] Silvers, Wasserman and Mahowald, *Disability, Difference, and Discrimination*, 187.

[2] There is evidence that attempts to evaluate quality of life in the past have been biased because those with disabilities were not part of the evaluation process. See Menzel, *Strong Medicine*.

that their lives be ended. A simple refusal to allow nonvoluntary euthanasia would have the effect of perpetuating their suffering. But, surely, the burden must be on those who would propose death as a solution to the problem that such persons face. There must be very careful procedures in place to ensure that we are rightly interpreting their nonverbal signals and that there are no other ways of relieving their suffering. We must ensure that we are not mistakenly exaggerating their degree of suffering because of our own fears of being similarly situated. The standard for such tests must be very high, and the alternatives to killing must be expanded and explored. We should be very wary of the ease with which we all unconsciously devalue the lives of persons who belong to oppressed social groups.

Such measures are particularly important in the case of decisions regarding people with severe disabilities, since the politicians and civil servants who are involved in developing policies and the doctors and nurses who would be involved in administering euthanasia, should it be permitted, are likely not experiencing serious disability. Hence, they may hold inaccurate and unrealistic assumptions about the quality of life of people with serious disabilities. While it is not possible to include people with disabilities as severe as Tracy Latimer's in policy formation, it is important to ensure that people with a wide range of disabilities have a place at any table where policies regarding nonvoluntary euthanasia are discussed.

4. THE ETHICS OF CARE

The previous discussion focused on the relations between groups. We argued that the existence of oppressive group relations requires reframing the arguments for and against permissive policies toward euthanasia and assisted suicide. But there is another stream of feminist ethics that also plays an integral role in raising important questions which are generally ignored by non-feminist approaches: the ethics of care. We move now to examine how permitting assisted suicide, and more importantly nonvoluntary euthanasia, may have an impact on the caring relations in which all people are embedded, grounding our discussion in a particularly feminist ethics of care. This discussion occurs at two levels: the interpersonal and the political.

The terms "ethics of care" and "care ethics" embrace a diverse range of theoretical perspectives. There are three particularly well-developed versions of care ethics, each articulated in a full-length monograph.

Chronologically, these are Carol Gilligan's *In a Different Voice* (1982), Nel Noddings's *Caring* (1984), and Joan Tronto's *Moral Boundaries* (1993). Each author understands the meaning of care and the scope of caring responsibilities differently.

Interpersonal Care

Gilligan proposes the idea of an ethics of care (or an ethics of responsibility) as a complementary ethical dimension to the traditional ethics of justice (defined as ethics based on universal moral principles). Gilligan finds that both men and women use an ethic of justice in some contexts, but, generally, only women and girls are inclined to invoke an ethics of care as a regular part of their moral considerations. She argues that moral life requires both modes of deliberation and that the difficult challenge for every moral agent is to learn which types of decisions merit which type of reasoning. In contrast, Noddings proposes an all-encompassing interpretation of care ethics. In her theory, caring is the only legitimate moral consideration. She claims that the only proper locus of ethical thought is the quality of relationships, not the nature of acts or judgments. Ethical behavior involves putting oneself at the service of others, seeing the world from their perspective, and acting "as though in my own behalf, but in behalf of the other."[1]

Gilligan and Noddings disagree about the scope of care ethics (partial for Gilligan, total for Noddings), about the nature of the caring relationship (valuing the preservation of relationships for Gilligan, valuing the interests of the one cared for in Noddings), and about the importance of caring for oneself (central in Gilligan, not important in Noddings). What they share is an insistence that personal relationships are of fundamental moral worth; they are at the center of moral life. Moreover, what is valuable about interpersonal relationships has to do with the very particular nature of the specific relationship, involving details about the particular persons involved and consideration of the importance of emotional connections. Within the two versions of care ethics offered by Gilligan and Noddings, then, specific contexts are of fundamental moral significance, and interpersonal relationships, including the complex emotions associated with them, are the focus of moral concern. We have a moral responsibility to foster conditions that permit positive relationships to thrive and to avoid actions that will undermine the quality of specific and generic human relationships.

---

[1] Noddings, *Caring*, 33.

Joan Tronto takes a different approach to care ethics. She does not focus on the realm of intimate, interpersonal relationships; rather, she explores the role of caring in the political sphere. Where Noddings constructs care ethics as superior to an ethics of justice, and Gilligan constructs it as distinct from but complementary to an ethics of justice, Tronto makes care a central component of justice. She argues that it is not a question of choosing care *or* justice, since they are essentially connected. Care is a central element of justice, and justice is an important guide to appropriate caring. Tronto's aim is to develop a vision of the good society within the realities of human beings engaged in various relationships of dependence and care. Her question is not whether a political structure should address relations of caring, but how to ensure this is done in a just way. This requires consideration of who cares for whom, under what kinds of conditions, and how we can ensure that the collectivity of the state provides for the human need for care.

Feminists who structure their ethics around analyses of oppression, as we do, have an ambivalent relationship to an ethics of care approach. All three care theorists described above acknowledge that care is a primarily "feminine" activity, i.e., that it is a form of behaviour that is generally expected of women but is considered remarkable in men. Moreover, all three acknowledge that women are particularly likely to have developed the skills and capacities necessary for carrying out the activities of caring: most women learn to be attentive to the needs and desires of others and most have developed, to some degree at least, the virtues associated with caring for others. As Sherwin has argued, there is significant danger in valorizing the virtues of feminine subordination.[1] The character traits necessary for effective caring are attentiveness to the needs of others, empathy, patience, self-sacrifice, and an ability to focus on the minute details of life. These are also, however, the virtues that are required of people in subordinate social positions. To survive, or even thrive, within a subordinate position, it is helpful to develop an acute awareness of the perspectives and interests of those who occupy positions of relative power. Members of subordinate groups tend to be valued for their ability to provide for the daily needs of those with more power without requiring the active attention of those in power. Insofar as the traits and demands of caring well make its practitioners more vulnerable to exploitation, and, thereby, to increase their vulnerability to oppression, we need to be wary of celebrating these paradigmatically

---

[1] Sherwin, *No Longer Patient.*

feminine virtues of care. Moreover, as Gilligan makes clear, unless embedded within a full ethics of responsibility, the emphasis on caring can easily result in a practice of concern for others with no appreciation of the need to care for oneself.

Hence, it is important to be clear that in this discussion we are concerned with an explicitly feminist ethics of care. In our view, a feminist ethics of care must be deeply embedded within a theory of social justice that seeks to identify and eliminate oppression. Like other care ethics, it is attentive to contextual details, but it gives primary attention to contextual details having to do with systemic patterns of oppression. Relationships are recognized as having moral significance, but a feminist ethics of care takes a critical perspective on these relationships. It looks beyond the interactions of interpersonal relationships to examine the impact of unequal power between individuals and between social groups. It is clear that not all relationships are worth preserving. In particular, a feminist ethics of care is eager to eliminate relationships built on abuse of the power attached to oppression; as an extreme example, relationships of sexual slavery should be terminated. Among those relationships judged worth preserving, many will require some substantial reform, such as those built around traditional gender roles. The goal is to transform relationships of power and dominance and to promote relationships of mutual concern and respect.

This means that when considering particular types of action and policies, it is essential that our ethical deliberations be sensitive to the impact of our decisions on various types of relationships. It is not sufficient to reflect only on the application of abstract moral principles such as respect for autonomy and beneficence; nor will it do to weigh only the consequences of our actions or rules. Both of these traditional moral perspectives proceed as if actions occur within a vacuum and are right or wrong according to some characteristic attached to the action. Even utilitarianism, which asks us to evaluate the consequences of our actions or policies, generally measures those consequences by their effect on discrete individuals. A feminist ethics of care insists that we also include consideration for the impact of these decisions on existing (and future) relationships between groups as well as between individuals.

In the context of the decisions involving Tracy Latimer and Sue Rodriguez, we need to reflect on how the decisions regarding their deaths affected actual relationships, and how the state's response to those decisions is likely to affect future relationships. Given Rodriguez's apparently full and clear understanding of her situation and her open, supportive network of interpersonal relationships, it seems as if her decision was fully explored with intimate others in her life. We assume that there was an opportunity for Rodriguez herself, and those whose well-being was important to her, to express their feelings and concerns in an atmosphere of trust and honesty. Presumably, no one was coerced into participation in an action they could not endorse. The event was timed such that Rodriguez had the opportunity to say meaningful good-byes to those who were important to her and to ensure they understood her reasons for the action she took. This seems to us to be an ideal way of proceeding in the tragic circumstances she found herself in, for her decision and action seem to have been embedded within the context of a network of caring relationships and were carried out in such a way as to leave no one feeling abandoned or guilty at the outcome.

Tracy Latimer is a more difficult case, however, for it seems that she was not a party to the decision making. In the opinion of her father and the professionals involved in her care, she was not capable either of engaging in complex abstract deliberations or of expressing her views on such matters. It seems that Tracy lived fully in the present, defined by her immediate sensations of pain and pleasure, and the pain increasingly seemed to outweigh the pleasure. In what we assume was an act of love and concern, her father made the decision to terminate her life as the only way he could see for ending her suffering. We do not question his love or his motivation. We are deeply concerned, however, about the implications of having the state tolerate such behavior on the part of parents.

Our concern is that all children are dependent on their parents for care and support, and it is the responsibility of parents to act in ways that will ensure that their children survive and thrive. Families are not egalitarian institutions, though many like to imagine them as such. At least while children are young and dependent on adults for the necessities of life, parents have significantly more power than do children in most families. In many cases, the norms of traditional gender roles also ascribe significantly more power and authority to men in nuclear families than they do to women, though in this case, equality between adult partners is at least possible. Power imbalances, whether necessary or gratuitous, are always dangerous. It is easy to exploit or abuse power, particularly when that power is deployed within the privacy ascribed to family life.[1]

We are very wary, then, of endorsing a pattern in which a parent, particularly the male "head of the household," assumes the responsibility of

---

[1]   Okin, *Justice, Gender and the Family.*

making unilateral decisions about the value of the lives of those living under his authority and power. It is far too easy to embed this practice within patriarchal norms that have served for centuries to entrench the power of the father to make all the important decisions for his household, and far too difficult to separate it from that oppressive tradition. To ask, or even to allow, a parent to assume responsibility for determining whether or not those under his "protection" are living lives they would judge to be tolerable is to invite parents to reflect on matters that improperly extend their power and pave the way to abuse of that power.

Families are primary social institutions within which people receive the care they need for survival. It is, therefore, essential that we seek to ensure that everyone is safe within that family structure. Families are not the only place for meeting individual needs: many needs must be addressed outside the family, but often, even these are predicated on having basic needs first met at home. (For example, transportation needs can be met by public transit, but the expectation is that people will ride public transit clothed, bathed, fed, and toileted.) The needs of different family members may be in conflict with one another, and sometimes interests of some members must be ceded to meet the interests of other family members. Thus, the needs of any single member are unlikely to be independent from the needs and interests of others. When one member has particularly demanding needs, as was the case with Tracy Latimer, some of the resources (emotional, physical, and financial) required to meet those needs may come at the expense of other family members. A parent responsible for caring for the needs of all family members may have a difficult time sorting out the relative weight to assign to the demanding needs of one member.

Even when the decision to end a child's life is made out of love and concern, as we are willing to grant was the case with Robert Latimer, it is an inappropriate role for family members to assume. The parent is not a neutral observer, capable of accurately perceiving and weighing competing claims within the family, but a particularly interested party shouldering a major part of the burden of meeting those complex needs. It is neither reasonable nor wise for a society to suggest that an appropriate response is to allow the responsible parent to resolve this tension by eliminating the life of a family member, no matter how desperate the family may feel.

If it is truly the case that there was no hope of a future life for Tracy that was not dominated by suffering, then it is necessary for society to find other means of addressing this rare and desperate situation. We need to establish an appropriate forum where appointed advocates who have no conflicting duties, responsibilities, or interests can make the case that continued life would be an intolerable burden for a particular individual. Whenever possible, these arguments must be made on the basis of evidence provided by the individual herself, and we must be very wary of making such decisions on behalf of those who cannot communicate with us about the complexities of an early termination of their lives. All family members should be included in the deliberations, and they should understand that their continuing relationships will be sustained in an atmosphere conducive to mutual trust and shared concern. If the person with the greatest power within a family is permitted to make his own decision about the value of continued life for others, the opportunities for healthy trust within the family are seriously undermined.

That being said, however, we need also to acknowledge that caring for a family member with severe disabilities can be overwhelming for some parents. In the majority of cases, the burden of providing the necessary care falls most heavily on the mother. We are mindful of the fact that sometimes the burden is beyond the ability of the parent(s) to manage. If society is to insist that the lives of children with severe disabilities and extraordinary suffering be maintained, it also has a responsibility to ensure that services and resources are available to assist the family in caring for such children.

Political Care

There is another aspect of care ethics that is relevant to these two important Canadian cases, namely its explicit recognition of the reality of dependency within moral life. Most moral theories place high value on independence. They are directed at agents envisioned as being rational, independent individuals in full control over their behaviour. Responsibility is limited by circumstances that limit the agent's control (coercion, compulsion, physical constraints); conversely, full responsibility resides with those who are fully capable and acting independently. Autonomy, or self-governance, is typically constructed as the highest moral ideal, and it is primarily a virtue of rational, self-directed individuals. Most mainstream discussions of morality have to do with the rights and duties of a member of a society made up of other rational, independent, self-governing individuals in their occasional interactions with one another.

Theories of ethics of care acknowledge explicitly that we are all involved in a complex network of interdependent relationships. Those based in feminist critiques of the liberal conceptions of self and autonomy do not valorize independence, or even imagine it exists. Rather, they understand the need to speak of different degrees and kinds of dependence and interdependence. Those with private automobiles can appear to be "independent" with respect to transportation, but only if networks of adequate roads, gas stations, and mechanics are in place. Those who are financially "independent" rely upon a complex international banking system to manage their money, as well as the countless workers who organize an infrastructure that delivers safe water, food, and other necessities to sites at which they can be purchased. Some people need more particular kinds of assistance than others, but no one is free from the need for care and support from others. The principal difference is that our social institutions and structures have been created in such a way as to provide for the needs of those who appear independent as a routine, normal matter of course. Those with "special" needs appear to require special accommodation since their care is not built into the very fabric of society. Until recently, public buildings were constructed to allow easy access for those without mobility or sensory impairments but excluded entrance by those in wheelchairs. Happily, changes in building codes have extended accessibility in new buildings, thereby increasing the "independence" of people in wheelchairs and those with visual impairments. Still, many public places find it inconvenient, expensive, or not aesthetic to make accommodations that expand accessibility, increasing the common perception that people with impairments are burdensome; the point is that the sense of "burden" is a matter of social choice regarding whose needs are routinely accounted for, and whose require special measures.

It is evident that there is a great deal of prejudice and hostility in our society against those with significant impairments. An ethics of care reminds us that dependence on others is not a reason to be devalued or considered less than a full member of the moral community. By making visible the way we are all dependent on others to varying degrees at various times of our lives, an ethics of care can help to undermine the tendency to exaggerate the moral importance of apparent independence. An ethics of care also pays attention to attitudes and emotions, since these are core features of both personal and impersonal relationships. Hence, it can help us to come to terms with the common tendency of many toward fear or loathing when they contemplate living with serious impairments. Such attitudes are particularly worrisome in the context of end-of-life deliberations, since it is entirely possible that those of us who are within "normal" ability ranges exaggerate the hardship of lives lived with significant impairments.

These considerations point to another important difference between the Rodriguez and Latimer cases. Sue Rodriguez herself provided the evidence that her life was approaching a level of hardship she found intolerable. She was able to tell us, in her eloquent fashion, that she anticipated reaching a point further on in her disease (notably, she was not yet at that point in her judgment when she spoke to the courts) when she would consider the suffering associated with her disease to be so severe she would not wish to continue living. Tracy Latimer, in contrast, was not able to tell us what she thought about continued existence. Her parents tell us that by a series of grimaces and other pain behaviours, she conveyed continuing, unrelenting suffering, and that is a pretty good indication of a life most of us would find unbearable. But we must be very careful here, since many people with disabilities report that others frequently tell them that they would judge life in their condition to be unbearable. Unless we can hear unambiguously the wishes of the person whose life is at stake, we run the risk of letting our own fears and guilty feelings of disgust project onto another's life in an inaccurate and dangerous fashion.

From the perspective of a feminist ethics of care, both Sue Rodriguez and Tracy Latimer were, first and foremost, members of our society and thereby entitled to equal concern and respect. Both had unusual, very apparent, and extensive special needs. Tracy, throughout her life, and Sue Rodriguez in the last months of her life, were not able to perform even the most mundane of tasks without specific assistance from others. Moreover, it seems that it was not possible to fully meet the needs of either of them even with significant amounts of personalized care. Sometimes, even with the best available care, there is no way to prevent significant suffering in the ordinary course of living one's life. Before concluding that it is simply not possible to meet anyone's needs, however, we need to reflect very carefully on what it would take to meet such extensive needs as Rodriguez and Latimer represent in a satisfactory fashion.

For this task, we turn again to the work of Joan Tronto to help us to explore different possibilities for responding to extensive needs such as these. Tronto reminds us that it is not sufficient to simply list needs and insist that they be met. We need also to consider who is to meet these needs and how their efforts are to be evaluated. Tronto makes vivid the complexities of care provision by unpacking the activity of caring into four distinct, though interrelated, elements or phases:

1. *Caring about*, or the recognition that care is needed. This phase involves recognition of a need and an assessment that care must be provided if that need is to be met.
2. *Taking care of*, in which someone assumes responsibility for determining how best to respond to the identified need(s).
3. *Care-giving*, the direct meeting of the need(s) in question through physical activities. In contrast to those involved solely with caring about and taking care of, care-givers are in direct contact with those receiving care.
4. *Care-receiving*, in which the person receiving care responds to that care. By their response, care recipients tell us whether the caring provided successfully relieves their needs without worsening their situation.

Note that all of these categories are types of activities, not emotional attitudes. The provision of care may be done in what is known as a "caring" way, with empathy for the situation of the care recipient, or it may be carried out as a job with resentment, inattention, or selfish goals. Tronto makes clear that care involves work, which may or may not be carried out in the context of love. In contrast to Noddings, she is far more concerned with the politics of care provision than with the emotional attitudes that accompany it.

As a practice, the four phases of care can be done well or badly. To clarify these distinctions, Tronto proposes four "elements" or virtues of care, which comprise the ethical part of an ethics of care: attentiveness, responsibility, competence, and responsiveness. Not just any care will do, and good intentions are not enough to ground an ethics of care; rather, the caring activity must take place with considerations of how the care is carried out in light of these virtues. To care well, there must be close communication among those engaged in the four phases so that the care can be provided in an integrated fashion, where each phase informs the others.

Tronto observes that there is a hierarchical relationship among the four phases of care. Typically, the most power, prestige, and authority attach to those making the executive judgments associated with caring-about and taking care of activities. Those who are involved in the hands-on labour of care-giving come primarily from social groups oppressed by virtue of gender, race, and/or class. (This is the sort of work assigned to women and to members of racial and ethnic minorities, i.e., to those with lesser status.) They deal with the messy physical aspects of care-giving activity. Public applause is generally reserved for those who raise the funds and organize the workers, those who invest mental rather than physical labour in the cause of caring. These are the tasks of caring about and taking care of. The appreciation of care-giving comes, if at all, from those who receive the care, but if the care is inappropriate, or if the resources provided are insufficient, or if the conditions under which it may be delivered are oppressive, then the care may not be adequate to meet the needs of the care-recipient. Under such circumstances, both care-giver and care-receiver may feel frustration and anger.

Those identified as in "need" of care, those designated as care recipients, tend also to be devalued in our productivity-oriented culture. They are often seen as weak, burdensome, and inclined to use more than their share of social resources. As we saw above, within a culture that valorizes independence, there is a tendency to presume that those in need of exceptional care must be unhappy with their lives.

Tronto recommends a political interpretation of care ethics because she understands that there are questions of power and privilege involved with determining whose needs get met routinely and whose must be treated as "special cases." In the context of the Rodriguez and Latimer cases, we have to ask who assumes responsibility to recognize the needs of others like them (care about), and who will be responsible for taking care of those needs once they are identified. Sue Rodriguez was able to identify her own needs and seek the support she needed. As far as we know, resources were made available to her to meet her needs reasonably well, as long as it was within the realm of human capacity to do so. She did not complain of a failure of resources to provide the actual care-giving she needed, though there are many other, less articulate patients with comparable needs who are unable to command the particular kinds of care-giving that they need. Caring about, and taking care of the needs of other persons with debilitating illness by ensuring that the resources are there to provide for effective care-giving by valued workers, should be a high priority of the state.

In the case of Tracy Latimer, again, things are more complex. She was not able to express her needs, except by indications of pleasure or pain. Within traditional families, it is usually part of the mother's role to identify needs of individual members and bring them to the attention of the father. His job is to take care of those needs by ensuring that care is provided. The actual care-giving typically falls back on the mother. It seems that Robert Latimer made the decision that Tracy's needs for a tolerably comfortable life could not be met, and, therefore, that the best way to respond to her needs was to arrange her death. He then set about causing that death. But this is a very unusual sense of care-giving, and an odd way to go about meeting needs. There is no scope for feedback from the care recipient, and no clear way of evaluating the appropriateness of the judgment. There is room, then, to question if the caring process has indeed broken down and the ethical components of an ethics of care have not been met. The competence of health-care professionals, the parents, and society in general to deal with Tracy's needs comes to the fore as a serious problem. The question of whose responsibility it is to determine how those needs are met arises, as does that of whether the people involved in the care process were responsive to the needs of Tracy and the voices of those with disability.

Again, it seems to us dangerous for the state to allow causing the death of a family member to be regarded as a legitimate means of care-giving. For the reasons discussed above, decisions of this magnitude cannot be regarded as purely internal family matters, for families have conflicting interests regarding the care needed by very disabled members. It is very dangerous to grant fathers the power of life or death over their children, even under extreme circumstances. That being said, the state does have a responsibility to support families with severely disabled family members. It must ensure that they have access to the resources necessary to meet the needs of these family members without exhausting the capacities of other family members. It must provide for financial, physical, and emotional support for care-givers as well as disabled family members. And it must do it out of a sense of community, not burden.

5. CONCLUSION

Our feminist reflections do not yield a clear resolution to the problems before us. They leave us with many questions unanswered and have added many new questions into the mix. The tension that arises from the perspective of social justice as to the role of oppression between groups is complex. An oppression-based approach raises questions that force us to explore the multiple ways in which oppression will affect the lives of those who are faced with end-of-life decisions. Before we give a ringing endorsement of permissive or restrictive policies, we must recognize and explore the oppressive context. While we intuitively think that a decision like Rodriguez's is unproblematic in isolation, the impact of social policy on oppressed groups is a far more difficult matter. The Latimer case raises even greater concerns, since oppression based on social attitudes toward disability and pain are deeply ingrained in our culturally dominant attitudes and assumptions, not merely in overt actions and laws that blatantly oppress. But it must also be acknowledged that unqalified societal prohibitions of assisted suicide and euthanasia may also serve to reinforce oppressive attitudes toward vulnerable groups who already lack full control over their lives. It is a tenuous balancing act, and only through discussion of the ways in which oppression affects those in vulnerable groups can any path through the complexities be forged.

One way of responding to these complexities is procedural, but we must be wary of who sets and implements the procedures in question. In the context of a system that already oppresses, there is reason to doubt the ability of those in power to create policies that will not continue that oppression, especially when the voices of those oppressed continue to be marginalized and ignored. Because policy, laws, guidelines, and standards of informed consent are constructed within already existing institutions of government and medicine, we worry that just being very careful about the guidelines we create will not be sufficient to address the moral difficulties with end-of-life decision making. As long as women and members of minorities fail to have adequate voice in the institutions that create policies, guidelines, and laws regarding practices involving end-of-life decision making, feminists will have cause for concern that the implementation of guidelines to prevent abuse will be insufficient. In order to reduce that risk it is important to introduce measures that will help to ensure that policy-makers listen carefully to the voices of those who occupy oppressed positions and ensure that their concerns are taken seriously. So the response that solving the problem of abuse is merely a matter of practical "details" is insufficient. In order to develop just policy, and indeed, in order to argue for such policy, attention to oppression cannot be merely given lip-service; it must be taken very seriously, in the justification and implementation of such policies.

Our conclusions are ambivalent, as we are torn in conflicting directions. We desire to protect the personal autonomy of individuals and particularly those in oppressed groups, yet we recognize that individual choices may have to be restricted when the contexts in which those choices are made are oppressive to certain groups. We desire to acknowledge that Robert Latimer's decision was apparently motivated by beneficence and love, yet we understand that the caring relationships in which we are embedded are subject to questions of justice and morality. Insofar as the feminist perspective we take highlights key aspects of care and oppression, it also highlights a crucial aspect of the decision to support permissive policies toward euthanasia and assisted suicide: the issue is not a simple matter of preserving autonomy or acting on beneficence. The issues surrounding these cases are more complex than standard arguments around them permit.

Recognition of oppression and care requires that we take stock of the relationships in which we find ourselves and consider how our values affect those relationships, both at an interpersonal and at a social level between groups. As interests conflict, it becomes necessary to examine whose interests are being met through the development of particular social policies, who will bear the burden of carrying out the policies, and how the social context of those in oppressed groups will be changed and altered by such policies. Attention to oppression and an understanding of the intersection of justice with care help bring to light crucial issues that must be addressed in the justification of policy, not merely in the pragmatic solutions to prevent abuses. The feminist approach we use takes the issues and concerns that traditional approaches claim are pragmatic problems, not principled ones, and points out how the pragmatic and the principled must both be dealt with before permissive policies toward euthanasia and assisted suicide can be fairly created and judiciously implemented.

REFERENCES

Cudd, Ann. "Oppression by Choice." *Journal of Social Philosophy*, 25th Special Anniversary Issue (1994): 22-44.

Frye, Marilyn. *The Politics of Reality: Essays in Feminist Theory*. Freedom, CA: The Crossing Press, 1983.

Gilligan, Carol. *In A Different Voice*. Cambridge, MA: Harvard UP, 1982.

MacKenzie, Catriona, and Natalie Stoljar, eds. *Relational Autonomy: Feminists Perspectives on Autonomy, Agency, and the Social Self*. Oxford: Oxford UP, 2000.

Menzel, P. *Strong Medicine*. Oxford: Oxford UP, 1990.

Meyers, Diana. "Intersectional Identity and the Authentic Self." *Relational Autonomy: Feminists Perspectives on Autonomy, Agency, and the Social Self.* Ed. Catriona MacKenzie and Natalie Stoljar. Oxford: Oxford UP, 2000. 151-79.

Monture-Angus, Patricia. *Thunder in My Soul: A Mohawk Woman Speaks.* Halifax: Fernwood Publishing, 1995.

Noddings, Nel. *Caring.* Berkeley: U of California P, 1984.

Okin, Susan Moller. *Justice, Gender and the Family.* New York: Basic Books, 1989.

Sherwin, Susan. *No Longer Patient: Feminist Ethics and Health Care.* Philadelphia: Temple UP, 1992.

Silvers, Anita, David Wasserman, and Mary B. Mahowald, eds. *Disability, Difference, and Discrimination: Perspectives on Justice in Bioethics and Public Policy.* New York: Rowman & Littlefield, 1998.

Tomsons, Kira. "Oppression: A Conceptual Analysis." Doctoral dissertation: Dalhousie University, Halifax, 2006.

Tronto, Joan. *Moral Boundaries: A Political Argument for an Ethic of Care.* New York: Routledge, 1993.

Wolf, Susan. "Gender, Feminism and Death: Physician-Assisted Suicide and Euthanasia." *Feminism and Bioethics: Beyond Reproduction.* Ed. Susan Wolf. Oxford: Oxford UP, 1996.

Young, Iris. *Justice and the Politics of Difference.* Princeton, NJ: Princeton UP, 1990.

PART IV

ASSISTED SUICIDE, VOLUNTARY EUTHANASIA, AND PALLIATIVE CARE

Chapter 12

ATTITUDES OF PEOPLE WITH DISABILITIES TOWARD PHYSICIAN-ASSISTED SUICIDE LEGISLATION: BROADENING THE DIALOGUE

Pamela Fadem, Meredith Minkler, Martha Perry, Klaus Blum, Leroy F. Moore, Jr., Judi Rogers, and Lee Williams[1]

In November 2001, when Attorney General John Ashcroft challenged Oregon's Death with Dignity law by prohibiting doctors from prescribing lethal doses of federally controlled substances to their terminally ill patients, he added new fuel to an already contentious debate in American society. Yet as deeply divisive as the issue of death with dignity (DWD) or physician-assisted suicide (PAS) legislation is in the United States, it has a particular history of polarization in the community of people with disabilities. The organized disability-rights community has historically taken a strong stand against such legislation, including mobilizing to defeat California's proposed Death with Dignity Act (AB 1592) in 1999-2000 and vigorously opposing Oregon's Death with Dignity Act, which went into effect in 1997 (Wolfe 1997). This opposition is based on recognition of the marginalized status of people with disabilities as a vulnerable population in American society due to well-documented historical and continuing stigmatization and discrimination (Zola 1979; Longmore 1987; Hahn 1988).

---

[1]   Originally published in the *Journal of Health Politics, Policy and Law* 28.6 (2003).

Such groups as the National Council on Disability (1997), and Not Dead Yet and ADAPT (both of which submitted *amici curiae* briefs in support of petitioners *Vacco v. Quill*, Supreme Court of the United States, October term [1995]; see Chapter 2, above) have argued that legislation permitting death with dignity or physician-assisted suicide would deny fair and equitable life choices to people with disabilities and so would lead toward a slippery slope resulting in unwanted and unnecessary deaths within this population. This position has been heard. Writing for the majority in two 1997 US Supreme Court cases, *Vacco v. Quill* and *Washington v. Glucksberg* (see Chapters 1-2, above), Chief Justice William Rehnquist prominently referred to arguments included in the amicus briefs filed by two disability rights organizations (*Washington v. Glucksberg*, 521 U.S. 702, 728-35 [1997]).

Although a strong position opposing DWD/PAS legislation frequently is put forward as representing the views and interests of the disability community, in reality this issue engenders deeply polarized positions on disability policy and advocacy within different community arenas (Batavia 1997; Wolfe 1997; Toy 1999; Taylor 2002) and there is considerable diversity of opinion. The use in this article of the dual acronyms DWD and PAS reflects the strength of that opinion within the community, extending as it does even to debate about the terminology that should be used in discussing such legislation.

In a Harris poll of 1,011 adults conducted in November 2001, findings for the subset of 171 people with disabilities revealed that more than two-thirds (68 per cent) would favor a law such as Oregon's, with 29 per cent opposing and 3 per cent undecided. This diversity was similar to that found in the full sample, where the corresponding figures were 65 per cent in favor, 29 per cent opposed, and 6 per cent undecided (Taylor 2002).

There also is anecdotal evidence that fear of criticism among people with disabilities who fail to support the publicized disability position opposing DWD/PAS legislation has led to a stifling of open discussion within the community. A 1999 survey conducted by *New Mobility* magazine, for example, resulted in a large volume of responses, with 37 per cent of those who favored the legislation also reporting fear of censure from their own community if they voiced such an opinion (Corbet 1999b). Although admittedly representing the experiences of a small and non-representative sample, such findings are of concern because fear of censure could contribute to the exclusion of broader disability-community representation in statewide and national policy-development bodies.

This article presents the methods and findings of a small participatory

action research (PAR) project on attitudes within the disability community toward DWD/PAS legislation, undertaken in the San Francisco
Bay Area in 1999-2001. Consistent with the principles of PAR (George,
Daniel, and Green 1998-99; Israel et al. 1998), members of the disability
community were actively involved in every aspect of the study, from setting goals and formulating interview questions to data collection and
analysis, and the findings are to be used for education and social change.

Although the findings of small, nonrepresentative, qualitative studies such as the one reported on here cannot be generalized to the larger
population, they can be useful in helping to uncover ignored or overlooked viewpoints and to further illuminate the complexity of the issue
under investigation within its social context (Strauss and Corbin 1990).
A goal of this study was to help broaden dialogue around this divisive
issue by, among other things, sharing the study findings among the
immediate community as well as within national public and professional forums. Through the inclusion of an empowerment process, the
study was designed also to help communities of people with disabilities,
particularly those in the San Francisco Bay Area, to find common
ground and become better positioned to be included in the ongoing
legislative and policy debate on physician-assisted suicide.

The choice of the San Francisco Bay Area as the study site was deliberate and significant. Although the Bay Area is atypical of the nation at
large in terms of its progressive political culture and its higher-than-
average levels of educational achievement, it also is home to a disproportionately high population of people with disabilities. Birthplace of
the Independent Living Movement (Shapiro 1993), the area continues
to be a center of disability-rights activism in the United States, serving
as national headquarters for many leading disability-rights organizations, including those putting forward a uniform community position
on the issue. Therefore, an exploratory study of attitudes toward
DWD/PAS legislation among people with disabilities in the Bay Area
was deemed methodologically useful as well as principally consistent
with the above-mentioned goal of qualitative research, namely, to
describe and interpret phenomena within the social context in which
the subject exists (Strauss and Corbin 1990).

BACKGROUND

Oregon is the only state to have legalized physician-assisted suicide. The
Death with Dignity Act (Oregon Revised Statutes 127.800-127.897

[Supp. 1996]), which Oregon voters passed in November 1994, faced a series of legal challenges and a second voter referendum, and it did not go into effect until November 1997. According to the Oregon law, residents of the state who are eighteen years of age or older, who are terminally ill with a life expectancy of six months or less, and who are not clinically depressed may request a prescription for a lethal dose of barbiturates from their physician. They must make this request twice, with two weeks between requests, and be able to self-administer the medication prescribed by their physicians.

California, Washington, and Maine also have considered but rejected ballot measures that would have legalized physician-assisted suicide. Following intense public debate on the subject, the high courts of Michigan, New York, Florida, and Alaska similarly ruled that there is no constitutional right to assisted suicide. The American Medical Association and the Catholic Church are among the powerful forces that have consistently lobbied against DWD/PAS legislation, and, as noted above, many prominent disability-rights organizations have worked alongside these larger groups as part of the opposition.

On 26 June 1997, the US Supreme Court issued two related rulings, *Washington v. Glucksberg* (521 U.S. 702 [1997]) and *Vacco v. Quill* (521 U.S. 793 [1997]), which firmly returned the debate over PAS from the federal courts to individual states. The majority opinion in both of these rulings specifically addressed the obligation of the state to protect especially vulnerable populations from the possible dangers of involuntary euthanasia, naming people with disabilities as members of one of the at-risk groups.

As mentioned above, two disability-rights organizations, Not Dead Yet and ADAPT, entered an amicus brief in both cases, extending the argument about the logical slippery slope and vulnerable populations. The brief argued that an increased burden on caregivers of the profoundly disabled, combined with a decrease in social and economic supports, would sufficiently lower the quality of life for people with disabilities and result in encouraging the disabled to choose PAS. This legal brief strongly asserted the impossibility of autonomy for people with disabilities because of the profound and lasting impact of social stigmatization. Indeed, many leading disability organizations and institutions, including the National Council on Disability, the World Institute on Disability, and the American Association on Disability, have official positions opposing DWD/PAS legislation. With varying degrees of complexity and sophistication, these organizations base their positions on the systematic devaluation of, and discrimination against, people with disabilities (National Council on Disability 1997; Madorsky 1997). The 1990 Americans with Disabilities Act (42 U.S.C. [1990]) was an outcome of and response to conclusive evidence of discrimination that constituted people with disabilities as a vulnerable population (Silvers 1998).

METHODS

This study involved qualitative, in-depth interviews with 45 respondents as part of a participatory action research process. Two of the three University of California at Berkeley research team members, and all six members of the project's Community Advisory Group (CAG), had substantial physical disabilities, thus facilitating the use of a true PAR approach.[1]

Defined as "systematic inquiry, with the collaboration of those affected by the issue, for the purposes of education and taking action or effecting social change" (George, Daniel, and Green 1998-99), participatory action research is committed to blurring the line between the researcher and the researched (Gaventa 1981) and the "strengthening of people's awareness of their own capabilities" as researchers and agents of change (Hagey 1997). PAR is particularly well suited for use in studies addressing controversial issues, which DWD/PAS legislation is for those in the disabled community. Whether employing qualitative or quantitative methods, PAR incorporates an asset-based approach to community organizing and capacity building and provides an opportunity for those with divergent opinions to work together toward a common goal, such as education or change.

This project met the criteria for participatory action research in several ways. The problem arose within the disability community itself, and the research was conducted largely by members of that community. The CAG, which met monthly from fall 1999 to spring 2001, comprised

[1] The authors gratefully acknowledge other members of the Community Advisory Group (CAG), Mary Pugh-Dean, and World Institute on Disability Representative Devva Kasnitz for their major contributions to all aspects of this project. Thanks are due also to Tatra-Li Beuttler for her help with data analysis and to Eve Muller for her early contributions as a member of the project team. We gratefully acknowledge the Wallace Alexander Gerbode Foundation for its belief in and support of this project. The anonymous reviewers, along with editors Mark Peterson and Mark Schlesinger, made many valuable suggestions that greatly strengthened the final version of the article. Finally, our deepest thanks go to the participants in this study for sharing their life stories and deeply personal beliefs and for contributing to a process that we hope will help enrich and strengthen the community of people with disabilities.

six people with disabilities, five of them informal leaders in the disability community and the sixth a researcher/representative of a leading disability advocacy organization (the World Institute on Disability [WID]). The CAG was actively involved in determining the criteria for sample selection, developing the research instrument, conducting interviews, data analysis, presenting the final report to the study participants, and follow-up dissemination and other action-phase activities.

Sample

A combination of methods was used to develop a sample that, while not random or representative, would include considerable diversity in terms of nature of disability, race and ethnicity, and socioeconomic status. Targeted sampling was used in which basic ethnographic mapping of the population helped to determine representation (Watters and Biernacki 1989). Through snowball and reverse snowball sampling, respondents were asked for the names of other people with disabilities who might wish to participate, particularly those who were likely to hold opinions about PAS/DWD legislation that were different from their own. Finally, local disability-community resources, such as independent living centers, outpatient rehabilitation services in local hospitals, disabled student services at local college campuses, and county social services and seniors' centers, were contacted and asked to post flyers and in other ways assist with recruitment.

To be included in the study, a participant had to be over the age of 21 and have a physical disability, either congenital or acquired, requiring accommodations and/or assistance with the activities of daily living (ADLs) or the instrumental activities of daily living (IADLs). People whose primary disability was sensory (such as deafness or blindness) and those who acquired a physical disability secondary to their primary diagnosis (e.g., HIV/AIDS or cancer) were excluded from participation. Individuals who were being treated for depression or who had been depressed during the past six months, or who had a history of suicide ideation or attempts, and those who had been disabled for less than four years also were excluded from participation in accordance with Institutional Review Board approval.

Consistent with grounded theory and other qualitative research approaches involving open-ended interviewing, sample size was determined by saturation, that is, the point in the interviewing process when similar attitudes and experiences begin to be repeated and substantively new information is no longer being uncovered (Glazer and Strauss 1967). The final sample included 27 women and 18 men who ranged in age from their early 20s to their early 90s and who had an average age of 46.[1] Sixty per cent of sample members were people of color, primarily African Americans and Asians, and more than half were single at the time of their interviews. Close to half of the participants had been disabled prior to age three, and all but six had been disabled for at least one-third of their lives. While education ranged from less than high school completion to an advanced degree, the greatest proportion of participants (44 per cent) were college graduates.

Instrument Development and Administration

A 29-item questionnaire consisting of both semi-structured and open-ended questions was developed and pretested by the UC-Berkeley team members and the CAG. The first half of the final interview instrument included questions about demographic background and the nature of the disability; daily life routines and life satisfaction; social support; perceptions of stigma, discrimination, and life control; and relationships with medical providers and to the health-care system. The second half addressed end-of-life decision making and feelings as well as opinions regarding death-with-dignity legislation.

The 60- to 90-minute interviews, which were taped and transcribed, took place at sites that were convenient for the participants, each of whom received a $50 honorarium for participating. Although pairs of team members were present at each interview to facilitate subsequent inter-rater comparison of coded responses, the interview was always conducted by a team member with a disability.

Data Analysis Methods

A code book was developed to numerically code those questionnaire responses that lent themselves to such analysis. Transcripts were each

---

[1] A total of 68 individuals expressed an initial interest in participating in the study. Of these, thirteen were excluded on the basis of the initial screening criteria, typically because they were suffering from depression or had a secondary, rather than a primary, physical disability. An additional eight were excluded in the later stages of the sampling process because they represented groups that were already overrepresented, that is, white women and middle-aged and older people (see Fadem et al. 2003 and Minkler et al. 2001 for more detail). Two individuals changed their minds about being interviewed, one stating that the topic was "too depressing" and a second fearing censure if her co-workers in the disability movement learned of her positive views toward DWD/PAS legislation.

coded independently by the two team members who had participated in the interview, and a high degree of inter-rater reliability was found (93 per cent).[1] In cases where there was disagreement over the coding of a particular response, relevant portions of the original redacted transcript were reexamined, discussed, and reconciled.

A qualitative data-analysis software program, QSR NUD*IST 4.0, was used to generate reports based on coded words (e.g., "terminal"), phrases (e.g., "easy way out"), concepts (e.g., autonomy), and numbered question responses. A subgroup of four CAG members and two members of the university research team independently reviewed redacted transcripts and NUD*IST reports by numbered responses to identify those patterns or themes that appeared across multiple questionnaires. Individually identified themes were compared and a master list was generated that represented those patterns identified by the majority (and typically all) of the participants. This master list was then presented to the full CAG for further discussion. The themes described below constitute the major findings.

Consistent with a key principle of participatory action research — returning data to the community (Israel et al. 1998) — study findings were presented first to the study participants at two luncheon meetings during which they were given an opportunity to comment on and question the findings, suggest alternative interpretations, and offer ways to use the findings to help address the needs and interests of the disability community (for a more detailed look at study methods see Fadem et al. 2003).

FINDINGS

Six key findings or themes emerged in this study: (1) the existence of a great breadth and diversity of opinion with respect to attitudes toward DWD/PAS legislation, (2) the importance attributed to self-determination and autonomy in the way people with disabilities live and die, (3) the pervasive experience of discrimination based on disability, (4) contradictions between personal experiences and abstract or political beliefs shaping attitudes toward DWD/PAS legislation, (5) misinformation about the Oregon law and its implementation, and (6) fear of talking about DWD/PAS legislation with other members of the commu-

---

[1] The inter-rater reliability score was calculated by dividing the total number of questions and subquestions on which coding discrepancies occurred (84) by the total number of questions asked (1,260). The three graduate student team members received training in coding, and sample coding sessions were held to help ensure that the process was applied uniformly.

nity, particularly if one held an attitude that contradicted the stated disability-community position.

A seventh finding was that many of the factors commonly believed to make a difference in attitudes toward DWD/PAS legislation did not hold up for this group of respondents as a whole. These factors included self-identification as a member of the disability community; race and/or ethnicity; religious or spiritual identification; relationship with one's physician; age; and gender. Although a detailed discussion of these factors is beyond the scope of this article (see Fadem et al. 2001), the most salient finding here was that, contrary to expectation, none of the above factors bore an association with the attitudes of sample members toward DWD/PAS legislation. Of particular interest was the finding that, of the nearly two-thirds of sample members who self-identified with the disability community, fully half reported having considerable ambivalence about the legislation, with the remainder only slightly more likely to oppose than to support it. In short, contrary to a widely held assumption both within and outside the disability community, people who strongly identified with the disability community frequently did not express the strong negative views about DWD legislation that have been put forward by activists as the disability community's position on this issue. Together with the observation that race and ethnicity, religious and spiritual beliefs, gender, and the other factors noted above bore no relationship to attitudes toward the legislation, this finding was instructive. For although the nature of the sample precluded the drawing of any conclusions about associations, the findings suggest that for the individuals interviewed, factors shaping attitudes toward DWD/PAS legislation cannot be reduced simply to the demographic characteristics noted above or to self-identification as a member of the disability community.

Great Breadth and Diversity of Opinion about DWD/PAS Legislation

A key component of the findings from this research is the wide range and diversity of opinion toward DWD/PAS legislation in this Bay Area sample. A member of the study's Community Advisory Group summarized this well when he observed,

> There seems to be one public position on behalf of people with disabilities about death with dignity legislation put forward by disability community spokespersons and groups, but when you

go deeper into the community there are many different opinions. An individual's opinion seems to depend on their own character, personal experience [of self or a loved one] with near-death or death, among many other things.

Positive opinions and support for legislation were expressed by close to 30 per cent of those interviewed. As one woman in her 30s said, "I do support legislation for compassion.... I believe in supporting legislation as long as there isn't the assumption that because you are disabled you don't want to be here." An almost equal number of participants were strongly opposed, though for many different reasons. In a few cases, opposition was based on religious or spiritual feelings. A man in his 30s thus said emphatically, "No way, I'm not letting anyone pull no plug... it's already written... only [God] has permission to do that.... I'm not going to vote for that law to come in, no way.... I'll go naturally."

For others, opposition reflected fears that such legislation would lead to misuse and/or jumping the gun, when a cure for a terminal illness might be right around the corner. A woman in her 50s described herself as "absolutely opposed" to legislation, explaining, "I don't think a bunch of people can sit around and come up with something that would be safe because there would always be some other people who would figure out ways around it."

For several participants, the reality of racism within society constituted a special reason for opposition to DWD/PAS legislation. A man in his 60s commented,

> I think there is too much room for abuse. Physicians getting rid of people they've done dirt to and covering up their mistakes. Helping people die who don't need to die. The statistics of dying in the civilian world are greater than on the front line. The [risk of dying on the] front line is 5000:1; out on the streets [it is] 200:1 for a black male.... Being a black male influences my thinking about this. Especially about dying in this society.

Perhaps the most striking finding about opinions toward DWD/PAS legislation was that nearly half of the study participants expressed ambivalence about such legislation. This ambivalence included a wide range of concerns, including an individual wanting to have the option for him or herself but not feeling comfortable with an institutionalized law; generalized mistrust of government and/or the health-care industry in general, particularly in regard to the devaluation of disabled people, people of color, and the poor; and the belief that one of life's most personal decisions should not be legislated either for or against. One participant, a man in his 30s who has lived with disability for more than half of his life, told us,

> I do not believe there should be any type of legislation. I also think there should not be legislation against it. It is a very personal decision. Some people are going to come to a point in their life where they want to end it. This is a very personal decision.

Other participants described a shifting line in the sand regarding their own or others' experiences with disabilities. As one woman in her 20s who is living with a degenerative disease said, "I haven't gotten to that point in my disability. If that time came that my disability progressed at a more rapid pace, I don't know what my decision would be."

Central Concern for Autonomy or Self-Determination

A desire for autonomy in decision making was a central, unifying concern expressed by nearly all sample members, regardless of their positions on DWD/PAS legislation. All respondents reported wanting their life choices concerning independence and autonomy to be respected. Similarly, all but one respondent also wanted assurance that if they were close to death, or were experiencing intractable pain or loss of cognition, their own opinion and choices about ending or continuing life would be respected. Many study participants stressed the importance of autonomy in end-of-life decisions, stating that life-and-death decisions should not be in the hands of doctors, family members, health maintenance organizations (HMOs), or other bureaucratic bodies. Many shared the experiences of friends and loved ones who they said "suffered needlessly"—whether disabled or not—when aggressive treatments for a terminal illness had prolonged pain and suffering (cancer and HIV/AIDS were mentioned most frequently in this regard).

Participants often expressed concern that disabled people may be especially vulnerable to being denied end-of-life choices because of the way they are devalued in society. There was widespread worry, for example, that doctors, HMOs, and others may hasten death because the lives of people with disabilities are not considered worthy or valuable. One woman with a congenital disability stated,

> I can't even think about physician-assisted suicide because it scares me—someone making a decision based on someone else's quality of life. In the past, when I was working [in] hospitals...I would hear other people ask [referring to people with disabilities], "What kind of life can they have?" That scares me.

Many respondents were concerned that people with disabilities may be denied choice because they are assumed incompetent to make their own decision—or because of their physical inability to execute a choice. As a man in his 50s remarked,

> I think a person should have a choice. Especially if they have a disability that they could not voice their concerns. People should have a choice in how we live and die. As long as there is communication and safeguards, the family and person are involved. They don't feel the plug is being pulled without their consent.

And in discussing the Oregon law, several interviewees argued that the requirement that medication to end life be self-administered effectively denies choice to those whose disability prevents them from using their hands or in other ways complying with this aspect of the legislation.

Perhaps the best summary of how a majority of participants perceive society's view of people with disabilities was simply stated by a man who remarked, "I would like the community to give people with disabilities more respect and more of a chance in life." This simple, deeply expressed desire for self-determination and autonomy seems closely related to the next key finding, the perception of discrimination based on disability.

The Prevalence of Disability-Based Discrimination

Almost 90 per cent of study participants reported that they had experienced discrimination based on their disability, whether from employers or potential employers, teachers, health-care practitioners, social-service or government agencies, members of the community, or their own families. Despite the fact that 60 per cent of sample members were people of color, experiences of disability-based discrimination were often recounted as having been as damaging as experiences of racism. This experience of discrimination and stigmatization was accompanied by a widespread mistrust of government and the health-care industry overall, including individual practitioners, HMOs, and health insurance companies. A man in his 70s told us, "I have heard people say to disabled people, 'Why don't you die?'" Another participant, disabled since birth, described herself by stating, "I'm probably an able-bodied woman's worst nightmare" and "I'm an expensive commodity" for HMOs concerned about "the bottom line."

This experience of discrimination had a profound impact on participants' opinions about DWD legislation and on their trust in society to respect the life (and death) choices that people with disabilities may make. One man, disabled since his teens and now in his mid-30s, noted,

> Some people say, "Oh, if I became disabled I would just want to end it." I truly believe that if people have community-based services they would have a fuller life and choices in their own life. Having able-bodied legislators understand that is difficult without [their] being patronizing. Even in progressive towns like San Francisco they still see it as, "We'll take care of you."

Personal Experiences Often at Odds with Abstract or Political Beliefs

A sizable proportion of sample members reported having had personal experiences or anticipating changes in their own lives that would cause them to have opinions at odds with their abstract or political beliefs regarding DWD/PAS legislation. As one participant remarked, "Largely I have a problem with it being legalized, which is distinct from my personal view for me—meaning there should be one law for me and then a general law for society."

Over half of the sample participants had a loved one who had died a painful or difficult death or had themselves faced a near-death experience, or had anticipated changes in their disability that challenged their own opposition to or ambivalence toward DWD/PAS. A woman in her 30s who has been disabled since birth explained to us,

> Unless [other people with disabilities] really go out of their way to learn more about this issue, more than likely they will be pro—you know—pro death with dignity, because they would know a lot more people like my grandmother [who suffered a painful cancer death]. And so, if you're not as politically observant, maybe, if you don't realize how vulnerable people with disabilities

can be to their health providers, you're going to be influenced by these dramatic stories, you know, and they are very dramatic.

Before being exposed to the "official" disability position, this young woman told us that because of her experience with her grandmother she was in favor of DWD/PAS legislation.

Abstract or political beliefs for many were largely based on perceptions of, or direct experience with, discrimination based on disability, race, or class. A distinction sometimes was made in this regard between ideal and real societal conditions. One participant in her 60s stated,

> If we lived in a different kind of society, you know, a much more humane, socially viable society...an egalitarian society where we wouldn't have to worry about doctors deciding, "Well this is— this Negro here ain't worth saving anyway," I could see lots of room for abuse. Lots of room for abuse with legislation like that. Since there's already so much abuse.

Misinformation about the Oregon Law and Its Implementation

A major theme that emerged from the interviews was the degree of misinformation and misperceptions about what Oregon's Death with Dignity Act actually stipulates, as well as who has obtained and used lethal prescriptions in the three years of implementation. For a number of participants, ambivalent or negative feelings about DWD/PAS legislation and the contradiction between personal experiences and abstract or political beliefs were compounded by misinformation concerning the nature and outcomes of the nation's first death-with-dignity law. A woman in her 30s commented,

> What I hear has not been very positive. I hear that people are sometimes almost forced into agreeing to end their life. And knowing that Oregon is probably not much better at providing health care services than it is here in California, you know, it's just an easy way out for health care providers out there to not have to give them more options to live a longer life.

Another participant remarked,

The studies show that in Oregon, once suicide was legalized, an expensive drug for pain was not covered by insurance companies. Their feeling was that if they are having all this pain they can just kill themselves. They have to see a doctor. Well, some shop for the doctor. It is a political statement for the doctors because they are affiliated with the Hemlock society.

The degree of misinformation was so pronounced that the university researchers and the CAG rewrote one of the interview questions early in the data-gathering process in order to provide basic information about the Oregon law before asking participants for their opinion of the legislation.

In discussing the law, respondents raised a number of interesting concerns. Several commented that the requirement that people with a terminal illness not be depressed was "a real catch-22," while others worried about the potential for physician error in estimating remaining length of life. Some participants also commented that the legislation was biased against those people with disabilities whose physical limitations prevented them from being able to self-administer a medication.

Participants were divided between those who felt that the Oregon law had adequate safeguards and protections against abuse and those who felt that the legislation was weak in this important respect. Finally, whether personally in favor of or against DWD/PAS legislation, a number of participants viewed the Oregon law as providing an additional option for people at the end of life, without putting pressure on them to exercise such an option. As a man with a congenital disability remarked,

> I don't think the legislation itself would externally put pressure on a person with a disability to kill themselves. It would simply give them the option. Besides, the Oregon legislation doesn't allow for a person with a physical disability, just the terminally ill.

Substantial Fear of Criticism from Other Disabled People

Over half of the participants in the study responded that they either had experienced, knew someone who had experienced, or feared they would experience criticism if they spoke out in favor of DWD/PAS legislation, regardless of what their own opinion actually was. A man in his 40s, who described himself as "not opposed" to such legislation, said,

I have seen and experienced the disabled community resenting each other for their differences. It is a waste of time. Just accept the differences and cooperate.... [DWD/PAS legislation] needs to be studied and weighed to include disabled people.... [Legislation authors] do not think inclusively about the severely disabled person.... [On the other hand] disability is not a terminal illness [and there's need for] strict controls of doctor judgments.

Similarly, a woman in her 40s who did oppose the legislation remarked,

I can see people with other opinions [about DWD/PAS legislation] being shut up. I don't think it is okay. I think they should be able to give their opinions. But I also see where something is so important and frightening you want to come with one voice.... I think we should have discussions about it.

As noted above, a question about self-identification with an organized disability community was included in the study instrument, and any association between the response to that question and opinions about DWD/PAS legislation was analyzed. This was done because of the widely held belief among both people with disabilities generally and many disability leaders specifically that people who so identify are more likely to oppose such legislation and to agree with the public disability position on this issue. Almost two-thirds of the respondents in this study described themselves as part of a community of disabled people. Of these, close to 60 per cent—regardless of their opinion about DWD/PAS legislation—had personally experienced or knew others who had experienced criticism for expressing support for such legislation or were fearful of expressing support because of the charged atmosphere in the disability community. This group held a range of opinions about DWD/PAS legislation, with the majority expressing ambivalence.

Of the over one-third of respondents who did not self-identify with the disability community, opinions toward the legislation were similarly diverse. And similarly as well, a high proportion (44 per cent) had directly experienced criticism or feared criticism for expressing an opinion in support of DWD legislation, regardless of what their own opinion really was.

The most succinct summary of the conflicted feelings within the disability community regarding the ability to openly discuss DWD/PAS legislation was reflected in the words of a woman in her 50s who was ambivalent about legislation:

> I can see this. There have been a few [disabled] people who wanted to end their lives, and the disabled community has come out in force against it. They think, "Oh no. That's what we fear, we fear people will pull the plug on us if we are in the hospital or another vulnerable situation." But I think we need to listen to all voices...to understand where they are coming from, given their situation.

DISCUSSION

The debate within the disability community about death-with-dignity/physician-assisted suicide legislation has taken place primarily in academic and policy arenas. Less often, and usually in response to a state legislative initiative or legal case, the discussion has broadened to include the lay public. This study attempted to provide an avenue for broadening the discussion within the community of people with disabilities to include some of those outside the traditional academic and policy-advocacy silos.

The study finding that a breadth of opinions about DWD/PAS legislation exists was consistent with the earlier mentioned results of a recent Harris poll (Taylor 2002) that found such attitudes to be highly diverse, mirroring in part the divergence found among the population as a whole. While lacking the generalizability of the Harris data, the qualitative nature of these findings complements the national poll by offering a more in-depth exploration of why some people with disabilities hold the views they do on this highly charged topic. Together with the Harris poll, this study was important precisely because the diversity of opinion about DWD/PAS legislation is largely ignored and denied by both current disability leadership and forces outside this community (Bickenbach 1998; National Council on Disability 1997; Longmore 1987). The denial from within the disability community may contribute to a form of elitism, or "outsider within" mentality, hampering open discussion and increasing polarization. The study findings emphasize the deeply personal and individual nature of how and why people form their opinions toward this legislation. Personal experiences with individual and institutionalized racism, the end-of-life experiences of friends and relatives, and discrimination based on class, gender, or disability were among the factors discussed as helping to shape and influence the positions held.

Within disability academic and policy-development circles, the debate over DWD/PAS legislation typically is framed around the ability—or inherent lack of ability—of a vulnerable population to exercise autonomy in life, as well as end-of-life, decisions. As has been noted, one of the positions asserts that, by definition, membership in a vulnerable group precludes any possibility of exercising self-determination (Longmore 1987; Bickenbach 1998). Carried further, this view affirms that any choice a person with a disability makes in support of DWD/PAS legislation is "morally coerced by the fact of socially limited options" (Bickenbach 1998). The opposing position, while acknowledging the reality of profound stigmatization of people with disabilities as a vulnerable group, recognizes the practical exercise of the right to self-determination for those whose physical impairments make the creative redefinition of autonomy a daily and lifelong necessity (Batavia 1997; Wolfe 1997).

Participants in this study expressed both of these positions, as well as a range of viewpoints in between. Indeed, the lack of a singular position, and the many nuances and caveats in the positions expressed, were an important hallmark of the study's findings. A central finding was that virtually all of the 45 respondents expressed the desire for autonomy in life choices, and all but one respondent (based on religious beliefs) also expressed a desire to choose whether or not to end their lives if faced with a terminal disease or other significant life-changing situations. The commitment to and struggle for autonomy by study participants, if similarly found in larger representative studies, may provide an important key to depolarizing the debate within this community. In this research study, the finding of a strong desire for choice was accompanied almost universally by an experience of disability-based discrimination.

The very high prevalence of such discrimination and stigmatization, and the fact that it frequently came from the participants' own families and communities, was another illuminating theme uncovered in this research. The mistrust of "the system" reported by many study participants reflected negative experiences with many levels of bureaucracy—from education to employment, social services, and health care. DWD/PAS legislation was viewed as coming from and representing the same power structures that are perceived to discriminate against and often deny autonomy to people with disabilities and that stigmatize and marginalize them on both the individual and the group level.

The high levels of disability-based discrimination experienced by participants, as well as the substantial amount of misinformation about the Oregon law, help explain another major finding of this study: many participants reported either personally having experienced, or knowing others who had experienced, criticism and/or the fear of criticism coming from within the community should they speak out in favor of DWD/PAS legislation. Some respondents, for example, raised concerns that public exposure of differences of opinion may further weaken the position of the disabled in broader societal arenas. Others, however, stressed the need for further opening up of discussion within the disability community to possibly counteract this fear. The latter perspective echoed the outcome of *New Mobility* magazine's 1999 reader survey on DWD/PAS legislation. As the editor reported at the survey's conclusion, although the poll had requested simple "yes" or "no" answers, a majority of respondents instead wrote long explanations of their thoughts and feelings (Corbet 1999b). Both the breadth and depth of interest in the *New Mobility* survey—and the considerable interest generated by the present study—may be indicative of a community that deeply desires to air its views and to engage more openly in this debate.

This study was hampered by a number of methodological limitations. The sample was small and nonrepresentative in nature and relied in part on snowball sampling, which can lead to bias in sample selection. The attempt to counter a critical dimension of such potential bias through a reverse snowball sampling technique was of only limited usefulness, as participants generally lacked familiarity with the DWD/PAS views of those they were referring to the study.

In addition, this research was conducted in an atypical region of the country in terms of educational levels, political affiliation, and the size and level of organization of the disability community. Although consistent with the context-specific analytic goals of qualitative research, the nature of the sample further precluded any generalization of the findings.

Limitations should be noted also in relation to two of the questions included in the survey. Although it is not uncommon in qualitative research to modify a question in response to knowledge gained (Denzin and Lincoln 1998; Strauss and Corbin 1990), the rewording of a question concerning opinions about Oregon's death-with-dignity law—after the first few interviews revealed considerable confusion about what the law actually said—was problematic. The modified question, which began with a listing of the law's major stipulations, was helpful to subsequent participants and increased the research team's ability to obtain data on people's reaction to the legislation. However, the need for a wording modification created difficulty in reconciling the few responses to the earlier questionnaire item with those given to the reworded version.

The wording of a second question proved challenging from a coding perspective as well. Respondents were told, "Some people with disabilities who support the idea of PAS or death with dignity legislation have experienced or feared they would experience criticism from other people with disabilities for expressing their support. Please describe your feelings or experiences." This wording of this question was intentionally broad in the hope that respondents who felt reluctant to share their personal experiences or feelings in this area might feel more comfortable discussing those of an acquaintance. The question appeared fruitful in that many respondents offered concrete examples to illustrate ways in which either they or others they knew had felt or feared criticism for expressing their views on this issue. That other study participants chose to return to this issue only after the formal interview had been concluded and the tape recorder turned off also indicates the potential usefulness of such broad and nonthreatening phrasing. In a few cases, however, the double-barreled nature of the question precluded a more precise teasing apart of the feelings and experiences that the study instrument was designed to capture.

Finally, the airing of a widely viewed, six-part series on death and dying in September 2000 on the local Public Broadcasting System station, a month prior to completion of the interview stage, may have contaminated the findings of the study. Several respondents interviewed after the airing reported that watching it had pushed them to think about and challenge some of their own views.

Despite these limitations, the study provided a unique look—of and by people with disabilities—at the views of a diverse group of members of this community regarding a controversial topic. The study further achieved its aim of broadening dialogue within the community. Many participants shared their copies of the study findings as a basis for discussion, a summary report was widely distributed within the disability community, and findings were presented at several national meetings. The project director and some CAG members also used the study findings as they worked to help found a new organization, Autonomy,[1]

---

[1] See the website at <http://autonomy-now.org>. [Since the original publication of this article, this URL has ceased to be active.]

which is designed to honor the desire for choice among people with disabilities.

CONCLUSION

As noted above, the findings of a small, nonrepresentative participatory action research study like this one cannot be generalized to the larger population. However, by helping to illuminate alternative viewpoints and by including within the sample a disproportionate number of people of color and others whose views are less frequently heard, such a study can help bring attention to the complexity of the issue being explored. In that light, this modest qualitative study suggests that, contrary to the most publicized position put forward by the organized disability community, individuals with disabilities may find DWD/PAS legislation to be a highly complex, difficult, and personal issue. It is further instructive that such high levels of complexity and ambiguity about DWD/PAS legislation were found in a study conducted in a part of the country where the organized disability community — with its emphatically stated position opposing such legislation — is particularly strong.

These findings underscore the need for further research, ideally using large representative samples of the US disabled population. The prospects for obtaining such a sample are made more difficult by the lack of adequate data collection where this frequently hidden population is concerned. The use of broad categories to define people with disabilities, for example, and the tendency to collect data based on the utilizing of county services, introduce biases in population definition, which in turn may limit the generalizability of findings. Improved data collection methods that more accurately define this population would enable researchers to better determine the attitudes of people with disabilities toward DWD/PAS legislation and related topics.

Additional research is needed also to further explore the reasons for the apparent disjuncture between the diversity of attitudes held by people with disabilities (as evidenced by the Harris poll findings and further suggested by this study) and the more unitary position expressed by many disability activists. Because the simple survey methods used for most public opinion polls often fail to tease out the ambivalence frequently embedded in expressions of support or opposition for items of interest (Feldman and Zaller 1992; Alvarez and Brehm 1995), such research should include a substantial qualitative component to help illuminate these feelings and concerns.

The findings suggest the need for further research as well on the meaning and embodiment of autonomy. The divergence expressed by some respondents between how they personally would like to be treated and what legislation affecting the broader category of people with disabilities should look like presents a classic case in point. Research that explores this potential disjuncture in more detail, and that considers it in relationship to court documents and other material presented by many disability advocacy groups, would be useful in expanding understanding of the complexities of notions of autonomy and how those notions are portrayed.

In sum, both more qualitative research and more large-scale studies using representative samples are critical to informed policy deliberations that take into account the attitudes and opinions of the often-discounted segment of the population comprising people with disabilities. In the meantime, however, the findings of this study, as well as earlier research (Zola 1979; Hahn 1988) showing very high levels of disability-based discrimination experienced by people with disabilities, may be useful in discussions about the legal and ethical dimensions of DWD/PAS legislation. Such pervasive experience with discrimination may help explain the considerable ambivalence expressed toward such legislation by many study participants and the strong negative position of the majority of disability community leaders. It further points to the necessity of public-health professionals examining their biases and becoming better educated about and sensitized to the real concerns of the disabled and other vulnerable populations regarding this legislation and other critical policy debates.

The lack of accurate information among study participants about the Oregon Death with Dignity Act and the results of its implementation, if corroborated in larger representative sample studies, would suggest the need for widespread education based on facts. Each year the Oregon Health Division issues a report on the implementation of the law. This yearly update is a concise and accessible tool for community education. Its findings reveal, for example, that, to date, the median age of those who have used the law is 69, and as in previous years, the majority of people requesting and using their lethal dose prescriptions under the law (84 per cent in 2002) had cancer (Oregon Health Division 2003). This report also provides an important counter to widespread misinformation, including the erroneous view that large numbers of nonterminally ill people with disabilities are victims of the law.

Physician-assisted and -hastened death regularly occurs in the United States without, except in the state of Oregon, any legal or ethical guidelines (Heilig and Brody 1998; Meier et al. 1998; Lee et al. 1996). At the same time, as Mayo and Gunderson (1993: 329) point out, "We have entered a period when laws which permit assistance in dying are being proposed on a fairly regular basis." Health-policy professionals can play a critical role in helping to further a true community discourse on this subject. Broad community-based discussions — including not only medical professionals, policy-makers, and bioethicists, but also and importantly members of various vulnerable populations — may contribute to setting aside biases and reaching greater consensus on this ethically contentious issue. This discussion must be informed by data available from the only state to have passed DWD/PAS legislation. Similarly, as the present research has suggested, the discourse also should include far more information concerning the depth and breadth of opinions and concerns of people with disabilities. A commitment to the full inclusion of people with disabilities, as well as other underrepresented vulnerable populations, at the policy table is necessary if a meaningful community dialogue is to be achieved.

Finally, the findings of this study have important implications for the disability community. As Roe et al. (1997: 313) have noted, "Strong communities know their history, understand how they are different than others, and find ways to honor their shared paths." It is hoped that the findings of this study, if made widely available to the community of people with disabilities, may make a contribution to broadening the dialogue and internally strengthening the community (Fadem et al. 2003). Such strengthening, it is hoped, may in turn better position members within the community to participate fully in future policy debates about death-with-dignity/physician-assisted suicide legislation.

REFERENCES

Alvarez, R. M., and J. Brehm. 1995. "American Ambivalence towards Abortion Policy: Development of a Heteroskedastic Probit Model of Competing Values." *American Journal of Political Science* 39: 1055-82.

Batavia, A.I. 1997. "Disability and Physician-Assisted Suicide." *New England Journal of Medicine* 336(23): 1671-73.

Bickenbach, J.E. 1998. "Disability and Life-Ending Decisions." In *Physician-Assisted Suicide: Expanding the Debate*, ed. M.P. Battin, R. Rhodes, and A. Silvers. New York: Routledge.

Corbet B. 1999a. "Editorial: Community Assist." *New Mobility: Disability Culture and Lifestyle*, August, 4.

———. 1999b. "Assisted Suicide: What Do We Think?" *New Mobility: Disability Culture and Lifestyle*, September, 44-46.

Denzin, N.K., and Y.S. Lincoln. 1998. "Introduction: Entering the Field of Qualitative Research." In *Strategies of Qualitative Research*, ed. N.K. Denzin and Y.S. Lincoln. Thousand Oaks, CA: Sage.

Fadem, P., M. Minkler, M. Perry, K. Blum, L. Moore, et al. 2001. "Summary of Findings Report — Attitudes of People with Disabilities toward Death with Dignity/ Physician Assisted Suicide Legislation: Expanding the Dialogue." Unpublished report. School of Public Health, Berkeley, CA.

Fadem, P., M. Minkler, M. Perry, L. Moore, and J. Rogers. 2003. "Ethical Challenges in Community Based Participatory Research: A Case Study from the San Francisco Bay Area Disability Community." In *Community Based Participatory Research for Health*, ed. M. Minkler and N. Wallerstein. San Francisco: Jossey-Bass.

Feldman, S., and J. Zaller. 1992. "The Political Culture of Ambivalence: Ideological Responses to the Welfare State." *American Journal of Political Science* 36: 268-307.

Gaventa J. 1981. "Participatory Action Research in North America." *Convergence* 14(3): 30-42.

George, M.A., M. Daniel, and L.W. Green. 1998-1999. "Appraising and Funding Participatory Research in Health Promotion." *International Quarterly of Community Health Education* 18: 181-97.

Glazer, B., and A. Strauss. 1967. *The Discovery of Grounded Theory: Strategies for Qualitative Research*. San Francisco: Sociology Press.

Hagey, R.S. 1997. "Guest Editorial: The Use and Abuse of Participatory Action Research." *Chronic Diseases in Canada* 18(1): 1-4.

Hahn, H. 1988. "The Politics of Physical Differences: Disability and Discrimination." *Journal of Social Issues* 44: 39-47.

Heilig, S., and R.V. Brody. 1998. "Physician-Hastened Death and End-of-Life Care: Development of Community-Wide Consensus Statement and Guidelines." *Cambridge Quarterly of Healthcare Ethics* 7: 223-25.

Israel, B.A., A.J. Schulz, E.A. Parker, and A.B. Becker. 1998. "Review of Community-Based Research: Assessing Partnership Approaches to Improve Public Health." *Annual Review of Public Health* 19: 173-202.

Lee, M.A., H.D. Nelson, V.P. Tilden, L. Ganzini, T.A. Schmidt, and S.W. Tolle. 1996. "Legalizing Assisted Suicide — Views of Physicians in Oregon." *New England Journal of Medicine* 334: 310-15.

Longmore, P.K. 1987. "Elizabeth Bouvia, Assisted Suicide and Social Prejudice." *Issues in Law and Medicine* 3: 141-68.

Madorsky, J. 1997. "Is the Slippery Slope Steeper for People with Disabilities?" *Western Journal of Medicine* 166: 410-11.

Mayo, D.J., and M. Gunderson. 1993. "Physician Assisted Death and Hard
Choices." *Journal of Medicine and Philosophy* 18: 329-42.

Meier D.E., C.A. Emmons, S. Wallenstein, T. Quill, R.S. Morrison, and C.K.
Cassel. 1998. "A National Study of Physician-Assisted Suicide and
Euthanasia in the US." *New England Journal of Medicine* 338: 1193-1200.

Minkler, M., P. Fadem, M. Perry, K. Blum, L. Moore, and J. Rogers. 2001.
"Ethical Dilemmas in Participatory Action Research: A Case Study from
the Disability Community." *Health Education and Behavior* 29: 14-29.

National Council on Disability. 1997. "Assisted Suicide: A Disability Perspective." Position paper, 24 March. Washington, DC: National Council on
Disability.

Oregon Health Division. 2003. "Fifth Annual Report on Oregon's Death with
Dignity Act." Salem: State of Oregon Department of Human Services,
Office of Disease Prevention and Epidemiology. Available online at
<http://www.oregon.gov/DHS/ph/pas/docs/year5.pdf >.

Roe, K.M., C. Berenstein, C. Goette, and K. Roe. 1997. "Community Building
through Empowerment Evaluation: A Case Study of HIV Prevention
Community Planning." In *Community Organizing and Community Building for Health*, ed. M. Minkler. New Brunswick, NJ: Rutgers UP.

Shapiro, J.P. 1993. *No Pity: People with Disabilities Forging a New Civil Rights
Movement.* New York: Time Books/Random House.

Silvers, A. 1998. "Protecting the Innocents from Physician-Assisted Suicide."
In *Physician-Assisted Suicide: Expanding the Debate*, ed. M.P. Battin, R.
Rhodes, and A. Silvers. New York: Routledge.

Strauss, A.L., and J. Corbin. 1990. *Basics of Qualitative Research: Grounded
Theory Procedures and Techniques.* Newbury Park, CA: Sage.

Taylor, H. 2002. "2-1 Majorities Continue to Support Rights to Both
Euthanasia and Doctor-Assisted Suicide." Harris Poll, No. 2. 9 January.
Rochester, NY: Harris International.

Toy, A. 1999. "Assisted Suicide: Issues of Life and Death." *New Mobility Disability Culture and Lifestyle* 10(72): 34-42.

Watters, J.K., and P. Biernacki. 1989. "Targeted Sampling: Options for Study
of Hidden Populations." *Social Problems* 36: 416-30.

Wolfe, K. 1997. "Assisted Suicide: Choice or Coercion?" *New Mobility: Disability Culture and Lifestyle*, April, 42-47.

Zola, I.K. 1979. "Helping One Another: A Speculative History of the Self-Help Movement." *Archives of Physical Medicine and Rehabilitation* 60: 450-56.

Chapter 13

OREGON'S EXPERIENCE: EVALUATING THE RECORD

Ronald A. Lindsay[1]

Since November 1997, Oregon has had in place a statute that authorizes physicians, under certain conditions, to provide terminally ill patients with a prescription for medication that they can take to hasten their deaths. Prior to the implementation of the Oregon Death with Dignity Act (ODWDA), opponents of assisted dying vigorously opposed the new law. In fact, implementation of the ODWDA—initially approved by voters in 1994—was delayed for three years by litigation that sought to prevent the law from going into effect, and opponents successfully campaigned to place a repeal measure on the ballot in 1997. Voters decisively rejected the proposed repeal (60 per cent to 40 per cent).

Those who opposed the ODWDA offered arguments similar to the arguments advanced by opponents of assisted dying elsewhere. These arguments included both ethical objections not amenable to factual refutation and predictions of various harmful consequences. For example, in addition to invoking the sanctity-of-life principle, opponents claimed that assisted dying could not be regulated properly and would result in a large number of patients being coerced or pressured into requesting assistance in dying (Callahan and White 1996; Kass 1993; New York State Task Force on Life and the Law 1994). In their 1996 article, Callahan and White unqualifiedly proclaimed that "it is impossible in principle and in practice to regulate ... [physician-assisted suicide] successfully" (2). Opponents also argued that following legalization, the quality of palliative care would decline (Kass 1989; Miller 1992; Teno and Lynn 1991), that the "vulnerable"—variously defined as women,

---

[1] Originally published in *The American Journal of Bioethics* 9.3 (2009): 19-27.

racial and ethnic minorities, the disabled, the poor, or some combination of these groups—would be adversely affected in disproportionate numbers by legalization (Annas 1993; New York State Task Force on Life and the Law 1994), and that once assisted dying was legalized, inevitably we would begin our fall down the slippery slope to legalizing assisted suicide on demand or nonvoluntary euthanasia (Doerflinger 1989; New York State Task Force on Life and the Law 1994; Pellegrino 1992).

A decade after implementation of the ODWDA, the weight of the evidence suggests that these predictions of dire consequences were incorrect. The records compiled under the ODWDA, the investigations by researchers, and the diligent but largely fruitless efforts of opponents of legal assistance in dying to generate evidence of abuse have all failed to establish the existence of widespread abuses (Goodwin 2004; Oregon Department of Human Services 2008; Sullivan, Hedberg and Hopkins 2001). Moreover, the overwhelming number of persons receiving assistance under the ODWDA are white, well-educated, and financially secure, and their gender approximates that of the general population (Oregon Department of Human Services 2008). With respect to palliative care, there is evidence that the quality of palliative care has actually improved in Oregon since the adoption of the ODWDA (Ganzini et al. 2000; Oregon Department of Human Services 2008). With respect to the dreaded slippery slope, there has been scant effort to expand the classes of persons eligible for assistance in dying or to loosen the regulations that physicians and patients must follow in order for legal assistance to be provided. The wording of the ODWDA remains virtually unchanged. Moreover, there is not a scintilla of evidence to suggest that the ODWDA has caused physicians, patients, or Oregonians in general to value life less.

Nonetheless, some who have evaluated Oregon's record maintain that it is too ambiguous to justify legalization of assistance in dying in other states (Steinbock 2005), while others contend that the evidence actually argues against legalization (Foley and Hendin 2002; Gorsuch 2006). Such conclusions confront us with an important methodological question: How are we to evaluate the evidence from Oregon? As argued below, the assessments of Oregon's experience by opponents of legalization are flawed, in part because they utilize improper criteria for evaluating Oregon's record.

In this article I will first provide a brief argument about the benefits of legalization and, in particular, will explain why the option of physician assistance in dying is so important for the terminally ill. Some may think this is well-trod territory, but the argument provided here draws attention to considerations that are sometimes overlooked. Moreover, we cannot properly evaluate the harms from legalization without weighing them against the benefits. I will then expand on my analysis of Oregon's experience, discussing four major concerns that have been presented by opponents: the supposed negative effects on palliative care, the alleged disparate impact on the vulnerable, the initiation of the slide down the slippery slope, and the problem of abuse, understood to mean the problem of persons receiving assistance improperly (for example, because they were coerced or not competent to request assistance). The problem of abuse will receive more attention because it is the strongest argument against legalization. In the last section I will propose an appropriate framework for analyzing the record from Oregon.

Before proceeding to my argument, a brief word about terminology. This article uses the terms *assistance in dying* or *assisted dying* rather than *assisted suicide*. Use of these terms does not stem from any squeamishness about suicide or a desire to gain a polemical advantage through use of euphemisms. Instead, this terminology reflects a desire for accuracy. The term *physician-assisted suicide* connotes an action in which the physician intentionally participates in bringing about the patient's death (Gorsuch 2006). Under the ODWDA, not only must the patient be terminally ill before requesting a prescription for a lethal dose of medication from his physician, but also the patient maintains control of the process throughout and decides when, if at all, he or she will ingest the medication. More than one-third of the patients who obtain a prescription under the ODWDA never take the drug; others ingest the drug months after it is prescribed (Oregon Department of Human Services 2008). Under these circumstances, it seems more accurate to describe the practice as *physician-assisted dying* than *physician-assisted suicide*.

Let us now turn to a summary of reasons why physician assistance in dying provides an important benefit to some patients.

THE IMPORTANCE OF PHYSICIAN ASSISTANCE IN DYING FOR THE TERMINALLY ILL

It is sometimes forgotten in the debate over assistance in dying that the ODWDA and similar proposed statutes apply only to the terminally ill and require physician consultation. Both of these factors are critical in assessing both the morality of the practice and the wisdom of legalizing assistance in dying.

Respect for autonomy is one reason for supporting legalization of assistance in dying, but it is not a sufficient one. To begin, no state currently prohibits anyone from ending his own life, so it is unclear why a general prohibition on assistance in dying constitutes a substantial infringement of autonomy. In the classic 1958 article against the legalization of assisted dying, Yale Kamisar made a similar point, arguing that the extent to which laws against assisted dying infringe on liberty and autonomy interests had been overstated because prohibitions of assisted suicide are directed against the person providing assistance, not the person receiving the assistance. Accordingly, it would seem that any person's interest in escaping a life found unacceptable to that person could be accommodated by a simple policy of noninterference. As Kamisar put it,

> Finally, taking those who may have such a desire [to die], again I must register a strong note of skepticism that many cannot do the job themselves... [A] laissez-faire approach in such matters [may be preferable to] an approach aided and sanctioned by the state. (1958: 1011)

Kamisar's contention has some merit if one focuses only on the physically robust. Indeed, offering assistance to those truly capable of doing "the job themselves" may improperly circumvent an important psychological barrier to hasty, ill-considered decisions — leaving aside any moral problems that may be raised by the offer of such assistance.

However, the issue being debated is *physician* assistance in dying for the *terminally ill*. Let us first consider the importance of terminal illness. Ending one's life without assistance is an option only for those with access to the proper means and the ability to use them. One crucial fact acknowledged only infrequently by the opponents of assistance in dying is that the State and its licensed agents control access to medications that are efficient in bringing about a peaceful death. Because the State maintains control of the dispensation of barbiturates and similar medications, a person must have access to firearms, knives, or other such means of death *and* possess the ability to use these means effectively to commit suicide without assistance. In the last stages of a terminal illness, "the patient is likely to lack the capacity to commit suicide on his own" (Posner 1995: 238). Many of the terminally ill are physically frail and have impaired mobility. One survey found that approximately 75 per cent of those Oregonians who obtained assistance in dying were confined most of the time to a bed or chair (Ganzini et al. 2000). For someone in such a situation, being denied assistance effectively results in that person's being kept alive against his or her will. The terminally ill have a much stronger liberty interest in assistance in dying because, unlike the physically healthy, they need assistance to die.

A person's terminal illness also provides some assurance that a request for assistance in dying is not the product of some hasty, irrational decision. A person who is dying is beyond the hope of any cure and is in an objectively verifiable condition. (The exceptional case of a mistaken diagnosis does not mean a diagnosis of terminal illness is not objectively grounded, no more than the rare mistake regarding the existence of a pregnancy implies that pregnancy is not objectively verifiable.) These patients are not volatile individuals reacting to serious but passing problems, such as rejection by a lover or taunting from schoolmates. Instead, they face an inevitable death. The statistics collected in Oregon confirm that virtually all those who have sought assistance have been in the terminal stages of cancer, amyotrophic lateral sclerosis (ALS), AIDS, or some other terminal, distressing condition (Battin et al. 2007; Oregon Department of Human Services 2008). Simply put, for those requesting assistance in dying, their choice is between dying peacefully now or dying within a short time after what they regard as pointless suffering.

Some may question my claim that the terminally ill cannot "do the job themselves," provided they act quickly. Granted, not everyone who has just been diagnosed with a terminal illness will lack the vigor necessary to end life by a gunshot to the head, hanging, or similar lethal actions. However, if we want the terminally ill both to live as long as possible *and* to consult with their physicians about alternatives to a hastened death, then legalizing assistance in dying is the best way to accomplish these objectives. A ban on assistance in dying pushes the terminally ill who are concerned about future suffering to end their lives while they are still able, without discussing their plans with anyone. Not only might some bring about their deaths while they still have months left to live, but also others may hasten their deaths unnecessarily because if they had been able to wait to make a decision about requesting assistance in dying, they would not have found their condition unbearable. In other words, assuming we desire a regulatory scheme that encourages persons to live as long as they find their lives worthwhile, a policy of permitting physician assistance in dying for the terminally ill is much more likely to accomplish this objective than is a ban on it (Posner 1995: 247-48).

The claim that legalizing assistance in dying actually encourages many to live longer, and some to forego hastening their death altogether, is not mere speculation. Oregon's experience confirms this. Although approximately 15 in 100 dying Oregonians seriously consider hastening their deaths, and although many of these discuss this option with their physicians, only approximately 1 in 100 decide to request assistance, and only approximately 1 in 700 actually use prescribed medication to hasten their deaths, with rates of death under the ODWDA in recent years ranging from approximately 13 to 15 per 10,000 deaths (Oregon Department of Human Services 2006: 4-5; 2008; Tolle et al. 2004: 111-18; Ganzini et al. 2000). Significantly, research surveys suggest that the rate of legal physician-assisted dying in Oregon may be significantly less than the rate of *illegal* physician-assisted dying in other, states, and there is evidence that illegal assistance in Oregon is extremely rare (Emanuel, Fairclough and Emanuel 2000; Emanuel 2002; Ganzini and Dobscha 2004; Tolle et al. 2004). Knowledge that escape from intolerable suffering is always available can diminish the felt need to hasten one's death, and allowing physicians to discuss all options with their patients promotes a thorough consideration of all these options, including alternatives to hastened death such as hospice care. Almost all of us want to live as long as we are able to squeeze something worthwhile out of our lives; we will not choose death unless we believe there is no alternative, and we will not choose death now unless we believe the option of a relatively peaceful death otherwise will be foreclosed.

Let us now consider the significance of the physician's role, and why it is important not just to allow assistance in dying, but to authorize *physician* assistance in dying. The role of a treating physician is crucial in the context of end-of-life care. Legalizing physician assistance in dying allows the terminally ill to discuss all aspects of their condition and treatment, including their anxieties and fears, with a knowledgeable and—one would hope—caring expert. Legalization encourages a frank exploration of options, permitting a patient to make an informed decision. Sensitive physicians will use the full extent of their training and experience in assessing the patient's condition and the prospects for effective alternatives to hastening death, such as palliative care. The physician's expertise is important in evaluating, in consultation with the patient, which alternatives might be feasible. Similarly, the physician's expertise is important for determining whether the patient is competent to make a decision concerning the course of treatment. Surveys indicate that Oregon physicians take seriously their responsibility of screening patients for signs of depression or impaired judgment (Ganzini et al. 2000). Forbidding physicians to discuss the option of a hastened death will not stop some patients from hastening their deaths; it will prevent them from receiving appropriate professional care.

In sum, legalizing physician assistance in dying shows both compassion and respect for the desire of the terminally ill to make critical decisions about the course of their own lives, whereas denying them the possibility of this assistance compels them to live in suffering. Moreover, legalizing this option brings added benefits, including increasing the likelihood that patients' decisions about end-of-life options will be informed and deliberate as opposed to uninformed and precipitous. Of course, individual rights always must be balanced against the common good. It is both legally advisable and morally permissible, if not obligatory, to restrict the actions of some individuals if these actions pose a significant threat of harm to others. On some occasions, these restrictions may even require significant infringements on personal freedom. It is time now to consider in more detail the experience under Oregon's statute to determine whether Oregon's record confirms or refutes the claims that legal assistance in dying inevitably results in serious harmful consequences.

THE EXPERIENCE IN OREGON

A Beneficial Impact on Palliative Care

Directly contrary to the predictions of opponents of legal assistance in dying, who argued that post-legalization physicians and other healthcare workers would expend little effort to alleviate the symptoms of the terminally ill—because these patients could just "go ahead" and die—there has been no evidence to indicate that the quality of palliative care in Oregon has diminished. To the contrary, there is evidence that the quality of palliative care has actually improved in Oregon since implementation of the ODWDA (Ganzini et al. 2000; Oregon Department of Human Services 2008). Many physicians have made a conscious effort to improve their knowledge of palliative care so they can offer appropriate treatment options to their patients (Ganzini et al. 2000; Ganzini et al. 2001). The reality is that in a state where assistance in dying is legal, physicians and other health-care workers are motivated to spend more time with patients in discussions about end-of-life choices, carefully exploring options and arranging for palliative care as an alternative to hastening death. Few treating physicians want their patients to choose hastened death as the first option.

Opponents of legal assistance in dying often try to frame the debate as a choice between effective palliative care and assistance in dying (Foley and Hendin 2002). This is misleading, to say the least. No responsible advocate of assistance in dying has ever suggested that we should de-emphasize palliative care. Furthermore, the evidence indicates that inadequate palliative care is not a significant motivation for requesting assistance in dying. It is striking that more than 85 per cent of the patients who have availed themselves of assistance in dying under the ODWDA were in a hospice, usually considered the gold standard for palliative care (Ganzini et al. 2006; Oregon Department of Human Services 2008). Patients are electing to hasten their deaths, not because they are receiving inadequate care, but because the care they receive cannot remedy their anxiety, frustration, hopelessness, and anguish.

No Disparate Impact on the Vulnerable

The argument that we should not legalize assistance in dying because of the disproportionately adverse, or "disparate," impact that the practice allegedly will have on various vulnerable groups has a very questionable moral premise—one that remains largely unexamined, despite the frequency with which this argument is advanced (but see Coleman 2002; Lindsay 2002; Spindelman 2002). To consider this an important argument against legalization, one must believe that it somehow makes a difference whether proportionally more blacks than whites, more women than men, or more poor than wealthy, for example, are pressured into choosing assistance in dying. When one thinks about this proposition, one should be able to see that it is not morally sound. What matters is whether someone has been coerced or pressured into requesting assistance in dying, *not* the race, sex, ethnicity, etc., of that person. Coercing a rich white male into requesting assistance in dying is just as morally repugnant as coercing a poor African American woman into making such a request.

In any event, we do not have to debate at any length the normative portion of the disparate impact argument, because Oregon demonstrates that it lacks empirical support. The persons who have received assistance in Oregon are overwhelmingly white (in fact, not one African American has received assistance); most are financially secure; most are men; and they are better educated than the population as a whole (Battin et al. 2007; Oregon Department of Human Services 2008). Even those who are doubtful about legalization have acknowledged that fears about abuse of the vulnerable have not materialized (Steinbock 2005). In fact, if there is any disparate impact, it may be felt by those patients who want assistance but who lack the education and confidence to assert their rights forcefully enough to obtain assistance. That is regrettable, but it may be the unavoidable price of having adequate procedural safeguards in place.

No Slippery Slope

Many predicted that once the practice of physician assistance in dying was legalized, neither Oregon nor any other state would be able to contain the practice of hastening death to competent, terminally ill patients. Instead, the practice inevitably would be broadened to include anyone who wants to die for any reason, or perhaps Oregon would legalize nonvoluntary euthanasia—the mercy killing of someone not presently capable of making her desires known—or even involuntary euthanasia.

It is beyond dispute that the tumble down the slippery slope has not occurred in Oregon. The same classes of patients are eligible for assistance in dying that were eligible in 1997. The law has not been broadened, nor has there been any serious effort to do so. Of course, the slippery slope argument is itself very slippery. Its advocates can always resort to the excuse that although the predicted fall into the abyss has not happened yet, it is just a matter of time. But no one has offered a persuasive argument why expansion of the practice to morally dubious cases is inevitable.

Some have tried, however. Consider this statement from the oft-cited report of the New York State Task Force on Life and the Law (1994: 100-01):

A policy of allowing assisted suicide or euthanasia only when a patient voluntarily requests an assisted death, and a physician also judges that assisted suicide or euthanasia are appropriate to relieve suffering, is inherently unstable. The reasons for allowing these practices when supported by *both* a patient's request and a physician's judgment would lead to allowing the practices when *either* condition is met...In particular cases, and more broadly over time, assisted suicide and euthanasia would be provided based on any serious voluntary request by a competent patient, regardless of his or her medical condition. (emphasis in original)

This reasoning is not sound. If legislation stipulates that two conditions are necessary for a certain action, why is the conjunction of these two conditions "inherently unstable"? Before being admitted to practice, lawyers in all states must establish both that they have the knowledge to be an effective lawyer (by passing a bar examination or graduating from an in-state law school) and the moral character to be an officer of the court. Since these requirements have been put in place, no state has decided to abandon either the knowledge or the character requirement, nor would there be a good reason for doing so. Similarly, there is no compelling reason to abandon either the ODWDA's requirement that the patient's request be voluntary or the ODWDA's requirement that a physician certify the patient as competent and terminally ill.

The argument of the New York State Task Force used a version of the slippery slope argument often called the *conceptual slope*; in other words, legalization for terminally ill patients will serve as precedent for offering legal assistance to other categories of individuals. There is also the *causal slope* version, which maintains that legalizing assistance in dying will bring about a material change in our attitudes, in particular by corroding our respect for life (Doerflinger 1989). One of the unnoticed flaws of the causal slippery slope argument is the implicit assumption that allowing assistance in dying necessarily shows less respect for life. But what is the justification for assuming that the operative attitude of those who favor assistance in dying for the terminally ill is a diminished respect for life? No empirical study suggests that those who favor assistance in dying have less respect for life. At least arguably, the primary operative attitudes are respect for self-determination, compassion for the plight of someone who is suffering, and a desire by (some) physicians to provide appropriate end-of-life care. Respecting the right of a terminally ill person to make his own decision about the course of his remaining days hardly seems to evince an attitude of diminished respect for life. Therefore, a key element of the causal slippery slope argument is missing. The projected progressive erosion of respect for life can hardly take place if it has not even started. Certainly, there is nothing to suggest that Oregonians have a diminished respect for life.

Effective Prevention of Abuse

We have disposed of three of the consequentialist arguments against legalization rather quickly, but, frankly, that is all the attention they deserve. The next argument has more weight. This is the argument that persons will obtain prescriptions even though they should not be receiving assistance, because they are not competent, they are being coerced or manipulated, and so on.

In examining the evidence from Oregon, we should first remind ourselves of the procedural requirements that must be satisfied before patients receive assistance (see Oregon Rev. Stat., secs. 127.800-995). To be eligible for assistance, patients must have received a diagnosis from their attending physician that they have a terminal illness that will cause their death within six months, and they must be capable of making their own health-care decisions. A second physician must confirm both the diagnosis of a terminal illness and the patient's competence. As a prerequisite to receiving assistance, patients must make a series of voluntary, verifiable requests that confirm that the desire for assistance is durable: the patient must make two oral requests for assistance, separated by at least fifteen days, and one written request, signed in the presence of two witnesses. To help ensure that the patient's decision is an informed one, treating physicians are required to inform the patient of alternatives to a hastened death, such as comfort care, hospice care, and enhanced pain control. Moreover, a patient must be referred to counseling if either the prescribing or the consulting physician believes she might be suffering from a psychological disorder that can cause impaired judgment. Provided these safeguards are followed conscientiously, the possibility that a noncompetent or coerced individual will receive assistance is small.

The procedural hurdles a patient must surmount prior to receiving assistance are not the only safeguards. The eligible patient maintains control of the process throughout. The patient may rescind her request, decline to fill the prescription she receives from her physician, or decide not to take the medication once she fills the prescription. As already indicated, many who receive a prescription never take the medication. As an additional safeguard, the patient must ingest the prescribed drug; the physician may not administer it.

The procedural requirements and safeguards of the ODWDA cannot, of course, guarantee that all requests for assistance are truly voluntary and informed. Nonetheless, it is striking that despite the microscope under which the Oregon practice has been examined, there is not one undisputed example of a coerced request for assistance or similar serious abuses. (Some disputed examples are discussed below.)

In addition to complying with the foregoing procedural requirements, physicians must maintain records of the process leading to the prescription and share them with the Oregon Department of Human Services. These records provide the basis for an annual, public report that provides details about both the number of patients who receive a prescription and the number who actually use the prescribed medication, as well as their medical condition and various other relevant data. The mandated records have been supplemented by interviews and empirical research carried out both by state officials and by private researchers (Ganzini et al. 2000; Ganzini and Dobscha 2004; Ganzini et al. 2006; Hedberg, Hopkins and Kohn 2003; Sullivan, Hedberg and Fleming 2000; Sullivan, Hedberg and Hopkins 2001; Tolle et al. 2004).

These records and research results are important for assessing some aspects of the abuse argument. Prior to legalization, opponents of legal assistance in dying predicted that physicians would place thousands of patients on a fast track to death, with the implication that many patients would be receiving assistance improperly. However, from the inception of the ODWDA through 2007, only approximately 570 patients received a prescription for medication that would assist them to die and — strikingly — only approximately 340 patients actually ingested the lethal dose of medication that was prescribed for them (Oregon Department of Human Services 2008). Oregon has not become a suicide mill.

In addition, there is no substantial evidence that someone who was noncompetent or not in a terminal condition received assistance (although a few patients have lived significantly longer than six months following their diagnosis). No physician or relative of the patient has been charged with improperly providing assistance or coercing the patient into hastening his death. With respect to data that might indirectly reflect pressure to request assistance, the state's reports reveal that only three of the patients who have ingested the prescribed medication, or less than 1 per cent, were uninsured, and only nine, or approximately 3 per cent, mentioned financial concerns as a motivation for seeking assistance in dying. (From the reports, it is not clear what these concerns might be; it may simply be that some patients believe any further treatment would be a waste of money, even when insurance covers most of the costs.)

Critics of the ODWDA have focused on a couple of cases that supposedly illustrate how easily the ODWDA's safeguards can be circumvented, namely the notorious cases of "Helen" (not her real name) and Kate Cheney (Foley and Hendin 2002; Gorsuch 2006; Steinbock 2005). (The case of Michael Freeland is sometimes cited as another example of abuse [Steinbock 2005], but it does not pass the threshold for serious consideration and will not be discussed here.) An objective appraisal of these cases indicates that they do not provide convincing evidence of abuse. I will not discuss all the details of these cases because the reader can readily access the other works that provide this information, but suffice it to say that the case of Helen is often cited as an example of "doctor shopping" and hurried decision making, among other problems (Gorsuch 2006). However, although Helen did switch physicians at least in part to find a physician who would be willing to help her hasten her death, the physician who refused to help her had not known her for very long; he was treating her only because her previous primary physician had recently left the practice (Goodwin 2004). As to the alleged rush to die (Helen was still mobile), the timelines set forth in the ODWDA were followed, and there is nothing to indicate that Helen was not terminal or that her decisions to request and to ingest the medication were not voluntary (Goodwin 2004). Do patients not have a right to seek a different physician if the physician who is treating them refuses to provide care that is legal and, as far as the patient is concerned, appropriate and necessary? If this had been a case involving withdrawal of life-sustaining treatment, would the same allegations of abuse have been made?

With respect to Cheney, some claim that her relatives, in particular her daughter, were eager to see her die and that Cheney may have been unduly influenced by her daughter (Foley and Hendin 2002; Gorsuch 2006). Again, a closer look at the facts reveals that these concerns are based on suppositions and a tendentious interpretation of events. A psychologist did describe the daughter as "somewhat coercive," but the same psychologist thought that Cheney was capable of making her own decisions. In addition, the director of the hospice program in which Cheney was enrolled subsequently interviewed her apart from her daughter, found her competent, and determined that her decision to request assistance was voluntary (Goodwin 2004). This conclusion was supported by a palliative-care expert who also interviewed Cheney.

If a physician or consultant describes a relative of the patient as "somewhat coercive," this certainly indicates that caution in evaluating the patient's request is appropriate. However, the record indicates that caution was exercised. If suggestions by a relative that a course of action might be appropriate always prevented a patient from subsequently following that particular course of action, this would work a revolution in medical care. Would those who cite the Cheney case as an example of an involuntary request have had the same reaction if the daughter had urged Cheney to reject assistance in dying, and Cheney subsequently decided to forego assistance despite the suffering her cancer was causing?

As to the alleged "eagerness" of Cheney's daughter to see her die (Foley and Hendin 2002: 157), this is a claim that lacks any support apart from the perceptions of those who made it. The evidence cited by Foley and Hendin is that Cheney's family honored her request to take the medication "now" after Cheney came home from a week-long stay at a nursing home. But if the family had resisted this request, would that resistance not have been coercive? Or is a relative's reaction only illicit if it is a reaction that respects the patient's desire for a hastened death? Foley and Hendin also make the interesting assertion that "[s]ending Kate to the nursing home was sending her a message that she was a burden." The millions of families who send their beloved relatives to nursing homes so they can receive better care might take issue with that assertion. The cases of Helen and Ms. Cheney are more revealing of the fierceness of the opposition to legalization of assistance in dying than they are of flaws in the regulatory framework.

In sum, what evidence there is does not indicate that abuse is common. Arguably, the evidence suggests that there has not been any case of abuse, but no definitive conclusion about the complete absence of abuse can be drawn. First, there may be abuses of which we are not aware. Second, as the cases of Helen and Ms. Cheney indicate, the inferences to be made from some cases are disputed. In light of the residual uncertainty about the existence of abuses, we need to consider how the evidence from Oregon should be evaluated.

WEIGHING THE EVIDENCE

Three of the four anti-legalization arguments based on harmful consequences can be refuted with confidence based on the data from Oregon. The "disparate impact on the vulnerable" argument is based on numbers, so numbers suffice to refute it. It is undeniable that the ODWDA has not been broadened, so the slippery slope argument also has been refuted. Refutation of the palliative care argument is not quite as straightforward, but there is no evidence that the quality or availability of palliative care has declined, some evidence that its availability and quality have improved, and substantial evidence that most patients are not motivated to request assistance because of inadequate palliative care.

This leaves the abuse argument. As indicated, there remains some uncertainty about the level of abuse, but that does not imply that we cannot make reasonable conclusions based on the available evidence. Opponents commonly make four mistakes in evaluating the evidence.

Improper Reliance on Individual Cases

It is common in the debates over assistance in dying for opponents to claim that no matter how compelling an individual's suffering may be, that does not imply that we should legalize assistance in dying; we need to consider the effects of legalization on the public as a whole. This is a valid point. In terms of evaluating the wisdom of legalization, the facts of any one case, while not irrelevant, are not dispositive. This point is equally valid, however, in evaluating the significance of alleged individual cases of abuse. Even assuming the safeguards of the ODWDA were circumvented in the cases of Helen and of Kate Cheney, this does not indicate that the safeguards have been circumvented in a large number of cases, much less that the ODWDA should be repealed and legalization resisted in other states. If we required perfection in any regulatory scheme that exposed persons to a risk of serious harm, we would not allow trucks on the road, meat in the stores, imported toys, or trial by jury.

Improper Skepticism about the Data and the Statute's Safeguards

Some opponents argue that scattered information about individual cases is all that can be used in evaluating the ODWDA because there is no reliable summary information. Furthermore, there is no reliable mechanism in place to report or control abuses because the Oregon Department of Human Services has no investigatory authority, there is no express requirement in the ODWDA to report abuses, and no identifying information is made public (Foley and Hendin 2002; Gorsuch 2006; see also Callahan and White 1996).

First, it is worth noting that opponents sometimes forget that the information compiled under the ODWDA has been supplemented by a number of empirical studies and surveys across several disciplines, including medicine, nursing, and social work. Obviously, even taken together, the official reports and the studies and surveys cannot provide a complete picture of Oregon's practice, but they can provide us with sufficient information to draw some reasonable conclusions, including the fact that most physicians are conscientious in screening patients and that the rate of legal assistance in dying in Oregon is remarkably low. If Oregon has created a culture of death and the safeguards of the ODWDA can be easily circumvented, this last statistic is inexplicable. If a physician can achieve immunity by marching a patient through steps that opponents maintain do little to control a physician's conduct, then the physician will utilize the ODWDA's procedures rather than risk prosecution. Frequent abuses would produce a much higher rate of assisted dying.

With respect to the alleged deficiencies in the statute regarding reporting of abuses, these criticisms ignore both the relevant social and legal background. That there is no express statutory requirement to report abuses does not in any way suggest that Oregonians should not report abuses to the proper authorities. Assisting a suicide remains a crime in Oregon; specifically, it is categorized as second-degree manslaughter (Oregon Rev. Stat., sec. 163.125). A physician who assists a patient to die can avoid criminal liability and administrative discipline if and only if she complies fully with the procedural requirements of the ODWDA. There is no need for a separate reporting requirement of abuses under the ODWDA, nor is there a need to invest the Department of Human Services with investigatory authority, because Oregon's criminal justice system and professional discipline system remain in place. Those concerned about abuses can report to the police, the local prosecutor, or the Oregon Board of Medical Examiners (BME) any physician who coerces a patient, who provides assistance to an incompetent, who does not engage a second, consulting physician, and so on. The BME maintains a website that permits concerned persons to submit complaints about physicians electronically. Given the diligent monitoring of practice under the ODWDA by opponents, it strains credulity to claim that abuses have not been reported or investigated simply because the ODWDA relies on existing state agencies to do their job.

Admittedly, not disclosing the identity of patients and physicians to the general public makes it somewhat more difficult to detect and report individual cases of abuse, but this nondisclosure policy does not constitute a significant obstacle to appropriate regulation. Those most likely to report abuses would be persons with intimate knowledge of the physician-patient interaction in question, so they would already know the identity of the participants.

Finally, the operating assumption of opponents appears to be that because the safeguards of the ODWDA *could* be circumvented by the unscrupulous or uncaring, this means they inevitably *will* be circumvented in a substantial number of cases. Typically, this is not the assumption on which we base our regulation of the work of health-care professionals. To the contrary, we assume that most will adhere to established standards of conduct with little direct oversight. The supposition that many Oregon physicians will be less than conscientious in the context of assistance in dying lacks any support beyond rhetoric.

Failure to Consider the Benefits of Legalization

Weighing the advantages and disadvantages of a proposed course of action requires one to take account of the advantages, but one would not know that from reading some of the arguments against legalization. Gorsuch (2006) has trivialized assistance in dying as a "lifestyle choice" (222), implying that its significance is roughly the same as a decision to take up golf. For those not blinded by ideology, however, the availability of assistance in dying is important for a substantial portion of the terminally ill, whether or not they actually decide to hasten their deaths.

Granted, there is no universally accepted metric for measuring and balancing the benefits to be gained from legalization against the risks to some resulting from possible abuses. Only a thoroughgoing utilitarian could indulge in the fantasy that we can assign precise values to these benefits and risks and then compare the two. But simply because we do not know exactly where to draw a line does not mean that there are no situations that clearly fall on one side of the line or the other. How many cases of coerced or nonvoluntary requests should result in reconsideration of the wisdom of legalization? A few cases of abuse should not require us to block or repeal legislation that provides a substantial benefit. In another regard, scores of coerced or nonvoluntary requests each year should produce doubts about whether assistance in dying can be appropriately regulated.

Fortunately, the record in Oregon is clear enough that we do not have to engage in a difficult balancing between the harms caused by abuses and the benefits provided to patients by the ODWDA. One cannot state with certainty that there have been no abuses under the ODWDA. But one can state with some assurance that the ODWDA's safeguards have prevented the level of abuses that opponents predicted and that would counsel against legalization.

Failure to Utilize an Appropriate Baseline for Evaluating the Risks of Abuse

I have already alluded a few times to our practice of allowing patients to forego life-preserving treatment. It is useful to compare this practice to legal assistance in dying and the alleged harms that result from legalization. In particular, in thinking about the tolerable level of abuses from legal assistance in dying, it is helpful to bear in mind the fact that competent patients have virtually an absolute right to refuse treatment, even when this refusal will hasten their deaths. Moreover, compared to the regulation of requests for assistance in dying under the ODWDA, there is negligible regulation of the withdrawal or withholding of life-sustaining treatment for competent patients. No law requires the patient refusing treatment to make a series of oral and written requests over a set period of time. No one is required to probe the patient's reasoning or to suggest alternatives to having the treatment stopped. And, typically, no investigation is carried out to determine whether the patient is being improperly influenced by relatives who are concerned about long-term care obligations or financial burdens. Because there is little oversight over this process, we can only guess at the number of deaths that have been improperly hastened, yet we have determined that the freedom to decide on a course of treatment is important enough that patients should be allowed this choice, even though the availability of this option probably results in some abuses, with fatal consequences.

Some may argue that the practices of assistance in dying and foregoing life-sustaining treatment are morally distinguishable, but if they are, they are distinguishable for reasons unrelated to the risks of harm attendant on the practice. One cannot consistently argue that assistance in dying is too risky, but concede that allowing patients to forego life-preserving treatment is not. This is especially true given that we have at least some reliable data indicating that abuses are infrequent under the ODWDA, but nothing comparable with respect to the nationwide practice of allowing patients to forego life-sustaining treatment. Opponents of legalizing assistance in dying often seem to suggest that the risks of harm from legalization are unique. They are not. We already allow patients to incur the risks of a coerced or nonvoluntary death so some might have the freedom to avoid the suffering associated with a prolonged death. Any appropriate analysis of the risks of legalized assistance in dying must take into consideration analogous practices we deem acceptable.

CONCLUSION

There are, of course, reasons for opposing legalization of assistance in dying other than the supposed harmful consequences of legalization. But to the extent that public policy on this issue is supposed to be informed by evidence regarding these alleged harmful consequences, the Oregon experience argues for legalization of assisted dying in other states, provided that these states follow a regulatory scheme similar to Oregon's. Significantly, at the time of this writing, citizens in Washington are attempting to put on the November 2008 ballot an initiative that would, if approved, result in adoption of a law substantially similar to the ODWDA.[1]

Admittedly, the fact that the ODWDA has been in effect for ten years without causing the dreadful consequences that opponents predicted does not guarantee that other states will have similar experiences. However, Oregon's record is more relevant for determining public policy on this issue than the armchair speculation of philosophers. The Supreme Court in *Washington v. Glucksberg*, 521 U.S. 702 (1997), urged that the debate over assistance in dying be conducted and resolved in the "laboratory of the states." Oregon's experiment has provided us with results that, while not definitive or free of all ambiguity, are sufficiently clear to provide guidance. It is time to apply these results to other states.

REFERENCES

Annas, G. 1993. "Physician-Assisted Suicide—Michigan's Temporary Solution." *New England Journal of Medicine* 328: 1573-76.

Battin, M., A. van der Heide, L. Ganzini, G. van der Wal, and B. Onwuteaka-Philipsen. 2007. "Legal Physician-Assisted Dying in Oregon and the Netherlands: Evidence Concerning the Impact on Patients in 'Vulnerable' Groups." *Journal of Medical Ethics* 33: 591-97.

Callahan, D., and M. White. 1996. "The Legalization of Physician-Assisted Suicide: Creating a Regulatory Potemkin Village." *University of Richmond Law Review* 30: 1-83.

Coleman, C. 2002. "The 'Disparate Impact' Argument Reconsidered: Making Room for Justice in the Assisted Suicide Debate." *Journal of Law, Medicine & Ethics* 30: 17-23.

---

[1]   [Editor's comment: This initiative was ultimately successful. Assisted suicide became permissible in Washington state in March 2009.]

Doerflinger, R. 1989. "Assisted Suicide: Pro-Choice or Anti-Life?" *Hastings Center Report* 19(1): S16-19.

Emanuel, E. 2002. "Euthanasia and Physician-Assisted Suicide: A Review of Empirical Data from the United States." *Archives of Internal Medicine* 162: 142-52.

Emanuel, E., D. Fairclough, and L. Emanuel. 2000. "Attitudes and Desires Related to Euthanasia and Physician-Assisted Suicide among Terminally Ill Patients and their Caregivers." *Journal of the American Medical Association* 284: 2460-68.

Foley, K., and H. Hendin. 2002. "The Oregon Experiment." In *The Case against Assisted Suicide: For the Right to End-of-Life Care*, ed. K. Foley and H. Hendin. Baltimore, MD: Johns Hopkins UP, 144-74.

Ganzini, L., and S. Dobscha. 2004. "Clarifying Distinctions between Contemplating and Completing Physician-Assisted Suicide." *Journal of Clinical Ethics* 15: 119-22.

Ganzini, L., T. Beer, M. Brouns, M. Mori, and Y. Hsieh. 2006. "Interest in Physician-Assisted Suicide among Oregon Cancer Patients." *Journal of Clinical Ethics* 17: 27-38.

Ganzini, L., H. Nelson, M. Lee, D. Kraemer, T. Schmidt, and M. Delorit. 2001. "Oregon Physicians' Attitudes about and Experiences with End-of-Life Care since Passage of the Oregon Death with Dignity Act." *Journal of the American Medical Association* 285: 2363-69.

Ganzini, L., H. Nelson, T. Schmidt, D. Kraemer, M. Delorit, and M. Lee. 2000. "Physicians' Experiences with the Oregon Death with Dignity Act." *New England Journal of Medicine* 342: 557-63.

Goodwin, P. 2004. "The Distortion of Cases in Oregon." In *Physician-Assisted Dying: The Case for Palliative Care and Patient Choice*, ed. T. Quill and M. Battin. Baltimore, MD: Johns Hopkins UP, 184-89.

Gorsuch, N. 2006. *The Future of Assisted Suicide and Euthanasia*. Princeton, NJ: Princeton UP.

Hedberg, K., D. Hopkins, and M. Kohn. 2003. "Five Years of Physician-Assisted Suicide in Oregon." *New England Journal of Medicine* 348: 961-64.

Kamisar, Y. 1958. "Some Non-Religious Views against Proposed 'Mercy-Killing' Legislation." *Minnesota Law Review* 48: 969-1042.

Kass, L. 1989. "Neither for Love nor Money: Why Doctors Must Not Kill." *Public Interest* 94 (Winter): 25-46.

———. 1993. "Is There a Right to Die?" *Hastings Center Report* 23(1): 34-43.

Lindsay, R. 2002. "Should We Impose Quotas? Evaluating the 'Disparate Impact' Argument against Legalization of Assisted Suicide." *Journal of Law, Medicine & Ethics* 30: 6-16.

Miller, R. 1992. "Hospice Care as an Alternative to Euthanasia." *Law, Medicine & Health Care* 20(1-2): 127-32.

New York State Task Force on Life and the Law. 1994. *When Death Is Sought: Assisted Suicide and Euthanasia in the Medical Context.* New York: New York State Task Force on Life and the Law.

Oregon Department of Human Services. 2006. *Eighth Annual Report on Oregon's Death with Dignity Act.* Available at <http://www.oregon.gov/DHS/ph/pas/docs/year8.pdf>.

———. 2008. *Summary of Oregon's Death with Dignity Act-2007 and Tables 1 and 2.* Available at: <http://www.oregon.gov/DHS/ph/pas/ar-index.shtml>.

Pellegrino, E. 1992. "Doctors Must Not Kill." *Journal of Clinical Ethics* 3: 95-102.

Posner, R. 1995. *Aging and Old Age.* Chicago: U of Chicago P.

Spindelman, M. 2002. "Legislating Privilege." *Journal of Law, Medicine & Ethics* 30: 24-33.

Steinbock, B. 2005. "The Case for Physician Assisted Suicide: Not (Yet) Proven." *Journal of Medical Ethics* 31: 235-41.

Sullivan, A., K. Hedberg, and D. Fleming. 2000. "Legalized Physician-Assisted Suicide—The Second Year." *New England Journal of Medicine* 342: 598-604.

Sullivan, A., K. Hedberg, and D. Hopkins. 2001. "Legalized Physician-Assisted Suicide in Oregon, 1998-2000." *New England Journal of Medicine* 344: 605-07.

Teno, J., and J. Lynn. 1991. "Voluntary Active Euthanasia: The Individual Case and Public Policy." *Journal of the American Geriatrics Society* 39: 827-30.

Tolle, S., V. Tilden, L. Darch, E. Fromme, N. Perrin, and K. Hedberg. 2004. "Characteristics and Proportion of Dying Oregonians who Personally Consider Physician-Assisted Suicide." *Journal of Clinical Ethics* 15: 111-18.

Chapter 14

PALLIATIVE SEDATION: AN ESSENTIAL PLACE FOR CLINICAL EXCELLENCE

Philip C. Higgins and Terry Altilio[1]

Palliative care, at its most comprehensive level, attends to the physical, emotional, social, and spiritual needs of patients and their families along the continuum of life-threatening illness. The idea that patients and their families might receive comprehensive care long before they actually face the end of life seems unfathomable in our broken health-care system. Yet on a day-to-day basis, clinicians across disciplines and across specialty practices have the opportunity to weave palliative-care principles into their work, addressing symptoms and suffering in a way that helps minimize fear and builds patient and family confidence in our ability to serve them.

While this article is about "palliative sedation," a complex clinical and ethical topic, it is also about the critical work of exploring the fears, memories, and myths that patients and families harbor regarding serious illness and death. It is about understanding the beliefs and values that infuse clinicians' experiences and combine with their expertise as they consider options for care at the end of life, only one of which might be palliative sedation.

Any discussion of palliative sedation necessitates an awareness of the political, legal, and policy-driven world in which we practice and live. In addition to our own internal expectations, increasing public, media, and legislative attention and accountability regarding end-of-life care drives the need for clarity, excellence, and advocacy for the best interests

---

[1]   Originally published in *Journal of Social Work in End-of-Life & Palliative Care* 3.4 (2007): 3-30.

of patients and families. Concurrently, upholding the core values of client self-determination and autonomy requires that social workers inform their practice with knowledge and inquiry, insuring that their participation in each clinical case reflects the meticulous process of comprehensive, individualized assessment of the multidimensional factors that shape the application of these values.

DEFINITIONS AND INCIDENCE

Many phrases used in the palliative-care dialogue have evolved in day-to-day exchange without a vehicle for consensus building. As the field grows, the need and desire to develop and standardize practice invites an analysis of the words that are chosen to discuss the complex medical, ethical, psychosocial, and spiritual dimensions and decisions that are at the heart of palliative and end-of-life care. The literature and research on the treatment of intractable physical and existential suffering with sedating medications reflect this process of articulating the implicit and explicit issues reflected in the language. Attempts are being made to bring clarity to the dialogue and build consensus and a base of commonality on which to design research and enhance practice.

The following are some of the words and phrases chosen to describe the use of sedating medications to manage intractable symptoms and suffering at end of life:

- sedation in the imminently dying (Carver and Foley 2000)
- terminal sedation (Chater et al. 1998)
- total sedation (Rich 2006)
- controlled sedation (Taylor and McCann 2005)
- palliative sedation (Cherny and Portenoy 1994)
- respite sedation (Rousseau 2005)

In an effort to clarify the consistency within the terminology, Morita, Tsuneto, and Shima (2002) published findings from a systematic literature review. While limited to only seven articles, findings suggested that sedation involved two core factors: severe suffering refractory to standard management and the inclusion of sedative medications to relieve distress. The authors concluded that "palliative sedation therapy" can be defined as "the use of sedative medications to relieve intolerable and refractory distress by reduction in patient consciousness" (452). They suggest that the variation in the literature may reflect sub-categories such as degree of sedation (total), duration (respite, inter-mittent), target symptoms (physical versus existential or psychological suffering), and target populations (imminently dying, terminally ill). The phrase "terminal sedation" is felt by some to add further confu-sion, as it might mean sedation for a terminally ill patient or infer seda-tion for the purpose of terminating a life (Chater et al. 1998). Another troubling phrase that pervades health-care environments and end-of-life communications is "hang a morphine drip." These words often have ominous and unspoken implications for clinicians, patients, and fami-lies that stretch beyond symptom management and need to be made explicit so that the intent and goals of this treatment are openly dis-cussed and myths and misunderstandings challenged.

The lack of a universal definition can act as both a cause and a con-sequence of clinician confusion and may be one factor that influences estimates of the numbers of patients who are reportedly sedated to manage symptoms and suffering at end of life. Rousseau (2005) posits a range from 2 to 52 per cent, while Cowan and Walsh (2001) estimate between 15 and 30 per cent. In addition to clarity of language, other fac-tors that may inform this variation in range include diagnostic issues; medical and ethical aspects; confusion related to the intent and goal of interventions; and cultural and religious factors that affect the clini-cian, patient, and family's relationship to the complex phenomenon of suffering. For example, is there consensus as to the meaning of "termi-nally ill" or "imminently dying"? What is the significance of the fact that much of the literature related to palliative sedation relates to oncology patients? Do some see cognitive compromise as an expected consequence of progressing illness, while others attribute such symptoms mainly to the medications used to manage symptoms or induce sedation?

For the purposes of a focused discussion and to create a theoretical and clinical background for this article, we will use the following terms and definitions:

- *Palliative sedation* involves a decision, in consultation with an informed patient, family, or agent to provide sufficient doses of medications to reduce consciousness in terminally ill patients with the goal of relieving physical symptoms, or existential or psychological suffering, deemed intractable after expert inter-vention. The intent is to relieve symptoms and suffering, not to hasten death (Cherny and Portenoy 1994; Rousseau 2005).
- *Suffering* is a unique and personal experience that involves

severe distress associated with threat to the integrity and intactness of the whole person (Cassell 1991). While suffering may or may not include physical symptoms, it must include consciousness. Emotional or existential suffering may not have a physical component, as in anticipation of death and the implicit threat to one's future (Peppin 2003).

- *Withdrawing/withholding of treatment* includes decisions about interventions such as resuscitation, mechanical ventilation, vasopressors, hemodialysis, transfusions, antibiotics, parenteral nutrition, and hydration.
- *Physician-assisted suicide* involves the provision of medications to a patient with decisional capacity, with the understanding that the patient may use the medications to hasten their death. While the clinician provides access to the lethal doses of medications, the act to hasten death is in the control of the patient, making it essentially different from both palliative sedation and euthanasia. Physician-assisted suicide is legal only in Oregon.
- *Voluntary euthanasia* is the intentional act of causing the death of another who is competent and has made the request. Euthanasia is illegal and may be prosecuted under laws that preclude murder or assisting in another's suicide. The intent is to end life.
- *Nonvoluntary euthanasia* is the intentional act of causing the death of another who lacks the cognitive capacity to make decisions due to conditions such as dementia, delirium, or coma. In situations where clinicians covertly decide that treatments are futile or judge that another's quality of life is not worth living, acts such as withholding treatments or increasing medications in the absence of symptom exacerbation, with or without knowledge or consent of family or proxy, would be another example of nonvoluntary euthanasia (Cohen et al. 2005).
- *Refractory symptom* refers to a symptom that cannot be managed despite expert efforts to identify a tolerable therapy that does not compromise consciousness (Cherny and Portenoy 1994). Undoubtedly subjective, this description may include physical symptoms such as pain, dyspnea, or agitation, as well as psychological and/or spiritual suffering.
- *Respite/intermittent sedation* involves sedating and then awakening patients after a predetermined time, with the goal of providing temporary respite from suffering (Rousseau 2005).

- *Imminently dying* refers to a prognostic assessment that a person is close to death—ranging from hours, days, or at most a few weeks (Jansen and Sulmasy 2002).

While consensus around definitions is a good place to start in addressing palliative sedation, many essential aspects of palliative care are woven through this topic. They include an understanding of the unique values, beliefs, and goals of the patient and family; excellence in the assessment of symptoms and suffering; and careful consideration of the ethical and legal precepts and psychological, social, and spiritual factors that influence patients, families, and professional caregivers. Beyond the lived experience of the patient, a decision to sedate influences the bereavement process and the legacy of the death as it is woven into the fabric of a family history. Was a person helped to avoid a death with uncontrolled pain? Will a bereaved family feel robbed of the remaining time with their loved one because sedation changed the quality of their time together? These are some of the complex and rich aspects of palliative care that are reflected in the debate that surrounds palliative sedation. It is a decision that is made in the present, but it also has an impact for the future of the families as well as the clinicians who collaborated in decision making and provided care for the patient.

LEGAL AND ETHICAL BACKGROUND

In 1997, the Supreme Court of the United States, in *Washington v. Glucksberg* and *Vacco v. Quill*, upheld New York and Washington state statutes prohibiting assisted suicide, unanimously ruling that there is no constitutional right to assisted suicide. The court was also unanimous in affirming that state laws are constitutionally valid in recognizing the distinction between prohibiting physician conduct that intentionally hastens death and that which may hasten death but is intended for other purposes such as relief of pain (Burt 1997). For many, the ruling signaled a constitutional right to palliative care, but for others, the Court's endorsement of sedation was essentially an embracement of euthanasia.

The ethical justification for sedation that may hasten death stems from the principles of double effect as well as respect for patient autonomy, individualized values and beliefs, and informed consent. Double effect is a Roman Catholic doctrine that evolved to provide guidance in circumstances where it is impossible to avoid all harmful consequences. Its four precepts require that

- the nature of the action is good or morally neutral;
- the good effect is intended with the possible negative effect foreseen but not intended;
- the negative effect is not the means to the good effect; and
- there exists proportionality with the good effect outweighing the negative (Rousseau 2005).

While many believe that palliative sedation is justified through application of the principle of double effect, there is considerable variance in the views and perspectives of experts.

CONTEXT AND CONTROVERSY

In palliative sedation, the intended outcome of treating refractory symptoms and suffering is thought to outweigh the possible negative consequence of hastened death. An additional negative effect that receives much less attention is the diminished consciousness that influences the end-of-life experience for both patient and family. When days of life are limited, the quality of time and the value of each exchange can be profoundly meaningful. Because the care team's role in facilitating the "loss of social selfhood" through diminished consciousness (Davis and Ford 2005) is essentially different from this same loss occurring as a consequence of natural disease progression, this outcome also warrants ethical and professional justification. Following the weighing of the risk and benefit, the losses to relationship and self-actualization are direct outcomes of sedation and require explicit consideration in clinical evaluation and discussions of informed consent (Lynch 2003).

It is important to recognize that the requirement for informed consent of patient and family does not preclude internal conflicts for staff, such as the physicians who write the orders or the nurses who administer the medications. In the home-care setting, family members may be asked to administer sedating doses of opioids or sedatives to manage symptoms such as agitation or myoclonus. The choice to diminish consciousness and the fear that death may be hastened are troubling ethical and moral dilemmas, and one need only consider the national dialogue and disagreement around the care of Terri Schiavo to savor the depth of feelings around these and related issues.

When "intent" is the basis for justification, one relies on the integrity and insight of the clinician as well as the patient, family, or proxy whose input helps to inform assessment and decision making. It presupposes not only that physicians and other participating professionals have expert knowledge, but also that their personal motives and needs do not unduly influence their recommendations and decisions or lead them to essentially abandon patients through the act of sedation. Just as patients and families can become exhausted and overwhelmed, professional caregivers experience a myriad of responses in caring for patients at the end of life (Quill 1993; Wein 2000). The clinician's feelings of failure and fatigue can have unconscious bearing on the complex process of decision making. In addition to the transparency necessary in these processes, transdisciplinary collaboration can enhance the shared nature of multidimensional assessment, encourage introspection, and potentially diminish the weight given to unconscious feelings and needs.

The concept of "intention" becomes more complex in cases of existential suffering or psychological distress, when patients are often alert, eating and drinking, cognitively intact, and possibly without any physical symptoms. Patients may feel unable or unwilling to face their dying and have an autonomous and covert intent to hasten their death. Ethical and clinical analysis would need to include a judgment as to whether existential suffering meets the standard of proportionality (Jansen and Sulmasy 2002). Some assert that just as one cannot kill the body in order to manage physical symptoms, so one cannot kill the existential self to manage existential suffering. Is it possible that sedation for existential suffering is a representation of a medicalization of end-of-life spiritual and psychosocial struggle (Davis and Ford 2005)? These considerations require reflection, knowledge, and communication with patients, families, and colleagues as clinicians struggle not only to maintain their moral, ethical, and professional responsibilities but also to insure that they do not abandon patients to their suffering (Quill and Cassel 1995; Rich 2006).

Orentlicher (1997) and Billings and Block (1996) argue that at times palliative sedation is tantamount to euthanasia. The issue is not whether it is morally and ethically appropriate to treat symptoms and suffering aggressively, but whether the combination of inducing unconsciousness and withholding food and water is the cause of death (Quill, Lo and Brock 1997). Without these combined acts, the person would live longer. While it is legally and ethically permissible to withdraw hydration and nutrition and allow death to occur, this is understood as essentially different from assisted suicide and euthanasia, because the person dies of the disease rather than through an act of a clinician. Orentlicher (1997) compares palliative sedation to the removal of a feeding tube in a person in a persistent vegetative state, who dies because the condition creates the inability to take in nutrition. In palliative sedation it may be that the clinician-created state of diminished consciousness renders the person unable to eat. The argument is that the principle of double effect justifies sedation but does not justify the withdrawal of hydration and nutrition, as this act does not treat symptoms or suffering. These clarifications and disagreements highlight the need to create processes that demand and document the critical assessment and thinking that informs each decision made in settings of uncertainty, blurred perspectives, and clinical or ethical complexity.

While there is debate related to artificial hydration and nutrition, there seems to be consensus that prior to sedation, a do-not-resuscitate order needs to be in place. It would seem incongruous to request an intervention that could potentially extend life while at the same time considering sedation for intolerable suffering. Confusion or lack of consensus around this option would redirect clinical attention from decisions about sedation to the myriad of factors that inform patient and family perspectives on resuscitation.

Another essential question is whether sedation does in fact hasten death. While the research is complicated by lack of consensus, retrospective, and anecdotal data (Rousseau 2000), the few studies that focus on this topic examine the use of opioids, analyzing patterns and types, mean doses, and effect of opioid use on survival. Sykes and Thorns (2003) found that when sedatives were given to cancer patients at the end of life and titrated against relief of a specific symptom, impairment of consciousness was not the objective, but rather it accompanied the use of medications. Generally sedation was used over a short period during the dying process and, in the context of specialist palliative care, was not associated with shortening life. The authors suggest that the principle of double effect is irrelevant to symptom control at end of life, and that invoking this ethical precept unnecessarily perpetuates the misconception that symptom control is inevitably associated with hastening death and possibly exacerbates a reluctance to provide relief to a very vulnerable group of patients.

Another interesting and challenging issue implicit in this discussion is the concept of an intractable or refractory symptom, the determination of which emanates in part from the expertise of the clinician. Those who do not know about such interventions as respite sedation, opioid rotation, adjuvant medication, and treatment of side effects may come to offer sedation simply because they lack knowledge of other options. Similarly, clinicians may have no expertise or experience to evaluate the potential effectiveness of invasive interventions that might provide relief. This same lack of understanding may result in clinicians' thinking that they have euthanized a patient when what they have done is aggressively treated symptoms appropriately or compassionately in the setting of end-of-life care.

How does one ensure that refractory symptoms and the consequent decision to offer sedation are not premature or a reflection of the inadequate training of clinicians, rather than a result of thorough medical, psychosocial, spiritual, and ethical analysis? Does the perception of palliation as "comfort care," the antithesis of "aggressive" intervention, invite a less rigorous approach to assessment and evaluation, which if done scrupulously might reduce the need for palliative sedation (Fainsinger 1998; Peppin 2003)?

This same conundrum factors into judgments about "imminent death." When prognosis is hours to days, the value attributed to the remaining time may be different than if there are weeks of life remaining. Patients with days to live may or may not choose to tolerate symptoms in exchange for conscious time with their families. If sedation is chosen, it impacts a shorter period of remaining life and there may be less chance that death will be hastened, if at all. When a patient's prognosis is a matter of weeks, there is a greater chance of hastening death and a longer period of time that families may need to be helped with complex feelings including ambivalence, impatience, relief, and guilt (Taylor and McCann 2005). Patients, families, and professionals involved in these discussions need to count on expertise in prognostication, just as all involved need to ensure expertise in multidimensional assessment of, and interventions with, symptoms and suffering.

IS THERE A ROAD TO CONSENSUS?

The recognition of the complexity of this intervention is reflected in the growing interest in developing consensus. In Japan, a national interdisciplinary committee including five palliative-care physicians, four nurses, two oncologists, two psychiatrists, two anesthesiologists, two bioethicists, a medical social worker, and a lawyer constructed a clinical guideline to be tested for efficacy. While there may be limitations consequent to cultural and legal differences between the US and Japan, the consensus nature of the process and the algorithms are important additions to a growing literature that discusses the complexities and provides guidance to the clinical work (Morita et al. 2005; Rousseau 2004, 2005). The European Association of Palliative Care has convened a panel of international experts, also with the goal of developing a consensus document related to these issues (Rousseau 2005).

Guidelines and consensus statements are important, as they lend guidance and add credibility to decisions that frequently may appear arbitrary, insular, isolating, or colored by subjectivity (Lo and Rubenfeld 2005). There is often intense emotional distress and internal struggle for patients, families, and staff when symptoms and suffering are intractable. The ethical, legal, medical, psychosocial, spiritual, and emotional aspects converge, and it is helpful to distinguish among the various facets of the narrative so that critical thinking infuses the process of decision making and the menu of potential interventions.

Palliative Sedation and Social Work Practice

Social workers have the opportunity to play a unique role in addressing the clinical and ethical issues that are embedded in the discussion of palliative sedation. Because palliative sedation in the setting of existential suffering and refractory symptoms is so complex, care teams must adopt a critical lens through which to develop a clear understanding of the terminology as well as the medical, psychosocial, spiritual, legal, and ethical issues that infuse each patient and family scenario and converge to influence the situation at hand. This is consistent with Miller, Hedlund and Murphy's (1998) three-tiered model for assessing and evaluating patient requests for assisted suicide, a model that looks not only at the interplay between desire for death and patient/family understanding about disease progression, symptom management, and related care concerns, but also at the cultural meaning of such requests and the unique psychosocial concerns that may also contribute to a desire for hastened death. A multifactorial assessment leads to a comprehensive range of potential interventions and is central to the person-in-environment perspective that infuses all good social-work practice. Such an assessment may be modified to respond in a crisis situation or applied over time, as in the patient case example discussed below.

The social worker's unique training creates a level of comfort and expertise in using this model to evaluate the clinical components implicit in any consideration of palliative sedation. Rather than unequivocally promoting or automatically rejecting palliative sedation as an intervention, the social worker who adopts a critical thinking, person-in-environment approach can work with the team to highlight the multiple factors to be explored in the setting of "intractable suffering," including the impact on patient, family, team members, and the social worker her/himself. Performing such a careful and multifactorial assessment enables us to identify the underlying root causes and conditions that guide health-care providers to appropriate interventions, which may or may not include palliative sedation.

The Case of Julia

Patient Narrative

Julia was a 75-year-old, Irish-American woman with flaming red hair and a personality to match. She grew up as the eldest of three daughters in a working-class family in lower Manhattan, the larger portion of her childhood colored by the Great Depression and World War II. Unlike some of her peers, Julia completed high school; like most, she did not attend college but instead went to work in a local factory to help support her family. Julia married young and soon bore two children. Her husband died in his forties and Julia never remarried, supporting her family with various clerical jobs and working into her seventies. Life passed by uneventfully until 2001, when she was diagnosed with lung cancer. The next two years witnessed several unsuccessful courses of chemotherapy and radiation, eventually resulting in admission to an acute-care cancer facility for pain and symptom management and, ultimately, end-of-life care.

Soon after arriving at the hospital, Julia began expressing a desire for hastened death. She struggled with the devastating impact of a disease that had taken away her long-cherished independence and left her instead with rather foreign feelings of helplessness and meaninglessness. She found herself in a self-described "limbo state," where she was neither well enough to live her life as she wished, nor sick enough to immediately die. Julia became increasingly withdrawn and isolated. The staff psychiatrist diagnosed mild depression and prescribed antidepressants. Julia continued to openly yearn for death or, at the very least, for a deep sleep that would take her away from her disheartening new reality. During weekly rounds, a team member raised palliative sedation as a future treatment option. Some members of the team agreed that, should other interventions fail, palliative sedation might be the only means of providing Julia with relief by inducing the sleep she so longed for, while others felt troubled by the thought of sedating a patient with no acute or unmanageable physical symptoms and who was not imminently dying.

Assessment
Assessing Julia's case through a multifactorial, person-in-environment lens reveals how the physical, social, spiritual, economic, cultural, environmental, personality-based, and psychological components of Julia's story, together with the roles and responses of her family and care-team members, may have contributed to her desire for hastened death.

Physical
Prior to her cancer diagnosis, Julia had few serious medical problems. Unsuccessful treatments left her with a limited life expectancy as well as lingering doubts about the ability of her care providers to successfully manage her illness and consequent symptoms such as pain and shortness of breath. While Julia had witnessed her husband's death from lung cancer, an experience that would greatly color her response to her own illness, it is significant to note that Julia's lung cancer marked the first time in her life that she herself had been incapacitated by disease.

Social
Julia was one of three sisters. Her older sister, with whom she was close, had died several months earlier, leaving her with one remaining sibling. Her husband's death from lung cancer in his early forties had made Julia a single mother who raised her son and daughter alone. Julia described a close relationship with her daughter and her daughter's family, but her relationship with her son had grown increasingly distant over the years. Her daughter's debilitating rheumatoid arthritis prevented her from performing many daily activities, including driving, which limited her ability to visit Julia. Julia described a supportive network of friends and coworkers, but work responsibilities and geography limited their ability to visit as well. This social history reflects many avenues for further assessment and intervention, including the deaths of Julia's husband and sister (the former from the very illness she now faced, and the latter very recently), her tenuous relationship with her son, and her potential for social isolation.

Spiritual
Julia described herself as a "lapsed Catholic," having stopped attending Mass and participating in other religious rituals over the years. How-

ever, she felt at peace with God. While Julia's religious background did not immediately manifest itself in her response to her disease, it is significant that Julia maintained a personal sense of spiritual connection. Exploration of her existential distress from a spiritual perspective might lead to greater understanding of the meaning of suffering, her connection with the transcendent, and its relevance to her wish for death.

Economic

While socioeconomic or financial status may seem insignificant in an assessment of this kind, both can play a role in a patient's, family's, or agent's wish for hastened death. Socioeconomic status may have an impact upon a patient or family member's trust in the ability and willingness of the health-care system to provide the best care, and lack of access to care may result in unaddressed health problems and untreated illness. Limited education and lack of access to medical information may have an impact upon patient and family understanding of disease processes or available treatments, both of which have the potential to increase fear and anxiety and compromise the ability to follow treatment protocols (Agency for Healthcare Research and Quality 2004).

Beyond issues of access to care, money and its use are influenced by personal values and beliefs. Some view their resources as a legacy to benefit their family and would not want to exhaust their resources to address an incurable illness. Conversely, and of greater concern, a family may have ulterior financial motives for keeping a loved one alive or for encouraging a loved one's death. Many of these issues did not apply to Julia, who, though working class, enjoyed access to good medical care and had no overt financial concerns. An important consideration for the astute clinician, however, would be to ensure that Julia's limited educational background did not interfere with her understanding of medical information and leave her with increased fear or anxiety around issues of prognosis and symptom management.

Physical Environment

The influence of the actual physical environment on a patient and family can be profound. Hospitals and other medical settings may increase fear and anxiety, or they may represent safety, reassurance, and hope. These symbolic associations may increase at the end of life, due to the potential for increased physical and emotional vulnerability and dependence of patients and families. While Julia's hospital enjoyed a reputation for quality care, members of the surrounding community also regarded it as "a place where people go to die." As such, Julia viewed her hospitalization with fear and resignation. It is important to consider how the staff in such facilities may interact with patients. Intentionally or not, staff may convey pity, sorrow, or discomfort through their verbal and nonverbal behaviors. Staff discussions overheard by patients and families can increase fear and anxiety or, conversely, relay a message of comfort and confidence. Finally, witnessing the deaths of other patients on a daily basis may have an enormous cumulative effect on patients who see their own future in the quality of the care and the deaths that surround them. Indeed, it is this final point that proved most relevant to Julia, who lay in her bed day after day staring into the room across the hallway. From this room Julia heard what she described as the agonized moans of patients in distress, patients unable to breath and racked by pain, but helpless to do anything about it. Julia had seen countless new faces in that bed during her first few weeks at the hospital. She imagined the lifeless, ravaged bodies of the prior occupants wheeled out of the room atop a gurney, covered head to toe by a white sheet, destined for the morgue. It would only be a matter of time, she feared, before her neighbors imagined the same thing about her.

Team and Family Members

Just as we assess the impact of the physical and social environment on a patient's suffering and consequent desire for sleep or hastened death, we must be equally mindful of the concurrent emotional reactions that arise for the patient's family and care team members when faced with a patient's request to die. The care team should treat patient and family as one unit of care, eliciting input and information from both and addressing any family distress that may accompany the patient's desire to die. Family members or decision-making agents may implicitly or explicitly suggest that clinicians hasten death or sedate the patient. It is crucial for the team to acknowledge these communications, with the goal of identifying the contributing factors and clarifying the perceptions and beliefs underlying these requests. It is important to explore whether it is the perceived suffering of the patient that generates such a request, or rather the suffering of the family member or agent in witnessing the patient's condition. This effort to clarify and partialize the clinical experience will focus the nature of interventions. Conversely, family members may ask that a patient in severe distress not receive pain medication that would affect her level of awareness, placing more value on keeping the patient conscious than comfortable. Once again, the beliefs, feelings, and perceptions of both patient and family need to be considered in the process of assessment, decision making and treatment planning.

Members of the care team may also have strong moral, ethical or religious responses to these complex situations. Care providers may feel like they are "failures," question their own effectiveness as clinicians, or doubt their ability to manage patient and family suffering, medically or otherwise. Significant countertransferential responses may arise, and responsibility lies with individual practitioners and teams to ensure that their clinical judgment is not unduly influenced by personal feelings or emotions resulting in interventions that are too hasty or aggressive or, conversely, too delayed or ineffective (Wein 2000). It is of paramount importance that care providers monitor and assess their own motives for offering or discouraging options, recalling the rights of patients and families to consider available treatments in an autonomous manner, free from provider bias, and with respect for the individual's assessment of his or her own quality of life. At the same time, it is important for team members to respect the roles and responsibilities of their colleagues, as each provider has a distinct "distance from the act" in any patient or family intervention. In cases involving the delivery of sedating medications, the nurse who actually administers the medicine will have an experience distinct from the doctor who prescribes or the social worker who addresses the family's emotional fallout. This highlights the importance of clear team communication and mutual appreciation of the skills, responsibilities, and values that different providers bring to patient and family care.

In assessing the reciprocal impact of Julia's family and care providers on her request for hastened death, several of the above issues are immediately apparent. Her family did not request hastened death or sedation and reacted very strongly when the team raised palliative sedation as a possible intervention for Julia's existential distress. Julia's sister initially questioned whether this type of sedation wasn't simply a form of euthanasia. Her daughter recalled her father's own traumatic death and wished to avoid the same for her mother, yet she did not want sedation or sleepiness to diminish the quality of their remaining time together. Members of Julia's care team, too, presented with a range of clinical, moral, personal, ethical, and emotional responses, expressing strong feelings about her request to die and the subsequent discussion of palliative sedation. The psychiatrist felt strongly that, given enough time, Julia's desire to die would be mitigated by effective antidepressant therapy.

The attending physician, too, struggled with the concept of sedation as a treatment for existential, rather than physical, suffering. Some nursing staff were familiar and comfortable with the therapeutic use of sedation, while others felt that sedation to treat any type of suffering was uncomfortably close to euthanasia. The social worker hoped that palliative sedation would be a treatment of last resort, and felt that the immediate clinical and ethical mandate was to carefully explore the feelings, thoughts, and fears behind Julia's desire to die before pursuing interventions that would dampen her consciousness. The treatment plan was influenced not only by the clinical issues but also by the anticipated length of time Julia was expected to live.

Personality
Beyond Julia's brash and seemingly self-explanatory exterior lay a complex and sometimes contradictory woman. Julia described herself as someone who had always enjoyed life and had many friends, but who also required solitude. Her wry and contagious sense of humor colored much of her worldview, but it also served to deflect, distance, and mask her discomfort and anguish. She was self-sufficient and independent, but vulnerable to the slights of those she loved. Above all else, Julia was a woman with a zest for life. Having lived her entire life in the driver's seat, only now to be faced with an illness that threatened her independence as well as her very existence, she would sooner get out of the car than sit helplessly in the passenger seat.

Psychological
In assessing requests for hastened death or sedation, comprehensive psychological evaluation—including assessment of depression and anxiety, the patient's worldview and perception of his or her advanced illness, the patient's coping mechanisms, and other emotional factors such as fear and hopelessness—is crucial. Julia had a distinctly pragmatic worldview. She was well aware of the pains and sorrows of the world and accepted them as unavoidable, if unbearable, facts of life. She attributed much of this view to her Irish-American cultural heritage. She did not struggle with the progression of her illness so much as with the prospect of remaining conscious to witness that progression come to its ultimate fruition.

It is helpful to understand the factors that help differentiate depression in the seriously ill patient. While there is an emerging literature concerning patients who request assisted suicide in Oregon [see, for example, Chapter 13 above], there is little research exploring the complex experience of patients, families, and staff when palliative sedation is requested or when it is offered as a treatment for refractory symptoms or suffering. The literature pertaining to patients who request assisted death can help inform this discussion if one assumes that each of these patient groups is ultimately requesting the same thing: relief of suffering. Miller, Hedlund and Murphy (1998) encourage social workers to complete a comprehensive assessment of patient coping history, underlying mental illness, significant depression, and other relevant psychiatric concerns in cases involving requests for assisted suicide; the same is necessary when sedation is being considered or hastened death is requested. While there is considerable emphasis placed on the importance of assessing depression in those who express a desire for death (Von Gunten, Ferris and Emanuel 2000; Block 2001; Billings 2000; Breitbart et al. 2000), many cite the difficulty of diagnosing depression in the terminally ill (Billings 2000; Muskin 1998; Werth and Holdwick 2000) due to the similar somatic symptoms found in both terminal illness and depression (Van Loon 1999). While Van Loon (1999) suggests an emphasis on psychological, rather than somatic symptoms, she acknowledges that this approach raises a subsequent dilemma by its assumption of a normative psychological response to terminal illness.

Hoffman (2000) emphasizes the possibility that an expressed desire for hastened death may have multiple contributing biopsychosocial factors. Farberman (1997) cautions clinicians against assigning inappropriate psychiatric diagnoses to dying patients, insisting that "[t]he first task … [must be] to separate the patient's prospective grief, fear of dying, fear of the unknown, and fear of pain from clinical depression" (545). Werth and Holdwick (2000) likewise underscore the need to explore a patient's reasons for desiring death in an attempt to understand the process by which she arrived at such a conclusion, rather than assume that it is irrational. Indeed, the clinician will often find that fear, rather than depression, often underlies a patient's suffering and desire for death. The exploration of worst fear and fantasies may lead to specific concerns such as loss of control, meaning or function; fears of dependence or being a burden; hopelessness; or loss of dignity (Billings 2000; Block 2001; Breitbart et al. 2000; Loscalzo and Jacobsen 1990; Quill, Lo and Brock 1997; Von Gunten, Ferris and Emanuel 2000). Kissane, Clarke and Street (2001) encourage assessment of dying patients for what they term "demoralization syndrome…a psychiatric state in which hopelessness, helplessness, meaninglessness, and existential distress are the core phenomena" (13). The authors assert that interventions other than sedation, including cognitive behavioral therapy, can be effective in addressing existential distress for patients who suffer from such a syndrome, and they likewise highlight a multifactorial approach in assessing such patients, whose "wishes, desires, impulses, and fears are governed by the context of their illness and the environment in which it is being managed" (19).

Understanding the patient's use of adaptive or maladaptive coping mechanisms to deal with those responses is just as important as assessing a patient's emotional and cognitive responses to progressing illness. Julia's desire for hastened death could, in and of itself, be considered either an adaptive or maladaptive coping mechanism. Seeing that there was no possibility of recovery and knowing that death was inevitable, Julia assumed the identity of what Muskin (1998) referred to as "the living dead," wanting to escape her limbo state and "get it over with." Some might view this desire as reflective of an inability to adapt to and cope with the emotional distress of advanced illness and the concomitant losses that advanced illness entails. It is equally important, however, to consider that such requests may also stem from other, more adaptive, sources. Van Loon (1999) writes,

> Some patients make statements about desiring death as a way of coping with their circumstances. These statements may be used to promote feelings of control, invite a discussion of existential concerns, or elicit help. Patients may also express these feelings in a more positive manner, saying, "I've lived a good life. I'm ready to go," as a way of inviting reflection on the meaning of life. (265)

A deeper and more comprehensive exploration involved listening and dialogue at a pace determined by Julia. This approach revealed a number of fear responses contributing to Julia's desire for death (Mount 1996). While she was withdrawn, isolated, and acknowledged intermittent feelings of depression, the root of Julia's fear and hopelessness lay in her unique personal history, quite beyond the realm of depression. Having witnessed the trauma of her husband's death from lung cancer, a death marked by severe agitation, incoherence, and shortness of breath, Julia could only imagine that a similar fate awaited her. She had no interest in taking her final, agonized breaths while tied down to a bed, suffocating to death as she believed her husband had done — indeed, as she had *watched* him do with her own eyes — and leaving her daughter with the same haunting legacy. The care team, for their part, anticipated the psychological toll of balancing Julia's fears and suffering against the option to blunt her consciousness. Did existential distress grounded in fear and hopelessness warrant as serious an intervention as sedation? How could the team measure or judge a subjective and elusive entity such as suffering? At what point would they feel they had safely exhausted all other options for treatment? Who was to say that sedation should be used only as a last-line approach? Was it possible that Julia's suffering would be assuaged by her evolving trust and the commitment of staff to aggressively manage her symptoms as she died?

Intervention
A wide range of interventions are available to social workers assisting patients and families where refractory symptoms and existential suffering beg a response, whether immediate or over time. Patients often share with social-work clinicians their thoughts and wishes about hastening their death and their fears related to the potential for suffering at the end of life. At the same time we often feel uncomfortable and ill equipped to discuss options for treatment of symptoms and suffering (Portenoy et al. 1997), creating the potential for patients to feel abandoned to clinician helplessness and the patient's own hopelessness. Social-work interventions can range from advocating for patients, families, and colleagues by facilitating open discussion of goals of care and available treatment options, to exploring ethical variables and ensuring that team assessment and intervention are comprehensive, holistic, and respectful of both the seriousness of the issues as well as the differences in values within the team and within unique families.

The care team's response to Julia's request — first evaluating her for depression and then prescribing anti-depressant medications — was medically appropriate. As the literature highlights, however, for the team to limit its response to a purely psychopharmacological treatment plan would fail to take the necessary comprehensive and critical approach to the problem. By partializing the variables that informed Julia's request to die, additional interventions became possible and necessary as the choice to sedate and compromise consciousness presupposes this expert evaluation and intervention (Cherny and Portenoy 1994).

Interventions that modify the patient's environment — ranging from something as simple as changing the position of a patient's bed, to something as daunting as changing the way providers use verbal and nonverbal language around patients and families — can serve to reduce fear and isolation and increase understanding. Accurate and effective documentation and consistent follow-up must reflect the critical thinking and comprehensive evaluation that informs ongoing decision making and treatment plans. Effective communication extends to the team as well as to patients and their families, as the complexity of these issues requires that dialogue be thorough, consistent, and ongoing. Psychotherapeutic and cognitive-behavioral interventions provide a wide range of possibilities for social workers both to enhance patient and family care and decision making and to assist colleagues. The continuation of Julia's story reflects the use of several of these interventions, along with consideration of palliative sedation as death became imminent.

Dignity Conserving Therapy
In Chochinov's (2002) model of dignity-conserving care, the author suggests that dignity can be maintained only when health-care professionals take a holistic approach, moving beyond symptom management and addressing the "physical, psychological, social, spiritual, and existential aspects of the patient's terminal experience" (2254). This emphasis on dignity must infuse the professional's innermost beliefs and attitudes:

> Acknowledgement of personal attributes, unique differences, and the essential or even subtle qualities each person embodies is fundamental to the preservation of dignity. When dying patients are seen, and know that they are seen, as being worthy of honor and esteem by those who care for them, dignity is more likely to be maintained. (2254)

Miller, Hedlund and Murphy (1998) posit that patients who seek assisted suicide may do so as a way of preserving personal dignity and maintaining control in the face of "humiliating circumstances" (32). Safeguarding a dying patient's dignity, then, encompasses not only seeing the patient as an individual with unique ideas about what "dignity" means, but also promoting the patient's sense of control and independence, which may help to alleviate the desire for hastened death. In addition, dignity is often represented in the behaviors and language used by health-care staff as they provide care, whether intimate physical care or counseling, and whether a person has capacity or is seemingly unaware.

Family Counseling and Education

In order to most effectively address patient requests for hastened death, the care team must also address the concerns of the patient's family, social-support network, and decision-making agents. When confronted by Julia's wish to die, her daughter struggled with the thought of no longer being able to verbally communicate with Julia. In private meetings with the social worker, she questioned why the support of a loving family wasn't enough to maintain her mother's will to live. Julia had always been her closest and most trusted confidante, but she now wondered whether their relationship held the same meaning for her mother as it did for her. At the same time, she could not help but pray that her mother's death would be more peaceful and dignified than that of her father. Julia's sister, too, had concerns that sedation would act against God's will in pushing her toward death before it was her time. Despite outreach efforts, Julia's son remained distanced from the situation.

Individual sessions with Julia's sister and daughter provided an outlet for the complex emotional responses each of them experienced. The team educated Julia's family about possible physiological changes and symptoms as her illness progressed. They discussed the concept of palliative sedation and reassured the family that the purpose of sedation, if necessary, was to manage intractable symptoms and not to hasten death. In the event that achieving adequate relief from existential or physical suffering necessitated a loss of consciousness, the team reminded Julia and her family of the ongoing responsibility to weigh the risk against the benefit of each intervention. The team actively described their ongoing commitment to relieve Julia's emotional and physical distress with varied interventions, including pharmaceutical, psychotherapeutic, and environmental approaches; if these provided an acceptable level of relief, then palliative sedation need not be a consideration. Perhaps simply knowing that palliative sedation was a viable option would provide Julia and her family with a sense of security and confidence that might diminish the anticipatory anxiety related to Julia's illness and eventual death. One of the hospital's Catholic priests also extended pastoral counseling to Julia's sister in an effort to address her concerns about the moral or theological acceptability of palliative sedation. Finally, the team social worker arranged a family meeting with Julia as a forum for all to express their feelings and concerns openly with one another and with the care team. Only Julia's daughter wished to participate, but the meeting provided another opportunity to answer questions, clarify concerns, and reframe palliative sedation as only one in a range of therapeutic options available to address Julia's suffering.

Legacy Activities
Given Julia's lack of interest in the present, legacy work and life review held the potential to give her a greater sense of meaning or purpose, while at the same time providing insight into her history as it related to her present coping. Despite her continued desire for death, Julia was eager to engage in life review. Initial sessions dealt mainly with life prior to the cancer diagnosis, and she enjoyed singling out moments and events that illustrated her independence and accomplishment. She was adept at using humor to offset those periods of her life marked by hardship, such as the death of her husband and the troubled relationship with her son, but with each passing session she grew more comfortable discussing these events without using humor to offset sad feelings.

Supportive Counseling and Cognitive Behavioral Interventions
Using effective listening skills, engaging in life review, and maintaining a dignity-centered model of care, the social worker established a level of rapport and trust and created a safe environment for exploration of underlying fears. As Julia began to discuss her husband's death, it became clear that fear of the dying process was a significant factor in her desire for death. Julia's pain was palpable as she shared the horrific details of her husband's death from cancer, marked by the memory of seeing her husband tied down to his bed as he took his final breaths. Julia feared that she would meet a similar end and, perhaps worse still, she knew the potential impact on her daughter who might witness her death just as Julia had witnessed that of her husband; thus she prayed for death to come soon.

Julia began to talk about the patients she had seen come and go in the room across the hall, patients who had died only after prolonged periods of apparent anguish, their deaths marked by moans and gasps that filled Julia with dread. Julia was terrified that she would die with this same level of distress. Von Gunten et al. (2000) touch upon this: "When evaluating psychological and social issues, the patient's fears about his/her future should be explored. Many patients have witnessed suboptimal care in others that fuels their fears of losing control, being abandoned, being a burden, or being undignified" (3054). In discussing therapeutic approaches with demoralized patients, Kissane, Clarke and Street (2001) encourage the use of cognitive behavioral therapy to counter and reframe patients' negative thoughts and beliefs. Supportive counseling with Julia paved the way for a more directive approach, which included reality testing as a means of addressing and reducing underlying fears and catastrophic thinking. The social worker reminded Julia about the advances in pain and symptom management since her husband's death, as well as the facility's expertise in this field. The treatment plan included engaging nursing and physician staff to provide end-of-life education, assuaging some of Julia's fears by reframing the moans and rattles she had been hearing as a normal, expected part of the dying experience which were more distressing for observers than for the patient her/himself. At the same time, Julia's expressed desire for death was reframed with staff as an invitation to respond quickly and effectively to escalating symptoms. Relaxation techniques were considered as a skill that would empower Julia toward self-soothing behaviors that might have an impact upon symptoms as well as anticipatory anxiety. She was asked to consider the possibility that physical dependence did not preclude her remaining independent and competent as she guided her care and assisted her family to integrate her death.

As Julia discussed her fears, she began to explore other aspects of dying, including her beliefs about the afterlife and the frustration of remaining for so long in a state of limbo between life and death. It became clear that Julia's desire to die had little to do with depression, but was instead based in rational, self-protective thought processes grounded in her lived experience. Providing Julia with a forum to explore the multidimensional aspects of her feelings and thoughts, rather than judging them as irrational or as a consequence of depression, enhanced the clinical understanding of her situation. Discussing potential options for care reduced her fears and allowed her to live out the end of her life feeling valued and validated, confident that impeccable symptom management would help her to avoid the horrific death she imagined.

Epilogue
After four to five weeks of requesting hastened death, Julia's behavior began to change noticeably. She became less vocal about her desire for death, more interested in seeing family and friends, and resumed eating after a lengthy hiatus from food intake. Julia had continued to receive anti-depressants during this period and met regularly with her social worker. She regained her ability to laugh. She continued to share her underlying fears and anxieties with increasing candor. Additional interventions

that were considered included focused breathing and imagery for shortness of breath (Gallo-Silver and Pollack 2000). Physical symptoms were actively evaluated, and she was treated with morphine for symptomatic relief. As her illness progressed and her lungs became more congested, Julia feared suffocation in addition to pain, and she was able to benefit from ongoing medical management, supportive counseling, cognitive interventions, and reassurance that her symptoms could be managed. Eleven weeks after her admission to the hospital, on a snowy Saturday afternoon, Julia's shortness of breath became markedly worse but was managed, as planned, by the nursing staff. She died shortly thereafter, peacefully, with her daughter at her bedside.

CONCLUSION

Confronting advanced illness and the end of life, no matter what the circumstances, can present challenges for patients, families, and providers alike. The US health-care system, as broken as it is, provides complex technological choices but does not allow the time or encourage the expertise that is needed to inform these choices. This does not preclude the responsibility of clinicians who choose to join with patient and families during this chapter of their lives, to strive toward excellence in providing care.

The process of facing one's own death is not simple, but rather requires careful decision making in the setting of comprehensive, multifactorial assessment. If we as providers find ourselves stymied by the myriad of questions and concerns that arise around end-of-life care, we need only put ourselves in the shoes of our patients and families. Imagine how ominous these uncertainties may be for those who do not dedicate their daily practice to care of the dying, but rather face these issues as a singular event with no second chances to get it right.

When considering sedation for patients at end of life, failure to notice the intricacies and uniqueness inherent in a given clinical situation may signal a need for additional learning or more thorough analysis on our part. Put another way, quoting Lynn (1997), "If you do not find it troubling, you aren't thinking hard enough." Enhancing our clinical practice is an ethical responsibility and allows us to assist patients and their families with clarity, expertise, and compassion. By solidifying our own thoughtfulness around palliative sedation, we can help patients and families to better understand the concepts embedded in this issue, thus empowering them to make informed decisions about the care that may or may not be offered and that they may or may not wish to receive. Developing this level of expertise is essential if we are to invite interdisciplinary respect and participate in a collaborative approach to end-of-life care that recognizes the clinical skills and knowledge that each team member brings to quality care for the dying.

REFERENCES

Agency for Healthcare Research and Quality. 2004. *National Healthcare Disparities Report: Summary*. Retrieved from <http://www.ahrq.gov/qual/nhdr03/nhdrsum03.htm>.

Billings, J.A. 2000. "Palliative Care." *British Medical Journal* 527(7260): 555-58.

Billings, J.A., and S.D. Block. 1996. "Slow Euthanasia." *Journal of Palliative Care* 72(4): 21-30.

Block, S. 2001. "Psychological Considerations, Growth and Transcendence at the End of Life: The Art of the Possible." *Journal of the American Medical Association* 285(22): 2898-2905.

Breitbart, W., B. Rosenfeld, H. Pessin, M. Kaim, J. Funesti-Esch, M. Galietta, C.J. Nelson, and R. Brescia. 2000. "Depression, Hopelessness, and Desire for Hastened Death in Terminally Ill Patients with Cancer." *Journal of the American Medical Association*: 284(22): 2907-11.

Burt, R.A. 1997. "The Supreme Court Speaks—Not Assisted Suicide but a Constitutional Right to Palliative Care." *New England Journal of Medicine* 337: 1234-36.

Carver, A.C., and K. Foley. 2000. "The Wein Article Reviewed." *Oncology* 598 and 601.

Cassell, E. 1991. *The Nature of Suffering*. New York: Oxford UP.

Chater, S., R. Viola, J. Paterson, and V. Jardis. 1998. "Sedation for Intractable Distress in the Dying." *Palliative Medicine* 12: 255-69.

Cherny, N.I., and R.K. Portenoy. 1994. "Sedation in the Management of Refractory Symptoms." *Journal of Palliative Care* 10: 31-39.

Chochinov, H.M. 2002. "Dignity-Conserving Care: A New Model for Palliative Care." *Journal of the American Medical Association* 287(17): 2253-60.

Cohen, L., L. Ganzini, C. Mitchell, S. Arons, E. Goy, and J. Cleary. 2005. "Accusations of Murder and Euthanasia in End-of-Life Care." *Journal of Palliative Medicine* 8: 1096-1104.

Cowan, J.D., and D. Walsh. 2001. "Terminal Sedation in Palliative Medicine—Definition and Review of the Literature." *Supportive Care in Cancer* 9: 403-7.

Davis, M.P., and P.A. Ford. 2005. "Palliative Sedation Definition, Practice, Outcomes and Ethics." *Journal of Palliative Medicine* 8: 699-701.

Fainsinger, R.I. 1998. "Use of Sedation by a Hospital Palliative Care Support Team." *Journal of Palliative Care* 14: 51-54.

Farberman, R.K. 1997. "Terminal Illness and Hastened Death Requests: The Important Role of the Mental Health Professional." *Professional Psychology: Research and Practice* 28(6): 544-47.

Gallo-Silver, L., and B. Pollack. 2000. "Behavioral Interventions for Cancer-Related Breathlessness." *Cancer Practice* 8: 268-73.

Hoffman, M.A. 2000. "Suicide and Hastened Death: A Biopsychosocial Perspective." *Counseling Psychologist* 28(4): 561-72.

Jansen, L.A., and D.P. Sulmasy. 2002. "Sedation, Alimentation, Hydration and Equivocation: Careful Conversation about Care at the End of Life." *Annals of Internal Medicine* 136: 845-49.

Kissane, D.W., D.M. Clarke, and A.F. Street. 2001. "Demoralization Syndrome—A Relevant Psychiatric Diagnosis for Palliative Care." *Journal of Palliative Care* 77(1): 12-21.

Lo, B., and G. Rubenfeld. 2005. "Palliative Sedation in Dying Patients: 'We Turn to It when Everything Else Hasn't Worked.'" *Journal of the American Medical Association* 294(14): 1810-16.

Loscalzo, M., and P. Jacobsen. 1990. "Practical Behavioral Approaches to the Effective Management of Pain and Distress." *Journal of Psychosocial Oncology* 8: 139-69.

Lynch, M. 2003. "Palliative Sedation." *Clinical Journal of Oncology Nursing* 7: 653-57.

Lynn, J. 1997. "'Passive Euthanasia' in Hospitals is the Norm, Doctors Say." *New York Times* p. 10.

Miller, P.J., S.C. Hedlund, and K.A. Murphy. 1998. "Social Work Assessment at End of Life: Practice Guidelines for Suicide and the Terminally Ill." *Social Work in Health Care* 26(4): 23-36.

Morita, T., S. Bito, Y. Kurihara, and Y. Uchitomi. 2005. "Development of a Clinical Guideline for Palliative Sedation Therapy Using the Delphi Method." *Journal of Palliative Medicine* 8(4): 716-29.

Morita, T., S. Tsuneto, and Y. Shima. 2002. "Definition of Sedation for Symptom Relief: A Systematic Literature Review and a Proposal for Operational Criteria." *Journal of Pain and Symptom Management* 24: 447-53.

Mount, B. 1996. "Morphine Drips, Terminal Sedation and Slow Euthanasia: Definitions and Facts, Not Anecdotes." *Journal of Palliative Care* 12: 31-37.

Muskin, P.R. 1998. "The Request to Die: Role for a Psychodynamic Perspective on Physician-Assisted Suicide." *Journal of the American Medical Association* 279(4): 323-28.

Orentlicher, D. 1997. "The Supreme Court and Physician-Assisted Suicide: Rejecting Assisted Suicide but Embracing Euthanasia." *New England Journal of Medicine* 337: 1236-39.

Peppin, J. 2003. "Intractable Symptoms and Palliative Sedation at End of Life." *Christian Bioethics* 9: 343-55.

Portenoy, R., N. Coyle, K. Kash, F. Brescia, C. Scanlon, D. O'Hare, et al. 1997. "Determinants of Willingness to Endorse Assisted Suicide, a Survey of Physicians, Nurses and Social Workers." *Psychosomatics* 38: 277-87.

Quill, T.E. 1993. "The Ambiguity of Clinical Intentions." *Journal of the American Medical Association* 329: 1039-40.

Quill, T.E., and C. Cassel. 1995. "Nonabandonment: A Central Obligation for Physicians." *Annals of Internal Medicine* 122: 368-74.

Quill, T.E., B. Lo, and D.W. Brock. 1997. "Palliative Options of Last Resort: A Comparison of Voluntarily Stopping Eating and Drinking, Terminal Sedation, Physician-Assisted Suicide, and Voluntary Active Euthanasia." *Journal of the American Medical Association* 278(23): 2099-2104.

Rich, B.A. 2006. "The Ethical Dimensions of Pain and Suffering." In *Pain Management at the End of Life*, ed. K. Doka. Washington, DC: Hospice Foundation of America.

Rousseau, P. 2000. "The Ethical Validity and Clinical Experience of Palliative Sedation." *Mayo Clinic Proceedings* 75: 1064-69.

———. 2004 (November). "The Ethics of Palliative Sedation." *Caring*: 14-19.

———. 2005. "Palliative Sedation in the Control of Refractory Symptoms." *Journal of Palliative Medicine* 8: 8-12.

Sykes, N., and A. Thorns. 2003. "The Use of Opioids and Sedatives at the End of Life." *The Lancet Oncology* 4: 312-18.

Taylor, B.R., and R.M. McCann. 2005. "Controlled Sedation for Physical and Existential Suffering?" *Journal of Palliative Medicine* 8: 144-47.

Van Loon, R.A. 1999. "Desire to Die in Terminally Ill People: A Framework for Assessment and Intervention." *Health and Social Work* 24(4): 260-68.

Von Gunten, C.F., F.D. Ferris, and L.L. Emanuel. 2000. "Ensuring Competency in End-of-Life Care: Communication and Relational Skills." *Journal of the American Medical Association* 284(23): 3051-57.

Wein, S. 2000. "Sedation in the Imminently Dying." *Oncology* 14: 585-92.

Werth, Jr., J.L., and D.J. Holdwick, Jr. 2000. "A Primer on Rational Suicide and Other Forms of Hastened Death." *Counseling Psychologist* 28(4): 511-39.